BOOKS BY WILLIAM BRAGG EWALD, JR.

The Masks of Jonathan Swift

Rogues, Royalty and Reporters: The Age of Queen Anne Through Its Newspapers (published in England as *The Newsmen of Queen Anne*)

Eisenhower the President: Crucial Days, 1951–1960

Who Killed Joe McCarthy?

WHO KILLED JOE McCARTHY?

William Bragg Ewald, Jr.

SIMON AND SCHUSTER   NEW YORK

Published by Simon and Schuster
A Division of Simon & Schuster, Inc.
Simon & Schuster Building
Rockefeller Center
1230 Avenue of the Americas
New York, New York 10020
SIMON AND SCHUSTER and colophon
are registered trademarks of Simon & Schuster, Inc.
Designed by Irving Perkins Associates
Manufactured in the United States of America

10 9 8 7 6 5 4 3 2 1

Library of Congress Cataloging in Publication Data
Ewald, William Bragg, date.
    Who killed Joe McCarthy?

    Includes index.
    1. McCarthy-Army controversy, 1954. 2. McCarthy,
Joseph, 1908–1957. 3. Statesmen—United States—
Biography. I. Title.
UB23.E93   1984   973.921′092′4   83–20307
ISBN 0-671-44946-X

TO MARY

Contents

PREFACE   8

   I   Milwaukee   11
  II   "Don't Join the Book Burners"   48
 III   "He Is an Interesting Fellow"   70
 IV   "I Will Not Get in the Gutter with That Guy"   115
  V   The Fried Chicken Lunch   162
 VI   "With You at the Helm"   224
VII   Accidents: *Lacrimae Rerum*   313

EPILOGUE: Who Killed Joe McCarthy?   379
SOURCES AND ACKNOWLEDGMENTS   386
INDEX   389

Preface

In the spring of 1954, Senator Joseph McCarthy of Wisconsin and the United States Army engaged in one of the most momentous and dramatic confrontations in modern history. Much has been written about it. But this book, *Who Killed Joe McCarthy?*, for the first time tells the story from its most significant contemporaneous records, the documents that were recorded day by day at the very time the events were unfolding. Neither the public nor most of the participants ever knew the contents of these documents, because for reasons of strategy in the conflict, they were locked up in the White House by order of the President. The substance of these impounded papers, with their often word-by-word monitoring, is here at last published for the American citizen, to whose heritage they belong.

I first became aware of the existence of these documents one summer afternoon in 1958 as I was standing in the outer office of Fred Seaton, Secretary of the Interior, to whom I was an assistant. We had both served earlier as members of President Eisenhower's White House Staff, and I had accompanied him to Interior. He motioned to a green metal filing cabinet with heavy security locks.

"See that cabinet? That's my 'Eyes Only' file. It's locked. And it's going to stay locked until I am told to open it by you-know-who." I understood "you-know-who" as a reference to his boss, the President of the United States.

In the spring of 1954, as the Army and McCarthy began trading charges and countercharges and the resultant Senate hearings loomed ahead, Fred had been serving as Assistant Secretary for Legislative and Public Affairs in the Department of Defense. Earlier he had held a high position in Eisenhower's 1952 campaign entourage, and he had thereafter been made the White House man in the Pentagon. Fred Seaton was, in fact, the only direct link on strategy between the men in the Department of Defense and the men in the White House.

To get ready to prove the Army's contention that McCarthy and his aides, chiefly Roy Cohn, had used improper methods to obtain special privileges for a former McCarthy staff man, G. David Schine, recently drafted into the Army, and to defend itself against McCarthy's charge that the Army was trying to whitewash the investigation of Communists in the Army Signal Corps, the Pentagon assembled a pile of sensitive documents—memos of conferences, memos from one official to another, and above all an abundance of transcripts of monitored telephone calls—all elucidating the events in question. These documents stretched from September of 1953 to April of 1954.

As the hearings began on April 22, 1954, the Army announced its readiness to introduce any and all of these documents in evidence. But before any transfer took place, in the fourth week of the hearings, suddenly, from the White House, came a presidential directive forbidding any further testimony by Army witnesses on conferences within the executive branch, or the release of any documents bearing on such conferences. Instantaneously, all relevant records in the Pentagon were gathered up and spirited across the Potomac to the White House against the possible threat of their being subpoenaed, on McCarthy's demand, by the investigating Senate committee. A few weeks later the White House returned the documents to the Pentagon, to the office of Fred Seaton, designating him their custodian by presidential order.

There they remained, virtually untouched, through the rest of the hearings. When, in 1955, Fred became Deputy Assistant to the President under White House Chief of Staff Sherman Adams, he took these files with him. The next year, when he became Secretary of the Interior, he moved them once again. And when he left Interior at the end of the administration, in January of 1961, he took them with him to his home in Hastings, Nebraska. There they stayed until his recent death, when his widow, Gladys Seaton, turned them over to the Eisenhower Library in Abilene, Kansas. These papers— written minute by minute through many dramatic weeks—form the backbone of this book, which reaches its culmination in the hearings themselves.

Reams of public documentation exist on the McCarthy period; congressional testimony fills many volumes, including three thousand pages on the Army-McCarthy investigation itself.

The record in the public press—newspapers, magazines, broadcast commentaries—runs to millions of words. And to the writing of books about McCarthy there has been no end, both by outside observers and by such firsthand participants as Governor Sherman Adams, Senator Charles Potter, McCarthy's Chief Counsel Roy Cohn, and Army Counselor John Adams.

I have read through thirty boxes of Department of the Army papers in the custody of the National Archives in Washington. And through Freedom of Information Act inquiries, I have been given access to papers of the Department of Justice and specifically of the Federal Bureau of Investigation which illuminate the relationship between Senator McCarthy and the bureau's director, J. Edgar Hoover.

As a member of President Eisenhower's White House Staff, as an assistant to Secretary Seaton, and as an assistant to the President in the preparation of his memoirs of his White House years, *Mandate for Change* and *Waging Peace,* I of course knew many of the participants personally. I have combed their unpublished files—diaries, memoranda, letters. I have conducted extensive interviews to supplement the written record.

All these sources are valuable, each one serving as a check on the other. But the crowning revelations come from the Seaton–White House cache. This trove not only contains the most sensitive Pentagon data; it also clearly and accurately shows how one particular governmental storm was contained, and demonstrates how the various participants in the first place became involved to sword point.

And in *Who Killed Joe McCarthy?* I have been able to put together, finally, an accurate sequence of events: what was going on hour by hour at the White House, in Senate offices, and at the Pentagon—a blow-by-blow unfolding of one of the most fascinating conflicts in American politics.

I

MILWAUKEE

On the afternoon of Thursday, October 2, 1952, a small private plane took off in darkest secrecy from Madison, Wisconsin, then headed south toward Peoria, Illinois. The day was clear, the flight uneventful. The plane carried three men.

The first was Walter Jodok Kohler, the Republican governor of the state of Wisconsin. The second was the recently elected Republican National Committeeman from Wisconsin, Henry Ringling—a forty-six-year-old small-town banker, an Elk, and a Mason, from Baraboo, the town where the Ringling Brothers Circus got its start. The third was Wisconsin's junior Senator, Joseph Raymond McCarthy, now campaigning for a second term.

The plane touched down at Peoria at about four o'clock that afternoon, and the three men headed for the Pere Marquette Hotel—stopover site for General Dwight D. Eisenhower, campaigning for the presidency of the United States, poised there before entering Wisconsin the next day.

Eisenhower hadn't wanted to go into Wisconsin after the September 9 Wisconsin primary—the election in which McCarthy buried his opponent, a maverick loner, attorney Len Schmitt of Merrill, Wisconsin. To do so, Ike feared, would seem like an endorsement of McCarthy and all his works.

"I told Tom Coleman [the state's powerful Republican boss] I'd go in before the primary but not after it," Eisenhower years later testily declared. But no one on his staff could ever recall an outright order. New York's Governor Tom Dewey, an early and powerful Ike supporter—who had lost the presidency to Roosevelt in 1944 and to Harry Truman in 1948—said Stay Away. But he was outgunned by the practical men in the entourage: you couldn't, they argued, insult a major state like Wisconsin by singling it out for a nonappearance. Moreover, it didn't make sense to go into any major state before the

11

primary dust had settled. Finally, the practical men argued: Don't let McCarthy seem to scare Eisenhower away.

So they scheduled the candidate into the state against his will, and now he was stuck with a *fait accompli*. As Eisenhower's Chief of Staff, Sherman Adams, later wryly observed, "The trouble with Wisconsin came from being there in the first place."

The three men, Kohler, Ringling, and McCarthy, pulled up outside the Pere Marquette. The Eisenhower team had taken over three floors of the hotel—the fourth and sixth for staff members, the fifth for the General, all three cordoned off by the Secret Service. Reporters and Republicans milled around the lobby. Kohler, Ringling, and McCarthy eluded them, quickly found themselves spirited up. in the back-alley freight elevator to one of the staff floors and then hustled along to the room of Republican National Chairman Arthur E. Summerfield.

Here was a man they could feel at home with—a Republican's Republican, a politician's politician. Short, brisk, stocky, Summerfield was a Chevrolet dealer from Flint, Michigan, a future Postmaster General of the United States; ever eager to nail Democratic "charges" with Republican "facts," whatever the subject—defense, Sputnik, recession, water and power, morality in the government and in the nation. (He would once try to sneak a bit of political propaganda into an Eisenhower speech at the annual Christmas tree lighting ceremony.) Art Summerfield was one who never let the bastards on the other side get away with anything.

Art was for Ike (he and the Michigan delegation had recognized a winner and signed on at a crucial moment in the Eisenhower-Taft battle at the Republican Convention in July), but he was also for votes, and Joe McCarthy meant votes: not only Wisconsin's 12 electoral votes, but votes coast to coast, in Irish Boston, in German Milwaukee, in Polish Chicago, in redneck Tennessee and southern-fried Dixie, in the wild West, everywhere but in the effete East. Joe McCarthy meant votes wherever red-blooded Americans responded in wrath to his headlined "revelations" that the U.S. Government was honeycombed with Communists, pinkos, and fellow travelers.

So now in corn-belt–coal-field Peoria (population 112,000, home of Caterpillar Tractor and Hiram Walker), Summerfield welcomed Kohler, Ringling, and McCarthy into his suite, and for a few moments they had a most agreeable chat. They understood one another.

At about five-thirty the phone rang: General Eisenhower would see the Senator.

• •

McCarthy had the body of a brawler—a five-foot-ten-and-a-half heavyweight with a muscular frame and the wrists and hands of a much larger man. The thick black hair of his youth had thinned, but he still refused to let photographers reveal that he wore glasses. As a boy Joe had played basketball—a rough game of it—and a rough game of baseball also: on one occasion his nose had been broken. His first day at Marquette University, without any previous experience in football, he unsuccessfully tried out for the team. He also played donkey baseball—a loutish game that entailed the riding of a donkey by all infielders, outfielders, and base runners. In one game when McCarthy's donkey refused to move from home plate, the beefy young man picked up the animal and carried him bodily to first base, the crowd roaring and cheering them on.

Joe McCarthy's ruling passion, however, was not team sports but the supreme loner sport, boxing. His father taught him to box at about the age of twelve. Soon he could scare other kids in the neighborhood into giving him a wide berth. In high school he taught boxing, as an overaged student, to the younger fry. And in Marquette he boxed, coached boxing, and even for a moment toyed with the thought of turning pro. In the Marines out on Guadalcanal he got into an unbelievable fight with a Boston hockey player—a fight that left both men sprawling on the ground covered in dust and blood. Quarreling with columnist–radio commentator Drew Pearson in December of 1950 at an elegant dinner dance at the Sulgrave Club given by the chic and glamorous Louise Tinsley Steinman, Mc-Carthy physically attacked Pearson, then gleefully phoned the *Washington Times-Herald* the details: he had, he said, just kicked Pearson "in the nuts."

McCarthy fought with his knees and his ham-handed fists, not his head. Those at ringside at Marquette saw him as a hard hitter, more a slugger than a boxer—slow, strong, and fearless, charging his opponent without worrying about defense. From boyhood he stood out as ambitious—"always driving, always driving." In the ring as out of it, he thrived on raw brute energy.

Like Richard Nixon, Joe McCarthy came from black Irish parentage. He was born November 15, 1908, on a 142-acre dairy farm near Appleton, Wisconsin, into a family of average income, the fifth child of seven. He dropped out of school after the eighth grade and started his own chicken farm with $65.00 he had saved. By the age of seventeen he owned 2,000 laying hens and 10,000 broilers. But in 1928 he got influenza, and the chickens got coccidiosis, which left them dead and him broke. The next year, picking up the pieces, he became the manager of a Cash-Way Market at Manawa, where he impressed customers as courteous and kind—a young man who "sparkled." In the fall of 1929, nearly twenty-one, he entered high school as a freshman. By Thanksgiving he was a sophomore, by mid-year a junior, and by Easter a senior. He piled four years' work into one, made mostly A's, and engaged in a torrent of extracurricular activities. In the spring of 1930 he received his high school diploma.

Entering Marquette in Milwaukee that fall, planning to become an engineer, he juggled an array of odd jobs to pay his way. He worked as a yardman, a janitor, a flypaper salesman, a manager of two service stations, where he would at times put in ten-hour days, and as a short-order cook in a beanery—a job that left him with a lifelong fondness for cooking.

In his third year at Marquette, he switched from engineering to law. Though he went to classes regularly, he rarely entered the library and read little. Largely he relied on a prodigious memory (he could recall names and facts for thousands of people photographed into his consciousness) and an ability to absorb the comments of his fellow students in study groups before examinations. Never—at Marquette or elsewhere—would he learn to write with a care for accuracy, to read with discrimination, to study, to analyze objective fact, to trace logical implication. He saw history and philosophy through a haze; as one Marquette alumnus years later asked incredulously, "Who the hell taught him ethics?" He also depended upon energy, rote recall, shortcuts, personal magnetism, and bluff.

He had studied debating as a freshman. Later, in law school, as a driving member of the Franklin Debating Club, he readied no arguments in advance, talked off the top of his head, faked his way in the absence of fact, and at times tore into his opponents abrasively, though he forgot the animosity quickly afterward and would buy a round of Cokes for the house. He recklessly bluffed also in the Delta Theta Phi fraternity house poker games—one of his gambling passions, to which he later added horses, roulette, and slot machines. A pattern began to form: make a play, a move, an assertion, a challenge, and then stand back.

He would bet on cards face down, or bet his last nickel in a wild shot at a bonanza. He never knew how much money he had. He borrowed, spent, gambled, and gave away dollar after dollar. Elected judge of the Tenth Circuit on April 5, 1939, several years after leaving

Marquette, McCarthy could join a card game at the Racine Elks Club at midnight, play straight through to seven-fifteen the next morning, shower, and show up at the courthouse to begin judging cases.

As a boy Joe had impressed neighbors as loud, fun-loving, extroverted, and hyperactive: he slept little, and at thirteen he rode a motorcycle at breakneck speed into a corn crib and broke his ankle. But they also remembered him as dark and handsome, with pale skin, blue eyes, black hair, and a slight brogue—an appealing adolescent. As a young man he retained his sense of wild daring: he once talked a girl friend into going up in a little plane, then secretly slipped the pilot some extra cash to make him do enough wild stunts to scare her to death while he himself roared with glee. He also impressed his acquaintances with his religious sincerity and his regular attendance at Mass. A priest befriended him and helped him learn Latin. His father always reminded him—evidently with effect—not to forget to say his prayers. He had a bashfulness with women and an inability to dance, both of which soon passed. He also had an occasional nervous giggle, which never entirely vanished. Even as a judge in Racine before the war, though fierce in combat and slovenly in dress (he would greet visitors in his stocking feet, wrapped in a bathrobe), he often struck acquaintances as tenderhearted and sentimental; as funny, generous, and persistently pious. He would say his rosary while speeding along the highway.

But already, as Samuel Johnson said of the historian Bishop Burnet, McCarthy was a man who took no particular pains to find out the truth. And from time to time he also moved to the outright fabrication of falsehood.

Though his judgeship deferred him from the draft, on June 4, 1942, at the age of thirty-three, McCarthy enlisted in the Marine Corps. The *Appleton Post-Courant* headlined that the judge had entered the armed services as a buck private. That was good enough for McCarthy, and in both the *Congressional Directory* and *Who's Who* he would later repeat this untruth. In fact, he received a direct commission as a first lieutenant on July 29, 1942, and was sworn in with that rank on August 4. Nearly a year later, as he crossed the equator on a seaplane tender, McCarthy in a rowdy initiation ceremony climbed down a ladder with a bucket tied to his right foot. He slipped. His left foot caught on the rung, and he fell backward, painfully fracturing it. In removing the cast an inexperienced corpsman by mistake used glacial acetic acid, chemically burning McCarthy's left leg and leaving a huge scar. Though McCarthy suffered no other injuries during the war, he made the most of this one. After some genuinely hazardous gunning and photo reconnaissance runs in the Solomons, he evidently forged a letter describing his heroism, to which he signed his commanding officer's name. The letter snaked its way through Navy channels. Ultimately it resulted in a citation signed by Admiral Chester Nimitz himself, instancing McCarthy's indomitable devotion to duty despite a "severe leg injury."

McCarthy had grown up a New Deal Democrat, voting for Franklin Roosevelt. In 1946, having switched to the Republican party, he ran for the United States Senate against veteran liberal Bob La Follette, Jr., and won. For a few years in Washington he busied himself with sugar and housing legislation and with an inquiry of interest to his German constituents, into the U.S. Army's alleged brutality toward the German perpetrators of the 1945 Malmédy massacre. The headlines, if any, came and went.

But a fire was beginning to burn in the land.

A year before McCarthy's election to the Senate, the United States Ambassador to China, Major General Patrick Hurley, had sent off a furious letter of resignation to President Harry Truman, claiming he was being undermined by pro-Communist Foreign Service officers in the State Department—men suspicious of China's ruling government under Chiang Kai-shek and tolerant of Chiang's Communist enemies under Mao Tse-tung. Hurley was a rough and tough Oklahoman with a flamboyant white mustache, born in the Choctaw Indian Territory, and a rumor spread he was so mean that he had once killed a mule with a two-by-four. Hurley hotly denied it: "I have never killed a mule with a two by four. Hell, I've never even killed a Foreign Service Officer."

At once Truman dispatched to China a far different man—the revered Army Chief of Staff during the war, General George C. Marshall—in a mission that ended with Marshall's urging Chiang's ruling clique to broaden their government to include both Chiang's Nationalists and Mao's insurgent Communists. With these events, the cloud of smoke surrounding the fire began to form and to move— a cloud of suspicion of men in high places, of men making American foreign policy, of men running the government. A confirmed Roosevelt-hater might, of course, leap instantly to the verdict that we had traitors in our midst, ever eager to sell out to the Communists. Most Americans rejected this conclusion. But then other clouds gathered and coalesced.

On October 20, 1947, the House Un-American Activities Committee, J. Parnell Thomas (Republican, New Jersey), chairman, opened hearings on Communist influence on the motion picture industry. Before fascinated viewers, Thomas—he would later go to jail for payroll padding and kickbacks—haled one celebrity after another into the huge klieg-lighted hearing room, so hot their makeup ran. Loyal witnesses, like handsome Robert Montgomery and winsome Ronald Reagan and debonaire Adolphe Menjou revealed pro-Soviet propaganda in specific films and Communist infiltration into the movie-acting profession. A group of accused—mostly writers—who soon became known as the Hollywood Ten, again and again took the Fifth: they refused to answer questions about their Communist associations, taking refuge in the amendment to the Constitution which protects a witness against self-incrimination. Some of these recalcitrants, when they insisted on reading prepared statements or making speeches, were strong-armed out of the room. "If you want to make a speech," Thomas called out after one of them, "you can go outside under a tree." The audience cheered.

The next summer—on July 31, 1948—congressional investigators pulled back another curtain, this time not on unnamed low-life bureaucrats in China, not on faceless screenwriters pounding their typewriters in Hollywood, but on the upper reaches of the executive branch of the federal government, and the spotlight caught in its beam the White House itself. Elizabeth Bentley, an admitted Communist wartime spy, took the stand and named three high-flying Communist colleagues: William Remington, a Department of Commerce official with major responsibility in licensing the export of goods to Iron Curtain countries; Dr. Lauchlin Currie, a short, gray-haired professional economist who had taught at Harvard and later become an administrative assistant to FDR, with "a passion for anonymity"; and Harry Dexter White, another Harvard Ph.D. A former Assistant Secretary of the Treasury, White had served as the chief technical expert for the U.S. delegation to the Bretton Woods Conference, which set up the postwar international monetary system; he had also helped draft the Morgenthau Plan for the postwar dismemberment of German industry. All three men, Miss Bentley alleged, had slipped secret information to Communist spy groups for transmittal to Russia.

Remington, Currie, and White flatly asserted their innocence (and within a few weeks White would die of a heart attack). But the man in the street was stunned. Entertainment, education, the very pinnacle of government itself seemed to be infiltrated by Communist cells.

Then, on August 3, the House Un-American Activities Committee revealed a new witness—Whittaker Chambers. He charged that from at least 1934 until 1938 he—himself a Communist—had trafficked in Communist intrigue with a man named Alger Hiss.

Hiss was a political darling. Tall, handsome, urbane, a Phi Beta Kappa graduate of Johns Hopkins and of Harvard Law School, a former law clerk to Supreme Court Justice Oliver Wendell Holmes, a bright young man with stars in his eyes who had entered the New Deal in Roosevelt's Agricultural Adjustment Administration, he had in 1936 joined the State Department. He had been an advisor to President Roosevelt at the Yalta Conference, where Roosevelt, Stalin, and Churchill had drawn the boundary lines of postwar Europe, dividing East from West. He had been the executive secretary to the Dumbarton Oaks Conference in Georgetown, where the United Nations charter was framed. He had been a principal staff man for the U.S. delegation at the 1945 San Francisco Conference, which successfully launched the United Nations Organization. Finally, at the age of forty-two in 1947, he had become the new president of Washington's distinguished Carnegie Endowment for International Peace. Armed with glowing letters of endorsement from the nation's establishment, including Sullivan and Cromwell's John Foster Dulles, the dean of Wall Street lawyers, Hiss was a "certified gentleman." He had all the tickets.

In stark contrast his accuser, Whittaker Chambers, had almost none. He was pudgy. He wore a rumpled suit. The points of his shirt collar splayed out over his lapels. Now forty-seven, he was the son of an actress and of a staff artist for a New York newspaper. He had studied at Columbia University. He had been a free-lance writer. He had translated *Bambi*, the children's classic by Felix Salten. In 1939 he had moved to the staff of *Time* and *Life*, ultimately becoming a senior editor, at $30,000 a year. En route, for thirteen years, from 1925 to 1938, he had worked for the Communist party. And, he told the House Committee, he had known Alger Hiss as a fellow member.

Hiss, on August 5, quickly denied all these fantastic allegations. Harry Truman, in a political reflex, attacked the investigators. He called the Republican-spearheaded hearings a "red herring" dragged in to divert attention from the inaction of the Republican-led "do-nothing" Eightieth Congress. Thus inadvertently he lined up with Alger Hiss's defenders.

But one member of the committee—young Representative Richard Nixon of California—thought he detected in Hiss's denials a curious evasiveness. (Indeed, one of Hiss's school friends said later that the one thing above all that turned him against Hiss was that Hiss never forgot anything in his life, and when he alleged under oath that he could not remember, "I could not believe him.") In separate testimony both Hiss and Chambers had recalled Hiss's bird-watching, both mentioning Hiss's elation at seeing the rare prothonotary warbler. On August 17, in executive session, Hiss finally confronted Chambers face to face, and after lengthy and tortuous shifts and evasions finally admitted to having once known his accuser, not as Whittaker Chambers, but as one "George Crossley." In mid-November Chambers, for the first time accusing Hiss of espionage, began producing copies of secret State Department documents he swore Hiss had transmitted to him. Some of these, on microfilm, Chambers had hidden in a frosty field on his Maryland farm in a hollowed-out pumpkin.

Although the statute of limitations for espionage had already run out, Chambers's documents dated from 1937 and 1938, and in the course of his testimony Hiss had sworn under oath not only that he had never turned over documents to Chambers but also that he had not seen "George Crossley" at all after January 1, 1937. For these assertions, on December 15, 1948, a federal grand jury indicted Hiss on two counts of perjury. On January 21, 1950, in a second trial—the first ended in a jury hung 8–4 against him—he was convicted. His old department associate, Secretary of State Dean Acheson, declared: "Whatever the outcome" of the appeal, "I do not intend to turn my back" on Alger Hiss. On March 22, 1951, Hiss would enter the penitentiary.

If you could not trust a man like Alger Hiss, whom could you trust?

That question as much as any other loosened the soil for McCarthyism; for the readiness of the public to believe the unbelievable; for each man's willingness to look over his shoulder at his most innocent neighbor, wondering; for a national mood of suspicion, doubt, distrust. And two other events intensified the hysteria.

First, in the fall of 1949, the West finally "lost China." This occurrence, to the suspicious, had its beginnings with the Hurley-denounced career foreign-service officers and continued with the Marshall mission, which advocated the inclusion of Reds in the Chinese government. In October of 1949, Mao and Chou En-lai and their victorious Communist associates formed the People's Republic of China, the most populous nation on earth; on December 8, 1949, Taipei, on the offshore island of Formosa, became the last stronghold of the fleeing Chinese Nationalists under Chiang Kai-shek. To those watching the globe and its shadow of creeping communism, the Yellow Peril had been added to the Red.

Second, less than two months later, on February 3, 1950, British authorities arrested a distinguished nuclear physicist, Dr. Klaus Fuchs, for espionage. Fuchs had worked on the atomic bomb in the U.S. He had betrayed atomic secrets, upon which rested the fragile security of the West, to Stalin's Soviet Union. Six days later McCarthyism began.

On February 9, 1950, the junior Senator from Wisconsin flew to West Virginia to deliver one of a group of routine Lincoln Day speeches to Republican audiences, this one to the Ohio County Republican Women's Club in Wheeling, West Virginia. He had in his pocket two speech drafts done by two sets of ghosts: one a dissertation on housing, the other a disquisition on a subject that was increasingly interesting him, like everyone else—Communists in government. For some months he had been flirting with the subject. He had run out of headlines. You could not talk about milk or the Malmédy massacre and make page one. The previous October 19 he had routinely inserted into the *Congressional Record* an article attacking the State Department and specifically one of its old China hands, John Stewart Service, whom he named as a pro-Communist scoundrel. McCarthy had also conferred with conservative advisors—including Father Edmund Walsh, Dean of Georgetown University's School of Foreign Service—who egged him on to the pursuit of domestic communism.

But even now, driving in from the Wheeling airport to the McClure Hotel, he was undecided. Which one should it be, he asked his welcomer, Francis J. Love, a former GOP congressman—communism or housing?

Communism, the answer came back.

So communism it would be.

The advance text McCarthy handed out contained little that was new (considerable confusion would later attend the Senator's exact spoken words and the numbers he used because the radio station that made a recording erased it after the broadcast). As pieced together by a couple of *Times-Herald* reporters—George Waters and Ed Nellor—it was largely a tissue of ideas from the *Congressional Record* and congressional hearings, a familiar rehash of the dirt on such targets as John Stewart Service and Alger Hiss. Three paragraphs on the State Department were derived from an article published a week earlier in the *Chicago Tribune* by one of its Washington correspondents, Willard Edwards.

One piece of *Congressional Record* source data went back a full 3½ years—a letter written on July 26, 1946, by Secretary of State James F. Byrnes to Representative Adolph Sabath of Illinois. Of 4,000 employees transferred to the State Department from various wartime agencies, Byrnes told Sabath, about 3,000 had already been screened. The screening of those 3,000 had resulted in recommendations against permanent employment for 285. Of those 285, so far 79 had been separated from the service. That arithmetic left a magic number: 206.

In the typewriters of McCarthy's ghosts, this dog-eared document now underwent a transmutation that lifted the Wheeling speech out of the ruck of oblivion and made it one of the cardinal documents of this century. For as the Senator reached the climax of his speech that night before his loyal audience of 275 members of the Republican Women's Club in the Colonnade Room of the McClure Hotel, his typed text read: "I have here in my hand a list of 205—a list of names that were made known to the Secretary of State as being members of the Communist party and who nevertheless are still working and shaping policy in the State Department."

Secretary of State Byrnes's letter had said nothing about Communist party membership. It contained no list of names. It did not make—could not have made—any mention whatsoever of the then Secretary of State, in 1950, Dean Acheson. Were those 205 still employed after 3½ years? Were they still making policy? Who knew?

Not McCarthy. He had a number—an old number. He had no names, in his hand or anywhere else.

From source to speech, McCarthy and his ghosts had made a leap. The boxer had thrown a haymaker. The gambler had stayed in the game with not even a pair of deuces. The Marine lieutenant who converted a freak accidental chemical burn into a wound of war, the Marquette debater who made up his evidence as he went along, the law student who never learned to question, sort, use a scalpel, divide and distinguish, analyze, or reflect had made his assertion, doubtless without knowing or caring about its implications. And now he stood back.

The reverberations shook the earth. For with that leap McCarthy took the Communist-in-government issue across a boundary—the boundary that divided fact from speculation, certainty from conjecture. California Congressman Richard Nixon and South Dakota Senator Karl Mundt had spoken darkly of subversion in high places. But they could go no further. McCarthy now claimed to identify specific individuals. He had given to airy nothings a local habitation and a name. And now he was stuck with his assertion.

And he had become a celebrity. He had made the big time. He had climbed into the ring, a challenger of the champions at the top of the executive branch. In the limelight he weaved and bobbed, one fist punching, the other grabbing for corroborating data. He reportedly phoned among others his old friend J. Edgar Hoover. That Wheeling speech, the Senator told the head of the FBI, caused headlines I never expected. Now I need the evidence to back up my charges.

Predictably, a State Department absolutist spokesman rejected McCarthy's charges out of hand. Flying on to Salt Lake City the next day, McCarthy, at a brief stopover at the Denver airport, found himself surrounded, encircled, circumscribed by reporters. What about the State Department denial?

McCarthy zagged: He had a list of 205 "bad risks" in the State Department, he said. But he'd left it in his other suit, in his baggage on the plane. Next he threw a left hook: If Dean Acheson would phone him in Salt Lake City on his arrival, the Senator would be glad to read the Secretary the list. He had toughed it out, but also, as Mark Twain said of Tom Sawyer, he had taken refuge in a lie. And immediately he took refuge in a second one. That night in a Salt Lake City radio interview he declared that in Wheeling he had said he possessed the names of "57 card-carrying members of the Communist Party" in the State Department.

He had thus jettisoned the Byrnes letter as his source and seized on another, which he used equally fraudulently: a two-year-old response by the Department of State to an allegation made by the House Appropriations Committee (under Chief of Staff R. E. Lee) that the Department harbored 108 "instances of inefficiency." Of those 108, the Department wrote the committee in March of 1948, 57 still had State Department jobs. Of those 57, half had already been cleared by the FBI; the clearance of 22 more was pending. Therefore, McCarthy concluded, 57 card-carrying Communists still worked in the Department of State in February of 1950.

That night in Salt Lake City he once again compounded his lies with a bluff: If Acheson would phone him there at the Utah Hotel, he would give the Secretary of State those 57 names if—but only if— Acheson would reveal their Communist activities to a congressional committee (i.e., violate a Truman order closing the executive branch loyalty files to congressional inspection). McCarthy of course knew Acheson would never violate Truman's order; he also knew the Lee report included no names—only numbers to identify individual cases.

The next day, in Reno, McCarthy traded up, from the Secretary of State to the President himself. When the Senator received from State's Deputy Under Secretary John Peurifoy a request for the names of the 205, McCarthy went over his head straight to Harry Truman in a letter for immediate release to the press by McCarthy's Washington office. He had a list of 57, he told the President, "available to you," but "you can get a much longer list by ordering Secretary Acheson to give you [the names] of those whom your board lists as being disloyal and who are still working in the State Department." Only 80 of 300 certified for discharge, McCarthy went on, had actually been dismissed. Those dismissals, he alleged, were achieved only "after a lengthy conversation with Alger Hiss"—an allegation for which McCarthy had no evidence whatsoever. If Truman refused to request Acheson to reveal all information on all suspects, "including those who were placed in the department by Alger Hiss," and if Truman should fail to revoke his orders sealing the loyalty files, he would in effect label the Democratic party "the bedfellow of international Communism."

Hiss, Chambers, Fuchs, and Bentley, in the mind of anxious Americans, had set the stage. McCarthy would now direct the show. He moved with cunning and craft. He knew what he was doing. When baffled reporters tried in vain again and again and again to pin him down on fact and number, he had his answer: as he told three of them at lunch in Milwaukee on February 18, "Listen, you bastards, I'm not going to tell you anything. I just want you to know I've got a pailful of shit and I'm going to use it where it does me the most good."

From Wheeling and Denver and Salt Lake City and Reno, he rolled on, a permanent floating press conference. Lights, cameras, microphones followed him everywhere. Nothing could keep him out of headlines now. On February 20 on the Senate floor he claimed he had a briefcase chock full of photostats of documents on the—at that moment—81 State Department Communist employees—documents straight out of the State Department files, given him by "loyal Americans" whose identities would remain forever confidential. In actual fact, he had only the Lee list, and he exaggerated and twisted that.

Starting March 8, before a Senate committee chaired by Millard Tydings (Democrat of Maryland), McCarthy attacked some familiar targets, including Harvard astronomer Harlow Shapley and John Stewart Service, and he named Johns Hopkins Professor Owen Lattimore as the "top Russian spy" in the United States. When J. Edgar Hoover, under Truman's order, released an analysis of Lattimore's FBI file to the committee, the senators could find in it no evidence of either communism or espionage. McCarthy repeated and widened his accusation: Lattimore, he declared in a Senate speech on March 30, is "a Soviet agent"; the State Department's Far East Division and Voice of America are controlled by pro-Communists; and Secretary of State Dean Acheson is the mere "voice for the mind of Lattimore." Three weeks later, on April 20, McCarthy moved to the top of the Pantheon—Acheson's predecessor as Secretary of State, George Catlett Marshall. This towering figure of World War II—a man who patterned himself on Washington and Lee, who had taken on the impossible China task—had been, in McCarthy's words, "completely unfit" to become Secretary of State. "It was a crime . . . a pathetic thing," McCarthy said, to put Marshall in charge of a man like Service.

On July 17 the three Democrats on the Tydings Committee—the Republicans refused to sign—branded McCarthy's charges and methods "a fraud and a hoax." But the public thought otherwise. A Gallup poll taken in late May revealed that only 29 percent thought McCarthy's charges were doing harm. Thirty-nine percent thought them a good thing.

By September 23, over Truman's veto, the Congress overwhelmingly passed the McCarran Act—the Internal Security Act of 1950—requiring registration by Communist-action organizations and authorizing the Attorney General to round up and put into detention camps any suspected subversives during a time of national emergency.

McCarthy roared on. When North Korea invaded South Korea he again raked the subversives in State: "American boys are dying in Korea," he declared, because "a group of unchangeables" in the Department had "sabotaged" the South Korean aid program voted by the Congress. By December 15, from the privileged sanctuary of the Senate floor, he was savaging radio commentator Drew Pearson as "the voice of international Communism," declaring that "anyone who buys a hat" from the Adam Hat Company (Pearson's sponsor) "is unknowingly contributing at least something to the cause of international Communism." The hat manufacturer was forced to end its sponsorship. By April of 1951, after Truman fired—for blatant insubordination—General Douglas MacArthur, the Supreme Commander of the UN forces in Korea, McCarthy confided to the Senate chamber that he smelled the "midnight potency of bourbon and Benedictine" that "may well have condemned thousands of American boys to death. . . ." Finally, in June, McCarthy charged George Marshall with high treason, with being part of "a conspiracy . . . so immense, an infamy so black, as to dwarf any . . . in the history of man. . . ."

Shooting from the hip, McCarthy sprayed charges in every direction: against the White House, the State Department, even his fellow members in the legislative branch (several U.S. representatives and senators had Communists on their staff, he declared September 19, 1951). Always in the headlines, he became a scourge to the far left, a savior to the far right. At this time he was also a perpetrator of boorish jokes. At one party he asked a guest to balance a marble on his forehead and drop it into a funnel stuck in the front of his trousers; as the guest struggled, McCarthy poured water into the funnel, roaring with laughter. He was a man who could excoriate his opponent one moment and then embrace him the next—even the "unspeakable" Dean Acheson, whom McCarthy once met by chance in an elevator and greeted with a cheery "Hi, Dean!" Increasingly, he was a man awash in booze, capable of downing a glass of whiskey with a tablespoon of orange juice for breakfast, or of swilling down a "sea of bourbon" at an all-night party, then sleeping for three hours, and waking up the next morning hot to go.

Although the junior senator from Wisconsin claimed that traitors were everywhere, there were still those whom he admired. At the Republicans' Chicago Convention in July 1952, he had told the reporters that General Douglas MacArthur "combines the best qualifications of the other leading candidates." But he would not campaign for MacArthur, he added, because the two front-runners, Taft and Eisenhower, were both outstanding men. McCarthy had power in the form of votes to bestow, and he soon bestowed them on General

Eisenhower. On October 2, Joe McCarthy went to Peoria ready to like Ike.

And why not? Ike, like McCarthy, came from the Middle West— from the wide plains of Abilene, Kansas. Ike, like McCarthy, grew up on a farm, on the few acres around his family's white clapboard house. Ike, like McCarthy, was a country boy who worked up the hard way, hauling ice at Abilene's Belle Springs Creamery. And Ike was a star-spangled American, a true war hero, a stalwart anti-Communist, a Republican.

A vast gulf, nonetheless, divided the two men—not just a gulf in age (Ike sixty-one, McCarthy forty-three) but a gulf in character, intellect, temperament. One of them was brash, brawling his way, both hated and idolized; the other was mature, above the fray, the honors of the world heaped upon him, first as Supreme Commander in World War II, then as President of Columbia University, then as Supreme Allied Commander in Europe, head of all the NATO forces. McCarthy was a slugger, a club fighter. Although Ike boxed as a boy in Abilene (once slugging it out with Wes Merrifield until both seventh-graders, bloody and beaten, simultaneously admitted defeat) and boxed as a cadet at West Point, and throughout his life remained combative, his first love was organization sports—baseball and football. Ike played smart ball: under his coach at Abilene High School he became a "chop hitter" like Ty Cobb, poking the ball between short and third or into right center. He also played serious ball: ". . . don't let them take my leg," he implored his older brother Edgar after an injury. "I'd rather be dead than crippled, and not be able to play any more." The game was all-important, and one played it with others in accordance with rules.

Especially Ike played football, the supreme organization sport. To get ready for the fall season at West Point, he worked out on the running track, did gymnastics to build up his muscles, and put on twenty pounds. He played left halfback until felled by a devastating knee injury in a game with Tufts. After that he coached football, teaching younger men how to become an effective team. And he always saw in the game a preparation for the future. He always looked with pride on the ex-footballers who had become outstanding leaders in battle—Bradley, Simpson, Patton, Van Fleet, Patch. Football, Ike believed, instilled in a man the feeling that victory comes from "hard—almost slavish—work, team play, self-confidence, and an enthusiasm that amounts to dedication."

Eisenhower was an organization man, a leader who could indeed command commanders, delegate power, draw out subordinates' ideas, hold their loyalty and trust, move millions along a common path toward a goal.

Like McCarthy, Ike played poker: not as a raucous, wild, devil-may-care bettor, risking everything on unpredictable chance; but as a student of Bob Davis, an old illiterate muskrat-trapper of Abilene, once a young deputy to the town's marshal, Wild Bill Hickok. Bob Davis taught adolescent Eisenhower how to play percentages, how to calculate probabilities—for example, his mathematical chance, if he held two kings, of getting a third or fourth one on the next draw; he turned Ike into so proficient a bettor that he continued to play for the next twenty years, winning steadily, until finally he had to give up the game because he was carrying off too much of his impoverished Army buddies' hard-earned money. Later, in Europe and in the White House, Eisenhower would play bridge the same way: with intense intellectual concentration (myriad are the long letters he wrote to friends analyzing strategies) and with keen, intelligent companions, exemplified best by General Alfred Gruenther, an internationally respected master of the game.

Eisenhower was a well-rounded man, not an intellectual but a man of trained intelligence. Unlike McCarthy, he had learned to write with precision and care. His secretary in the old State, War and Navy Building—now the Executive Office Building—next to the White House, remembers his revising, revising, revising, of reports, always with a purpose. He wrote speeches for silver-tongued Douglas MacArthur in the Philippines. He edited typescripts with intensity, driving always for exactitude, logic, and correctness of qualification, scratching out and penciling in words in a tiny, always impeccably accurate hand. In rare moments he would surprise friends with bits of his reading, quoted with feeling. At the end of the victorious 1952 campaign, one of his key advisors, Bernard Shanley, listened with astonishment as Ike recited two stanzas of Gray's "Elegy Written in a Country Churchyard," ending with "The paths of glory lead but to the grave." And unlike McCarthy, Eisenhower had learned to reflect, to order, and to weigh the facts—weigh them, for example, in June of 1944, as a storm raged and the Allied forces watched and waited in suspense, poised for a cross-channel assault on the beaches of Normandy.

He was neither ideologue nor hater nor zealot, but a man of great common sense and moderation. In 1945, at the end of the war,

Eisenhower commanded the American sector of Berlin; an equally tough general—and a committed Communist—Georgi Zhukov, commanded the Russian sector. The two of them, as Eisenhower said later, made up their minds to cooperate "in our little local place there," to set an example, a demonstration "that even two nations," however diametrically opposed, could "get along if they would both recognize the folly of not getting along."

Dwight David Eisenhower was born in Denison, Texas, and grew up in Abilene. But in 1952 as president of Columbia University (he had gone on leave to SHAPE), Eisenhower lived at 50 Morningside Drive on Manhattan Island, the candidate of the Eastern Establishment: Time, Inc., the *New York Times*, New York Governor Thomas E. Dewey, Marshall Plan Administrator Paul Hoffman, New York big business—all the powerful plutocrats that Ohio Senator Bob Taft said had ganged up on him and snatched away the Republican nomination, which was his by every right.

Like his great hero, General George Marshall (the man who had jumped Ike over scores of officers with greater seniority and made him powerful and famous as a war commander, knowing, as John Eisenhower once observed, that "Dad would produce"; the man whom Ike revered above all others he had ever met, and he'd met them all, from FDR to Winston Churchill to Charles de Gaulle), like George Marshall, Eisenhower modeled himself on the image of Robert E. Lee and George Washington—to him the "greatest man the English-speaking world ever produced."

Like Washington (who in a fury could, with his bare hands, beat a clutch of drunken, brawling soldiers into submission) and Lee (who at times had to be physically restrained from rushing into battle) and Marshall (who at night at VMI would "run the block," going AWOL after hours to court the future Mrs. Marshall), Dwight Eisenhower was not made of sugar candy. In discipline at West Point in a class of 162, he ended up 125th. He once commented on a classmate: He'll never get anywhere; he never breaks a rule.

Ike had much in common with his great friend General Blood-and-Guts George Patton. As young officers in Panama, Ike and George heard of some bandits in a nearby forest who would at night waylay and rob innocent travelers along a lonely road. The two of them armed themselves to the teeth, put their hands in their pockets, and in the dark of night walked nonchalantly down the dangerous trail hoping—just hoping—the bandits would make an appearance. Perhaps forewarned, the bandits never did. "Someday you're going

to be dictator of this country," Patton once confided to Ike, looking
hopefully into the future, "and I want to be your right hand man."
Years later—after the war, after Patton's death, and after Ike had
become not dictator of the United States of America but President
of Columbia University—he would still insist on his right as a citizen
to take a walk of an evening, even in the wilds of Morningside
Heights, hard by Harlem. And he would always carry a service re-
volver with him. A few years later, after he became President, most
people knew that he liked to begin cabinet meetings with a prayer;
few knew that after one such meeting he had burst from the cabinet
room, turned to his appointments secretary, Tom Stephens, and exploded, "Jesus Christ, we forgot the prayer!"

Ike was a man of fire, but unlike McCarthy, he was a man of
colossal discipline, discipline that reined in that burning élan and
bent it to the service of causes greater than himself, from the Army
to the United States of America to the NATO alliance to the family
of man. These he served with high seriousness and single-minded-
ness. He couldn't see how you could call a man an SOB one minute
and then turn around and shake hands with him the next. He did
not live by personal attack on others. He served organizations; he
espoused policies. He would criticize other organizations and different policies. But not individuals. He never named names, even
Joseph Stalin's. When speechwriter Emmet Hughes brought him an
early draft of his first State of the Union message—a draft that contained a direct punch in the nose for the Soviet dictator—Ike struck
it out. "It's always possible I'll be meeting and negotiating with him
some day." Even less would Eisenhower lash out mindlessly at
chance targets of opportunity.

So there in Peoria's Pere Marquette Hotel two men headed for
their first confrontation. One was a man who habitually recognized
that he was part of an organization to which he had responsibility,
an organization that imposed limitations on his powers and whims
and personal predilections. The other was an undisciplined individual, a loose cannon on the deck. Ike could win hearts. He could
handle an opposing Army. But how would he control what looked
like a mongrel, untrained and yapping at his heels? The General
saw the Senator as a scandal, a national disgrace mishandled by the
Democrats, especially President Truman, who sullied his office by his
tendency to grapple in the ring with someone beneath him. Eisenhower did not see Joe McCarthy as a personal threat.

The two men were meeting in the world of partisan politics, the world of McCarthy, not of Eisenhower. Ike's partisanship had virtually begun and ended at age six when as a young Republican, he carried down the main street of Abilene a crude lantern—a cotton cloth soaked in coal oil—in a torchlight parade for William McKinley. He had gone into military service, marching in Woodrow Wilson's first inaugural parade, serving in Washington under Douglas MacArthur in the years of Herbert Hoover and Franklin Roosevelt, consorting with Roosevelt and Churchill during the war, responding to Harry Truman's summons to head the NATO forces. Assured that he could win the nomination for President as either Democrat or Republican, as late as February of 1952 Eisenhower had not yet agreed to become a candidate. He struggled over a conflict of loyalties, to NATO as a lifetime soldier, to the United States as a presidential candidate. As he struggled with this conflict at SHAPE headquarters, actor Robert Montgomery had brought him a passage from Stephen Vincent Benét's *John Brown's Body* which struck home. God has evidently made my duty clear to everyone else, Abraham Lincoln says; "it might be thought He would reveal it me." Eisenhower's arm had been twisted by a persistent and persuasive young Massachusetts senator, Henry Cabot Lodge. He had been moved to tears by a film brought to him at SHAPE by world-renowned aviatrix Jacqueline Cochran, which showed thousands upon thousands of citizens crowding Madison Square Garden in a spontaneous, emotional, and rousing show of hope that he would run. And finally in February of 1952 in London, where he had gone to attend the funeral of King George VI, Eisenhower had yielded to the iron persuasion of General Lucius Clay—hero of the Berlin airlift—and finally agreed to run for President on the Republican ticket. He had come home in June of 1952 and launched his campaign with a speech in an Abilene downpour that none could fault: "It came out," one amused critic averred, "for home, mother, and heaven."

That was the kind of platform on which Ike wanted to run and unite the country. Instead, immediately, he had found himself in the scurvy world of practical hardball politics. On July 11 he won a first ballot victory over Robert Taft—a near thing, as Wellington said of Waterloo—that left many scars in the party. Lucius Clay, Herbert Brownell, and a smoke-filled room of Republican regulars selected—from a little list approved by Ike—his running mate: California Senator Richard Nixon. Insecure in politics, Eisenhower met at his

Morningside Heights home with defeated Ohio Senator Robert A. Taft, who emerged from the meeting with a declaration of agreement to make drastic cuts in the federal budget, an agreement that would come back to haunt Eisenhower later. By the end of August, his campaign was "running like a dry creek." By the end of September, he found himself up to his elbows in the Nixon fund controversy—the allegation that Nixon had a secret fund filled by rich contributors which kept the Republican Vice Presidential nominee in a life-style far above his means—a controversy that ended only with a full-scale investigation that revealed Nixon's fund totaled only $18,235 and went into postage stamps, envelopes, and other campaign paraphernalia; and a nationwide television broadcast by Nixon himself—the famous Checkers speech—in which Nixon bared his financial records, proved himself "clean as a hound's tooth," and converted his candidacy from a burden on Eisenhower into a powerful asset.

Eisenhower remained above the fray of the Nixon controversy. He tried to remain above it all with McCarthy also. He thought he could dispose of the issue by a declaration of principle—an outright condemnation of guilt by association. He couldn't. He felt also that he could dispose of McCarthy's attacks on General Marshall by a vigorous defense. So when reporters at a Denver news conference on August 22 asked about Marshall and his alleged treason, Ike exploded: "There was nothing of disloyalty in General Marshall's soul. . . . I am not going to support anything that smacks to me of unAmericanism. . . . George Marshall is one of the patriots of this country. . . . Maybe he has made mistakes. I do not know about that, but from the time I met him on December 14, 1941, until the war was over, if he was not a perfect example of patriotism and loyal servant of the United States, I never saw one. If I could say any more, I would say it, but I have no patience with anyone who can find in his record of service for this country anything to criticize."

Campaigning in September in Indiana, Eisenhower found himself on the stage near Republican Senator William Jenner—a red-baiter as virulent as McCarthy, and more foul-mouthed, a mudslinger who called General Marshall "a front man for traitors." Suddenly, with photographers standing at the ready, Jenner approached, grabbed Ike's arm, and lofted it high in the air. Ike habitually disliked back-slapping. And at Jenner's touch he recoiled. Afterward he confided to Bernard Shanley: "He's just slimy."

Through all these weeks before his coming to Peoria, Eisenhower's gorge had been rising. His staff had fouled up; he hadn't wanted to go into postprimary Wisconsin in the first place. Now, poised for the entry, at five-thirty on October 2, he had no choice. His train would be rolling across the state the next day. And its despised junior Senator was coming to call.

The elevator stopped at the General's floor. McCarthy stepped out. He walked with great difficulty, every move an agony. Back in July he had undergone an operation—duplicating one in boyhood—for maxillary sinusitis. Shortly thereafter he complained of severe stomach trouble. Once again he had undergone an operation, this time for a herniated diaphragm. It had cost him eighteen pounds and left him with a painful scar running from his stomach to his shoulder, and a slight twitch of the head. Into the bargain, he had injured his back jumping out of a car. All things considered, he had no business traveling to see the General at all. But he *had*, in violation of his doctor's orders. He was forever violating doctors' orders, getting up out of hospital beds, staying up all night in reckless poker games, burning the candle at both ends, pushing and punishing his powerful body.

As McCarthy left the elevator, a lone Eisenhower aide, General Robert Cutler, recognized the Senator, came forward to help him, assisted him into a stiff-backed chair, and got him a drink of water. Then, taking McCarthy by the arm, Cutler walked him down the empty hallway to Eisenhower's suite, escorted the Senator in, closed the door, and waited outside.

General and Senator met in the suite's principal room—a combination living room and dining room. Off it a small vestibule with a couple of chairs separated this room from the outside hall. And in that vestibule sat two men. The first was Thomas E. Stephens—Eisenhower's appointments secretary through most of his eight presidential years. A New York lawyer, Stephens was also a veteran of many a Republican campaign, from Wall Street attorney Herbert Brownell's campaign for the New York State Assembly in the 1930s to the 1944 and 1948 presidential races under Brownell's campaign direction, to the crowning 1952 search for Eisenhower delegate votes at the Republican Convention. On nitty-gritty political questions, Thomas E. Stephens *was* Dwight D. Eisenhower: he was shrewd, experienced, knowledgeable. He hid this acumen under deadpan humor. He was the kind of prankster who once ordered a couple of huge exotic dogs from Tibet, had them brought into the country, and then shipped them to an unsuspecting Kansas senator. He once purchased a mynah bird, phoned the pet store to complain that it couldn't talk, listened to the salesman offer a substitute of proved loquacity, and then demanded: "Well then, put him on the phone." Once he walked down Sixteenth Street from his apartment to his White House office, passed the Russian embassy, extended a loud greeting to a yardman, received no reply, repeated the performance the second day, again received no reply, and on the third day yelled out enthusiastically, "I got your message." He chuckled over the fact that he never saw the man again. Stephens would fill his apartment with gags, including a chair bearing a small brass plaque that read: "If Abraham Lincoln's bodyguard had been sitting in this chair at Ford's Theatre as he was supposed to, history would have been different." When Ike would go on vacation in the mountains of Colorado, one could frequently find Stephens in the company there of an old gold panner named Arlo, with whom he formed a fast friendship.

Tom Stephens sat in that vestibule throughout Eisenhower's meeting with McCarthy and to this day remembers nothing about it. To one and all he has always claimed he was sleeping.

The second man in the vestibule was another Irishman, Kevin McCann. McCann had been brought up in Chicago, trained by the Jesuits in Cathedral Latin High School and at Saint Mary's of the Lakes University. He became an industrial engineer and publisher of weekly newspapers around Chicago. He entered the army as a private, went to OCS, served in New Guinea, became an assistant to Under Secretary of War (later Secretary) Robert Patterson, then to Dwight Eisenhower, and in 1948 left the Army with the rank of lieutenant colonel. He wrote speeches for Eisenhower, helped Ike write *Crusade in Europe,* and in 1951 went to SHAPE headquarters. Tall, gaunt, spring-coiled, with nervous energy exploding in laughter or a groan, a no-nonsense Eisenhower idealist, McCann wrote with precision and sonority. He liked to make life interesting, and he collected bright personalities about him, from Jinx Falkenburg to *Washington Post* reporter Eddie Folliard to Joe McCarthy.

Shortly before his death in 1981, McCann disclosed in detail his vivid recollection of the Eisenhower-McCarthy confrontation. "I never heard the General so coldbloodedly skin a man. He spoke with white hot anger and just took McCarthy apart. The air turned blue—so blue I became embarrassed and finally had to leave." What did McCarthy say? "He just grunted and groaned. He said damn little. He was not a heavyweight, and when he was personally attacked, he just went into shock. When he emerged, I felt sorry for the guy. He had just been in the hospital. And I know he came to Peoria against his doctor's advice."

McCarthy recovered quickly, however. He—and only he—got to the press.

"What happened in the meeting?" Bill Lawrence of the *New York Times* asked.

"We had a very very pleasant conversation," McCarthy replied. And that false report entered the public mind.

As soon as McCarthy left Eisenhower's suite, the General called in Governor Kohler. They talked briefly about the campaign. Eisenhower seemed relaxed. An eat-and-run buffet dinner followed (Ike had to deliver a talk that night). Kohler, Eisenhower, and Cutler ate at one small card table. Other aides—Gabriel Hauge, McCann, Jim Hagerty and General Wilton Persons—scattered around the room. McCarthy was not invited. During dinner Eisenhower said nothing to Kohler about McCarthy or the conversation. McCarthy waited for Kohler back in Summerfield's room.

After dinner McCann and his daughter Marie conveyed McCarthy to the campaign train, "took him to his compartment, and told him to stay there." At ten-thirty that night it pulled out of the station and headed toward northeast Wisconsin—toward the country where in 1854, in the town of Ripon, a crowd of restless reformers had met to put together a new political entity called the Republican party, uniting Whigs, Democrats, Free Soilers, and Abolitionists; toward the country where now, a century later, a man called McCarthy had his roots and made his home.

It would be a long day, that day of Wisconsin campaigning, October 3. McCarthy always dressed slovenly, leaving dirty socks and underwear strewn about his rented room in the home of his administrative assistant Ed Kiermas, wearing grimy shirts and frayed and shiny suits. But at breakfast, on the train that October morning, Marie McCann was especially shocked at his physical appearance: pain in his walk, a big grease spot on his tie. McCarthy got no breakfast; by the time he—and McCann and Kohler—made their appearance, the dining car had run out of food. "We got only some damn coffee," McCann ruefully recalled.

For hour after hour that day McCann "babysat" the Senator. "I would not let him out of my sight." McCann had known him for years, from the time before the war when McCarthy had been a big

Wisconsin Democrat. Now on the train they just reminisced. Mc-Carthy rambled on about Wisconsin. Art Summerfield came in with news of the indictment of a Communist woman. "Tell the General that," Kohler urged McCarthy, but the Senator was keeping his distance from Eisenhower. ("He probably got his courage back later out of a whiskey bottle," McCann later speculated.)

First stop, at 9:00 A.M.: Green Bay (population 53,000), home of the Packers and of Vince Lombardi, to whom winning was the only thing; a city that turned out paper and paper products and boasted the largest cheese-processing center in the U.S. From the back plat-form of Ike's car—the last one on the train—McCarthy was intro-duced to the crowd of about 3,000. He left the platform before Ike appeared, but hovered inside, listening. Eisenhower announced that he agreed with McCarthy on the purpose of "ridding this Govern-ment of the incompetent, the dishonest and above all the subversive and disloyal. . . . The differences between me and Senator Mc-Carthy are well known to others. But what is more important, they are well known to him and to me, and we have discussed them. . . . Our differences have nothing to do with the end result that we are seeking. The differences apply to method." Inside, McCarthy shook his head. Ike urged the election of Republicans one and all.

At nine-fifteen the train pulled out.

Next stop, at 11:00 A.M.: Appleton (population 34,000), Mc-Carthy's hometown, a wealthy dairy and livestock area, and the home also of Lawrence College, which would soon send its presi-dent—Nathan Marsh Pusey, an outspoken anti-McCarthyite—to the presidency of Harvard. McCarthy himself introduced Eisenhower this time. Eisenhower made no mention of McCarthy. Governor Kohler sat on the platform, between the two men, "insulated," the Governor amusingly recalled later, "by Kohler."

Next stop: Neenah-Menasha, twin cities (population 12,000 each) on Lake Winnebago, a paper-making capital with eleven paper mills. Ten minutes there, then on to Fond-du-Lac, a town of 30,000 people with seventy factories and a big output of dairy products.

The morning ended. At two-fifteen that afternoon the train ar-rived at its destination, Milwaukee (population 637,000), a city made famous by Schlitz; home of McCarthy's alma mater, Mar-quette University; and the scheduled site of a major Eisenhower ad-dress that night before a rally of 13,000 boisterous Republicans.

Publicly, it had been a bad scene, with Ike's reiterating: "You elected him; I don't agree with him." Somewhere along the track the train had given a sudden jerk: Ike, lying down trying to catch a few minutes' rest, banged his head. He felt groggy the rest of the day.

Privately, October 3 had been an even worse scene.

For throughout the morning a backstage battle had been raging. Specifically, it had been a battle over seventy-four words, a single paragraph in the draft for Eisenhower's speech that night: "Let me be quite specific. I know that charges of disloyalty have, in the past, been leveled against General George C. Marshall. I have been privileged for 35 years to know General Marshall personally. I know him, as a man and as a soldier, to be dedicated with singular selflessness and the profoundest patriotism to the service of America. And this episode is a sobering lesson in the way freedom must not defend itself."

Deliberately, intentionally, those words had been designed to slap McCarthy in the face in his own backyard. In his presence Ike would disown the lie, the demagogic assault on Marshall, the ruthlessness of the Senator's private anti-Communist crusade. The idea of including those words had come to Eisenhower some days earlier from Arthur Hays Sulzberger, the publisher of the *New York Times*, who by one account actually wrote them, and who without question, in a face-to-face meeting, personally urged them on the General and won Eisenhower's enthusiastic acceptance.

Lean, graying, sixty-one, liberal and respected, Sulzberger had married the daughter of the boss, Adolph Ochs, and had for seventeen years led the *Times* onward and upward as the nation's number one newspaper, the voice of independent progressivism, of the internationalist Eastern Establishment. His friend and fellow New Yorker, Dwight Eisenhower, president of his alma mater, Columbia University, owed him a lot. In February of 1952, breaking with the paper's past practice of announcing for a candidate only after the political conventions, and fearing the nomination of midwestern isolationist Robert Taft, the *Times* had come out for the election of Eisenhower. In those heady days, liberal Republicanism resurgent was receiving widespread liberal applause: from radio commentator Elmer Davis, columnist Walter Lippmann, the *New York Herald Tribune*, and above all the *New York Times*. Up at Harvard, still a very young man-on-the-move, McGeorge Bundy—collaborator with Henry Stimson on his memoirs and brother of Dean Acheson's son-in-law—spearheaded Ike's drive in the Yard. The country had had a surfeit of Harry Truman, midwesternism, crooks and cronies, and mediocrity in government, and opinion leaders like Sulzberger welcomed the new progressive Republican white knight. In their view Eisenhower had only one problem, to shake himself free of clinging McCarthyism, and this punch in the nose would do the trick.

The time for it would be October 3, 9:00 P.M. The place would be the cavernous Milwaukee Arena, filled with yelling loyalists. The subject would be anticommunism: tough anticommunism, no-nonsense anticommunism, but anticommunism that moved by due process, that separated fog from fire, that respected civil liberties. It was anticommunism smear-free. And it was anticommunism that drew a sharp line around the region of McCarthyism.

To shape the speech another ikon in the world of eastern publishing, Clare Boothe Luce, discovered in the Time, Inc., empire a passionate young liberal, Emmet John Hughes. Emmet did not ride the campaign train. He worked back in Eisenhower headquarters in the Commodore Hotel in the heart of Manhattan, under the supervisory eyes of Herbert Brownell, C. D. Jackson, and Harold Stassen, writing, writing, writing, turning out words that mirrored his own life—Princeton *summa*, ardent Catholic, passionate independent, internationalist devoted to new initiatives in foreign policy, mesmerized student of Italian painting—singing and soaring words, rich in music and persuasiveness.

His heart had leaped up when, in a brief conference, Eisenhower had told him about the plan to put an anti-McCarthy paragraph into the Milwaukee speech. And Hughes had produced a bell-ringing text. Sulzberger knew what that text contained. Some members of Eisenhower's staff aboard the train also knew. But the press did not. In fact, the press worried: How far would Ike go in endorsing McCarthy?

Aboard the train, the *New York Times* principal political reporter, veteran liberal Bill Lawrence, wondered. Bull-shaped, muscular, with a football guard's aggressiveness and a dogged tenacity, a seasoned political reporter, thirty-six-year-old Lawrence hated McCarthyism—as he would later hate Nixonism—root and branch. But as a great practicing reporter he got along fine with McCarthy. (In fact, when McCarthy later dug up damaging dirt on Eisenhower's Air Force Secretary Harold Talbott—that Talbott was using Air Force stationery for quasibusiness purposes—McCarthy leaked it to his old friend Lawrence, and Lawrence helped force Talbott's resignation.)

New York Times publisher Arthur Sulzberger had told *Times* reporter Lawrence nothing about the anti-McCarthy paragraph. Lawrence would learn about Sulzberger's hand in it only from the *Times*'s managing editor, Turner Catledge, back in New York long after Election Day.

But Nebraskan Lawrence had long known a key aide on the Eisenhower train, Fred Seaton—owner of a string of newspapers and radio stations through the Middle West. So he asked Fred: Will Ike give McCarthy an unqualified endorsement? And Fred gave Lawrence an answer that crossed a crucial invisible line of confidentiality: Eisenhower will endorse McCarthy at Green Bay. But don't form any final judgment until you hear Eisenhower's major speech in Milwaukee. Because that speech includes a defense of General Marshall—a defense in which your publisher is very much interested.

With these words the Marshall paragraph went public. Why did a veteran Nebraska newspaper publisher—wise in the ways of reporters—leak that lethal fact? With hindsight, years later, Ike's press secretary, Jim Hagerty, could comment, not without smugness: "Staff people shouldn't talk about drafts." But Fred Seaton did nothing out of rashness. When he confided in Lawrence (1) he must have assumed that because Sulzberger knew, Lawrence would inevitably know; and (2) he must have taken a calculated risk to hold a powerful reporter from a powerful paper in line behind the Eisenhower candidacy. After all, Seaton must have reasoned that morning in the Wisconsin farmlands, the paragraph would soon become public knowledge anyway, because Hagerty was about to begin stenciling copies of the text for release.

But words are fragile. As the train rolled inexorably toward Milwaukee and the showdown, Governor Walter Kohler of Wisconsin asked to see a copy of the speech.

Kohler was no McCarthyite. At this time forty-eight years old, he had started out as a businessman in the Kohler plumbing-fixture empire, after he had been sent East to Andover and Yale for polishing. He was a small-bore man: nothing especially eventful, he once admitted, happened to him as he worked his way through various jobs in marketing and engineering at the Kohler company, founded by his grandfather. But with the coming of World War II things began to happen. He shipped out to the Solomon Islands. His marriage broke up. Returning from the wars, he entered another family enterprise, the Vollrath Company, founded by his great-grandfather, and became its chairman. Then he moved into politics. Republican, of course: he had attended every state convention since 1929, when his father began a two-year term as Wisconsin's governor.

Under the watchful eye of Wisconsin's "Mr. Republican," party boss Tom Coleman, Kohler ran for the governorship in 1950 and won. Popular, decent, and moderate in office, he deliberately put a distance between himself and McCarthy, whom he personally disliked (rich against poor, Andover against Little Wolf High School, Yale against Marquette) and whose methods he deplored, especially his slanders against Marshall, not to mention the demagogic vibrations the Senator habitually set off. No politician, Kohler once said, should arouse in people the kind of frenzy that McCarthy evoked.

Back in 1946, when Kohler had appeared as a possible rival to McCarthy for the Senate race, the two men had discussed Kohler's divorce. By one account McCarthy threatened to make it a campaign topic and thus kill Kohler with Catholic voters, of whom Wisconsin had scads. Kohler always dismissed the threat. But he admitted that McCarthy, ever devious, might well have claimed to reporters that he had thus scared Kohler out of the race.

In December of 1951, when two thousand of McCarthy's jubilant backers held their big gala precampaign blowout in Milwaukee, Wisconsin's Republican Governor Walter Jodok Kohler pointedly stayed away. Indeed, he seriously considered challenging McCarthy in the 1952 GOP primary. And anti-McCarthy backers began to rally around: Mrs. Ogden Reid of the *New York Herald Tribune* family traveled to Wisconsin to urge the Kohler challenge. Officials of the Wisconsin Federation of Labor promised money and votes.

But in January of 1952 Kohler announced that he would not run for the Senate but would instead seek reelection as governor. Henry Reuss—a declared candidate for the Senate on the Democratic side— pronounced the obituary: "I had hoped that Governor Kohler would carry out the promptings of his conscience and give the decent Wisconsin Republicans a chance to clean up a national disgrace within their party primary."

But Kohler hadn't. And he had his rationalizations. The people who urged him to run against McCarthy were mainly Democrats, and there was no point in playing into their hands. If he had run against McCarthy, he would have split the Republican party wide open and possibly helped elect Democrat Adlai Stevenson as President. By August of 1952, Kohler, practical politician, had managed to swallow his misgivings and made his peace with Joe: "You can't write McCarthy off," he publicly declared. "You can like him or dislike him, but . . . all the things he has said about the Communists in government stack up to the point where there is too much smoke to repudiate McCarthy." As Ike himself came to realize that October day in Wisconsin, Walter Kohler was not "a forceful individual."

Ike's candidacy, nonetheless, owed him a lot. In 1951 Kohler's mentor and friend Tom Coleman—a passionate pro-Taftite—implored the Wisconsin Governor to back the Ohio Senator for the presidency. But Kohler demurred. Despite some qualms about having a military man in the White House, he questioned Taft's international experience and thus inclined toward Eisenhower. In September of 1951, Kohler visited Eisenhower at SHAPE headquarters. All his reservations vanished. He signed onto the Ike bandwagon with enthusiasm. When Coleman, heading the pro-Taft forces in Wisconsin, later implored Kohler to go to the 1952 Republican National Convention as a delegate committed to Taft, Kohler refused. As a result he did not attend the convention as a delegate for anybody. (In fact, Kohler's pro-Eisenhowerism split the Kohler family itself: his sister-in-law went to the convention as a loyalist for Taft.)

Kohler had a major influence, however, on that convention's outcome. A few days before it opened in Chicago, the nation's governors met in conference in Houston. There Kohler and a group of other pro-Ike Republican governors had a get-together in the hotel room of New Hampshire Governor Sherman Adams to talk strategy. The Eisenhower-Taft contest was heading for a screaming climax. Neither side had enough delegate votes to win. In several states—notably Texas, Louisiana, and Georgia—rival Taft and Eisenhower delegate groups were moving toward Chicago, each demanding certification as their state's voting representatives. Already Taft people controlled the Republican National Committee and the mechanics of the convention: old Walter Hallanan of West Virginia would be temporary chairman: old Joe Martin of Massachusetts would be permanent chairman; old Douglas MacArthur would deliver the keynote oration.

So back in Manhattan, Herb Brownell—Dewey's campaign manager in 1944 and 1948, now Ike's principal delegate hunter—had been devising a change in convention rules. This change would keep contested Taft delegations, seated in temporary convention seats, from voting one another into permanent seats. As the meeting in Adams's hotel room went on, Governor Tom Dewey of New York picked up the phone and called Brownell. They talked over this possible change in the convention rules. And somewhere, someone—

Dewey himself always credited *Houston Post* publisher Oveta Culp Hobby—came up with the idea of having the Republican governors, assembled in Houston, put out a "clean hands" declaration—a blunt endorsement of the proposed rules change at the convention. In the upshot Dewey's friend Kohler got out a pencil, drafted up the endorsement, and persuaded nearly all his fellow Republican governors to sign on, starting with such Eisenhower stalwarts as Dewey of New York, Alfred Driscoll of New Jersey, Val Peterson of Nebraska, Dan Thornton of Colorado, John Lodge of Connecticut, and Arthur Langlie of Washington, but including also such fence-sitting favorite sons as Earl Warren of California and Theodore Roosevelt McKeldin of Maryland.

The governors' adoption of this "clean hands" manifesto foreshadowed the adoption of the rules revision—the Fair Play Amendment—at the convention a week later. The vote on the Fair Play Amendment—which joined the Eisenhower forces with those of the "favorite son" states, notably California, Minnesota, and Maryland—not only led to the seating of the Eisenhower delegates; it also demonstrated that Taft lacked a majority in the convention. And that demonstration led to the first-ballot nomination of Dwight Eisenhower. Ike owed Walter Kohler a huge debt.

Kohler was mindful of this debt. And he was also politically scared. Wisconsin was McCarthy country. In the September primary Joe had swamped his opponent, Len Schmitt, by 516,000 to 214,000 votes, rolling up 100,000 more votes than all his Republican and Democratic opponents combined. And McCarthy wasn't Kohler's only problem: Wisconsin was also Taft country. Ike had not even entered the April 1 Wisconsin Republican primary. Taft had all its delegates. Wisconsin's "Mr. Republican" Tom Coleman—silver-haired, genteel, powerful—served as Taft's floor manager at the convention. (Like Kohler, Coleman had come up in business, in 1927 succeeding his father as head of the Madison-Kipp Corporation.) If Taft lost at the convention, Coleman had let it be known, he would go on to Europe—take a walk. And he did. Passions cut deep. "If Taft had won the nomination in Chicago," Cabot Lodge never doubted, "our boys would have walked out," Bull Moosers resurgent. Neither side, Ike's nor Taft's, had ever forgotten 1912, when conservative William Howard Taft snatched the Republican nomination from Teddy Roosevelt. Sherman Adams, Ike's floor manager, forever remembered the livid rage of Ohio's senior Senator John Bricker as Ike's votes went over the top—"the worst day of my life," Bricker said—a livid rage that, generalized among Republican conservatives, plagued Adams to the end. And to this day some who remember those distant times will still identify themselves as "Taft men," unregenerate to infinity.

Walter Kohler, frail reed in the wind, felt the force of all these driving passions. Like any good politician, he thought the election might hang on a thread. For a quarter century no Republican had won the White House. The party—and everybody else—had reasoned they had the 1948 election in the bag, and look at what happened to Tom Dewey. The 1952 Democratic nominee, Governor Adlai Stevenson of Illinois, even with Ike as his opponent, had aroused wide enthusiasm. Intelligent, charming, idealistic, to millions Stevenson was "a new voice in American politics, the most authentic arrival out of Illinois since Abraham Lincoln." Wisconsin had 12 electoral votes. They could possibly, Kohler reasoned, throw the result of the election either way.

So Walter Kohler asked to see a copy of Ike's Milwaukee speech. Sherman Adams, Kohler's old friend from Houston, agreed. The Wisconsin Governor, and speechwriter Kevin McCann, sat down to read it through.

And there it was: the Marshall paragraph—the slap at Joe.

In the frenzy of the moment Kohler could come to only one conclusion: Take it out. Why jeopardize Eisenhower's chances in Wisconsin, he implored, by throwing in that out-of-place paragraph? Why risk defeat for the whole Republican state ticket? Why come here and pick a fight with a home-grown Wisconsin political hero? Everybody knows how Eisenhower feels about Marshall. That's not in question. This paragraph is just gratuitous—out of place in this speech. Besides, with so much smoke, how can you be sure, really sure, that McCarthy is all wrong?

As the argument raged, Kohler had eager allies. Republican National Chairman Art Summerfield, of course. A month earlier he had stuck by Richard Nixon through thick and thin; he may be a son of a bitch, he had claimed, but he's our son of a bitch! You'd never catch Summerfield sacrificing party solidarity for principle. And big Bill Knowland, senior Senator from California, an Oakland newspaper publisher, a heavy plodder, humorless, devoid of grace notes, a man who barreled down the Senate Office Building hallways with such hand-swinging relentlessness that one observer remarked: "Put a pile of books under each arm, and you stop him dead in his tracks." You knew where Bill Knowland stood: An unambiguous reactionary, a man who could whip up a California crowd with the pro-Chiang slogan "Back to the mainland!," a toy of the China lobby, a free-enterprise right-winger. Knowland would have stood shoulder to shoulder with McCarthy at every turn but for one thing: McCarthy's carelessness with fact. Sure, the State Department contained Communists. No doubt about that. But get the names and addresses straight. On the imperative of accuracy, McCarthy and Knowland parted company. But Knowland never belonged as an Eisenhower insider.

On that October Wisconsin morning, Knowland was suddenly called off the campaign train (perhaps, he later speculated darkly, by some of McCarthy's opponents who knew where Knowland stood and what he'd argue for); he had to fill in as an emergency substitute for a suddenly incapacitated Republican speaker in Ohio. Trusting no one, he grabbed a paper and with pencil in longhand wrote out his advice to the General: Leave that Marshall paragraph out. He folded the paper, handed it to his wife (they had been married twenty-five years; he could count on her), and left her with explicit instructions: "Deliver this only to Eisenhower himself, nobody else." He didn't trust—would never trust—the palace guard.

Bill Knowland was an outsider; his credibility was questionable. Jerry Persons was an insider; his was impeccable. What would be his advice on the Marshall paragraph?

Major General Wilton Burton ("Jerry") Persons had known Eisenhower for more than twenty years, from the time when Ike was a major in the Army. In 1933, when Eisenhower was serving in the office of Army Chief of Staff General Douglas MacArthur, and Persons in the Office of the Assistant Secretary of War in charge of congressional relations, they'd done some business together. Persons continued in congressional liaison through the thirties and throughout the war, when he served in that demanding capacity under the demanding Army Chief of Staff George Marshall. Ultimately he ended up on Ike's staff at SHAPE.

To Ike, Persons was a "born diplomat." He was a conservative from a distinguished Alabama family; his brother served as governor of the state. Jerry had lost some of his deep-fried southern accent, but he still pronounced his name "Poissons." And as election results poured in at the end of Ike's second campaign in 1956, he would delight his fellow White House staff members with the announcement that Montgomery, Alabama, "the cradle of the Confederacy . . . had just voted for a Republican for the first time in its history!"

He exuded southern charm. He knew that to "get along you have to go along." When Lyndon Johnson controlled the Senate—and thus the fate of legislation—during Ike's presidency, Jerry Persons could be seen at a gala dinner jumping up and down to open and close the window behind the imperious Texas Democrat to assure his comfort.

Persons had the light touch. On Saturdays he would come into the White House in screaming loud jackets and blaring argyle socks. And once when a sobersided budget bureau spokesman was making a presentation on rivers-and-harbors projects of the Corps of Army Engineers, and a mischievous staffer looked at the map, noted the great cluster of power dams down in Alabama, and peremptorily demanded to know: "Why do you have all those dams down in Alabama? Alabama doesn't have any rivers." Persons shot back: "We're diggin' one!" But underneath the banter and the relaxed southern veneer, he was "taut as a bow string," sharp, shrewd—a man who in conducting business between Pentagon and Hill throughout the war habitually talked on two telephones at once.

He was a genius in engineering assent. Whatever Eisenhower wanted from the Hill, Persons would break his back to deliver—right, left, or center. Though at times as a southern conservative he evinced a lingering sympathy for McCarthy's purposes, of all the men on Ike's campaign train, Persons had done more than anyone else to protest McCarthy's onslaught against Persons's beloved former boss George Marshall. Persons resented it bitterly. McCarthy knew of that resentment because Persons had personally told him so, in a confrontation that had lasted nearly four hours. "I thought at times he was going to withdraw [that attack]," Persons recalled in an interview years later. Typically, Persons told McCarthy exactly what he thought. And typically he remembered that McCarthy was "very decent" about Persons's stand: "I never had any words or trouble with McCarthy." Like Walter Kohler, a practical politician, Persons habitually added up the numbers, totaled up the vote. His mind worked by arithmetic, not ideology. He came out against the Marshall paragraph.

So on one side of the argument there stood Governor Kohler, Senator Knowland, Chairman Summerfield, and General Persons. And on the other side? Not much.

Young Emmet Hughes was back in New York, writing. His boss, C. D. Jackson, high in the Time-Life organization, who later would condemn the compromisers and beg Eisenhower to bat McCarthy in the teeth, never got into the act. Jim Hagerty, a Dewey liberal, for some reason didn't weigh in.

Only two on the train strongly resisted the paragraph's deletion, both liberal Republicans. One was Brigadier General Robert Cutler, like his friend Jerry Persons devoted to General Marshall—under whom he had served, also in congressional liaison, during the war— and praised by Marshall as "a rose among cabbages." Bobby Cutler was a Boston Brahmin, president of the Old Colony Trust Company. A Phi Beta Kappa at Harvard, he had been elected to Porcellian, preceded by four brothers. He'd studied Shakespeare under George Lyman Kittredge, Milton under William Allan Neilson, and English composition with Harvard's revered Dean Briggs. Dean Briggs became Cutler's mentor. In his English 5, Cutler wrote his second novel, *Louisburg Square*, which after his graduation was published by Macmillan and followed by yet another novel, *The Speckled Bird*. After Harvard College, Cutler went on to Harvard Law School, made the prestigious Harvard *Law Review*, and graduated *cum laude*. A devout Anglican with a fastidiousness with words—and a raunchy mind that made him resemble Jonathan Swift more than any other man I have ever known—Cutler in his Boston elegance had no use whatsoever for Wisconsin's marauding junior Senator. Cutler was a man boiling with indignation. But he was no infighter.

Beside him stood a younger fellow Harvard man, Dr. Gabriel Hauge, who in the campaign wrote speeches and would ultimately become Eisenhower's chief White House economics advisor. Hauge came from Moorhead, Minnesota, the son of a Lutheran minister. Gabe was portly, round-faced, owlish. He was also rock-solid of conscience and brilliant and academic of mind. And he loathed McCarthyism as much as he idolized Eisenhower. He had seen McCarthy get into the elevator to go up to meet with the General in Peoria, and the sight had made him sick. No one would challenge Hauge's sternness of conviction, his absolute rectitude. (Kevin McCann once recalled with some amusement that through a mixup in the campaign scheduling, his daughter Marie somehow got put into Hauge's room, to the mystification of callers who heard her answer the phone and wondered incredulously what Gabe was up to.) He had even toughened up the Marshall paragraph a little. But he was young, a recent Ph.D., and an editorial writer from *Business Week*. And he was simply outgunned. "Who was Gabe Hauge," he once asked rhetorically in an interview, "to stand up against the Governor of Wisconsin, the Senior Senator from California, and the Republican National Chairman?"

The power tilted, overwhelmingly, toward McCarthy. The point man—Eisenhower's Chief of Staff on the train, the man to whom the General looked above all others for counsel—was of course Governor Sherman Adams. Adams, himself an anti-Taft Republican liberal, in his heart of hearts knew exactly where he stood: he had no more use for McCarthy than did Cutler and Hauge. Moreover, Adams never shied away from a fight. He had tangled with Chairman Summerfield over the Nixon fund incident: "General Eisenhower doesn't have sons-of-bitches running with him on his ticket." And he had tangled with Summerfield when Jenner had come forward and manhandled Eisenhower; he told Summerfield exactly what he thought of his failure to keep that kind of episode from happening. And he told him in "unlady-like" New Hampshire lumberjack phraseology. But Adams had a warm spot in his heart for Walter Kohler. He listened to Kohler's practical political reasoning. And he came down on Kohler's side.

Adams, Kohler, and Persons met with Eisenhower. In retrospect Adams always believed he made a mistake. "I should have taken Hauge in with me," he reflected long afterward in an interview. But he didn't. He didn't give Ike a chance to hear the opposite side.

Adams began to outline the background of political reality, starting with Taft and Tom Coleman. Eisenhower quickly broke in: "Are you telling me this paragraph should come out?"

"Yes."

"Take it out." Adams recalls the reply, as peremptory as if Eisenhower were sentencing a man to death. The deed was done.

Hauge and Cutler were sitting in the back of the train. Adams came back to see them.

"The paragraph is going out."

Hauge could not believe what he was hearing. He protested.

"It's been decided."

Eisenhower himself appeared. "You could tell the ordeal he'd been through," Hauge later recalled in an interview. "He was purple down to the root of his neck, and glowering."

Hauge asked Eisenhower for confirmation.

"Yes." The menacing tone of his voice "shut off all possible argument."

Gabe Hauge would never forget that moment—the one time when he felt ready to get off the train and quit. He never forgot the overpowering practical political advice that had overwhelmed his opposition. And he never forgot that, in retrospect, he had been proved right, the others wrong—"all wrong. . . . The audience in Milwau-

kee that night," he recalled—and he was absolutely on target—
"would have cheered Eisenhower on anything. They cheered every
sentence, they cheered the pauses, they cheered the commas, they
cheered the periods. He could have called for the impeachment of
Senator McCarthy, and they would have cheered. . . ."

Eisenhower, supreme organization man, had bowed to his organization. And the organization had failed him. Here he was, Hauge
observed, the General getting this advice that afternoon. He was
used to taking advice from informed advisors. These people were
friends of his. They were supporters of his. They were working their
hearts out for him. He accepted their advice. And they let him down.

The damage was done. But at this precise moment no one knew
the half of it. Because when Eisenhower and Adams arrived at the
decision, they did not know that the Marshall paragraph was already in process of going public, from Fred Seaton to reporter Bill
Lawrence, to the world.

They did not know what Lawrence would do with that fact: that
he would couple it with a lie—an assertion that McCarthy himself, in
the Pere Marquette Hotel, had personally gone over the Milwaukee
text with Eisenhower and had personally persuaded him to drop the
paragraph about Marshall. Such an assertion obviously did not come
from Eisenhower or McCann. It therefore in all likelihood came
from Bill Lawrence's principal source throughout this episode, Joe
McCarthy. And on the evidence it contained not a word of truth. In
a letter to Merlo Pusey of the *Washington Post* dated February 2,
1955, Kohler maintained that McCarthy did not see the Milwaukee
speech in Peoria or anywhere else in advance—did not see it until it
was released to the press. Later, in his oral history reminiscences,
Kohler went even further, asserting that on McCarthy's return to Art
Summerfield's room after his confrontation with Eisenhower, he
said nothing whatsoever about the contents of the Milwaukee
speech. Kohler himself—far closer to Eisenhower than McCarthy
ever was or would ever be—did not see the speech text until the following morning, when he had to ask to see it.

Seaton leaked. McCarthy lied. The result was inevitable: Lawrence's allegation on page one of the October 4 *New York Times* that
Eisenhower had bowed to McCarthy's urging and dropped his defense of the revered George Marshall.

Forever afterward Eisenhower would almost apoplectically deny
the accusation. But the scar would never disappear. McCarthy had
won the initial skirmish.

II

"DON'T JOIN THE BOOK BURNERS"

Eisenhower became President in a landslide, ending twenty years of Roosevelt and Truman. Within weeks of his victory he stole away from his New York residence in the dark of night to fly to the far battlefields of Korea to redeem his campaign promise that had decided the election: "I shall go to Korea."

A great change was getting underway on the national and international scene. Now it would be Ike standing up to Stalin: the Norman Rockwell Kansas General and NATO Commander squaring off against the murderer from the Caucasus, the neo-Attila scourge of Europe. The new President's first inaugural address would draw the line: "Good is pitted against evil, darkness against the light." The forces of Chiang's Nationalists, previously blocked from attacking the Chinese mainland by the U.S. Seventh Fleet, would be unleashed. The Acheson-Kennan containment doctrine—the product of what the new Vice President of the United States had called in the campaign the "cowardly college of Communist containment"—would be abandoned and a new doctrine of rollback—the liberation of Europe's captive peoples by peaceful means—would be erected in its place. Harry Truman's mess in Washington would be cleaned up, the crooks and cronies jailed and banished, the Communists in high places fired.

A new era of executive-congressional amity would begin. Cooperate with congressional investigating committees, Eisenhower told his cabinet on January 30. Get to know, officially and socially, the chairmen of the committees closest to your departments, Eisenhower's legislative liaison chief Jerry Persons underscored; handle personally all patronage requests coming from any congressman.

Eisenhower had a blue-ribbon cabinet team: John Foster Dulles of Wall Street's prestigious Sullivan and Cromwell law firm for State, George M. Humphrey of Cleveland's powerful M. A. Hanna and Company for Treasury, Charles E. Wilson of General Motors for Defense, Herbert Brownell of Wall Street's Lord, Day and Lord for Justice, plus Henry Cabot Lodge of Massachusetts for UN Ambassador.

One by one in the weeks after the election, amid busy comings and goings at Ike's residence on Morningside Heights, their names were given to eagerly waiting reporters in a succession of portentous announcements.

In ludicrous harum-scarum contrast, several miles downtown, at a cocktail party at Times Square's Astor Hotel, another staff was being assembled.

Joe McCarthy had won a second term in the Senate. The Republicans had won control of the Eighty-third Congress: an 8-vote lead in the House, a one-vote lead in the Senate. McCarthy would therefore become chairman of the Permanent Subcommittee on Investigations of the Senate Government Operations Committee with an increase in personnel and a doubling of its 1952 funds. So he would be hiring new staff members. He had heard of a bright and eager young attorney in the office of Harry Truman's outgoing Attorney General, and he wanted to meet this Roy Cohn.

And so they met: at eleven o'clock on a December night in McCarthy's suite at the Astor, dozens of partying gowned and dinner-jacketed ladies and gentlemen milling about, McCarthy himself jovial and gregarious in the midst of it all, relaxed in patent leather shoes, tuxedo trousers, and a pair of suspenders over an undershirt.

"My God, I'm glad to meet you," McCarthy burst out. "But you can't possibly be one tenth as good as everyone says you are. I just want to find out what's public relations and what's real."

At twenty-five, Roy Cohn had already established an incandescent record. When Roy was nine his father, a prominent Bronx Democrat, Judge Albert Cohn of the New York State Supreme Court, took him to Washington, where he met Associate Supreme Court Justice Benjamin Cardozo and earnestly outlined to President Franklin Roosevelt his views on the packing of the Supreme Court. He entered Columbia College, and under the forced pace of the wartime years graduated with both an A.B. and a law degree at the age of twenty. He revealed a brilliant mind and photographic memory. While he waited until his twenty-first birthday to take the New York bar exam, he served as a photostat operator in the office of the U.S. Attorney for the Southern District of New York. And on the day he became a member of the bar, he was sworn in as an Assistant U.S. Attorney. In this position he helped convict the top-drawer leaders of the U.S. Communist party for violation of the Smith Act, which, enacted in 1940, made it a crime to advocate the violent overthrow of the government; William Remington, the Department of Commerce employee identified by Elizabeth Bentley as a Communist spy, for perjury; and Julius and Ethel Rosenberg for espionage—the theft of atomic secrets. Cohn assisted the McCarran Internal Security Subcommittee in its probe of Communists among the Americans working at the U.N. Along the way, he also picked up some experience in prosecuting counterfeiters and traffickers in narcotics. In July of 1952, ten minutes out of New York Harbor on a boat headed for Europe and vacation, he got a ship-to-shore phone call: Truman's Attorney General was calling, offering him a job. So in September of 1952 the young man went to Washington to work for James P. McGranery as a special assistant to the Attorney General of the United States. Occupying space formerly held by three junior department lawyers, acquiring a private cable address and telephone line to his Wall Street law firm—Curran and Stim—from which he continued to draw a salary, Cohn worked on the indictment of Owen Lattimore on perjury charges, which had come out of investigation by the McCarran committee.

Cohn was five feet eight inches tall, 160 pounds, with dark complexion and dark hair, which he slicked back. A boyhood accident had left him with a scar on his nose. He had sleepy, hooded eyelids. But everything else about him mirrored intensity, ambition, rapidity of mind and speech. Already he had friends known for conservatism and power: the Hearst Columnist George Sokolsky, a right-wing tiger and an old friend of Cohn's father; the clattering commentator Walter Winchell; and, from 1952 on, an institution within the Justice Department, FBI Director J. Edgar Hoover. Cohn also had choice enemies, produced by his abrasiveness, his unwillingness to suffer fools gladly. Over time, McCarthy's close friends from rural Wisconsin came to detest Roy Cohn.

On the day after New Year's 1953, McCarthy announced Cohn's appointment as the Chief Counsel of the Investigations Subcommittee. FBI Director Hoover, Vice President Nixon, and about twenty Senators showed up for a private party to celebrate.

Less than a year earlier a friend had invited Cohn to lunch with a young man named G. David Schine. They had become close friends, occasionally double-dating. Upon joining the subcommittee, Cohn soon recommended that McCarthy hire Schine as an unpaid "Chief Consultant."

G. David Schine, twenty-five, was rich, the son of a multimillionaire owner of a string of hotels, theaters, and radio stations across the country. After serving for a postwar year as a civilian employee— a purser—in the Army Transportation Service, and after graduating from college, he became president of Schine Hotels, Inc. He had a Manhattan office at Fifty-seventh and Park. He indulged in a variety of tastes for nightclubs, starlets, and fancy cars; he claimed the world's largest collection of cigars.

His family had sent him to Fessenden and Andover, where he made respectable grades, and then to Harvard, where he not only did well but also sported a black convertible equipped with a telephone.

He was handsome: tall, slim, blond; in the words of the unsympathetic *New Yorker* correspondent Richard Rovere, "sallow, sleekly coiffed, and somnolent-eyed," in a "style that one used to associate with male orchestra singers." Schine had indeed once served as press agent for the Vaughn Monroe orchestra and had even indited a couple of desperately blue-mooded ballads, including one called "Please Say Yes or It's Goodbye," which ended with a prosecutorial couplet: "So I'm asking you to tell me how things stand. A simple 'yes' or 'no' is all that I demand." He knew his way around.

At the beginning of 1953 nobody had ever heard of him, except perhaps those guests at a Schine hotel who chanced to riffle through a publication left in every room—a six-page pamphlet entitled "Definition of Communism," a work that despite its misdating of the Russian Revolution, the founding of the Communist party, and the start of the first Russian five-year plan; its misnaming of Lenin; and its confusion of Stalin and Trotsky, Marx and Lenin, and Kerensky and Prince Lvov, stood as exhibit A of author Schine's credentials as an authority on Communist ideology.

One day the whole United States of America would learn the size of G. David Schine's feet—13. But at the moment young Schine was, to paraphrase Archibald MacLeish, "rich, rich, and no one had heard of him." His draft board had classified him 4-F.

In all this organizing of staff there had been a slight hitch. McCarthy had heard of another bright young man—equally unknown— heard of him from his father, a McCarthy campaign contributor, the Honorable Joseph P. Kennedy, father of John F. Kennedy (just elected senator from Massachusetts) and former United States Ambassador to England under Franklin Roosevelt. Jack's younger brother Bobby wanted a job. Lean, sharp, he had not by a long shot acquired that humanitarian warmth of heart for the downtrodden—the poor, the underprivileged, the blacks, the American Indians, the Hispanics, the elderly, all the forgotten little people—that would one day make him a political hero to a new generation of alienated students and an older generation of dispossessed political liberals, heirs of the old New Deal. But he already had a countervailing quality they would equally admire—ruthlessness. He had it in abundance.

"Bobby hates like I do," old Joe once declared, admiringly singling this one out of his gregarious brood. The others had other virtues—good looks, loyalty, a sense of honor. Bobby was tough—tough as nails—tough as Joe.

He was twenty-seven, about the age of Cohn and Schine. He had graduated from the University of Virginia Law School, doing his own work, writing his own papers. As president of the Student Legal Forum at Virginia he had brought Joe McCarthy to the campus as a speaker. Now he wanted a job, and old Joe Kennedy had just the one in mind—Chief Counsel for his friend Joe McCarthy's subcommittee.

The subcommittee already had one general counsel—holdover Francis Flanagan, an ex-FBI agent. It was about to get a chief counsel—Roy Cohn. So Bobby was given a position as Flanagan's assistant with—to placate old Joe—the assurance that he would eventually move up into Flanagan's place (he never did). When reporters confronted McCarthy with the organizational confusion (What's the difference between a chief counsel and a general counsel?), Joe just smiled. He didn't know, he said. He was not an organization man.

It was a heady time for the crusading anti-Communists and liberal-baiters—Republican or Democrat—on the Hill: Cohn and Schine and Bobby Kennedy, their ex-FBI cohorts, their boss McCarthy. Strong currents of public opinion buoyed them up. A congressman named Busby detected that composer Aaron Copland had once consorted with Communists; Copland's *Lincoln Portrait* was dropped from the inaugural concert. Chancellor Henry Heald of New York University declared on the eve of the inauguration that the preservation of academic freedom did not require the presence of Communists on university faculties since they were not free agents. One citizen wrote to maverick Senator Wayne Morse, who had made things tough for a number of prospective Cabinet appointees: "After your talk today and after so great an inaugural address by Dwight D. Eisenhower, our President, I condemn you as a Communist. Prove to me otherwise." That man happened to be drunk, and his wife hastily wired Morse an apology. But he had only slightly stretched the limits of tolerable opinion.

However fast the new reformist administration moved, McCarthy and his staff could always flog it on; faster, faster; more, more; hang the evidence; get the bastards.

John Foster Dulles, the new Secretary of State, wanted to clean up the State Department. Now sixty-five years old, the son of a Presbyterian minister in Watertown, New York, he had gone to Princeton (Phi Beta Kappa), the Sorbonne, and George Washington University Law School, and had ultimately become senior partner at Sullivan and Cromwell and the dean of New York's Wall Street lawyers. He was descended from two earlier Secretaries of State—John Watson Foster (under Benjamin Harrison) and Robert Lansing (under Woodrow Wilson)—and he had been studying diplomacy since 1907, when he had attended his first international peace conference at The Hague.

Foreign policy advisor to New York Governor Thomas Dewey in the presidential campaigns of both 1944 and 1948 (in fact, designated Secretary of State by Dewey in a moment of euphoric confidence in a smashing 1948 victory over Harry Truman), Dulles was a devout churchman who during World War II chaired a Federal Council of Churches commission on the postwar peace. A Republican delegate to the United Nations General Assembly and architect—as a special ambassador under Dean Acheson—of the 1951 Japanese peace treaty, Foster Dulles was an unambiguous anti-Communist of intellectual brilliance and philosophical tenacity.

He knew, and read, and reread the root arguments in the central documents germane to the titanic ideological debate between the world's two major thought systems. He had always at hand on one side Stalin's *Problems of Leninism* and on the other, *The Federalist Papers* and the Bible. To him, as a wise man, the debate was at bottom not economic, not military, but intellectual, philosophical, and moral.

To such a man a more flexible, urbane, and relaxed appreciation of the struggle—as found at times in the liberal press and universities and indeed in the State Department's Foreign Service—was unthinkable. From the outset—indeed, in his first communication to more than sixteen thousand State Department and Foreign Service people—he asked their "positive loyalty" to the new administration. And in his first broadcast address to the nation, he cited the "shocking revelations which showed that some Communists and sympathizers had found their way into high places and betrayed secrets— even that of the atomic bomb. I can assure you that all the resources of Government, and that includes the FBI, are going to be employed to be sure that any such people are detected and cleaned out." He wanted to cooperate—as did Nixon and Persons—with McCarthy. And McCarthy, hearing of Dulles's appointment in November of 1952, had reciprocated: "I like Dulles. I think he is a good American."

Dulles knew that security measures sometimes slipped. Throughout the federal government the new administration would tighten up the process. Under Eisenhower's Executive Order 10450 of April 27, all federal employees not previously investigated would be, not just those in sensitive departments. The old Truman double yardstick was discarded: in it an employee could be fired if he was found to be disloyal in any agency or if he was found to be a security risk in a sensitive agency. Instead, a single government-wide criterion was established: Is the employee's employment, it was asked, clearly consistent with U.S. national security? Federal employment, Eisenhower and Brownell believed, was a privilege, not a right.

Even before this change in regulations, Dulles set up a new job, Under Secretary of State for Administration and Operations, charged with the specific responsibility of "house cleaning" the State Department. He gave the job to a hardheaded businessman, Donald B. Lourie, president of the Quaker Oats Company of Chicago. From a Chicago friend Lourie, by chance, heard the name of Scott McLeod, a young former FBI agent and administrative assistant to crusty conservative Republican Senator Styles Bridges of New Hampshire. Lourie and McLeod had lunch in Washington. They hit it off fine. Lourie offered McLeod a job as the Department's security chief. McLeod accepted it and eagerly set to work. In his first three weeks he got rid of twenty-one alleged sexual deviates. He and a cluster of ex-FBI agents crawled all over the department examining file cabinets, opening desks, and scrutinizing what employees were reading, both during and after hours. By late 1953, McLeod could announce the removal—on various grounds—of 306 citizen employees and 178 aliens.

But not enough for McCarthy.

For one thing, he found Dulles unacceptably soft on one of the old China hands, John Carter Vincent. In 1951, Dean Acheson had demoted the Director of the State Department Office of China Affairs, O. Edmund Clubb, and permitted him to retire; he had fired another China expert, John Stewart Service, after the Civil Service Loyalty Review Board found "reasonable doubt" of Service's loyalty. In contrast, Dulles had permitted John Carter Vincent to resign, citing his "poor judgment" but clearing him of all loyalty and security charges and allowing him to retain his pension. McCarthy couldn't believe his ears. "Under no circumstances," he declared, "should anyone like Vincent, having been rejected by the Loyalty Board, be entitled to any pension."

Next, Eisenhower and Dulles insisted on making a couple of—to McCarthy—bad appointments.

First, Harvard President James Bryant Conant as U.S. High Commissioner in Germany. Here was the sane, slender, bespectacled high priest of the great citadel of anti-McCarthyism—a world-famous chemist, a man respected ungrudgingly by the sniffishly fastidious and captious inhabitants of Widener Library and the Yard, a man uncompromising in his commitment to the scientific method and freedom of the mind—headed toward a key outpost on anticommunism's easternmost front. McCarthy could not stomach the prospect. Though he knew Conant had the Senate votes to confirm, he wrote Eisenhower a private letter attacking the nomination.

In his White House memoir *Mandate for Change*, Eisenhower wrote that McCarthy made "wild charges" against President Conant. This phrase "wild charges" left McCarthy's minions all shook up. McCarthy's defender William F. Buckley, Jr., protested in print that he knew the charges were not wild because he had written them himself, but dammit, he couldn't find his copy of the letter. In his 1968 book on McCarthy, Roy Cohn, following Buckley, similarly disputed the word "wild." Both Buckley and Cohn were right. McCarthy's letter was a model of Buckleyan temperate and reasoned objection. In it the Senator opposed Conant's nomination because of Conant's wartime concurrence with the Morgenthau plan to destroy all German industry; his advocacy of a 100 percent tax on inheritance; his opposition to parochial schools (this would kill him in Catholic Germany, Buckley argued); and last but not least his resolute opposition to the investigation of Communist infiltration into American universities—all reasonable grounds for argument. McCarthy told Eisenhower he would vote, but not speak, against the nomination, because Conant would certainly go to Germany, and a fight against him would help only the Communists.

Thus McCarthy's evenhanded exposition. The word "wild" slipped into Eisenhower's text as the result of a sparking-up by editors who couldn't imagine that any of McCarthy's charges were not wild.

The second bad nomination, in the view of McCarthy, was Charles E. ("Chip") Bohlen as Ambassador to the Soviet Union.

"Prince Hal in Shakespeare's *Henry IV, Part I*," the poet Richard Wilbur once observed in a faculty conference at Harvard, "strikes me as the typical white-shoe boy getting gentleman's Cs and sowing his wild oats in Scollay Square before going on to a brilliant career in the State Department." This offhand comment in many ways fits Bohlen's description of himself and his life in his 1973 book *Witness to History.* Born in the family's summer home on one of the Thousand Islands in the Saint Lawrence River, son of a gentleman of leisure, Bohlen had been a boy who delighted in the winter sports and chocolate of Switzerland, a preppie at St. Paul's, a Harvard A.B. of no particular distinction. He had entered the Foreign Service largely because the alternatives—Wall Street, banking, business, the professions—bored him. An autobiographer who characterized his diplomatic posts by their perquisites (Prague: accessibility to skiing; Paris: the delights the city offered a young bachelor; Moscow: the importation of a French chef), Bohlen comes across, in part, as a representative of a type. One cannot help recalling Anthony Eden, who in his memoirs repeatedly seems to say, in effect: As we bathed in the pleasant pool and sipped cocktails before a lovely lunch, the news from the battlefield grew steadily worse.

Further, one feels that in his book Bohlen tries to have it both ways. He reveals, for example, that he had disagreed with Dean Acheson on the Communists' intentions in the Korean War, believing that Truman and his Secretary of State overreacted, since Stalin had no great expansionist designs. He writes that he had disapproved of the unnecessary Truman-Acheson "militarization" of NATO. He writes self-approvingly that as State Department Counselor he had cleared a speech of his friend and fellow diplomat George Kennan. That speech, after the 1952 election, hit head-on Secretary of State–designate Foster Dulles's commitment to the rolling back, instead of the containment, of communism. Bohlen had no use whatsoever for Dulles's insistence on "positive loyalty" to the new administration, which, he wrote, disgusted and infuriated most of his friends in the Foreign Service. In a word, Bohlen shared—his book smugly and candidly reveals—the liberal's usual objections to major features of the Eisenhower-Dulles foreign policy, conspicuously to Dulles's "narrow-minded" pursuit of an "anti-Communist crusade."

But none of this really mattered. The overriding fact was that Chip Bohlen was a tough, seasoned, trained, authentic authority on the Soviet Union—the country, its government, its policy. He spoke fluent Russian. He was a man of intelligence and courage. And he would play his part straight, as a genuine professional of impeccable integrity, speaking his mind.

So Eisenhower and Dulles stuck their necks out a long way for him, selecting him not as a policymaker (Dulles specifically ruled out this kind of responsibility, shrewdly sensing Bohlen's alienation), but as an on-the-spot observer of keen and analytical mind.

On February 27, Eisenhower sent Bohlen's nomination to the Senate. Early in March, Scott McLeod learned that the FBI investigation of Bohlen—the first ever made on him in his quarter-century career—had turned up some derogatory information. McLeod told Dulles. He also told McCarthy. By March 13, McLeod's former boss, Senator Styles Bridges, was announcing that top people in the administration were asking Eisenhower to withdraw the nomination.

McCarthy roared. Here was the very model of the striped-pants cookie-pushing diplomat headed for the Kremlin itself as our man in the lion's den. Like Alger Hiss, Bohlen had served at Yalta (as President Roosevelt's advisor and interpreter), at the very conference where, in the McCarthyites' view, Roosevelt had sold Eastern Europe and its captive peoples down the river to Stalin.

Dulles called Bohlen into the office of the Secretary of State. Sitting beneath portraits of his predecessors, a large lighted globe nearby, the Secretary asked, "Is there anything in your past that might be damaging?"

"No."

"I'm glad of that. Because I couldn't stand another Alger Hiss."

Dulles read through the full-field investigation summary on Bohlen, and on March 18 the two men drove up to Capitol Hill to confront the Senate Foreign Relations Committee. They drove up in separate cars, at Dulles's insistence: better not to be photographed together. Bohlen made a mental note, which later surfaced in his book: "His remark made me wonder if he would have the courage to stand up to the McCarthyites."

He need not have worried. Dulles came out foursquare: "There is not a whisper of a suggestion that I have been able to turn up," he told the committee, "throwing any doubt at all upon his loyalty or upon his security as a person." Although Dulles conceded under questioning that McLeod had not cleared Bohlen, the committee approved the nomination 15–0, and those fifteen included such rock-ribbed conservatives as Bourke Hickenlooper of Iowa, Robert A. Taft of Ohio, and Bill Knowland of California.

McCarthy became ominous. Eisenhower would withdraw the nomination, he declared darkly, if he saw the "entire file" on Bohlen. On March 19 in his news conference Ike backed Bohlen to the hilt. McLeod phoned his friend Jerry Persons at the White House; because Dulles had overruled him on the Bohlen clearance, he thought he should resign. Dulles talked alone with McLeod; the security chief remained stubborn. And the next morning a "darned accurate account" of their conversation, in Dulles's words, appeared in the *Washington Times-Herald.* Dulles told Hagerty. The press secretary agreed with the Secretary of State: either McLeod or Dulles would have to resign. "The characters are minor but the issue is great," Dulles declared. "It will decide whether McCarthy, Bridges and Jenner are dominating the executive branch of this Government." By phone the President backed Dulles: if necessary, fire McLeod.

Sherman Adams, however, warning of the explosion that would surely come, argued for a second chance. Persons had tried to reason with McLeod; Dulles should give McLeod a hearing—let him explain. But, Adams added, "If the boy does not come clean, you cannot keep him."

Dulles and McLeod conferred. A contrite McLeod repented his indiscretion. And—now on probation—he kept his job.

Meanwhile, McCarthy demanded Dulles be put under oath and questioned further by the Foreign Relations Committee. He branded as false Dulles's contention that the Secretary and McLeod saw eye to eye on their "final evaluation" of Bohlen: McLeod and Dulles do *not* agree on Bohlen, McCarthy declared. And "McLeod is a very truthful man."

On March 23, the Senate debate began. McCarthy demanded that Bohlen be given a lie detector test, that Dulles and McLeod be brought before the Foreign Relations Committee simultaneously in a Hiss-Chambers type of confrontation. But the ruckus began to die down when the Senate agreed to a proposal by Robert Taft—against FBI precedent—that one senator from each party would read through the FBI file on Bohlen and report back. The Foreign Relations Committee picked Taft for the Republicans and John Sparkman (Adlai Stevenson's 1952 vice presidential running-mate) for the Democrats.

The two senators read the FBI summary only—J. Edgar Hoover assured them that it included all relevant information from the raw file—and reported back on March 25. "There was no suggestion anywhere by anyone," Taft said, "reflecting on the loyalty of Mr. Bohlen in any way, or any association by him with Communists or support of Communism or even tolerance of Communism." Eisenhower again defended Bohlen at his news conference the next day as the best-qualified man, describing him as an acquaintance "for some years" whom he'd visited in his own home "with his very charming family," and even joined in a game of golf. The next day Bohlen was confirmed 74 to 13. But when a reporter asked Robert Taft, who had masterminded the Bohlen drive, whether that struggle meant a break in relations with McCarthy, Taft had an eloquent polysyllabic answer, "No, no, no." The Majority Leader had won a victory, but he didn't want any more. He let the White House know: "No more Bohlens."

As that front quieted, another began to crackle. Dulles and Harold Stassen—administrator of the foreign aid agency—had undertaken to discourage the United States' Allies from trading with Communist China. Greek-owned ships flying the British flag, for example, were delivering cotton, fertilizer, and other nonstrategic products to Red Chinese ports. Not enough for McCarthy and his young aide Bob Kennedy. Suddenly, on March 28, 1953, at a televised news conference, McCarthy, Kennedy at his elbow, announced he had made an agreement with Greek shippers in New York, the owners of 242 cargo vessels, to end all trade with Red Chinese and Soviet Block ports. Instantly Stassen flared up: McCarthy, he declared, was undermining foreign policy. Hastily Vice President Nixon—ever the bridge between left and right—set up a McCarthy-Dulles lunch. After ninety minutes in the Secretary's dining room, the two came out with a joint communiqué. Dulles, throwing a bone, praised McCarthy for acting in the "national interest." McCarthy, bowing to the Constitution, admitted that the President had among his prerogatives the right to conduct foreign policy. He promised to give the administration any further facts he might collect on ships headed for Communist countries. Soothingly, Eisenhower at his next news conference tried to cool things down. Harold, he said, meant "infringe," not "undermine." And of course, he added, under our scheme of things McCarthy could not in any way "negotiate" a treatylike agreement. So why should anyone be upset?

McCarthy didn't stay hitched. He tried to get Greek shipowners in London to join his boycott. They refused. McCarthy accused Stassen of torpedoing his efforts. "More Americans," he declared over television, "will die because of the decision of these Greek ship-owners in London." Later he revealed that the Greek owners of 53 more ships had "volunteered" pledges to his subcommittee, bringing to a total of 295 the Greek-owned vessels no longer trading with the Reds.

On May 5, Dulles warned against the imposition of a total em-bargo on Allied trade with the Communists. Then, at the suggestion of Missouri Democratic Senator W. Stuart Symington, McCarthy asked Bob Kennedy to draft a letter to the President asking a simple question: What is U.S. policy on trade, specifically with Red China, our shooting-war enemy in Korea? The White House, hearing of this, considered it at a staff meeting on May 22. The presidential advisors split. National Security Assistant Bobby Cutler and Cold War Planning Advisor C. D. Jackson urged that the administration not ignore McCarthy's attempt to embarrass the President. But the legislative-liaison conservatives Jerry Persons and Jerry Morgan, joined by Governor Sherman Adams, held back. The public, they argued, opposes trade with Communist China. The subject is too complicated a one to use for straightening out McCarthy. Once again Nixon came to the rescue: You've fallen into a Democratic trap, he told McCarthy, and McCarthy got the point. He ordered his letter withdrawn before it was ever officially "received" at the White House. And for a brief moment calm once again descended.

But not everywhere. Foster Dulles had set out to promulgate a new policy for the International Information Administration (IIA), a semi-autonomous organization, approximately 40 percent of the State Department population, with responsibility for the United States overseas information effort by radio (the Voice of America), libraries, motion pictures, and promotional exhibitions—an organiza-tion that people like John Taber, Chairman of the House Appropria-tions Committee, knew as "decidedly pinko."

Dulles did not want to defend the mistakes of the past adminis-tration. Like C. D. Jackson, the President's Assistant for cold war policy, the Secretary of State saw the Voice of America "not in very good condition"—an organization that, in C. D.'s words in a Febru-ary 19 memorandum, through "mal- and mis-management has gone bankrupt"; one that needed to "be thrown into receivership, the bad boys kicked out, completely reorganized." Likewise Dulles wanted to clean out and straighten up the IIA's overseas libraries, some two hundred of them in more than sixty countries.

To many, the idea of "straightening up" a library is anathema. A library should be a repository for books—all kinds of books. To depart from this prescription is to abrogate the First Amendment, to deny freedom of the press and opinion, to infringe on the most sacred of our liberties.

But, as Dulles recognized, American libraries overseas have some limitations. For one thing, they are small. They have a finite budget. And they have a specific purpose. That purpose—different from the purpose of a public library in any American town, large or small—is to present valid evidence that will win for the United States foreign friends and an understanding of our ways, and elicit some measure of sympathy for our policies and actions. So selection becomes significant. What books and what periodicals should these libraries stock? Specifically should they, at taxpayers' expense, disseminate the writings of Communist or near-Communist authors?

Following the latitudinarian policies of the Truman administration, on February 3 the State Department made a pass at an answer: Soviet-endorsed authors—for example, Howard Fast—who wrote favorably about the U.S., a policy directive declared, might have a "special credibility" with key foreign audiences.

McCarthy leaped to ask questions about this, attacking the directive as an encouragement of subversion. He haled Howard Fast before his subcommittee and, after Fast refused to answer questions about communism, got off the cheap shot that Eleanor Roosevelt had "helped" circulate Fast's books. (She had, indeed, invited him to lunch at the White House nine years earlier.) On February 19 Carl McCardle, Dulles's Assistant Secretary for Public Affairs, canceled the old directive and came up with a new one. This banned from overseas libraries the books of "Communists, fellow travelers, etc." A month later Dulles issued still another directive. Though this one deleted the menacing "etc." of the previous marching order, it specifically edicted the withdrawal of works by Communist authors and of individual issues of periodicals containing "material detrimental to U.S. objectives."

The librarians energetically obliged. They discarded, shredded, and even burned books that they thought the directive proscribed, including works of Vera Micheles Dean, Theodore H. White, mystery writer Dashiell Hammett, Lillian Hellman, Jean-Paul Sartre, Bert Andrews (head of the Washington Bureau of the *New York*

Herald Tribune and an old pal of Richard Nixon), and Whittaker Chambers. Dulles later announced that only eleven books had actually been burned, presumably in embassy incinerators; the others disappeared otherwise. Into the bargain, during the spring of 1953 the State Department fired hundreds of IIA employees, eliminated some VOA foreign-language programs, and even closed some libraries down.

But despite the zeal of the administration reformers, McCarthy's far outstripped it. Charging into the IIA as soon as the opening whistle blew (his subcommittee's hearings started February 13, 1953), he pursued and hounded its employees. He questioned Roger Lyons, head of the Voice of America's religious programming, to determine the depth of Lyons's alleged atheism or agnosticism. His subcommittee made public the testimony of a young lady who charged that one Troup Mathews, editor of the French section of the Voice of America, had tried to recruit her into a Marxist collective-living community, and he then denied Mathews a public platform to demonstrate his repudiation of free love. McCarthy attacked Reed Harris—a former OWI employee and recently acting head of the IIA—because as a student at Columbia University years earlier he had written a book called *King Football*, which upheld the right of a Communist to teach in a college. By mid-April, Harris had resigned. Allegedly terrified of persecution by McCarthy, a VOA engineer, Raymond Kaplan, jumped in front of a truck and committed suicide. The Senator grilled James Wechsler, editor of the liberal *New York Post*, on his membership in the Young Communist League between April of 1934, while a student at Columbia, and December of 1937, and accused him of still peddling the party line: "You have not broken with Communist ideals." Even as balanced a man as Robert Taft largely approved of all of this; the VOA, he said, "certainly was full of fellow travellers." He found McCarthy's investigation "very helpful and constructive."

On the White House staff, C. D. Jackson, nonetheless, urged standing firm. It would be a "bad idea," he wrote Foster Dulles on February 19, to liquidate the VOA. Such an action would be read as "panic" by the administration and especially by the Secretary of State, as a result of McCarthy's attacks.

McCarthy hounded not only people. He also hounded books. Hearing from eager witnesses that the overseas Information Center libraries still harbored Communist writings, he dispatched Cohn and Schine to Europe to root them out. The trip, starting in April, became in the press accounts a continual floating farce. A flock of reporters followed them everywhere. "We were derided," Cohn wrote, "as Innocents Abroad." The two committed and energetic young men had gone through a steep learning curve. Before the VOA hearings started back in February, Cohn and Schine, working out of Schine's family apartment at the Waldorf, had mapped strategy with their IIA underground informants (their "loyal American underground") and grilled prospective witnesses. Now, on April 4, they started out on 18 days that would shake the news media of the Western world.

They spent 40 hours in Paris, 17 in Bonn, 19 in Frankfurt, 23 in Belgrade, 24 each in Athens and Rome, 60 in Munich, 41 in Vienna, 6 in London. In a whirlwind of motion they descended on the Information Center libraries, zeroed in on the card catalogs, collected documents, interviewed embassy staff members, and held one press conference after another. A few weeks after they returned, Theodore Kaghan, Acting Deputy Director of the Office of Public Affairs in the U.S. High Commission for Germany, resigned. Kaghan had once roomed with a Communist in school. He had refused to give McCarthy the names of his left-wing friends in the 1930s. And he had derided Cohn and Schine as "junketeering gumshoes."

All in all, it was an ugly spring in our national life, a time of hate, doubt, and division. And these features were epitomized above all not by the hearings, not by the relentless savaging of witnesses, not by the transcontinental sleuthing of McCarthy's two young scourges, but by a case that McCarthy habitually refused to mention, despite its allure, out of fear of a charge of anti-Semitism—the case of convicted atomic spies Julius and Ethel Rosenberg.

The Rosenbergs had joined the Communist party in 1934. Ten years later Ethel Rosenberg's brother, David Greenglass, became a machinist at the atomic weapons center at Los Alamos, New Mexico. In January of 1945 he gave the Rosenbergs rough sketches of the high-explosive lens used to detonate the atomic bomb. In June he gave a conspiratorial courier, Harry Gold, more sketches of the lens. In October of 1945, after the bombs dropped on Hiroshima and Nagasaki, Greenglass gave the Rosenbergs crude sketches of the A-bomb itself, plus explanatory notes. Four years later, in 1949, the British atomic physicist Klaus Fuchs confessed, implicating Gold, who also confessed, and who in turn implicated Greenglass. In June of 1950, Greenglass confessed, in January of 1951 the Rosenbergs were indicted for conspiracy, and in March of 1951 a jury found them guilty. Gold got 30 years, Greenglass 15, Fuchs (in England) 14, and the Rosenbergs, who refused to confess, got the death sentence. They had become the first persons ever sentenced to execution during peacetime in the United States on the charge of espionage. In February of 1952 an Appeals Court upheld their conviction, and in October the Supreme Court refused to review the appeal. An appeal for executive clemency went to President Truman on January 10, 1953, and on February 11 President Eisenhower denied it. On May 26 the Supreme Court again refused to hear the Rosenbergs' appeal, and on June 16 it denied their plea for a stay of execution, set for that week.

Throughout that spring Eisenhower agonized over the executive clemency decision. The arguments raged around him: that the sentence was too severe, the other spies getting 30 years or less; that the Rosenbergs were the only ones who stubbornly did not confess; that execution would make them martyrs; that clemency would discourage confessions. The Communists claimed the Rosenbergs were innocent anyway, framed by virtue of being Jewish; Gold and Greenglass, they said, had cooperated in order to save their own skins. Even the head of the Bureau of Prisons, James Bennett, opposed the execution of a woman as unchristian, as destructive of the continuity of the human race.

Picketings, mass meetings, and petitions swirled about the White House. On June 16, Eisenhower wrote his son, John, stationed in Korea, a long letter laying out argument and counterargument: that it went against the grain to execute a woman; that in this instance the woman seemed the stronger of the two partners; that clemency would merely encourage the Communists to recruit women as spies in the future. Above all, Eisenhower found compelling the fact that the Rosenbergs had received fair and exhaustive hearings in court. A group of ministers requested an appointment to plead with the President for clemency. The White House staff urged a turndown. Ike refused. He met with the churchmen and answered their arguments one by one. "It was the most dramatic thing I ever saw him do," his appointments secretary, Tom Stephens—a man not given to hyperbole—remembers.

At that precise moment in the history of the United States, almost anything could become believable—an allegation that McCarthy spoke Russian; a rumor that conspirators were plotting to assassinate the Senator. Hate mail to the White House prompted the Secret Service to double the security around the President's grandchildren.

Even a relaxed and sane and liberal-minded Eisenhower staff member like Bern Shanley could believe—he confided in his diary—that at Eisenhower's meeting with the religious leaders one of them, a rabbi, might attempt to shoot the President. That particular rabbi, Shanley told the President, is a Communist, and a full-fledged Communist would want above all to murder the President. During the session with the four ministers Shanley sat close to Eisenhower, never taking his eyes off the rabbi's hands.

On the night of June 19 the Rosenbergs were executed. As the world awaited word of their deaths from Sing Sing prison, demonstrators surrounded the White House, in ugly, sickening contrast: one mob imploring mercy, weeping and praying; one mob reveling in the kill, yelling: "Two fried Rosenbergers coming up."

Throughout that spring of 1953 ignorant armies clashed by night. Absolutists of right and left charged and crashed in the shock of combat. Guilt by association (if you ever had a Communist roommate in college, you're guilty) closed and locked with innocence by accusation (if McCarthy attacks you, you're by definition clean). At bottom, the problem was intellectual and moral: the failure of reason, the indulgence in excess. Valid grounds existed for inquiring into the appointment of Conant to Germany—grounds outlined in McCarthy's letter to Eisenhower, as drafted by William Buckley—and of Bohlen to Moscow. As Robert Taft himself wrote to Don Rowley, the publisher of the Ashtabula *Star-Beacon* on April 15: "The opposition to Bohlen was not started by McCarthy, and he was in no sense the leader of that opposition. It is a perfectly reasonable opposition, and I would have joined it myself except that I did not think the position of Ambassador to Russia was any sufficiently important position to make an issue of it. Bohlen was one of the four or five men who made the decisions at Yalta, which the Republican Party had condemned properly for many years."

Valid arguments existed for scrutinizing the competence and intellectual convictions of the employees of the IIA, an agency that existed to export intellectual messages, thereby winning friends for the United States. And valid reasons existed to examine the content of those messages, whether broadcast over the Voice of America or conveyed to readers by books on Information Center library shelves. It was stupid to spread Russian propaganda; our best public relations effort was to tell the truth.

McCarthy and his minions, however, in pursuit of Communists, drove over the edge of the cliff. Bohlen became a study in loyalty, possibly treason, complete with threats of a lie detector test and a replay of the Hiss-Chambers confrontation. The examination of individual IIA employees often turned into bullying, harassing, and hounding of little people—usually with their hands tied behind them—for silly mistakes, titillating sexual episodes, and college-day indiscretions. And the Cohn-Schine tour of books and authors demonstrated, in the end, only their ludicrous lack of training, knowledge, and capacity to conduct such a philosophical inquiry.

The requisite was to hold the center; to restore the capacity to divide and distinguish. Dwight Eisenhower knew this. Consistently he refused to mention the Senator by name, despite abundant prompting, which included one call to "fire McCarthy," and the far more persuasive pleas of his brother Milton that he "tear McCarthy to pieces."

Milton was the family liberal, and one of the two or three men in the world whom Dwight Eisenhower admired most. He had entered government service in the days of Calvin Coolidge, beginning in the State Department and then moving into Agriculture. During World War II he became a reliance of Franklin Roosevelt and served at the apex of the Office of War Information. Following a stint as President of Kansas State University, by 1953 he headed Penn State. And in his arguments he brought the full force of his background in the career civil service, the New Deal years, and the academic world to wide-ranging and frequent and impassioned discussions of McCarthy and McCarthyism with his brother.

But Ike refused to concur.

He foresaw the knee-jerk response of a constitutionally coequal branch of government, suspicious of encroachment on its turf, and majority-populated by a combination of Democrats and anti-Administration Republicans. "You want me to make a martyr of McCarthy," Ike asked Milton, "and get the whole Senate to stand behind him just because a President has attacked him?"

And Ike had another reason. McCarthy, he argued, wanted publicity. Repudiation by the President would give him more publicity than he could garner by any other tactic.

"Senator McCarthy," Eisenhower wrote in his diary on April 1, "is, of course, so anxious for the headlines that he is prepared to go to any extremes in order to secure some mention of his name in the public press. His actions create trouble on the Hill with members of the party; they irritate, frustrate, and infuriate members of the Executive Department. I really believe that nothing will be so effective in combating his particular kind of troublemaking as to ignore him. This he cannot stand." The presidential silence thus became not a subterfuge of defense; it became a strategy of attack.

Ike continued to countenance attempts toward conciliation—for example, a dinner in May of 1953 laid on by Nixon, Persons, and Deputy Attorney General William Rogers, which was designed to lure McCarthy back onto the "team." With a one-vote majority in the Senate, how could they write off Joe and his friends? But underneath, Eisenhower smoldered. Ike "loathed McCarthy as much as any human being could possibly loathe another," Milton remembered after his brother's death, "and he didn't hate many people; but he felt McCarthy was a curse on the American scene. . . ." When, in an early White House receiving line, McCarthy, ever obstreperous, engaged in loud, gauche, and tasteless banter with Assistant Press Secretary Murray Snyder about his beautiful blond wife, Betty, the President snapped to Murray: "That goddamned Joe McCarthy!" In his April 1, 1953, diary entry Eisenhower confided that he was considering the formation of a new party, bringing together all the sensible people in the great middle band of American politics. And though he promptly rejected this, he did declare his determination to win away five or six from the "McCarthy-Malone axis"— linking Joe's name with that of another unspeakable right-wing Republican, Senator George Malone from Nevada—and thus reduce that "splinter group to impotence." He didn't want to run again in 1956, he had told Bern Shanley, who recorded the conversation in his diary; he would run again for only one reason—to defeat McCarthy.

On June 1 he confided to his diary his awareness of the terror that McCarthy's "calling names and making false accusations" aroused in Europe. And then on June 14 in a commencement speech at Dartmouth College, all the repugnance overflowed—all the pent-up anger at the extremism of McCarthy and the obstreperousness of Cohn and Schine.

"Don't join the book burners," he told his Dartmouth audience. How can we combat communism unless we know what it is? Go into your libraries and read anything you want.

By July 1, Eisenhower had begun to draw some lines. At his news conference that day he said he thought it foolishness to distribute books overseas that advocated the violent overthrow of the U.S. Government. But he would not discard detective stories written by proscribed Dashiell Hammett. When reporters told him librarians overseas had been doing so, the President refused to approve: "I think someone got frightened." Within a week the State Department issued a new directive, which McCarthy called "completely ridiculous," permitting the libraries to stock books by Communist authors which served democratic ends.

In his impromptu outrage at Dartmouth, speaking from a rough set of notes, Eisenhower had sounded a theme voiced with greatest eloquence a week earlier down at Harvard's Sanders Theatre by an old OWI colleague of Milton's who was delivering the annual Phi Beta Kappa lecture—the theme that McCarthy's excess, his intellectual and moral failures, mounted an attack on our most precious freedom, the freedom of the mind.

Elmer Davis, the Harvard speaker, was a former Rhodes Scholar, a newspaperman whose favorite book was Catullus in the original Latin, a reporter who could write a round-by-round description of a heavyweight fight, or a novel, or a satire. Davis had for months criticized McCarthy in his seven-o'clock fifteen-minute radio broadcasts, in his slow Hoosier twang, sometimes citing incisive fact, sometimes poking fun. When a Senate committee discovered that McCarthy had accepted $10,000 from the Lustron Corporation—a manufacturer of prefabs—for a thirty-seven-page article on housing, Davis observed: "Well, I used to be in the magazine business. And back in those days nobody would have paid that kind of money for an article on housing. Even by McCarthy—or, indeed, Shakespeare."

Now at Harvard his attack began with heavy irony: "A century or so ago, a Harvard graduate wrote a hymn whose opening line, plausible enough when written, turned out to be one of the most inaccurate forecasts ever set down: 'The morning light is breaking, the darkness disappears.'" Davis proceeded to consider the questions in the lecture's title: "Are We Worth Saving? And If So, Why?" And he returned an eloquent answer: "What we have to offer, to the contemporary world and to the future, is a method—and the freedom of the mind that makes method possible. Not an infallible method, but the best yet discovered for reaching increasingly closer approximations to the truth. It will never offer its conclusions with such assurance as does dialectical materialism. . . . It can only say, We have kept the door open for exploration of all possibilities, consideration of all objections, application of all possible tests; and this is what seems to be true. . . . What makes Western civilization worth saving is the freedom of the mind, now under heavy attack from the primitives—including some university graduates—who have persisted among us."

And he concluded with an arresting citation from the Old Testament: "I should perhaps have begun this sermon with a text, a text taken from the fourth chapter of the first book of Samuel . . . the mutual exhortations of the Philistines before the battle of Ebenezer. 'Woe unto us!' they said when they realized that the Israelites had brought the Ark of God with them to battle. 'Woe unto us! Who shall deliver us out of the hands of these mighty gods?' But then, realizing that nobody else was going to deliver them, they said to one another, 'Be strong, and quit yourselves like men; and fight.' And they did fight, and delivered themselves.

"So may we, but only if we quit ourselves like men. This republic was not established by cowards; and cowards will not preserve it."

Against this darkling backdrop a local draft board had acted. It had reclassified G. David Schine. He had been 4-F because of a slipped disc. But Drew Pearson had phoned Schine's draft board and demanded a reopening of his file. The doctors had done a reexamination, and now, in early July of 1953, the Selective Service had put him in 1-A.

Schine had an immediate response: he would get a direct commission as an officer in one service or another. He enlisted the assistance of Cohn and McCarthy. They made inquiries, set up one appointment after another. But Schine knew that time was running out. He wanted to hold up his hand, to take the oath as an officer in the United States Army. He'd drive right down to the Pentagon that very afternoon. But all in vain. The Armed Forces looked at his background. They looked at their regulations and requirements. Then one by one—first the Army, then the Air Force and the Navy—they informed him—through channels—that he did not qualify for a direct commission.

III

"HE IS AN
INTERESTING FELLOW"

"Ike always left an escape route open," his astute press secretary, Jim Hagerty, once told me, "both for himself and for the other guy." Eisenhower steadfastly refused, ever, to traffic in personalities, to become engaged, one-on-one, *mano a mano*, with an adversary—any adversary. In the 1952 campaign he had never made a personal target of Truman. He had uttered the name of his 1952 Democratic opponent, Adlai Stevenson, not at all. And as President he would not personally attack even Joseph Stalin.

He saw himself as Dwight Eisenhower, President of the United States, serving a constitutional purpose, occupying a constitutional role, a role greater than himself; not as Dwight Eisenhower, single citizen, free to speak out and strike out at will and by whim. He had a responsibility to abstract principles; these he would talk about and enunciate. He would not clutter his discharge of this responsibility by brawling with an opponent, however much he had once reveled in it, in the ring and on the gridiron.

"[The President] does not initiate leadership," another equally astute White House aide, C. D. Jackson, noted on July 8, 1953, in the candid secret diary he was keeping. "But he wants energetic, alert staff to bat things up to him, and when he approves he will lead." Dwight Eisenhower in the war and in the presidency was supremely an organization man. He delegated authority to able lieutenants, trusted them, held them responsible, sharply questioned them to test their knowledge and conviction, and at times accepted their conclusions above his own. In the 1952 campaign, when he deleted the George Marshall paragraph from the Milwaukee speech, his organization was a tiny knot of loyal advisors: a former governor of New Hampshire, a longtime congressional liaison wizard, an editorial writer for *Business Week*, the President of the Old Colony

Trust Company, a former press secretary to Governor Dewey of New York, each one with a berth on a frenzied railroad train criss-crossing the country. Now, after inauguration, Eisenhower's organization was the entire federal executive establishment: at the center the White House Staff with Governor Adams as its chief, Jerry Persons in congressional liaison, Jim Hagerty as press secretary, Tom Stephens as appointments secretary, Bern Shanley as special counsel, Gabe Hauge as economics advisor.

The next concentric ring included Cabinet officers: *e.g.*, Dulles at State, Humphrey at Treasury, Wilson at Defense, Brownell at Justice. And each of these had its sublayers of under secretary or deputy secretary; assistant secretaries—all presidential appointees; bureau chiefs; and career civil servants—some two million of them, largely inherited from Roosevelt and Truman. The Pentagon, of course, was a special case, four departments in one. The umbrella Department of Defense capped the whole: beneath it lay separate departments of the Army, headed by Robert Stevens, the Navy, headed by Robert Anderson, and the Air Force, headed by the engineering tycoon and Dewey confidant Harold Talbott.

In peace, as once in war, Eisenhower informed and relied on his organization. For one thing, it afforded him detachment—freedom to maneuver, opportunity to choose the ground for doing battle, the capacity to offer the citizenry not only a protagonist in the center of events but a standard to which all men of good sense could in the end repair.

Fealty to principle; aversion to personality; reliance on organization—the history of the decline and fall of Joseph McCarthy is in major measure a history of these features of the Eisenhower presidency at work.

In Milwaukee, Eisenhower had followed his organization. It had given him bad advice. He had taken it. It had backfired, and McCarthy had scored a knockdown. At Dartmouth, Eisenhower in outrage had asserted obedience to a principle—the principle of the freedom of inquiry: "Don't join the book burners." When reporters at his next news conference pressed him to utter the hated Senator's name, Eisenhower with equanimity refused. He wasn't, he said, talking personalities. McCarthy himself said the shoe didn't fit him (as Elmer Davis observed, he had never himself actually touched a match to a book). But no one could misread the event. Ike had pierced his target.

The organizational process which had given Eisenhower bad advice in October 1952 in Milwaukee now gave him good advice in July 1953 in Washington. On June 18 one J. B. Matthews had become the new Executive Director of McCarthy's subcommittee staff. One of the last things he'd done before signing on was to author an article for the July issue of *American Mercury* entitled "Reds and Our Churches," which started off with a real grabber: "The largest single group supporting the Communist apparatus in the United States today is composed of Protestant clergymen." The magazine hit the newsstands. Word reached the White House. A group of Eisenhower's aides huddled in Sherman Adams's office. Phone calls were made to Catholic, Protestant, and Jewish leaders of the National Conference of Christians and Jews. As step one in the agreed-upon stratagem, they fired off to the White House a wire condemning the Matthews attack. The moment it arrived the mailroom bucked it to Special Counsel Bern Shanley. And there momentarily it lay: he had not participated in the scheme. It was soon rescued, however, and brought to the President, along with a Hughes draft of a presidential reply, a forceful condemnation of sweeping accusations of disloyalty against any entire group of American citizens.

Time was of the essence. McCarthy, feeling heat from other quarters, was planning to fire Matthews himself, without benefit of presidential stimulus. As Ike, now privy to the scheme for the first time, enthusiastically edited the draft, McCarthy was making his way through the Capitol corridors to announce Matthews' departure. After a frenzied phone call with Hughes, Bill Rogers and his old friend Richard Nixon waylaid the Wisconsin Senator and held him for crucial minutes in vapid conversation. By the time McCarthy released his announcement, Ike's angry condemnation had gone out over the news service wires.

No names were named. The staff had done its work. And Ike had once again, as at Dartmouth, scored.

The next day, in protest against a Republican majority vote to give McCarthy sole authority on hiring and firing the subcommittee staff, the three Democrats on the committee—John McClellan of Arkansas, W. Stuart Symington of Missouri, and Henry M. Jackson of Washington—resigned. They were joined three weeks later by Robert Kennedy, who wrote his friend McCarthy a gentlemanly letter and left his post as assistant counsel.

At the outer fringes of Eisenhower's organization, McCarthy and his staff continued to nibble away. Through the summer weeks they conjured themselves to no one target, digging like wildcatters for any payout.

They made a pass at the CIA, specifically at William P. Bundy, the son-in-law of Dean Acheson and a $400 contributor, so they discovered, to the legal defense fund for Alger Hiss, who like Bundy had all the right school ties and connections. McCarthy growled when Central Intelligence Director Allen W. Dulles stood firm, with the active help of Richard Nixon, against an uproarious excursion into his hypersecret agency and refused to let Bundy testify before McCarthy's committee. And the McCarthyites howled when the State Department gave Bundy a passport and thus let him slip out of the country for an assignment far overseas.

They went after a U.S. citizen in the employ of the Polish delegation to the United Nations. They took a look into the Government Printing Office, and got the scalp of a man who allegedly had had access to a lot of top secret Atomic Energy Commission and CIA documents. He was soon dismissed.

Forays of this kind died as the seams of low-grade ore petered out. But then McCarthy hit pay dirt—a long lode that seemed to stretch to infinity.

On Friday, September 4, G. David Schine phoned Jack Lucas, appointments aide to Secretary of the Army Robert Stevens. McCarthy, Schine said, wanted Stevens to see him privately at ten-thirty in the morning on Tuesday, September 8, and afterward attend a subcommittee hearing.

Five days earlier McCarthy had gone public with his latest target—the United States Army. His subcommittee had been holding closed hearings at the Foley Square Court House in New York City. And at the end of each session McCarthy would go out and give a little summary to a clutch of reporters. Two Army civilian employees, he told them, had admitted their Communist ties though denying Communist party membership. One of them, he said, was a woman in purchasing, a second was a man also in the Quartermaster Corps, and the third was a security guard in the Signal Corps who allegedly had signed a nominating petition for a Communist gubernatorial candidate in 1946. One witness, identified by McCarthy to the reporters as "Mrs. Commissar," had admitted having worked with the lady in purchasing, whom McCarthy identified as "Miss Q," back in 1947–48 but refused to say whether she knew Miss Q as a Communist. McCarthy was outraged. Miss Q, he told the press, had worked for the Quartermaster Corps since 1949 or 1950, after having served as secretary to a member of the National Committee of the United States Communist party. He ordered testifying Army officers to produce the names of the officials who had cleared the suspects. And he demanded the suspension of Miss Q, who, when queried about her Communist party ties in the 1940s, had taken the Fifth.

The Army suspended the security guard, said by McCarthy to be a "rabid Communist Party sympathizer": he had threatened to murder a witness scheduled to testify against him. But the Army refused to give the names of the clearance officials, citing a 1948 Truman Executive Order, still in effect. McCarthy was beside himself. Whoever certified the loyalty of Miss Q, he said, was either "incompetent beyond words, or in sympathy with Communism." He was outraged at Miss Q's chief, Colonel Robert A. Howard, Jr., commanding officer of the Quartermaster Inspection Service Command, for refusing to say whether he personally believed a Communist should be—as Miss Q had not yet been—suspended from government service.

McCarthy had moved up the ladder. On September 3 an acolyte on his staff named Hawkins got on the phone to Joseph W. Bishop, Jr., acting counselor (chief legal officer) of the Department of the Army, and announced: "Our chief consultant wants to speak to you. Will you hold the line?" (One story—perhaps apocryphal—had it that two subcabinet officers failed to hold an urgent conversation for two full days because neither secretary would put her boss on the phone first.) Hawkins, however, had Bishop on the line, awaiting the Great One. He also had—though he undoubtedly didn't know it—Bishop's secretary, pencil sharpened, ready to take down everything said. (One thing the Pentagon had was manpower—plenty of people poised to monitor; up on the Hill those tiny overworked staffs couldn't take the time to keep detailed records.) Now came a new voice: "This is David Schine. We are holding these hearings, and we have before us Colonel Howard. The Chairman of the Committee, Senator McCarthy, asked me to find out whether you had advised Colonel Howard not to state his opinion whether a Communist should or should not be suspended. Is that true?"

Bishop backpedaled. "Do you mean any Communist? Maybe it would be plainest if I told you what I did tell Colonel Howard. . . . I called his attention to the provisions of the Presidential directive of 3 April 1952 which says, I am quoting, 'No information shall be supplied as to any specific intermediate steps . . .'" Schine cut him short. "I know that directive. Did you tell him that he should not say whether he felt that this person should be suspended?"

"Not if his personal opinion is the same thing as his official opinion."

After a question to establish exactly who Bishop was and where he worked, Schine continued: "You know for the past couple of days we have been trying to get information . . . and we can't seem to get any action from the Army in this matter, and we don't quite understand. We think it is bad public relations on the Army's part."

Bishop tried to protest: "As you know, Mr. Schine, we are bound . . ."

Schine cut him off again: "I don't care if you are bound or not. The fact is you are doing a great disservice to the Army."

"I can only say that we have no discretion. We are under a directive from higher up. . . . I do want to emphasize that we will be glad to cooperate in making available to the committee any information which is authorized by directives from higher authority."

"Thank you." End of conversation.

Bishop put down the phone and called H. Struve Hensel, General Counsel for the entire Department of Defense. Then, in Stevens's absence, he called Acting Army Secretary Earl Johnson and told him about the call from Schine and about the grounds for his legal advice to Colonel Howard—the Truman directive of April 3, 1952, which said, "No information shall be supplied as to any specific intermediate steps, proceedings, transcripts of hearings or actions taken in processing an individual under loyalty or security programs." In Bishop's view, Colonel Howard, having responsibility for action taken on "Miss Q," could not separate his personal from his official opinion. Acting Army Secretary Johnson concurred and told Bishop to keep Hensel informed. Bishop thereupon dictated a memo for the record and sent copies to thirteen offices around the Pentagon.

The next day, Friday, September 4, on the eve of the Labor Day weekend, McCarthy and his staff moved up to the Secretary of the Army himself. They had subpoenaed General Miles Reber—head of the Army's Office of Legislative Liaison—to appear at ten-thirty on the morning of Tuesday, September 8, in room 357 of the Senate Office Building to tell them who cleared "Miss Q" and the security guard. McCarthy was insisting that he wanted no FBI information or no disclosure of sources. But he did want Stevens to come to his office before the hearing, and once the hearing began he wanted the Secretary of the Army personally present. The Secretary, McCarthy was told, had left Washington for the long weekend—gone to his ranch in Montana. But as soon as he returned, Stevens' aide Colonel BeLieu would give him the Senator's message. Thus began the confrontation between the legislative and the executive branches of the government.

Robert TenBroeck Stevens, Secretary of the Army, fifty-four years old, was born July 31, 1899, in Farmwood, New Jersey, close to his later home in South Plainfield, where he had lived most of his life. The son of John Peters Stevens and Edna TenBroeck Stevens, he was heir to the factories and fortune of J. P. Stevens and Company, Inc., the textile company founded nearly a century and a half earlier by his ancestor, Nathaniel Stevens.

Robert had gone to Andover and Yale. After graduating, he had entered the family business first as a mill hand, then as a salesman, and on his father's death in 1929 he had become the company's president. He had presided over acquisition, expansion, and explosive growth. When he took over, the company was doing $25 million worth of business a year. By 1939 that figure had more than quadrupled. And by 1952, when Robert Stevens resigned as chairman to become Army Secretary, it had multiplied more than thirteen times, to an annual $335 million.

Stevens moved easily in the upper reaches of the blue-ribbon corporate world. He served, *inter alia,* as a director of General Electric, General Foods, New York Telephone, and Owens-Corning Fiberglass, and as a trustee of the Mutual Life Insurance Company of New York, Roosevelt Hospital, and the Rockefeller Foundation. With his fellow tycoons he frequented New York's prestigious clubs—the Links, the Merchants, and the Union League, as well as, of course, the Yale Club—and he had been elected chairman of the Business Advisory Council, the predecessor of today's Business Council, the most exclusive business executives' group.

Noblesse oblige. At times of national emergency, he had always responded. In World War I he interrupted his studies at Yale to serve as a second lieutenant in the Field Artillery. In the early days of the New Deal, he went to Washington as an administrative representative in the industry section of the NRA. In 1934 he became a director of the Federal Reserve Bank of New York, ultimately rising to the post of chairman. Even before Pearl Harbor he had entered a special course at the Command and General Staff School at Fort

Leavenworth, Kansas; upon graduation he was assigned to the Office of the Quartermaster General with the rank of colonel. He served as Director of Purchases from 1943 to 1945 and came out of the war with the Legion of Merit and the Distinguished Service Medal. In 1950 he received honorary doctorates from both Lafayette and N.Y.U.

He was a distinguished man. He of course had known GM's Charlie Wilson from the Business Advisory Council. But Stevens had taken no active part in the 1952 campaign, he had not met Dwight Eisenhower until December of that year, and he always modestly said that he never knew exactly why Ike had chosen him as Secretary of the Army.

When his nomination went to the Senate, he—like Defense Secretary–designate Charlie Wilson and Air Force Secretary–designate Harold Talbott—had an awkward problem. He agreed to sell all his holdings in companies doing business with the Defense Department. But he dearly wanted to hold on to his stock in the J. P. Stevens Company—stock worth some $1.4 million. "I am steeped in sentiment and tradition with respect to the company that bears my father's name," he told the Senate Armed Services Committee. But the senators remained unmoved. And on January 20 he agreed to divest himself of his holdings and at once received their blessing.

He had taken the helm of the Pentagon's largest military department with customary vigor. On entering office he announced he would fly to Tokyo to get firsthand information on the reported shortage of ammunition in Korea. And during the spring of 1953, he visited the Joliet Arsenal, the Louisiana Ordnance plant near Shreveport, and the Seventh Army in Europe as well as the Eighth Army in Korea. Hanson W. Baldwin, a veteran Pentagon watcher for the *New York Times*, reported in July of 1953 that the Army liked Stevens's manner and his managerial ability. People up on the Hill admired him as an energetic, personable, and affable man who, with his lack of side, easily won friends. And Ike liked him: in a moment of pique with Air Force Secretary Talbott, the President confided to Bern Shanley that he wished he'd given Air Force either to Navy Secretary Bob Anderson—already beginning an unbroken ascent in Ike's admiration—or to Bob Stevens.

Thus in his first months the new Secretary of the Army worked his way methodically and effectively through busy days in his big office on the Pentagon's E wing with its sweeping view of the Lincoln Memorial, its big desk flanked by the American and Army flags, and its portraits of predecessors Henry Stimson and Frank Pace on the walls, along with a framed front page of the Paris edition of the *New York Herald Tribune* for May 23, 1927, the date of Lindbergh's arrival, which Stevens had witnessed as a young man and had never forgotten.

An occasional press article would provide a glimpse into Stevens's private life. He had a pretty, slender, blond wife, the former Dorothy Goodwin Whitney, whom he'd married thirty years earlier. They had five children: one now with the Stevens firm in New York; one with the Army in Germany; one a Virginia farmer who eventually married the daughter of Lewis Mumford; a daughter, Joan, a CIA employee who lived with her parents; and a young son away at prep school. The Stevenses rented a furnished mansion off Rock Creek Park in Washington, and they made no waves. No one ever monitored the phone calls that came in from Mrs. Stevens or Joan or any of the boys. Back home in Plainfield the Secretary of the Army had served as a deacon of the Crescent Avenue Presbyterian Church. On the surface and to the core he was—always had been—a Christian gentleman.

He was trim, with thinning gray hair; ruddy-cheeked; and easy-smiling. He was a patriot who always observed Flag Day, a "straight arrow," one of his assistants once described him, "right out of *McGuffey's Reader.*" People liked him, and he liked them; he got along and wanted to get along. He walked respected, wealthy, with large accomplishments behind him. Yet his name was not a household word. Nine months after his swearing in, Governor Dewey's office would phone asking for Secretary of the Army Thomas Stevens, confusing his name with that of the White House appointments secretary. In his impeccably tailored double-breasted gray flannel suit, quiet striped tie, polished buckled black shoes and dark horn-rimmed glasses, he remained a man nobody really knew.

Indeed, undetected by the press and eyed with some apprehension by those closest about him in the Pentagon, Stevens had been getting off to a shaky start. In his textile business he had had a large organization around him which protected him and with which he felt comfortable. In the Pentagon he had a far different organization—largely holdovers from the predecessor regime, hundreds and hundreds of men and women to be viewed with suspicion, tested, and if necessary replaced. As a result the brand-new Secretary found himself relying on a handful of individuals who passed the test of trust, not on the full organization chart with its assigned responsibilities.

Stevens, for example, didn't like to make speeches. So he soon began turning over speaking engagements to his office administrator, a young lieutenant colonel named Kenneth BeLieu, whom he had inherited, scrutinized, and come to rely on, instead of assigning the platforms, as a service secretary ordinarily would, to a four-star general. Stevens found himself awash in the wild world of political patronage. For a while he turned that job over to the uniformed Colonel BeLieu too. Stevens couldn't penetrate the arcane mysteries of military jargon. "Do you understand this document?" he would ask BeLieu. "You sign it."

But the Secretary didn't worry. He had a lot of Republican friends, not only in New Jersey but outside—for instance, in Wisconsin, where he'd put money into the campaign of Senator Joseph McCarthy. Nobody was going to hurt him. And if any difficulty did arise, he really didn't need that big, dubious organization to help him, anyway. He could take it on all by himself.

Stevens enjoyed his ranch in Montana—a faraway spread near the town of Harlowton—where he could hunt and ride and get away from it all.

On September 7, Labor Day, when Stevens returned to Washington, he not only had McCarthy's summons awaiting him; he also found on his desk a memorandum from Joe Bishop. Because Colonel Howard would be appearing before McCarthy's committee at 10 A.M. the next day, Bishop urged that Howard receive a specific order not to give the committee any information in violation of existing presidential directives—those promulgated by Truman, still in effect. Among others, Bishop went on, Struve Hensel and Assistant Attorney General J. Lee Rankin concurred in this recommendation. In addition, Hensel strongly advocated that "the highest authority" within the Department of the Army—i.e., Stevens himself—should sign the directive to Colonel Howard. The directive went out that very day, signed by Earl Johnson.

The grounds for the Army's refusal were unexceptionable: not only to preserve the security process and the objectivity of its participants by keeping them from endless congressional inquisitions on why they had decided one way and not another; but also, and above all, to protect accused innocents from a public dumping and airing of all allegations against them, whether truths, half-truths, or lies.

The next day, Tuesday, September 8, as requested, Stevens phoned McCarthy. All was sweetness and light. Stevens had to attend a major military funeral, and so at the morning's open hearing he missed seeing McCarthy attack Major-General Miles Reber, head of the Army's Legislative Liaison Office, who along with the others had advised the Army to abide by the old Democratic directive: "Don't give me that, General. . . . I can't conceive that the President, who is elected on a platform of opposition to Communism, would whitewash those who are responsible." At noon, however, Stevens, McCarthy, and subcommittee member Everett Dirksen (Republican of Illinois) had lunch together. Stevens agreed to review the Army's refusal to reveal the security-clearers' names. And he sat in as a spectator at the afternoon's executive session.

About lunchtime the next day Deputy Attorney General Bill Rogers phoned Stevens: "I feel like McCarthy calling you."

As the Deputy Attorney General uttered these bantering words, they were heard not only by the Secretary of the Army but also by a youngish, half-bald man with rimless spectacles and a bow tie who sat just outside the Secretary's office door, his phone held cradled on his shoulder by a rubber gadget, his hand fleetly converting the conversation into Gregg shorthand in his stenographic notebook.

John J. Lucas, Jr., appointments clerk to the Secretary of the Army, was a career civil servant. He had sat outside the door of the Army Secretaries for a long time, all the way back to December of 1949. Earlier, for three years during the war, he had taken notes and made transcripts of the meetings of the Joint Chiefs of Staff.

He was fast, accurate, and meticulous. After graduating from Northwestern during the Depression, he had gone to school—by day and by night—to learn shorthand. He had won a 200 Gregg diamond medal. He didn't miss much of any significance. Day by day he would summarize, on separate little memo slips, the highlights of who called the Secretary and whom the Secretary called and about what. And the most significant calls he would index, on three-by-five cards. This elaborate and fussy Dickensian process enabled Lucas to do his job as appointments clerk: instantaneously, as a call unfolded, he would spot actions to be taken as a result of the call and set those actions in motion—for example, alert the chauffeur, order the plane tickets, make the hotel reservations, get the speech preparation started, all for a trip to Chicago the Secretary had just discussed. But the process, as a by-product, also eventuated in a gold mine, in his untranscribed notebooks—a rolling contemporaneous record of thousands upon thousands of words spoken by and to the Secretary, day by day, minute by minute, month after month. Even when Lucas went to the men's room, got entangled in other duties, or took a vacation, the records relentlessly continued to accumulate, in the shorthand notes of his two backups—Stevens's personal secretary, Mrs. Jane R. Pike, and a Department of the Army shorthand reporter who had another full-time job, Theodore R. Rhodes.

That ominous noontime in September, Rogers and Stevens chatted for a few minutes about a non-McCarthy problem. "Hold on," Rogers suddenly interrupted, "Adams is calling me." The whole organization was wired for sound. The White House phone network—the miraculous White House switchboard its nerve center—extended not only through 1600 Pennsylvania Avenue but throughout the offices of Cabinet members. Sherman Adams and others would phone Stevens directly, skirting the Pentagon switchboard. Calls on that line, connected to a special white phone at Stevens's desk, Appointments Clerk Lucas and the others couldn't monitor. They also couldn't hear anything said over the internal buzz-box system that linked, for example, Stevens and the counselor of the Army. These calls were merely logged in; one knew when a call was made but not what was said. One didn't monitor upward, only horizontally or downward. The President's personal secretary, Ann Whitman, for example, would at times monitor calls of the President; nobody monitored the line on the other end with one exception: Foster Dulles's secretary, Phyllis Bernau. Other Cabinet officers would not only refrain from putting a secretary on the line with the President; they would ordinarily not even permit anyone in the room while he spoke with them.

Finally, after a long-holding pause, Rogers came back on Stevens's line: "How are you getting along with jumping Joe?" the monitoring began after the interruption.

"To be honest, perfectly well. Yesterday I was willing to give way on several things, but on major things like the Executive Order of the President, we'll stand tightly and see."

Rogers, wise in the ways of the Hill, concurred: "Half the battle is having good relations."

Before nightfall McCarthy had dropped yet another contribution to the salubriousness of those relations: he revealed the existence of a document, bearing the Army's imprimatur, used to educate troops and titled "Psychological and Cultural Traits of Soviet Siberia." "Clear-cut Communist propaganda," he called it, citing the presence in its bibliography of the writings of a well-known left-leaning author, Corliss Lamont. McCarthy demanded to know who had approved it.

One rung up the ladder from the Department of the Army, in the office of Defense Secretary Wilson, the Department's general counsel, Struve Hensel, watched these events with increasing uneasiness. At 4:45 P.M. on September 10 he phoned Stevens. "You've seen what's breaking in the papers," he began. He'd been talking with Assistant Attorney General Lee Rankin, he continued, and the two of them had agreed that "we must have an overall policy, and that the Attorney General must get in and so must the White House." The Attorney General at the moment was away, Rankin said, but as soon as he returned, Rankin assured Hensel, "We will sit down with some [people] from State and others and get a policy."

While this effort at shoring up proceeded in the Army, McCarthy was demanding that an officer appear before his committee on Monday, Tuesday, or Wednesday of the next week to tell all about the pernicious pamphlet. The committee had given the Army no list of the questions it might ask, and at four o'clock on Saturday, September 12, the Army Chief of Staff, General Matthew B. Ridgway, phoned Stevens: "General Partridge, our G-2, has been . . . giving consideration down there as to which officer ought to go or whether he himself ought to go."

"These hearings are going to be in New York?" Stevens asked.

"That's right, the committee is in session there through next week."

Stevens also had to go to New York on Monday. "I was just wondering one thing," he said. "I was just beginning to turn this over a little bit in my mind and I was wondering whether it would make any sense to go up there and see Joe or the staff and see what it is they want and when they want it and get the thing on the track."

At this precise moment the Pentagon organization itself began to undergo two changes—changes that, unremarked at the time, would throw long shadows into the future.

First, up in the office of Secretary of Defense Wilson a career man—Andrew Berding—was leaving as chief of press relations, and a new man was coming into a new post—Assistant Secretary of Defense for Legislative and Public Affairs. "I told them," Berding once recalled, "that no one man could oversee both the press and the Congress, but that if anyone could, it would be the man they'd selected, Fred Seaton." Fred, a Nebraska newspaper publisher, had served out an unexpired term in the Senate. After the Milwaukee speech episode, his leak to Bill Lawrence of the Marshall paragraph and the campaign, Fred had gone home to Hastings, Nebraska, to run his newspaper and radio empire. He wanted nothing in government. But now they needed him. And at ten-fifteen on the morning of September 15, Bob Stevens joined in congratulating Fred as he was sworn into his new job.

Second, in the Department of the Army, another key official, Joe Bishop, who had been serving as the department's acting counselor—its chief legal officer—was leaving government service to return to private law practice, and Bob Stevens was looking for a replacement. At 3 P.M. that same afternoon Stevens phoned Bill Rogers over in Justice to get his advice, not only as Deputy Attorney General, but as a veteran of the Hill with a shrewd knowledge of congressional committees and their staffs. Specifically, he wanted Rogers's advice on one John Adams—an assistant to Struve Hensel whom Hensel was recommending for the Army's top legal job. "I have no knowledge of his legal ability," Rogers told Stevens, "but Adams knows his way around on the Hill and has many friends."

That evening Stevens flew to New York—with Secretary Wilson and Treasury Secretary George Humphrey—for a dinner in Stevens's honor, and at 9:45 the next morning, at McCarthy's request, he breakfasted with the Senator at the Waldorf Towers suite, 30A, of the parents of David Schine.

Stevens went into the meeting fortified by the assurance, face-to-face from Charlie Wilson himself, that Wilson approved the Army Secretary's refusal to knuckle under to McCarthy's demands, with one exception. Stevens, Wilson said, should give Joe the names of the officers who had recommended against the elimination of one particular McCarthy-alleged homosexual. Joe reported on their discussion to the press, and the next afternoon, September 17, Fred Seaton phoned Stevens.

"I couldn't help," he said, "being curious about your own appraisal of the situation the other day in New York."

"I still continue to have my fingers crossed," Stevens replied, "but so far the thing has gone along surprisingly well. I followed along

the lines we discussed the other day. . . . I agreed to give him the
names of the people that had reviewed that one case. . . . I refused
of course on the loyalty files and things of that kind. Joe was definitely pleased with the conference; so I felt I had accomplished
quite a bit. I feel that at the moment he is very strong for the Army
and the way we are operating with him. . . ."

Fred Seaton knew where he was going. But he always had a ready
reserve of flannel and salve. And now he laid them on. "I thought
you must have done a bang-up job with him. He complimented you
highly." Then, underneath, came the key question—one little sharp
rock in a wide pond of pleasantry: "The only thing I was surprised
at was that he said he had established a liaison." Establishing a
liaison with a key Senate committee was, at least in part, Seaton's
turf. Was this some kind of end run?

Stevens explained: "You see, I am getting a new Department
Counselor, and I think we will have it settled tomorrow. [Mc-
Carthy] said, 'We don't want to bother you all the time, but we
want to have somebody reasonably close to you that we can call
when we have something.' When I get him set up here, which will
be certainly by Monday, then I was going to say to the Department
Counselor that one of his jobs is that if McCarthy calls up, and I
am not here . . . , you take it on and see what it is, and we will
talk about it later. That is all I meant. . . . We will keep that coordinated with you in any way you want. In other words, we will
not go off here by ourselves. And everything I have attempted to do
so far with Joe has been along [this] line—I have taken it more on a
Department of Defense level really because what is good for the
Department of the Army in this regard is good for the Department
of Defense and vice-versa. . . ."

Seaton had his answer. But his parting shot, couched in jocosity,
still mirrored the jurisdictional uneasiness that had prompted the
conversation: "I think . . . you have done such a good job that
you may find yourself a representative of everybody in the Department of Defense, Bob. Have you thought of that?"

Stevens replied straight-arrow: "No. But we must, if we can, have
a good relationship. We would rather have a good one than a bad
one; and if I can at any time be of any service in any area of the
Department of Defense on that particular thing, I, of course, would
be glad to try to do it."

"I was," Seaton concluded, "half serious and half facetious."

Stevens had not told Seaton Adams's name. But only minutes

before their conversation, the Secretary of the Army had had a call from Hensel, Adams's boss, wanting Stevens's decision. One last check, Stevens told him. "I think he could do the job," Stevens said, "and I like him." That check made, at one-fifty the next afternoon, Friday, September 18, Stevens phoned Adams with the offer. Adams at once accepted, and they agreed he would start a week from the coming Monday—September 28.

Ken BeLieu had been running a little background check on Adams. It had come up with mixed signals—nothing earthshaking but enough to suggest the prudence of a few further inquiries. Too late. "I've made up my mind," Stevens told his aide, "and he's accepted. Anyway," he added, "if he can't do the job, we can always fire him."

Watching from the sideline as the events of that week unfolded, John Adams, experienced in the ways of the Hill, could only have felt foreboding at what he was getting into. It was a week of frantic phone calls between Washington and New York—efforts to reach Roy Cohn again and again without result, fruitless efforts to get Schine to return a call, mysterious allusions in conversation between Colonel BeLieu and McCarthy's office to a "personal matter," all capped by planning for a committee hearing on the tract "Psychological and Cultural Traits of Soviet Siberia," and a grilling of its perpetrators in Army Intelligence.

An investigation had brought to Stevens's office at 4:25 P.M. on September 17 the name of an obscure Army officer who had inadvertently leaked the name of the pamphlet's author. Almost at the same instant Cohn phoned from New York. He had two questions: (1) What time on Monday would it be convenient for the Secretary to have the hearing? (2) Because time was running out, did the Secretary's office have any word on the still-unspecified "personal matter"?

The hearing on the pamphlet was finally set for 10:30 A.M. in room 357 of the Senate Office Building. At the last minute, as Stevens was going down the stairs, Lucas caught him and told him of a switch to Room 101, to throw the press off the trail. The doors closed on the executive session. The lead witness, the head of Army Intelligence, took the stand. And the massacre began.

Cohn: "Could we get your full name for the record?"

General Partridge: "Richard C. Partridge. P-A-R-T-R-I-D-G-E. . . . [Commanding] G-2 of the Army."

Cohn wasted no time. "You have heard the testimony [on the pamphlet in question]. What the committee is particularly interested in is the origin of this report. Why was it . . . used? Are any of them still around, still being used?"

Partridge began to explain. McCarthy jumped in: "Do you approve of the pamphlet?"

Partridge: "I don't approve of everything, but I think it is an honest attempt to do what it says it is trying to do."

McCarthy: "Do you know that [it] quotes directly verbatim Stalin's book in describing the workings of Communism?"

Partridge: "That has been stated."

McCarthy: "Without attribution to Stalin?"

Partridge: "That has been stated, I believe."

McCarthy: "You come here and say it is a good, honest attempt. I wonder how much you know about the book. Do you know that this book quotes verbatim from Joe Stalin, without attributing it to him, as a stamp of approval of the United States Army? Are you aware of that?"

Partridge: "I don't know that it quotes from Joe Stalin or not."

McCarthy: "Don't you think before you testify you should take time to conduct some research to find out whether it quotes Joe Stalin and other notorious Communists? Don't you think you are incompetent to testify before you know that?"

Partridge: "No, sir."

McCarthy: "I don't want someone here who knows nothing about this document, just giving us conversation. . . . Do you know who Harriet Moore is, General?"

Partridge: "Only in a general way."

McCarthy: "You only know Harriet Moore in a general way and you are head of G-2?"

Partridge: "Yes."

McCarthy: "You can't mean that. . . . You are the head of G-2? . . . One of your tasks, of course, is to dig out and expose Communist influences. That is correct, isn't it?"

Partridge: "That is correct."

McCarthy: "To make sure Communist agents will not be used by our enemy to infiltrate our forces. In other words, to keep Communists from infiltrating into the United States forces. Isn't that right?"

Partridge: "That is correct, sir."

McCarthy: "And you say you only know Harriet Moore in a general way?"

Partridge: "I know very little except that she contributed to the [books] we have been discussing. . . ."

McCarthy: "Did you know that before you came into this room?"

Partridge: "No, sir."

McCarthy: "What did you know about her before you came into this room?"

Partridge: "Nothing."

McCarthy: "Nothing at all?"

Partridge: "No. . . ."

McCarthy: "Do you have a staff that could properly inform you?"

Partridge: "Yes, sir."

McCarthy: "Why don't you have them inform you before you come down here? You come down here and say it is an excellent book. You don't know that Communists were used and quoted. You make the Army look awfully silly."

Next, McCarthy and Cohn worked over a man named Samuel McKee, who had headed a little committee that had approved the pamphlet.

Cohn: "Have you read Karl Marx?"

McKee: "I once read *Das Kapital*."

Cohn: "Have you read Lenin?"

McKee: "Excerpts."

Cohn: "Do you know the difference between Marxism and Marxism-Leninism?"

McKee: "Many of these fine distinctions of Communism I don't know."

Cohn: "That is no fine distinction. That is a distinction involving the United States of America. . . ."

Sitting in the closed-door audience, Stevens heard all this and McCarthy's ominous concluding words: "We will want both of you back here Monday." And the Secretary got to his feet: "Could I make one brief statement? I am most appreciative of the opportunity of being here. I think it is fair to say from my evaluation of the answers given to your questions that they are not very satisfactory to the committee. However, I would like to say, in fairness to General Partridge and Mr. McKee, I think they have tried to get before you the facts, right or wrong, to the best of their ability. There has been no effort to withhold whoever the author might be, who served on the committee. It seems to me, therefore, on the ground of attempt to cooperate, they have made that attempt, even though their answers might not have been satisfactory."

He had made a lame and feeble disclaimer. From McCarthy it drew only a retort: "I may say, Mr. Secretary, I have been shocked beyond words by the appearance of the gentleman here. He came here to testify in regard to a document which has been labeled by a student on the subject as a work of a Communist agent. We know that much of the contents of it is [the] work of identified Communist agents. Why Partridge comes here to defend that and say in effect that he intends to continue more of the same, to me that marks him as completely incompetent. He may be an excellent field commander. . . . Mr. Secretary, we need more than cooperation from a man like General Partridge. We need someone who has some conception of the danger of communism. . . ."

Partridge had not covered himself with glory. Even Roy Cohn didn't particularly want to stomp on him in the forthcoming public hearing. At twelve twenty-nine on September 23 he phoned Stevens about putting the General on the stand: "What are we going to do with General Partridge? . . . He is the head of G-2, and maybe he won't be doing much if we make the head of G-2 look awfully silly."

Stevens hesitated to beg off. "I don't like to say to you, 'Please don't call a fellow.'"

But Cohn knew what would happen if Partridge appeared: "You might want a nice gentle fight, but once you get in the ring and start taking a couple of pokes, it gets under your skin. . . ." Neither he nor Joe, Cohn knew, could resist the smell of blood and fear: "I think it would be a lot of fun. You know I am an old big-game hunter. . . ." In further conversation two days later—in which Stevens confided to Cohn his intention to take Partridge out of his job—they agreed the General would not show up to testify unless Cohn called. (A laconic note in Jack Lucas's log on Friday, September 25, records the substance of a phone conversation between Stevens and Bishop: "General Partridge is coming in to [Bishop's office] this afternoon for woodshedding by [Bishop] and General Reber. [The Secretary of the Army] may go down.")

On the morning of September 28, however, a red-hot Roy Cohn was again phoning the Secretary.

"Who is playing tricks on us?" he demanded. "It was our understanding that [Partridge] would not come."

Stevens tried to explain that a subsequent McCarthy public utterance had seemed to void the understanding.

Cohn brushed it aside. "When we have an arrangement, I will

stick by it no matter what Joe says or anybody says. And our understanding was that he would not be called. Now the guy walks right in, in the front witness row . . ."

Crestfallen, Stevens could only backtrack. "I am awfully sorry about this because the way you have played with me has been 100 percent. . . ." Later that day, after checking, Stevens retreated even further: "You were completely correct," he phoned Cohn, "and I muffed the ball." They closed with pleasantries about Stevens's attendance at McCarthy's wedding, a gala event, with all the high and mighty—executive and legislative; Republican and Democrat—scheduled for the morrow, in Washington's St. Matthew's Cathedral.

There the forty-three-year-old Wisconsin Republican and his twenty-nine-year-old bride, Jean Kerr, his secretary and assistant, exchanged their vows. The Roman Catholic cathedral was filled to capacity, and outside thousands of onlookers, standing in the bright sun, whistled and applauded the bride and bridegroom. The Reverend William J. Awalt, in gold and scarlet, performed the ceremony and at its end read a cablegram bestowing on the event the "paternal and apostolic blessing" of the Pope.

The bride, a Catholic convert from the Presbyterian church, wore a filmy white veil and a long-trained gown of ivory satin and lace. Senator McCarthy, for once properly dressed, wore black cutaway, striped trousers, ascot, and, in his lapel, a sprig from the bridal bouquet. The New York Times reported that the groom did not kiss his bride at the ceremony or on the cathedral steps, but that she "whisked a trace of her lipstick from his lips" as they arrived by limousine for a reception at the Washington Club. There the newlyweds greeted their guests in front of a white marble fireplace; then all moved into another room, where nonalcoholic fruit punch and a four-tiered wedding cake were waiting.

It had taken so long to seat the nine hundred guests in the cathedral that the ceremony had begun fifteen minutes late. President and Mrs. Eisenhower sent regrets, but Vice President and Mrs. Nixon, and Sherman Adams, Wilton Persons, and I. Jack Martin of the White House Staff attended. So did Jack Dempsey.

A day later, with Joe and his bride off on their honeymoon, Cohn again phoned Stevens, breathless with portents of things to come: "That thing I told you about, I will probably be ready to tell you about in a day or so. It is a pretty big situation. I will check the final word on it tonight. . . ."

• •

Cohn and McCarthy had a new lead, a tip on the possible existence of a Communist spy ring within one of the Army's most sensitive organizations—the Signal Corps Center at Forth Monmouth,
New Jersey. This two-thousand-acre establishment employed nearly
eight thousand civilians, plus people from the uniformed services
devoted to research, development, and training. The installation's
laboratories included the Army's main radar research center, the
Evans Signal Laboratory at Belmar, ten miles north of Fort Monmouth itself.

As the investigation began, it at once encountered a roadblock.
The Commanding General at the Fort, Kirke Lawton, was refusing
to cooperate. So on the afternoon of October 2, two McCarthy staff
members—Cohn and Frank Carr, the new Executive Director who
had replaced the controversial J. B. Matthews—called on Stevens to
protest. Stevens heard them out, then reached for the phone to put
in a call to General Lawton, a sturdily built man in his midfifties. He
had held his post for nearly two years now, and he found himself—like
Partridge—suddenly on the carpet. Stevens came right to the point:
"Is there any rule in effect . . . that none of these people down there
can talk to any of the committee people from the Congress?"

"That is right. They cannot, without your authority."

"I am working with the committees of Congress to try to get some
constructive things done and working on a basis that I am perfectly
satisfied to give that permission. And I now authorize you in my
name to give permission in any case that may be involved. . . . I
do not want to put any strings on that. This is an instruction in
effect now, as I understand it."

Lawton protested: "No. This is the first authority I have had here
to allow anybody here to talk about any of these cases to anybody."

"As long as it is one of the committees of Congress, I would like
them to go ahead, and I am sure nothing but good will come out of
it. . . ."

Lawton now raised a problem: "From [their] own personal
knowledge [they] can testify, but the files have a lot of FBI stuff
in them."

Stevens now backed off, making one exception: Don't release any
of that.

Cohn and Carr listened with satisfaction. They left, and Stevens
at once phoned Lawton's boss, Major General George I. Back, head
of the entire Signal Corps.

"I just called up General Lawton at Monmouth," Stevens began, "because I found out—I am sure that he was acting in what he thought was the proper way—he had refused to let anybody up there talk with any of this Congressional Committee that has been looking into this business of infiltration. I have been handling myself this relationship of the Army with the so-called McCarthy committee, and I think, General Back, getting along reasonably well. . . . And so I took the liberty of calling Lawton and telling him that I would like very much to have him make available to an accredited representative of the committee . . . anybody they wanted to talk with up there."

Back sidestepped: "I am surprised to hear that he denied them."

"There was nothing written on it," Stevens answered. "There was sort of an oral instruction. . . . But I thought it was advisable, rather than bring the wrath of the committee on the Signal Corps, the Army, or myself, that it would be better, if we have some trouble there, just to open the thing up and let them talk to anybody they want to. . . ." Then Stevens made an admission: "It is the only time I have made a call like that since I have been in this job; and the reason I did it was that I had several people sitting right here in the office from the committee, and they were pretty unhappy about the thing, and I thought the really best way to clear this thing up and get them in good humor is to call General Lawton. . . ." Finally a little stiffening of the spine: "I am not going to sell anybody in the Army down the river. I will stand up and fight just as hard as anybody, but I think we will come out better if we do cooperate with them."

Back concluded with a salute: "I would like to add that all of us are sure we are going to be defended by you. There is no one that doubts that, sir."

John Adams, now on the job, had hit the ground running. Already he was setting to work on the Monmouth problem: observing the interrogation of witnesses in executive session in New York, and reporting back to Stevens; taking on phone calls from Roy Cohn; writing the Assistant Chief of Staff, G-2, to speed up the investigations on pending security cases and setting deadlines for summary reports; urging a doubling of the number of people who screen security cases in order to cut down the time they sat in the office of the Secretary of the Army.

On October 6, the Army announced that "several" Signal Corps

laboratory employees at Monmouth had been suspended for security reasons. The next day one of them, Aaron H. Coleman, identified
himself as a suspended radar specialist, denied he was a security
risk, and charged that he was being suspended because of the people
he knew in college days, including Morton Sobell, a convicted member of the Rosenberg conspiracy. On October 9, McCarthy cut short
his honeymoon to come back to get in on the Monmouth probe. On
October 12, hearings began in New York City, and the next day the
first big news began to break. An ex-Army officer, McCarthy told
reporters, had testified that many top secret Signal Corps documents
were missing. Committee member Everett Dirksen, in a speech in
Chicago, asserted that twenty-six of the fifty-seven missing documents—they had to do with radar, he said—had been located in East
Germany. And even Defense Secretary Charlie Wilson sounded
ominous: the Army, he said, was conducting its own investigation
at Monmouth, and the problem "looks like it might be worse than
just a security leak."

Stevens came up to New York to observe the October 13 hearings
at Foley Square. He invited one and all to lunch at his nearby
Merchants Club. That evening he attended an expansive dinner
party—with, among others, the McCarthys, Cohn's parents, Schine's
parents, and Schine—given by Cohn in a private dining room at the
Waldorf. The next morning Schine picked Stevens up at his hotel
and drove him to the courthouse.

There they found Aaron Coleman on the witness stand and their
jovial fellow guest of the previous evening, Joe McCarthy, in high
dudgeon. By mistake, the committee had earlier been allowed to see
and study Coleman's personnel file. They requested a copy. But
when it arrived, they discovered it had been stripped of what they
wanted, what they never should have seen in the first place, under
the Army's regulations—the security information on Coleman's alleged malfeasance.

Coleman, who had known Julius Rosenberg at New York's City
College and once attended with him a Young Communist League
meeting, had gone to work at Monmouth before the war. During
wartime service as a Marine, Coleman had written a friend back at
Monmouth, asking him to mail him—out of channels—a copy of a
radar manual he had helped write. The censors, reading Coleman's
mail, blocked his attempt to secure this document of radar secrets.

Returning to Monmouth as a radar scientist after the war, Coleman received permission to take home forty-eight declassified doc-

uments. He stuck them under his bed. When Army security came to check, they discovered among the mass of declassified papers two still stamped "Confidential." For this indiscretion the Army had fined him two weeks' pay, mothing more. And in the years that followed, until he came under security suspicion in 1953, he had risen to the top of an extensive organization responsible for R and D on large-scale antiaircraft systems—weapons to be used worldwide against atomic bomb attack. McCarthy, now holding in his hand a bowdlerized record on such an inviting target, cried foul. And John Adams soon turned over the missing information; security had already been violated, he said, the damage already done.

The next day, October 15, McCarthy had still more red meat for the reporters. Coleman's college friend Julius Rosenberg, he told them, had set up a wartime spy ring at Monmouth which might, he speculated, still be operating. He insisted that informant David Greenglass, then in Lewisburg Penitentiary, be interviewed. And he urged the Secretary of the Army to speed the return to the U.S. of a German scientist who, he said, had given information to the Air Force on the use of Monmouth data in an East German laboratory. Even the good gray *New York Times* purveyed the news: "Rosenberg," it headlined, "Called Radar Spy Leader."

Hot on the heels of this headline, Army Under Secretary Earl Johnson—a Wisconsinite—was phoning Stevens: "Walter Kohler, Governor of Wisconsin," he said, "is in town. He has asked us to have dinner with them tonight, along with Joe McCarthy and his wife."

Stevens answered, relaxed: "I call him your Senator, you know. . . . I think it would be a good thing to do."

"As a matter of fact," Johnson went on, "I couldn't meet him on a more favorable basis. . . . I didn't want to do it without checking with you because I didn't know what went on in the hearings."

Stevens, the soul of equanimity, replied: "The Army is getting along fine with Joe. He is getting headlines and is entitled to them. Fundamentally, he has been fine with us. . . . I think you will enjoy it. He is an interesting fellow, and she is a very attractive person. . . ."

John Adams had remained in New York, staying at the Commodore Hotel at the government rate of ten dollars a night, to monitor the hearings. As he would frequently do at the Senate cafeteria in Washington, he broke bread regularly with Cohn and Carr. Now, on October 16, a muggy, overcast day, Adams joined a little group of McCarthy's friends—including reporter Willard Edwards of the *Chicago Tribune* and Governor and Mrs. Walter Kohler, she in a gaily decorated hat—in a hot, windowless makeshift hearing room at the Foley Square Courthouse to hear McCarthy go after his prey.

Adams listened a while, then went out to a pay phone and called Stevens: "General Back and General Lawton were here today, and we had a couple of their Indians to tell these people everything they could, which was bothering them, about the documents. . . . There was a fellow in a couple of days ago, I think previous to the time of this hearing, whose name was [Greenblum], who had been identified by [Joseph] Levitsky [another Monmouth suspect] as a carpool rider with Julius Rosenberg. He came back in today and was extremely uneasy and excited and frightened; and McCarthy and Cohn did a good job of scaring him more. He was scared to death, to the point where he could hardly talk. So they sent him to the other room to sit for an hour; and he came back in and asked to change his statement; and he told them that he had known that Levitsky was a Communist. . . . He has gone back in, about ten minutes ago. They are going to try to run him all afternoon to see if he will ramble and range and [fit] the little pieces in. That is how they are going to spend the afternoon—possibly tonight also.

"Tomorrow afternoon McCarthy and Carr are going up to Lewisburg. They finally got Bill Rogers to let them go in to see Greenglass. . . . We have been very clubby the last few days. I have been spending practically every night in some saloon. . . ." That day for the first time, Adams remarked in passing, McCarthy had taken up Stevens's offer and had lunched at the elegant Merchants Club near the courthouse, using Stevens's membership.

All this clubbiness aside, men elsewhere in the organization were looking at some hard facts. That same day Assistant Attorney General Warren Olney phoned Adams's assistant, John Saltonstall, to report that the Internal Security Branch of the Department of Justice's Criminal Division had been following the "Monmouth matter" and had found no evidence whatsoever of any criminal violation. So fortified, the Army the next day took its stand, declaring that it had no evidence that Monmouth data had reached East German Communist hands, and reminding one and all that during World War II the allied nations had exchanged such confidential data under lend-lease. McCarthy swung back. He would, he warned, probe the Air Force's ending the FBI investigation the previous

March on the ground that the Air Force had evidence that the defecting East German scientist-informant was not to be believed.

This public exchange triggered a phone call Monday, October 19, between Stevens and J. Edgar Hoover.

"I was a little bit disturbed last Friday," Hoover complained, "when some of those generals [appeared] in regard to having that matter referred to the FBI. As I was advised by the committee before the testimony, we agreed that it would be perfectly proper for whoever testified from the Armed Services to indicate that the thing had been referred to us. . . . But the General went only half way. He said it had been referred to the FBI, period, and left out the fact that the Air Force [subsequently] asked us to discontinue it. [The Air Force] made some check, and I think . . . talked to the informant and the informant . . . admitted to them that the entire matter had been fabricated. And then they passed it on to us and asked us to discontinue the investigation. . . ."

Stevens apologized, then switched the subject: "I am going up tomorrow to Monmouth with McCarthy. Strange thing: I had planned this trip several days ago, and I found out he was planning to go; so I called him, and we are going together." And then Stevens for the first time looked wistfully toward a possible resolution of his current headache: "I think he perhaps is willing to turn this back to the Army with the information he has so that we can take the responsibility for following it from here on in."

Later that day he talked with New Jersey Republican Senator H. Alexander Smith, who was planning to meet the flight. "You have checked with Joe then," Smith asked, "and you and Joe have got [the details] worked out?"

"No," Stevens replied somewhat testily, "this is my trip. Joe is going with me. I don't see why I should check it with Joe."

"He understands that?"

"I haven't discussed it with Joe at all. I don't see what difference it makes. . . ."

In these conversations with Hoover and Smith one senses the first faint hint of resistance to the Committee's maraudings. Joe might have deserved his headlines, but the problem was getting out of control. Stevens obviously wanted to stop the publicity. And so did John Adams. At twelve thirty-five that afternoon Adams phoned Stevens to say that, in talking with Republican Committee member Senator Karl Mundt on another subject, Adams had expressed concern over continuation of the hearings and hoped it would be possible to find some way of getting McCarthy to lay off so that the Army could look into the subject itself. Mundt, Adams said, replied that he was planning to have lunch with McCarthy and would try. "If this doesn't work," Stevens rejoined, "we'll work on McCarthy tomorrow ourselves."

John Adams had been a good soldier, a good reporter, and a hard worker. He was no ball of fire. He never got far out ahead of his boss, urging him on to more and more aggressive action. But week by week one senses his doing the legwork, gathering the facts, methodically digging the trench in which the Army would ultimately take its stand. Stevens had opined to Hoover that perhaps McCarthy would play ball and go hunting elsewhere. But it was Adams who made the first overture, through Karl Mundt.

He was doing the job Bob Stevens had given him—the job not of a general but of a lead scout. And in that job he was miscast.

Stevens had ignored his organization, specifically the part of the organization responsible for interacting with the Congress—the Office of Legislative Liaison. He had chosen to take on McCarthy hand to hand, either by himself or through his alter ego Adams, with both men standing there all alone in the jungle, face to face with Joe or Roy or Frank or young Dave.

John Gibbons Adams was not of the Establishment, not a Wall Street lawyer like Foster Dulles of Sullivan and Cromwell or Herbert Brownell of Lord, Day and Lord. And few men could have contrasted more sharply with his new boss, the Secretary of the Army, formerly of the Business Advisory Council, formerly of Andover and Yale, formerly chairman of the board of an old family firm.

John Adams was born in Ashland, Kentucky; educated in the public schools of Sioux Falls, South Dakota; graduated in 1935 from the University of South Dakota Law School; and hired into the criminal branch of the office of the South Dakota Attorney General. On his father's death he took over his oil distributorship in Sioux Falls, and shortly after Pearl Harbor went on active duty with the Army, in which he served nearly four years as a staff officer. First as an infantry lieutenant and then as a major, he had fought in North Africa, Italy, and France and had received a Bronze Star.

He had made a hobby of Republican politics. Immediately after the war he came to Washington as director of Young Republican affairs for the Republican National Committee, and in 1947 he entered government: first, through South Dakota Republican Senator

Chan Gurney, as staff director of Gurney's Senate Armed Services Committee, where he once or twice met McCarthy during the tenure of the Republican-led Eightieth Congress; and then, in 1949, as an attorney-advisor in the Office of the Counsel to the Secretary of Defense, moving up by 1952 to the post of Deputy General Counsel. Through this record one sees some flashes of courage and gallantry, as well as a seam of political common sense.

In his new job he didn't drive—or ride in the rear seat of—a battleship Packard. He owned a three-year-old Ford convertible, and from his apartment he sometimes took the bus to work. He and his wife Margaret—a lovely, quiet girl from rural Virginia—got up at 4 A.M. with their infant daughter. He sold no stock, made no sacrifice, in order to take on public service. He was a career man. And in 1953 in his new job, at the age of forty-one, he made more money than ever before in his life—$13,000 a year.

Like Robert Stevens, John Adams was mild of manner. But underneath he concealed a mordant visceral emotional intensity. And ironically like Stevens, John Adams was a man nobody ever really knew.

The trip to Fort Monmouth went off as planned. The Senator and the Secretary together inspected the radar research center. Stevens that day announced that more than twelve Fort Monmouth civilians had been suspended as security risks. McCarthy praised Stevens and Commanding General Lawton for the action they had taken. Stevens praised the concept of teamwork. McCarthy, however, despite Adams's and Stevens's agreed intent, was not persuaded to stop investigating.

Now the "personal matter" mentioned repeatedly in Cohn's phone calls surfaced. All those mysterious allusions, to a subject too sensitive for the organization's monitoring, broke into the open. The induction of G. David Schine was at hand, and on the morning of October 21, the day after the Fort Monmouth visit, he phoned Stevens from New York.

"I am sorry I missed you yesterday."

"I thought you were coming down," the Secretary of the Army said to the Chief Consultant.

"I was all set to go, and the pilot told me at the last minute that the fog wouldn't permit the plane to take off."

"In New York?" Stevens asked, incredulous. "While there was a little in Monmouth, it was perfectly all right for flying. I would rather have talked with you in person than to have called you on the phone; but since I didn't get you in person, and I am about to leave on a quick trip to California, I wanted to call you and tell you I have reviewed this whole situation with Mr. Wilson [the Secretary of Defense]; and it adds up to this: Neither he nor I can see an appropriate way to avoid the basic training. We feel that is almost a must in the situation as it exists. And after going over the situation three times now insofar as you are concerned, it is my honest conviction that that is the wise thing to do, Dave; and having done that, then I think there is an excellent chance that we can pick you up and use you in a way that would be useful to the country and to yourself."

Stevens had made a commitment. Then he qualified it: "Just what that would be, I don't know. I can't define it now because I haven't gotten to that point. But it is something on my mind, and one that I would make every effort to carry out. I personally would like to arrange it . . . that you would come into [the] Army or military establishment in such a way that you would use the knowledge and ability you have in certain fields. . . . I had a good visit with Mr. Wilson. We discussed it at considerable length, and we both felt it would be a big mistake to attempt in any way to do anything unless you had taken the basic training; then we feel our hands are free to make some kind of a plan that would work out satisfactorily for you and for the Government and for everybody."

Schine did not melt in elation. He wanted to know where Stevens would be going in California.

"I will be all over the place. . . . If you would like to get a hold of me, if you will call this office, they will be able to tell you just how to do it."

So they left it this way, in Schine's words: "I hope you will have a nice trip, and we will probably have to talk this over at greater length some time." End of conversation between the Secretary of the Army and its prospective private.

On October 22, one of McCarthy's staff men, ex-FBI agent Jim Juliana, returned from Germany; there he had taken testimony from the dubious East German defector, testimony in which he asserted that Soviet officials not only had access to the Monmouth radar information, but that they had even joked about how easy a time they'd had in getting it. McCarthy gave this account to the press. He pooh-poohed the possibility that the documents could have reached the Soviet Union under wartime lend-lease. And he got his headline: "McCarthy Charges Soviet Got Secrets."

The next day he handed the reporters some more: "An ex-Marine officer," he declared, not naming Aaron Coleman, "may have been the direct link between the laboratories and the Rosenberg spy ring." On October 26 the newsmen got the word from Schine: 27 civilian employees at Monmouth had been suspended by the Army. On October 15 it had been 10, on October 20, 12. Now it was 27.

At three twenty-eight the next afternoon Cohn phoned for Stevens from New York. Stevens was talking on the White House line. Cohn asked to be transferred to Adams. They talked, and afterward Cohn talked with Stevens. The committe, Cohn said, was having a problem with General Reichelderfer, now head of the Army Security Agency at Arlington. (Reichelderfer had made the decision not to kick out Aaron Coleman in 1946 when the Army had found documents in his room.) Moreover, McCarthy, Cohn said, was going to insist on calling members of the Screening Board—in the office of the Secretary—that had reversed some suspensions. And the conversation ended on a sensitive subject: "Our young friend." Next Tuesday, November 3, was the day of his induction.

"I have got two ideas in my head." Cohn told Stevens. "The main thing I am concerned about, since nothing else can apparently be done, since we are in the middle of this thing here, we would like him around for a while." So Cohn suggested Schine might be furloughed for a couple of weeks to stay on the job with the committee.

His other idea: "I am thinking of this [possible CIA job] again. Have you given it any further thought?"

"No," Stevens replied. "It was more or less on ice until you or Dave brought it up again."

"For a while anyway," Cohn replied, "it might be a good idea because, with us going into the [Monmouth] shop over there with such intensity, it might avoid embarrassment all around. I talked to Joe, and I talked to Dave, and they would be willing. The question is, could the people over there pick him up right away?"

Stevens was not sprinting ahead: "Do you want me to talk with [CIA chief] Allen Dulles? I think I might do it."

Cohn had got what he wanted. "I would appreciate that. It would give us a start on the thing if you would talk to him informally. Tell him Joe has been talking to you informally, and we have this problem here, and how does it fit over in their place? I would appreciate this."

"All right, Roy."

At once Stevens had Jack Lucas set up the appointment. He would go see Allen Dulles the next morning at eight-fifteen.

The attempt didn't pan out. At nine forty-seven the next morning Stevens put in a call for Cohn. No luck. At ten-forty Cohn called back: The CIA can't use "Dave," Stevens told him. They have to train people, and so they want them for a long period; moreover, they have a policy of not taking men eligible for the draft.

Well, Cohn wanted to know, couldn't something be done for Schine once he'd been drafted? "I," Stevens answered, "can probably do a better job on that than [the CIA] could. Now on the furlough business it would be possible to make him available in the New York area for a couple of weeks at the beginning of his service period." But he added that this would be only temporary duty with the First Army, not an assignment that Stevens would extend. And there, for the moment, it rested.

An hour later Seaton phoned. Diplomatically he probed the backbone: "On the McCarthy thing—on his request for those loyalty records—as far as I am personally concerned, I think that now does become a matter of principle. And if I can be of any help to you in fighting that one . . ."

Seaton was looking at the Army's apparatus for making security checks on its civilian employees: the Security Screening Board, a "grand jury" which, after examining results of FBI investigations, made a recommendation to the Secretary of the Army for or against a suspected individual's clearance; the Hearing Boards, at every major command, composed of military and civilian employees of the Navy and Air Force, which conducted the actual hearings; and the seventeen-member Security Review Board, which made a concurring or dissenting recommendation to the Secretary, who himself made the final decision.

"I am just going to tell Joe no in a nice way," Stevens replied. "I am working well with McCarthy, and I will say yes to stuff that makes sense and no to what does not. I will say no on the record of the people who were on the panel. . . . Our interpretation is that under existing Executive Orders we cannot give this stuff out."

"I think you have another thing," Seaton went on. "If Joe gets into this situation, you play hell in getting anyone to serve on those boards."

"We can order them to serve."

"But then," Seaton rejoined, "you will always have inclination to settle things the way he wants them settled."

A difference had now surfaced. "I don't know," Stevens replied. "I don't know whether the President's Executive Order which was written by Truman was right or not. I am inclined to think it should be modified by President Eisenhower. He has not seen fit to do it yet. I have had this out with Joe since I started on this job. He understands I am not going to violate what I conceive to be the intent of that Executive Order." Then the conciliatory summing up: "I am confident of this, Fred; [there] is nothing to worry about in my relations with Joe and that committee. We have a good working relationship, and I have reason to believe that Joe wants to maintain it. . . . Joe does not have too many friends around the Administration; and since I have been completely honest and frank with him, and I would agree to everything that made sense and [not] to what does not, the fact that I am going to turn him down will be nothing that will upset me or the relationship."

"I want to say," Seaton replied smoothly, "I have nothing but complete admiration for the way you have handled that situation." Characteristically, he took out a little insurance: "I don't know that I am a good judge of that situation, but I nevertheless think you have done a magnificent job."

Stevens preened himself and then made an admission: "I am disappointed I haven't gotten him off our back by now, and I would if Joe was the only one we had to deal with." For the first time in the contemporaneous record he had intimated that Cohn was becoming the driving force, the nettle, the problem maker on the other side.

"If Joe is sincere," Seaton observed, "then we have nothing to fear. But if he gets to be completely a demagogue on this subject, then we will."

Stevens came to McCarthy's defense: "Joe never fails . . . to tell [reporters] how much he thinks [of] the way we have gone about this thing and the way we are trying to clear it up. He may decide he will make an issue out of this. And if he does, it will get back to where we were the very first day, where Joe indicated that if I didn't give him the loyalty files, he would take it up with the President. I said, 'Joe, that is your privilege; but . . . let's see what we can do without putting any more on the President.' I have tried and have succeeded in completely keeping this away from the White House for two months."

"I want you to know I am sympathetic," Seaton responded. "I don't want to butt into your business." Thus he paid obeisance to bureaucratic niceties. But then he returned to his initial message: "I think you have a matter of fundamental principle. . . . I don't want the public to think we don't have loyalty review unless McCarthy says we should have. That is the one thing I am leery about and why I am tickled to death you have said no, you are not going to produce [the loyalty records]. . . ."

"I am keeping my eyes wide open, and I am not going to let Joe take me for a ride."

"You are too smart to let him make a satellite out of you."

At Stevens's request, Adams next took some readings. He talked further with Hensel, Seaton, and Lee Rankin on Stevens's interpretation of the Presidential directives—the interpretation by which he would refuse to reveal the names of members of various boards; refuse to name who had sat on a particular panel for a particular individual; and refuse to let members reveal information about hearings in which they had taken part. Hensel concurred 100 percent. Seaton agreed, adding, Adams reported, "that before we take any definite steps on the matter we [should be] certain that the Department of Justice will concur in any decision we make. I think he [Seaton] is wary because he does not want us to find ourselves standing alone in the tempest." No problems: Assistant Attorney General Lee Rankin not only concurred; he "strongly urged that if we find it necessary to make a public announcement . . . that we are not going to permit the McCarthy Committee to interview our board members, we should go further than heretofore and issue a statement pointing out the reasons why such a prohibition is necessary, instead of merely using the Executive Order as a shield. Such a statement should make clear what the hazards and dangers to the loyalty program would be if names of board members were to be indiscriminately revealed and members made subject to examination and review by Congressional Committees for their actions. I am having such a statement prepared in draft form, and it will be ready for your consideration early next week."

The McCarthy Committee wanted to wave the dirty linen; Stevens wanted to wash it. That very day, October 30, Cohn was announcing to the press the subcommittee's intention to interrogate those board members.

"The massive awakened forces": McCarthy at bay taking the oath. (WIDE WORLD)

"I just hope it is all concluded very quickly. That's all." President Eisenhower faces reporters. (WIDE WORLD)

Private G. David Schine, Senator Joseph R. McCarthy, Chief Counsel Roy M. Cohn. (WIDE WORLD)

The Tennessee Bulldog: Committee Counsel Ray H. Jenkins confronts
McCarthy and Roy Cohn. (WIDE WORLD)

"Someone let Stevens walk right into a bear trap." The Army Secretary after the Fried Chicken Lunch, surrounded by (left to right) Republican Senators Everett Dirksen of Illinois, Joseph McCarthy of Wisconsin, Karl Mundt of South Dakota, and Charles Potter of Michigan. (WIDE WORLD)

"No comment." Army Secretary Robert Stevens refuses to explain to reporters why he agreed to the Memo of Understanding at the February 24 Fried Chicken Lunch. (WIDE WORLD)

"*I shall never accede to the abuse of Army personnel.*" Secretary of the Army Robert Stevens (right), in White House Press Conference, repudiates his apparent capitulation to McCarthy at Fried Chicken Lunch. White House Press Secretary Jim Hagerty (left) and Deputy Defense Secretary Roger Kyes listen. (WIDE WORLD)

"*You first*": Welch and McCarthy. (WIDE WORLD)

Carr, McCarthy, and Cohn as the Senator reveals a purported letter from FBI Director J. Edgar Hoover. (WIDE WORLD)

"Not until this moment . . ." Joseph N. Welch hears McCarthy attack the loyalty of Frederick Fisher, a member of Welch's Boston law firm. James St. Clair sits at Welch's right. (WIDE WORLD)

Weariness: McCarthy and Frank Carr. (WIDE WORLD)

Welch's "lucky case," with James St. Clair looking on. (WIDE WORLD)

*"We made those decisions":
Governor Sherman Adams,
Assistant to the President,
Eisenhower's "alter ego."*
(WIDE WORLD)

Boring in: Welch cross-examines McCarthy. James St. Clair sits at left.
(WIDE WORLD)

*"Now was the time." Two anti-McCarthy hawks—Eisenhower's Cold War Policy Assistant C. D. Jackson and speechwriter Emmet J. Hughes, both from the Time-Life organization. (*WIDE WORLD*)*

*"Always for armistice": Major General Wilton B. ("Jerry") Persons, Eisenhower's legislative liaison chief. (*WIDE WORLD*)*

"He was a smoothie." Fred A. Seaton, Assistant Secretary of Defense for Legislative and Public Affairs, warily scrutinizes reporter during questioning. Pentagon press chief Herschel Schooley looks on. (WIDE WORLD)

"Bare-faced lies." Assistant Secretary of Defense H. Struve Hensel threatens to sue McCarthy if the Senator repeats his charges against Hensel without invoking congressional immunity. (WIDE WORLD)

The "shamefully cut-down picture" of Stevens and Private Schine. (WIDE WORLD)

Army Counselor John G. Adams testifies as McCarthy and Cohn look on. (WIDE WORLD)

IV

"I WILL NOT GET IN THE GUTTER WITH THAT GUY"

At eight forty-five on the morning of Monday, November 2, General Arthur Trudeau, the new G-2, head of Army Intelligence, stopped by to tell his boss, the Secretary of the Army, he was now on the job. Like the hapless astrologer of the same name—Jonathan Swift's victim in the uproarious *Bickerstaff Papers*—General Partridge, the old G-2, had been removed to another assignment. Partridge—who didn't know a quotation from Stalin when he saw it, who foisted "Psychological and Cultural Traits of Soviet Siberia" on innocent GI's, who fecklessly tried to defend it against attack by ideological opportunists and barracudas—this poor Partridge had fallen on a corner of the field, bloodied and then abandoned, like many others, by McCarthy and Roy Cohn.

At eleven forty-six that morning Cohn phoned Stevens. All was going well. They agreed Dave Schine would be put on duty with the First Army—i.e., in the New York City area. And if anything should go wrong, Stevens told Roy, he wanted Cohn or Schine to call him; his office would know where he was. He would have all in readiness when Schine reported for induction: "I will guarantee you that." And he wanted "you boys" to have lunch with him again on Friday.

The next day, November 3, G. David Schine entered the United States Army as a private. He was put on fifteen days' temporary duty in New York City—the scene of the McCarthy Committee's closed-door hearings on Fort Monmouth—in order to finish up his subcommitte work.

No ripples. Nonetheless, on Wednesday, November 4, Stevens wrote to Attorney General Herbert Brownell for buttressing. He wanted the United States Department of Justice, in writing, behind

115

the United States Army in its push-me-pull-you scrimmaging with McCarthy. Stevens began:

> The Senate Permanent Investigations Subcommittee has on several occasions in the past, requested that the Department of the Army furnish reports and other . . . information developed by investigations conducted in connection with the Army loyalty-security program. In addition, the subcommittee has also recently requested that the Department of the Army provide to the subcommittee the names of persons who sat on particular panels of Army security screening, hearing, and appeals boards, and has further requested that the Department of the Army make available such persons and other board members whose names are already known to the subcommittee to testify. . . .

Stevens then asked four crisp questions:

1. Does [the Eisenhower] Executive Order 10450, paragraph 9C, or any other Executive Order, or any Presidential Directive, prohibit the Department of the Army from complying with the request of the subcommittee for reports and other investigative material . . . ?
2. Does the [Truman] Presidential Directive of 3 April 1952 or any other Presidential Directive or any Executive Order prohibit the Department of the Army from complying with the requests of the Subcommittee for names of security board members who sat on particular panels?
3. Does [the Eisenhower] executive Order 10450, the [Truman] Presidential Directive of 3 April 1952, or any other Executive Order or Presidential Directive prohibit members of Army security boards from giving the subcommittee reports and other . . . information as to any specific intermediate steps . . . or actions taken in processing an individual under loyalty-security programs?
4. If no Executive Orders or Presidential Directives prohibit compliance with the requests of the Subcommittee . . . , may the Secretary of the Army decline to comply with the requests of the Subcommittee . . . and may he direct that members of security boards not comply with any requests or subpoenas issued by the subcommittee seeking information of the kind described above?

Stevens closed with a reminder of urgency: "The Army is going to be required to take action on these matters in a very few days, and your advice and recommendations are needed. . . ."

The letter crossed the river to the Justice Department building on Constitution Avenue. And there it sat a while. At the moment Brownell had more urgent things on his mind. On November 5 he talked by phone with the President. He was planning to make a speech tomorrow in Chicago, he told his boss, at a distinguished luncheon club—the Executives Club. He was going to talk about internal security—about the new security regulations. And he was going to use as an example Harry Dexter White, the former Assistant Secretary of the Treasury in the administration of Harry Truman.

Herb Brownell had grown up in Nebraska. But he'd gone to Yale Law School and become a Wall Street lawyer—a prestigious partner in the hushed, deep-pile-carpeted lower Broadway offices of Lord, Day and Lord. He wore his authority and clout lightly. He had a ready and gentle smile, smoothness of motion, a slight paunch, and a quick, tough Phi Beta Kappa mind behind a façade of good-humored unflappability. He was a politician—a veteran of the toughest school of politics in the United States, New York's—and was probably the shrewdest, most skillful, and most experienced in Eisenhower's entire entourage. He had served at Tom Dewey's right hand during the New York Governor's campaigns against Franklin Roosevelt in 1944 and Harry Truman in 1948. He had served as Chairman of the Republican National Committee and faced down a withering attack from right-wing Taftites who claimed he and Dewey had taken them down the road into ignominious defeat. After that he'd wanted to hang up his political gloves for good and concentrate exclusively on his law practice. But his good friend Lucius Clay persuaded him to journey to reluctant candidate Dwight Eisenhower's SHAPE headquarters in March of 1952. Eisenhower persuaded Brownell to take on the job of lining up Eisenhower votes from the delegates to the July 1952 Republican Convention, even without promising Brownell that he would become a declared candidate. And Brownell had set to work. He, as much as any other single man, had made Dwight Eisenhower President of the United States. Brownell knew the delegates ("I had helped their wives wash dishes in their kitchens for more than twenty years"). He weaned away votes from the uncommitted and also from the massive numbers who had given their hearts to Eisenhower's powerful and distinguished opponent, Senator Robert Taft of Ohio. Brownell devised the Fair Play Amendment—the change in convention rules that prohibited contested delegates, temporarily seated by the pro-Taft National Committee—from voting one another into permanent convention seats. He had lined up delegates from three crucial favorite-son states—California, Maryland, and Minnesota—behind this amendment. He had thus demonstrated to the entire convention that

Taft lacked a clear-cut majority. And that demonstration opened the way to Eisenhower's nomination. After that, Brownell went back to Wall Street; he knew from there on out it would be downhill all the way. He had returned after Election Day to join with Lucius Clay in selecting Eisenhower's entire cabinet.

Brownell was a liberal. As the Supreme Court considered the school desegregation case—*Brown* v. *Board of Education*—in late 1953, Brownell persuaded the President, against Eisenhower's clear objections, that the Department of Justice had a responsibility to submit an *amicus curiae* opinion to the court. And Justice did: a powerful affirmation of the right of a child not to be forced to attend a segregated school, a document that ended up with extensive editing by Eisenhower himself.

Brownell was no rounder-up of subversives and near subversives and innocents alike in the name of national security. In his own words, he "hated McCarthy's guts—had no use for him whatsoever." But Brownell was not a soft-liner on security risks. He didn't believe that anyone attacked by McCarthy became *ipso facto* innocent. Brownell had devised Eisenhower's Executive Order 10450 of the previous April, tightening up the Truman system, making government employment a privilege and not a right, setting a single standard—national security—in place of the Truman tests for security and loyalty.

Like other liberals in the administration—Cabot Lodge, Jim Hagerty, and C. D. Jackson, for example—Brownell believed in cleaning up the government, in restoring the citizens' faith in the trustworthiness of its employees, and in upholding due process throughout. Without apology he would announce the number of security risks dismissed by the administration—some 1,500—since it took office.

That was the subject of his Chicago Executives Club speech. And he had found for it an appalling exhibit A.

"Harry Dexter White," he intoned in his mild nasal voice, "was a Russian spy. He smuggled secret documents to Russian agents for transmission to Moscow. Harry Dexter White was known to be a Communist spy by the very people who appointed him to the most sensitive and important position he ever held in government service. . . . I can now announce officially . . . that the records in my Department show White's spying activities . . . were reported in detail by the FBI to the White House by means of a report delivered to President Truman through his military aide [then] Brigadier General Harry H. Vaughan."

White had joined the Department of the Treasury in 1934. In 1940 he had become Director of Monetary Research and in 1945 an Assistant Secretary of the Treasury. In December of 1945 the FBI had delivered its first report on White to Truman. Early in 1946, Truman had nominated White to become Executive Director of the United States Mission to the International Monetary Fund. On February 6, 1946, the Senate unanimously approved the nomination. The FBI sent Truman a second report. The White House again did nothing. In April of 1947, White resigned from government service. Accused in 1948 by Elizabeth Bentley, on August 13 of that year he had denied any connection with a Communist spy ring, as she had charged, or with the Communist party. Three days later he had died of a heart attack.

Out in Independence, Missouri, Harry Truman rode roughshod over this history and Brownell's charges. He knew nothing about any FBI report, he told reporters. Neither did Harry Vaughan, he said. And he added that when he found out White was disloyal, "we fired him."

Suddenly the spotlight of anti-Communist attention had swiveled away from McCarthy and onto Brownell.

While the Attorney General was lunching with the Executives in Chicago, McCarthy and the "boys" had been lunching with Stevens and Adams at the Pentagon. They doubtless spoke of Monmouth and of Schine. But not one scrap of contemporaneous evidence exists to reveal what exactly they said about these subjects—or anything else. The course and content of their conversation would become the subject of bitter contention—and conflicting recollections—in the months ahead. But on the evidence written at the time, only one fact is irrefutable: that the next day, Saturday, November 7, shortly after noon, McCarthy phoned Stevens.

"Bob," the Senator began, "did that work out all right to your satisfaction yesterday?"

"Yes, it did, Joe. And I appreciate your taking a very broad view of the thing."

"We both have the same interest, and we both are working at the same job."

"I was worried at first," Stevens admitted, "but the way it wound up I was satisfied with it, and I want to thank you."

McCarthy switched the subject: "I would like to ask you one personal favor. For God's sake don't put Dave in Service and assign him back to my committee. . . . One, I couldn't get away with [it] any more than a week. The newspapers would be back on us, and you would have to send him back into uniform anyway. Two, this thing has been running along so cleanly so far they have not been able to beat your brains out. There is nothing the left-wingers would like better. They don't like this cooperation between the committee and the Army. And the third thing, they would say I asked for him.

"He is a good boy, but there is nothing indispensable about him. From my desk today I can pick up letters from perhaps a half dozen . . . mothers whose boys are in worse shape than Dave; and it would be embarrassing. . . .

"If he could get off weekends . . . It is one of the few things I have seen [Roy] completely unreasonable about. He thinks Dave should be a general and work from the penthouse of the Waldorf. . . ."

Stevens hastened to differentiate between the Senator and his aide. "That is where my problem has come from, right from the start. You never have done or said anything that spurred me on this situation at all, other than to take a friendly interest."

McCarthy confirmed the difference: "Roy was next to quitting the committee. . . . And for God's sake don't tell . . . anything about this, because he would go right back and tell Roy."

"I would rather not tell anybody anything," Stevens replied. "I am not going to do anything except to have him go through the regular thing—maybe a weekend here or there, or something of that kind. . . ."

McCarthy agreed: "If you put him into service to work with the committee, all [hell] would break loose, and the President would be calling you not to play favorites. . . ." But then he bent a bit: "I think, for Roy's sake, if you can let him come back for weekends or something so his girls won't get too lonesome—maybe if they shave his hair off, he won't want to come back. . . ."

For the first time in the contemporaneous documents, in the records set down at the time of the event, a tiny crack had opened in the monolith, a brief glimpse of daylight between McCarthy and Roy Cohn. But McCarthy and Stevens, still friendly, still saw eye to eye.

Within three days, on Tuesday, November 10, Schine reported to Fort Dix, New Jersey, to start basic training. And Cohn lost no time in requesting from the Fort's Commanding General the first in a high pile of weekend—and weeknight—passes for the private, their purported purpose, committee business.

Meanwhile, back in Washington, bouncy, conservative Congressman Harold Velde, Republican of Illinois, perceiving a ball loose on the field, scooped it up, leaving McCarthy, for the second time in a week, a mere spectator. Velde's House Un-American Activities Committee, asserting its jurisdiction, issued three subpoenas: one for Supreme Court Associate Justice Tom Clark, Attorney General in 1946, whom Brownell had charged with knowledge of the FBI report on White's treason; one for former Secretary of State James Byrnes, who also, Brownell said, knew; and one for Harry Truman himself.

Suddenly, Eisenhower was not only uneasy; he was vulnerable. His Attorney General had propelled him into the midst of a constitutional crisis—into a quarrel between the rights of the Congress, embodied in Republican Velde and his committee, and the rights of the executive, embodied in Eisenhower's Democratic predecessor, Harry Truman. Here was a clear confrontation of executive and legislative power. A presidential news conference was coming up, and Eisenhower couldn't dodge.

With the reporters waiting to pounce, at nine-fifteen on the morning of November 11 the President phoned his Attorney General. In his news conference, the President said, he would tell the reporters that Brownell had serious evidence of a high-up Truman official with Communist leaning, and the President felt Brownell would violate his duty if he did not reveal the fact. We know, he said, that the report on White came to the White House. (Evidence now in Brownell's hands, Eisenhower's phone monitor—Ann Whitman—wrote parenthetically into the record, shows that the report went to Truman himself; Foster Dulles has a memorandum which indicates as much.) Both Eisenhower and Brownell agreed the subpoena to Truman was a mistake. In Ike's view, the country should accept Truman's word on his recollection.

At 11 A.M. the reporters assembled in the Indian Treaty Room on the third floor of the Executive Office Building across the street from the West Wing of the White House. The thrust of the first question went right to the mark: Would you have subpoenaed Truman? Eisenhower sidestepped deferentially:

"Once before, before this group I tried to make it quite clear that I am not going to be in the position of criticizing the Congress of the United States for carrying out what it conceives to be its duty.

"It has the right of course to conduct such investigations as it finds necessary, but if [I am asked] my personal reaction, I would not issue such a subpoena."

Edward Milne of the *Providence Journal-Bulletin* followed up:

"Mr. President, do you yourself feel that former President Truman knowingly appointed a Communist spy to high office?"

"You are asking me for opinions, of course, based on nothing else except what I have told you and what I have read in the papers. No, it is inconceivable; I don't believe that—put it in this way—a man in that position knowingly damaged the United States. I think it would be inconceivable."

Possibly nettled by press marginalia that divined a rift between him and Brownell—Eisenhower had affirmed Truman's integrity; Brownell had impugned it—the President at his Cabinet meeting the next day laid any such rift to rest. He had, he told the others around the table, consulted the Attorney General before his press conference. He would back his Cabinet members to the hilt. The real question, he went on, was whether White was the kind of man who should have been appointed to a high position in the first place. Elsewhere in the meeting, Eisenhower took another swipe at Truman: the best politics at home, he iterated, is to do "the right thing" overseas, even though it might temporarily alienate extremists. In the past administration, he instanced, officials frankly admitted playing politics against their wiser judgment on at least one major issue.

But above all in that Cabinet meeting Ike tried, as always, to move to higher ground. It was now State of the Union season— those grueling weeks when the executive branch hammers out its legislative requests for the coming year, to be announced in the President's kickoff address to a joint session of the Congress early in January; it was the Eisenhower administration's first and biggest chance to get new laws on the books, to shake itself free of the past, to chart a new course for the country on everything from taxes to dams to health insurance to housing to agriculture. The State of the Union message, Eisenhower told his colleagues that day, should "emphasize the Administration's determination to provide for the needs of all Americans, particularly the 'little fellow' and those in need. The Budget Message should contain specific provisions for such measures as small business loans and slum clearance: good intentions must not remain mere words."

Not everyone at that moment could feel so upbeat as the President. Learning that the old liberal warrior Elmer Davis had stopped broadcasting for no immediately obvious reason, Dean Acheson, now handsomely ensconced in the private practice of law at Covington and Burling, wrote Davis a gloomy note: "I do not know whether my depression is lessened or deepened by your message that it is blood, rather than economic or political, pressure that takes you out of the play just when only you can do justice to the mean stupidity which now seems to govern our affairs."

At three-ten that November 12 afternoon Fred Seaton phoned Stevens. The Secretary of the Army was holding a press conference the next day. The two men went over possible questions. Fort Monmouth headed the list, and sure enough produced headlines: the Army's investigation of the Monmouth laboratories, Stevens said, showed no evidence whatsoever of "current" espionage; thirty-three employees had been suspended; of these several had already been reinstated; the rest would have a fair hearing; and there were no missing Signal Corps documents that had not already been found.

Surveying the front pages and reading McCarthy's mild comment ("I'll let the hearings speak for themselves. So far I haven't tried to evaluate the testimony"), Seaton the next morning, Saturday, told Stevens he thought the press conference "went off all right." He spoke too soon. Later that same day McCarthy, in Portland, Maine, for a speech, declared that the existence of two separate investigations—his and Stevens's—was creating confusion in the public mind. The failure of Stevens's investigation to find evidence of espionage, he went on, "makes it necessary to open public hearings almost immediately." Forecasting that those hearings might be televised, he added, "I suggest you watch the motley crew that will parade across the witness stand."

Harry Truman—accompanied by Byrnes and Clark—had rejected the Velde subpoenas, on the ground of separation of powers. On nationwide TV and radio on the evening of Monday, November 16, the former President of the United States had his say. To this moment, the men at the top of the Democratic party had reined in their attacks on the Republicans, giving the new administration the traditional courtesy of several months to get its act together. Adlai Stevenson, the 1952 Democratic presidential candidate, had spoken with characteristic gentlemanliness. U.S. prestige, he had declared on August 20, had suffered as a result of McCarthyism. And on September 15 he had expressed his "anxiety lest the shaping of our policy may be slipping from the respected hands of President Eisenhower into the hands of men less concerned with strengthening our alliances abroad than with appeasing our isolationists at home."

Even Truman had—somewhat—held himself back. "We gave them their chance, and they threw it out the window," he told a cheering

Labor Day crowd in Detroit. "Now let's go after them and get this thing corrected." But now in his broadcast on November 16 he was slashing away, giving them hell as he had in the 1948 campaign.

With heavy sarcasm, underscoring with contempt the name Mr. Herbert Brownell, *Jr.*, whom he denounced for "cheap political trickery," Truman declared that he had first learned of the accusations against White in early February of 1946, when Harry Vaughan and Jimmy Byrnes brought him White's FBI file. He had, he said, discussed this with Treasury Secretary Fred Vinson, who discussed it with Tom Clark, the Attorney General, and they'd come to a decision: let White's appointment to the International Monetary Fund take its course; a change, they believed, would have alerted others under FBI investigation. They decided further to limit White to membership on the IMF Board of Executive Directors and not to support his election to the organization's top managerial post. Brownell lied, Truman charged, when he said Truman knew White was a spy when he appointed him to the IMF job. Brownell lied, Truman said, when he denied his attempt to impugn Truman's loyalty. And Brownell, Truman said, had consciously deceived Eisenhower about the purpose of his speech. The Eisenhower administration, Truman charged, had "embraced . . . McCarthyism."

The next day J. Edgar Hoover testified before the Senate Internal Security Subcommittee. On February 21, 1946, Hoover declared—in flat contradiction of Truman—that Vinson, Clark, and Hoover had discussed three alternatives, given the imminence of White's accession to the IMF job; fire him; let Truman tell him he didn't want him to serve; let White go into the IMF job under FBI surveillance. Clark and Vinson agreed only to give Truman these three alternatives. Hoover testified he had told Clark it would be "unwise" to let White remain in government; he never agreed to White's transfer to the IMF; in fact, he said, the transfer "hampered" the FBI's surveillance of White.

"At no time," Hoover asserted, "was the FBI a party to an agreement to promote Harry Dexter White and at no time did the FBI give its approval to such an agreement."

White was dead. The conflagration over him would soon die. A few days later Eisenhower put his own capstone on the episode in a letter to one of his closest confidants, General Alfred M. Gruenther, now head of the NATO forces in Europe: "I can see no flow in the entire line of argument and exposition that was presented publicly by Attorney General Brownell and J. Edgar Hoover."

• •

One spark, however, from Truman's November 16 broadcast flew off and burned McCarthy. As always, McCarthy would strike back. But first he had to get Bob Stevens for his denial of current Monmouth espionage.

From Roy Cohn, Stevens had learned of McCarthy's wrath. He saw the onrush of retribution—open hearings. He knew he had to move. He suggested, as usual, lunch, this time—because McCarthy was in New York—at the Merchants Club. The Secretary made the trip. At noon on November 17 the Secretary and Senator dined. Cohn, Carr, Adams joined them. And so did a surprise McCarthy ringer—conservative columnist and Roosevelt-hater George Sokolsky, who in 1917, in his midtwenties, had gone to Russia to report on the revolution firsthand and had in the decades since become the "high priest of anti-Communism." In an adjoining room a TV set was tuned into Herbert Brownell's testimony on Harry Dexter White before the Senate Internal Security Subcommittee. And with this in the background the group got down to business: hammering out a press release, through draft after hand-scrawled draft, that papered over their disagreement.

At last they succeeded. A crowd of reporters swarmed into the stately club, laying TV cable and grinding dirt into the carpeting. Stevens faced them. When he'd said he had no proof of current espionage at Monmouth, he explained, he had meant only that the Army probe had found no such proof; he was not reflecting on what McCarthy's investigation might have turned up. He agreed that spying at Fort Monmouth might well have continued after the war as late as 1951. And he charged the newspapers with having misquoted him.

The luncheon now over, McCarthy and Roy Cohn and Stevens hopped aboard the Secretary's private plane for a short flight to McGuire Air Force Base, right next to Fort Dix, the site of basic training for former Chief Consultant Schine. All would stand by smilingly while the Army's present private had his picture taken with the Army's Secretary. Such is the power of the investigative arm of the legislature.

Perhaps, as Stevens had said, the reporters had misquoted him. But he was making a no-win charge, as Fred Seaton shrewdly—and diplomatically—told him the day after the press reports appeared.

"The fellow that did the most misquoting," Seaton said, "was Homer Bigart of the New York *Herald Tribune*. . . . Hersch

Schooley [the Defense Department's able and respected chief public information officer] spotted that at your press conference and said [Bigart] didn't take any notes." But then as a good newspaperman Seaton added an admonition: "The only unfortunate part is that some of the other press members are a little heated up because they think your statement indicted them a little unjustly."

Stevens bridled: "I again was misquoted. I never used that [word "misquoted"] because I think it is a bad one. . . . I don't think it is a good idea to go out and say you [have] been misquoted."

"The Washington *Post* had it as a misquotation charge."

"Is that in the paper this morning?" Stevens asked.

"Yes sir," Seaton replied. "They have done document reporting on this, taken from the transcript. . . . The *Post* went to a column and half . . . to justify its reporting. . . . These boys in the main are friendly to you, and that helps you, but they are awfully touchy. . . ." As a Cabinet officer, Stevens had three clear tasks—to run his department, to get along with the legislative branch, and to control his public relations through the news media. Mistakes in any of the three areas could topple him from his position.

As Stevens and Seaton talked over Stevens's attempt to placate McCarthy, John Adams continued working to widen and deepen the Army's defenses. He was not only trying to get Justice Department backing. That day, November 19, he wrote for help to Struve Hensel in the Department of Defense. If members of hearing boards out in the field are not to reveal information, Adams said, that order should come from the Secretary of Defense himself. Any panel hearing charges against an Army employee is made up of military and civilian people not from the Army itself but—under Eisenhower's Executive Order—from the Navy and Air Force. Only instructions from the Secretary of Defense—not from the Secretary of the Army—could bind all three services.

That morning, November 19, as McCarthy readied his response to the Truman attack, the papers were headlining a second presidential attack, this time from the incumbent. At the usual Wednesday White House press conference, when Alan Emory of the *Watertown Daily Times* asked how significant the President thought the exposure of Communist infiltration in the government under previous administrations would turn out to be in next year's congressional campaign, Eisenhower answered: "I am proceeding with my associates as strongly and as earnestly and as thoroughly as I can in that direction, and I am certainly earnestly trying to do it without doing injustice to any individual, because I don't believe that we can afford to destroy inside what we think we are protecting from the outside.

"Now, I hope this whole thing will be a matter of history and of memory by the time the next election comes around. I don't believe we can live in fear of each other forever, and I really hope and believe that this administration is proceeding decently and justly to get this thing straightened out."

Stevens and Adams obviously would have concurred. They believed in fair play.

On November 16, Monmouth employee Carl Greenblum had identified himself as the "mystery" witness who had broken down in tears under McCarthy's questioning a month earlier. He had gone public, and some truculent cracks he made inevitably came up in the discussion at the Merchants Club luncheon the next day.

"At the luncheon," Adams reminded Stevens at eleven thirty-eight on November 19, "there was the remark made about Greenblum, who made some nasty remarks to the newspaper. You said, 'Aren't we suspending that fellow?' I came away with the impression that we were going to suspend him."

"I didn't intend to convey that impression," Stevens replied, "because I don't want to do anything except what the facts justify. With that martini in one hand and concentrating on Joe with the other hand, I probably didn't give it much thought."

"We have got nothing on the guy at all," Adams reminded the Secretary.

"We can't stop people from talking. After all, this is a country of free speech. If Mr. Greenblum or somebody else wants to blow his lid, if we took an action based on that statement, we would be in trouble, wouldn't we?"

Replying that same day to Senator Herbert H. Lehman of New York, who had inquired about one suspended Monmouth employee named Lawrence Suchow, Adams wrote: "Under existing Presidential directives and Executive Order 10450, the Army is precluded from commenting one way or the other concerning the security situation of a particular employee. These prohibitions are designed, among other reasons, for the protection of the individual employee. Under these restrictions it would be improper to reveal reasons for the transfer of Mr. Suchow or to indicate one way or another whether security is involved.

". . . Many intermediate steps short of actual suspension are taken during the course of processing individuals under the security program. All employees who are suspended for security reasons are given a full opportunity for a hearing before an impartial Security Hearing Board composed of civilian employees and officers. The recommendations of the Hearing Board are then reviewed by an Army Security Review Board, and the ultimate decision is made as to whether the individual should be retained in employment. . . ."

Even though Stevens and Adams were committed to fairness, the outlook for probity and balance wasn't encouraging.

Roy Cohn was planning a slam bang parade of the "motley crew" in long procession, single file. "By telephone Friday," John Adams wrote Stevens on Saturday, November 21, "I developed from Roy Cohn that the hearings in New York on Tuesday and Wednesday . . . will follow a pattern somewhat as follows:

"First, there will be read into the record a transcript of the interrogation of David Greenglass taken at the Lewisburg Penitentiary. As you know, Greenglass never worked at Monmouth, but was on duty as an enlisted man at Los Alamos. However, he knew of the Rosenberg espionage in the New York area. We have never seen the Greenglass interrogation.

"Following the Greenglass testimony, Colonel Lotz, a Signal Corps officer who has been working with the Committee at their request . . . will be put on the stand . . . to identify from the Rosenberg 201 file the types of equipment with which Rosenberg worked during his employment. I presume from this they will attempt to tie in the fact that Rosenberg got certain of this classified equipment out of the custody of the Army and into espionage channels.

"Cohn has stated that Lotz will be asked to describe generally what the Signal Corps responsibility in the development of radar is [and] . . . to describe a proximity fuse (Greenglass testified that Rosenberg once boasted of stealing one from an Army contractor while inspecting his plant). . . .

"Following Colonel Lotz, Joseph Levitsky will be put on the stand. He is a 1951 Monmouth employee who now claims the Fifth Amendment, and was identified as being very close to Rosenberg. He will be followed by Vivian Glassman, often called a Rosenberg courier. . . . Following Levitsky and Glassman, Max Elicher will be put on the stand. He is a former Communist, and a cooperative witness. He will identify all of the Communists he used to know, and will make a very good impression.

"Following Elicher, it is now planned to put Mrs. [Louise] Sarant on the stand. Her husband was a reported Rosenberg courier, and escaped from the United States just before capture and is presumably now in the Soviet Union. Mrs. Sarant . . . claims the Fifth Amendment.

"Following Mrs. Sarant, Harry Hyman will be put on the stand. . . . He is not a Monmouth employee, but reportedly has been making 10 to 15 telephone calls a day to various people at Fort Monmouth for many weeks past. Hyman repeatedly claims the Fifth Amendment, and Cohn contends that he is their solid proof of espionage. As to getting Hyman's testimony, McCarthy has not so far relented as to let us have these later transcripts, although there is still a possibility that he may ultimately do so (not before next Tuesday, however).

"Following the foregoing presentation, all of which will be . . . designed to prove that there have been many Communists and spies and people who claim the Fifth Amendment in and around the Monmouth area for many years past, the case of Aaron Coleman will be developed. They will undoubtedly make much of the documents which were taken out of the post by Fred Kitty and turned over to Jack Okun and by him mailed to Coleman while Coleman was on active duty with the Marines in Florida, where he (Coleman) contends he used them to further train himself as a radar officer. This is the situation on which the Department of Justice was interrogated as to the possibility of an espionage case being developed, and replied that the Statute of Limitations (three years) had already run. The taking and mailing to Coleman took place during . . . wartime, and the inquiry was not placed with the Justice Department as to the possibility of an espionage case being developed until 1951.

"Cohn thinks that the foregoing matters will take the better part of two days, and that after Thanksgiving intervenes, there will be a diversion of Committee interest to the existence of red cells in various industrial plants. . . . All of the Monmouth hearings are now scheduled to be televised and undoubtedly will get wide coverage. One of our greatest problems will be . . . to get Army people to make no comment whatsoever and to state only that the Army stands on the statement that the Secretary made following the conference with Senator McCarthy last Tuesday. I intend to attend both days of the New York hearings. . . ."

Compounding all the other headaches at Monmouth was the Commanding General himself, Kirke Lawton. He had started out as a roadblock in the way of Cohn and Carr. Now he had flipped 180 degrees. By October 14, in his closed-door testimony, he was implicitly praising the McCarthy committee's energy and derogating Stevens's lassitude in the rooting out of Monmouth's subversives. By October 31 his zeal was beginning to appear ridiculous.

Stevens phoned Lawton's boss, the Chief Signal Officer, Major General Back: "I am a little concerned over General Lawton's continuing to suspend people at Monmouth," Stevens told him. "While all the commanders in the field are told that I want them to use their discretion, I feel he is going too far over the other way and . . . is suspending people we haven't got anything on and we will have to take back."

Back got the message: "Yes sir, I understand. . . . I will communicate with him right away, Mr. Secretary."

Stevens hadn't finished: "When he suspends a fellow because he lives next door to a person who he thought was a Communist, that just isn't going to do us any good. It is going to make us look foolish. . . ."

Now, three weeks later, Stevens was getting even more disturbing under-the-table reports. At 11 A.M. on November 24 he talked with a fellow New Jerseyan, Republican Congressman Jim Auchincloss, calling from the Hill.

"I have got a confidential report I have just received from my district about the Commanding Officer at Monmouth," Auchincloss confided, "and I would prefer not to give it over the telephone to you. . . ."

"I will come over, . . . Jim."

At five-seven that same afternoon John Adams reported from New York. After six weeks of behind-doors sessions, the public hearings had started, in Room 110 of the Foley Square Courthouse, the scene of the trial of Julius and Ethel Rosenberg. In the hot glare of camera floodlights, Roy Cohn had introduced into the record the affidavit of imprisoned David Greenglass with its ominous open-ended "as far as I know [these espionage] operations never stopped and could very possibly be continuing to this very day." Lotz had given his factual rundown. Levitsky had taken the Fifth. But Adams and Stephens saw no reason to worry.

"We got along all right," Adams told his boss. "[Joe] is going to Wisconsin tomorrow. . . . And he is talking about long hearings . . . going to continue after we get back from Thanksgiving, but I am hopeful that there are no such things. . . . Cohn says there won't be."

"How is Roy?"

"He is pretty good. I don't anticipate any difficulty."

"[Columnist George] Sokolsky was just in here for about an hour," Stevens said. "I had a good visit with him . . . although I am not exactly clear why he came in. I sort of felt he was on a mission. . . . He talked about Dave [Schine] quite a bit, and maybe his idea was to find out whether anything could be done for Dave. . . . He said he knew Joe very well, and I made note of his phone number. . . ."

"We might," Adams mused, "get Sokolsky to see if we can get him to back off."

Suddenly Stevens changed the subject: "John, one thing that is growing in my mind is that I think I want to make a change in Lawton at Monmouth. . . . I had Back in this afternoon and told him some of my misgivings, and he is going to have Lawton down, probably this evening. . . . I am not going to take any precipitate action. But I have heard some rumors about what he has said around Monmouth, and I just wanted to alert you. . . . Lawton is apparently so much in the good graces of Joe that if we should remove him, Joe wouldn't like that. On the other hand, if Joe could get a change made, that is a feather in his cap. I thought I would let you know that I am moving . . . in the direction of a change . . . , to put somebody in there that is new on it, and can approach it soundly and objectively and with stability. . . ."

Adams cautiously questioned his boss: "You run into the situation that if this goes on, where are we going to put all these generals?"

"What do you mean?"

"We take Lawton, and we take Partridge."

"Let me tell you," Stevens replied, with the kind of testiness he showed from time to time toward Adams. "Anybody who is incompetent is going to be replaced, and I don't give a damn whether we have a place for him or not. If a person is incompetent—and I am beginning to think [Lawton] is—and he has already had a reprimand . . . if what I have heard today, or any portion of it, turns out to be true, I am going to relieve him immediately."

"I know," Adams answered, "he has made some statements that are pro McCarthy. . . ."

On the evidence of the phone transcript, neither man had any inkling of what would happen in the next four hours.

The night before, President Eisenhower had received the America's Democratic Legacy Award at a B'nai B'rith dinner honoring the fortieth anniversary of the organization's Anti-Defamation League.

The Dwight Eisenhower who had accepted this invitation was the Dwight Eisenhower who short weeks before, he wrote in his diary, had received in the Oval Office Norman Thomas, the perennial presidential candidate of the United States Socialist party, and had listened with patience and understanding to Thomas's bitter complaints about State Department security chief Scott McLeod's blurring the distinction between a Socialist and a Communist; about the abysmal morale in the Foreign Service; and about the fact that "we have been making a ridiculous show of ourselves" overseas "in giving a splendid example of both futility and stupidity. . . ."

To a nationwide television and radio audience, Eisenhower spoke off the cuff as he had at Dartmouth. And as at Dartmouth, he let his antagonism to an unnamed McCarthy glare through the surface of his remarks. By an able staff, he started out, "I have been briefed and briefed and briefed. I have heard more lectures on civil liberties, the people who have stood for them, the dangers to them, and what I should say, then you can imagine." But he was rejecting all this advice in order to reiterate just one thing: We are proud to be Americans "because from the beginning of this nation, a man can walk upright, no matter who he is, or who she is. . . . I was raised in a little town of which most of you have never heard. . . . It is called Abilene, Kansas. . . . Now that town had a code, and I was raised as a boy to prize that code. It was: Meet anyone face to face with whom you disagree. You could not sneak up on him from behind, or do any damage to him, without suffering the penalty of an outraged citizenry. . . . And today . . . you live after all by that same code in your ideals. . . . In this country, if someone dislikes you, or accuses you, he must come up in front. He cannot hide behind the shadow. He cannot assassinate . . . your character from behind, without suffering the penalties an outraged citizenry will impose. . . . If we are going to continue to be proud that we are Americans, there must be no weakening of the code by which we have lived; by the right to meet your accuser face to face . . . ; by your right to go to the church or synagogue or even the mosque of your own choosing; by your right to speak your mind and be protected in it. . . ."

Don't join the book burners, don't castigate the whole category of churchmen as traitors, don't assassinate a man's character without giving him the right to due process: no one who could read or hear or watch a television screen could mistake the connection between the general theme and the specific villain.

The day after Ike spoke, McCarthy was getting ready to answer Harry Truman on nationwide TV and radio. As the hour of McCarthy's evening broadcast approached, Seaton talked with Stevens about a possible McCarthy target of opportunity. A McCarthy staff member, Seaton said, wanted to know whether a man named Lloyd Lehrbas was employed by the Army. "We got this friendly tip . . . that they were trying to make an issue of Lehrbas because they said he was once associated with Dean Acheson."

"I know plenty about it," Stevens responded. "I know he was on MacArthur's staff for about four years. . . . I have looked into him carefully, and in my opinion he is okay. . . . I had been forewarned that [McCarthy] might mention this in his speech tonight. . . ."

McCarthy didn't. In vintage style, he went after Truman: Truman who had given a definition of McCarthyism "identical, word for word, comma for comma, with the definition adopted by the Communist *Daily Worker*, which originated the term McCarthyism"; Truman whose administration had been "crawling with Communists," who had kept them "in high positions of power with access to vital secrets"; Truman who was responsible for "the trickeries, the betrayals of an administration whose foreign policy was so carefully shaped by the Alger Hisses, the Harry Dexter Whites, the Owen Lattimores, the Dean Achesons, the John Carter Vincents"; Truman under whose presidency "the number of people under Communist domination" increased from 180 million to 800 million.

Then McCarthy turned a new corner. He went after Eisenhower. "A few days ago, I read that President Eisenhower expressed the hope that by election time in 1954 the subject of Communism would be a dead and forgotten issue. The raw, harsh, unpleasant fact is that Communism is an issue and will be an issue in 1954. . . . I would . . . like to remind those very well-meaning people who speak about Communism not being an issue that Communism is not isolated from other great evils which beset us today."

He paused for a little sop to the Republican record: ". . . so infinitely better than [that of] the Truman-Acheson regime that there is absolutely no comparison." Then he took off the gloves: "We still have John Paton Davies on the payroll after eleven months of the

Eisenhower Administration. . . . John Paton Davies, . . . part and parcel of the old Acheson-Lattimore-Vincent-White-Hiss group which did so much toward delivering our Chinese friends into Communist hands"; a man who "was unanimously referred by the McCarran Committee to the Justice Department in connection with a proposed indictment because he lied under oath about his activities in trying to put—listen to this—in trying to put Communists and espionage agents in key spots in the Central Intelligence Agency."

Then to McCarthy's biggest charge of all: ". . . the failure of my party . . . to liquidate the foulest bankruptcy of the Democrat Administration—" the continuation of U.S. foreign aid to countries that trade with Red China, a country that still holds prisoner Americans captured in the Korean War.

"How does that affect you? As of today, some money was taken out of your paycheck and sent to Britain. As of today, Britain used that money from your paycheck to pay for the shipment of the sinews of war to Red China. . . . It is time that we, the Republican Party, liquidate this bloodstained blunder of the Acheson-Truman regime. . . . What can we do about it? We can handle this by saying this to our Allies: if you continue to ship to Red China while they are imprisoning and torturing American men, you will get not one cent of American money.

"If we do that, my good friends, this trading in blood-money will cease. . . ."

It was *echt* McCarthy. The brawler had come out flailing. Nettled by Truman, goaded by Eisenhower, he had thrown haymakers—thrown them at random, abandoning himself to the unpredictable. To Eisenhower's press secretary Jim Hagerty, McCarthy's performance that night was "sheer fascism."

Sheer fascism or not, McCarthy this time had hit the State Department and the White House, not the Pentagon. After the broadcast, which originated in a New York studio, John Adams accompanied McCarthy and Cohn to the Stork Club. And the next day in the Department of the Army business went on as always. At ten-fifteen in the morning Stevens was returning a call from Jim Auchincloss: more intelligence from New Jersey on Lawton. "They have a story coming out today," Auchincloss warned. "I thought you ought to know it."

"I have the gentleman in question here in the building," Stevens replied. "I am going to talk with him in a few minutes."

The evidence against Lawton was becoming clearer. In four

tightly closed lectures in November for selected military and civilian people at Monmouth, General Lawton, Stevens's informants alleged, had, among other things, praised McCarthy for forcing Stevens to tighten the rules governing the suspension of suspected subversives; declared that anyone taking the Fifth was a Communist; and implied that particular universities tended to indoctrinate students with leftist ideas—for example, City College of New York, Columbia, MIT, Harvard, Wisconsin, and Minnesota.

Lawton denied the first two charges. But his personal observations on the thinking of graduates of those specific colleges—how their thinking conflicted with military tradition—led some of his hearers to conclude, doubtless without his so intending, that he was condemning these schools as fountainheads of communism.

To Stevens, firing was indicated. At twelve thirty-nine he phoned Adams, who was waiting at a pay phone in a restaurant near the Foley Square Courthouse. They talked about Lawton. At two-five they spoke again.

"I talked to Joe about that matter," Adams reported, "and the reaction is not too encouraging. He has the attitude that he himself would try very hard not to say anything about it, [but] that he would be pressed into a position where he might have to comment, and he feels that the comment would be adverse and would put us right into the situation we were [in] after that press conference of last Friday, and it would be much wiser to wait for a couple of weeks. . . . They think that it would be interpreted . . . as a direct slap. . . . Joe says he is not, of course, attempting to administer (Cohn says, 'The hell he isn't'). . . . He recognizes your right to do that, but he feels at this time and the present atmosphere of these hearings, that the interpretation made by the press would be adverse. . . . He is going to Wisconsin and . . . will be back in Washington in a week or ten days. . . . Roy says he thinks he can do a lot of talking and get the thing straightened out if we don't do it right now."

Stevens acquiesced: "I will try to hold off. I can't commit myself because there might be some developments down there that would make it mandatory to take prompt action, but if you are talking to him again, you can tell him I will hold off until we have a chance to discuss it further. . . . I definitely would not want to do it in the light of this conversation. . . ." McCarthy's savage shot over nationwide TV hadn't shocked the Secretary of the Army: it hadn't even shortened his forbearance.

•   •

But in the Executive Office Building next to the White House, McCarthy's diatribe at last drew a ferocious response. After all the weeks and months of gray prose, of hushed maneuvering, one finally sees a document scarlet with outrage, mordant with moral indignation.

"Listening to Senator McCarthy last night," Presidential Assistant C. D. Jackson wrote Chief of Staff Sherman Adams, "was an exceptionally horrible experience, because it was an open declaration of war on the Republican Party of the United States by a Republican Senator." At last, Jackson fervently hoped, McCarthy's "flagrant performance" would open the eyes of some of the President's advisors who seemed to think McCarthy was a good fellow at heart—like Mao, just an agrarian reformer. "Every egghead in the United States," Jackson thundered, can "rise to a fever pitch when Brownell talks about Truman. . . . Can't a single Republican Senator work up some temperature when McCarthy refers to Eisenhower as he did?"

Five months earlier Jackson had had a long talk with Governor Adams about his concern over presidential leadership and the merits of no longer being mealy-mouthed about McCarthy: "Not suggesting pitched battle or gutter brawl," Jackson wrote in his secret diary, "but when Joe off base such as ship deal, or when President makes book burning statement, the next act should not be hastily to take it all back. . . ." Now Jackson became a raging bull in the hushed West Wing china shop.

Above all members of the White House Staff, C. D. Jackson was a man of rhythm and vibration. Tall and balding, now fifty-one, he had been educated in Switzerland and at Princeton. In 1931 he joined the empire of Henry Luce, rising to become successively the first general manager of the new *Life* magazine, then vice president of the parent Time, Inc., organization, and publisher of *Fortune*. He and equally towering fellow executive Andrew Heiskell enjoyed striding long-legged down Fifth Avenue shooting rapid-fire witty French conversation over the head of little Roy Larsen, their Harvard-educated colleague, struggling to keep up with their words and their pace.

Jackson liked people. He treated everybody alike, from the board chairman to the janitor. He could talk about anything—politics, international relations, the theater, Vespas. With a kindly gruffness, he would disarm a young man entering his office seeking help: "How good a writer are you really? What do you really want to do, apart from playing a concert at Carnegie Hall?" Wherever he went, with his enthusiasm, his booming laugh, his ebullience, he would light up the room. And he would invariably end his letters—a pleasure to read for their spontaneity, articulateness, and abandon—with a swinging close: "All the best, C. D."

He loved music—loved it with a passion—and musicians. He served devotedly as a member of the boards of the Boston Symphony and the Metropolitan Opera. And he and his wife, Gracie, had a country place near Tanglewood; a beloved haunt with two massive Steinways side by side, where they would invite friends, put a drink in their hands, seat them in elegant comfort with a sweeping view of the Berkshires out the picture window, and let them luxuriate in the duo piano performances of the Jacksons' longtime friends, the celebrated team of Vronsky and Babin—luxuriate in the magic of money and music.

He was a cosmopolite, a raconteur, a *bon vivant,* a sophisticate. Ike and Mamie Eisenhower's tastes, their son John once remarked, were "strictly cornball." Bring in Fred Waring and his Pennsylvanians, let them reel off a scattering of rollicking male choruses closing with their rendition of Malotte's Lord's Prayer, and among the members of the White House Staff there would be not one dry eye. Except Jackson's. "Pageantry excellent, food mediocre, Fred Waring boring," Jackson once noted in his diary after such a state occasion. "Consider [the] Lord's Prayer in close harmony sacrilegious."

In the 1952 campaign Jackson, along with Harold Stassen and Herb Brownell, had watched over a little speechwriting operation—largely Emmett Hughes—in New York City's Commodore Hotel. Jackson had carried Hughes's draft of the Korean War policy speech from there to the campaign train; read it in its entirety to Eisenhower and a few aides, with great dramatic flair and portentous emphases, coming down impressively and movingly on the clincher, "I shall go to Korea." Subsequently, when Eisenhower at dinner suggested that Jackson show the text to Tom Dewey, seated nearby, Jackson, fearing a negative vote, stiff-armed both the presidential candidate and the powerful New York Governor with a presumptuous reminder that one does not discuss speech texts over dinner.

In the White House, where Jackson served as Eisenhower's Special Assistant on cold war—or psychological warfare—policy, he would draw on his experience from wartime days, when he helped

direct Allied propaganda in Europe against the Axis. He hated bureaucracy, had no staff, operated out of his brain, out of his back
pocket, and loved cloak and daggerism. His diary abounds with note
after note about spook after spook coming in for breakfast, lunch,
dinner, or cocktails to "talk about things"—mysterious goings-on—
frequently in Czechoslovakia or Rumania or East Berlin. He seemed
in character when photographed in a cloud of cigarette smoke. He
was a publicist and idea man, not a scholar. His habitat was Sixth
Avenue, not Harvard Square. (Indeed one wag, aware of the power
of this particular publicist, averred we were living in the "age of
C. D. Jackson.") His ideas came over cocktails, not out of the stacks.
After he left Washington he had his spacious yellow office high
above Manhattan Island lined with shelf after shelf of new books; a
visitor might wonder how many he had read. He was not a plodder;
he was a conduit: Karl Popper's heavy two volumes on *The Open
Society and Its Enemies* impressed him; and not by accident did a
major Eisenhower address—the U.N. speech after the American
landing in Lebanon in 1958—close with a plea for the world's
adoption of the "open society."

The C. D. Jackson journal or log, which he kept during his sojourn
in the White House, crackles with candor—candor about the President, Foster Dulles ("two-timing maladministration"), the Joint
Chiefs of Staff, everybody. For example:

> *June 23, 1953* "[In discussion of possible Presidential confer-
> ence with foreign leaders] President went into his 'just three
> old friends, no agenda' act. Dulles and [Under Secretary of
> State Walter Bedell] Smith manfully brought him back to
> reality several times. . . . President understood all right,
> but very irritated at Dulles' apparent suggestion he didn't
> know how to handle high-level *tete-à-tetes.*"
>
> *October 29, 1953* "NSC. Engine Charlie [Wilson] at his worst.
> . . . Half hour hassle over 'emphasis on' versus 'including.'
> President's temper really rose."
>
> *November 9, 1953* ". . . Lunch—during which Joe Dodge went
> into a devastating stream of consciousness about Engine
> Charlie."

Jackson, though liberal, was no soft-liner on security, foreign or
domestic:

> *June 20, 1953* "On Korea[:] Vehemently opposed Cutler's sug-
> gestion of retreat to Pusan Perimeter. Advocated calling off
> armistice and attacking. Psychological moment in view [of]
> internal Communist difficulties."

November 19, 1953 "Lunch—Joe Harsch [of the *Christian Science Monitor*] and Byron Connell, bearded Britisher writing biographer [of] Douglas Fairbanks, Jr. . . . Big hassle on Harry Dexter White matter. Harsch very eggheady; Connell puzzled because so much difference between British and American procedure. Tried to put everything into context, and got Harsch to agree that if he could get rid of his built-in prejudice I had made a case. Permitted myself crack that in the long run this whole affair may prove a blessing in Brownell clothing. Wonder how long before that hits the press."

December 14, 1953 "Forest McCluney—to tell me that he would like to be Secretary of the International Monetary Fund. Promised I would present his name, but nothing more to, [Treasury Secretary] George Humphrey. This is a well-surrounded slot occupied by Harry Dexter White, and White's men are still well entrenched. Might be good idea to have tough young man like McCluney get in there."

Like Milton Eisenhower, C. D. Jackson hated McCarthy. And like Milton, whom McCarthy once in short order (1) attacked as a Communist and (2) jovially embraced before a large crowd in a Wisconsin restaurant, Jackson had been astonished on August 28 when he "ran into . . . McCarthy on . . . plane trip. Amazed to be greeted with 'Hello C. D., how are you?' despite never having even seen the man before, and vice-versa. Seemed very friendly, and wished me all sorts of luck, etc. Wonder if it's kiss of death!"

The day after Thanksgiving, three days after McCarthy's nationally televised outburst, as the President's personal secretary, Ann Whitman, sat at her desk and noted that in remarks at Catholic University the President had had to reject the idea of a speech on Benedict Arnold because of the McCarthy issue, across West Executive Avenue, Jackson was dictating his diary to his secretary, Marie McCrum, unburdening himself of troubled reflections: "Tuesday night McCarthy made sensational radio and television talk. My impression was aside from open season on lambasting Truman, that McCarthy had a) declared war on Eisenhower; b) by subtle innuendo had accused Eisenhower of the same thing that Brownell had accused Truman of; c) had attempted to establish McCarthy as Mr. Republican; d) had attempted to establish McCarthyism as Republicanism, and anybody who didn't agree was either a fool or a protector of Communism. Wonderful syllogism—I am the only effective rooter-outer of Communists; there are still Communists in Government (Davies); this Government headed by Eisenhower; therefore, unless Eisenhower roots them out my way, he is a harborer of Communists.

"Wednesday, James Reston phoned to talk about this, and I told him I knew nothing about it, as President out of town and I had no discussion on the subject. He asked me personally what I thought, and I replied that I thought McCarthy had declared war on the President. . . .

"Thursday, Reston's piece included reference to one White House official who felt that this was declaration of war on President.

"Friday, Hauge reported that at Jerry Persons session on this subject, Persons very upset by all this because declaration of war 'would make it more difficult to get McCarthy and his allies to vote for Presidential program,' and I was identified with statement, probably because I had sent Persons copy my memo to Sherman Adams. . . .

"Can't understand his line of argument. Consider it disastrous appeasement which began September [*sic*] 1952, when the campaign train crossed Wisconsin border and the boys persuaded Eisenhower take out reference to General Marshall in his Milwaukee speech. That was the beginning.

"This has been Milestone Week for more than one reason.

"All the vague feelings of unhappiness I have had regarding 'lack of leadership' over the past many months, which I have always put down, really bounced up this week, and I am very frightened."

Two days later, on Sunday, November 29, Jackson wrote again: ". . . Had talk with Foster [Dulles], who was profoundly perturbed about McCarthy business, because it messes up his affairs. He is worried about presidential leadership. He intended to talk to the President first thing Monday morning about what the line should be on McCarthy because of the attack on the State Department. He also told me two terrifying facts—1) as of Thanksgiving Day the President had not read the McCarthy speech or been briefed on it. Dulles—: 'The President asked me if I thought he should read it.' Fact number 2) as of Sunday afternoon Herbert Brownell had not read the McCarthy speech. This place is really falling apart."

Outside Jackson's knowledge Eisenhower did read the speech and phoned Dulles: "[McCarthy] attacks the truce [in Korea]—attacks us because we don't go and get unaccounted prisoners. Does he want to declare war today?"

Back to the office Monday morning November 30 to Jackson, in his diary, "BLACK MONDAY." For the first time since the McCarthy outburst and the Reston story the White House staff was meeting.

Hagerty chaired. "Unfortunately," Jackson wrote in his diary, "neither Persons [at home ill] nor Adams [in Canada seeing about the tariff on oats] present. Hagerty opened up by mentioning the recent Reston, Folliard and Harsch pieces, each one of which contained anonymous attribution to White House personnel. He cautioned against talking, saying that it inevitably was embarrassing to the President, etc., etc. Incidentally, Hagerty was very low-pitch and temperate about whole thing.

"After moment of dead silence, I said that I had told Reston on the telephone the item he had in quotes, namely that McCarthy had declared war on the President—and that this gave me an opportunity to say some more on the subject.

"I went into the matter completely, including going back to campaign speech in Milwaukee when Marshall reference deleted. Warned them that this Three Little Monkeys Act was not working and would not work, and that appeasing McCarthy in order to save his seven votes for this year's legislative program was poor tactics, poor strategy . . . and poor arithmetic, and that unless the President stepped up to bat on this one soon, the Republicans would have neither a program, nor 1954, nor 1956.

"Immediately Jerry Morgan, Homer Gruenther, and to a lesser degree Jack Martin, jumped in on the opposite side. Only two to speak on my side were Willis and Harlow.

"Also I made proposition that the President substitute television appearance Wednesday for his scheduled press conference and face up before the nation to this declaration of war. Was appalled to discover that it had been planned to cancel the press conference and have the President go to Bermuda [conference with British and French leaders] having said nothing. Big rhubarb. Finally agreed to have press conference. The men have really separated out from the boys."

This comment, though understandable, was misleading. The staff didn't divide sharply into black and white, liberal and conservative. Individuals crossed lines, did the unexpected.

To be sure, Jerry Persons usually ended up on the conservative side, mediator rather than advocate. So did Jack Martin, a shrewd, whimsical Cincinnati lawyer who had for years served on the Hill as administrative assistant to the conservatives' Mr. Republican, Senator Robert A. Taft. After Eisenhower defeated Taft at the 1952 convention, Martin had warned his boss against the trickery of the Eisenhower crowd. But after Taft's death in July of 1953, as Martin returned to Washington from the Senator's burial in Ohio, two of his close White House friends met him at the airport and offered him a job on the President's staff. Martin worked for Eisenhower from that moment until 1958, when the President appointed him a judge of the United States Court of Customs and Patent Appeals. And he worked for him with unswerving devotion and loyalty.

Martin was no closet McCarthyite. He had known McCarthy from his days with Taft. He had gone one morning to McCarthy's apartment as an emissary of the President to plead with the Wisconsin rogue elephant to stop his obstreperousness; to give the White House the names of all suspected Communists; and to let the Justice Department, without publicity, investigate the allegations. He had returned empty-handed. Whatever measure of sympathy he might have had for McCarthy's purposes—not his methods—Martin served a single man now, the President of the United States. He was Jewish, he was funny (he once labeled a bill to raise Government salaries the "Jack Martin relief bill" and once added to his wife Barbara's list of chores to start the day, "Kiss Jack goodbye"), he was smart, and he was honest.

Jerry Morgan, who also reported to Persons, also usually stood shoulder to shoulder with Martin. A graduate of Harvard Law School and a brilliant lawyer, the architect of much of the text of the Taft-Hartley labor-management relations Act of 1947, Morgan was a man of deliberateness, care, and rigorous logic; a deep, thoughtful voice; and at times—particularly after several drinks and a long evening—a puckish sense of humor. ("If I had his district" he once said of the congressman from Beverly Hills, "I know how I'd campaign: door to door.") Like Persons and Martin, Morgan focused first not on ideology but on legislation, and the votes to enact it.

So, one might expect, would Bryce Harlow, whom Persons had brought into the White House in January of 1953 and who in October of that year succeeded Emmet Hughes, who was returning to *Time* magazine, as Ike's chief speech-writer. Bryce came from Oklahoma. As a staff man on the Hill he'd come under the tutelage of conservative Democrat Carl Vinson of Georgia, the powerful Chairman of the House Armed Services Committee, whom Bryce had served with the fidelity of a son. He had worked for Marshall and Persons during the war. And by 1953 he had logged fifteen years of Washington service—service that made him a trusted confidant of a host of senators and congressmen on both sides of the aisle.

Thus the putative conservatives. And ranged against them one would ordinarily expect to find these liberals: Sherman Adams; Press Secretary Jim Hagerty and his Assistant Press Secretary, Murray Snyder, a Brooklyn newspaper reporter who'd cut his teeth on New York State Republican politics; Brownell's chief assistant in the 1952 delegate search, Appointments Secretary Tom Stephens; and Bernard Shanley. A multimillionaire son-in-law of John Thomas Smith, one of the executive giants of General Motors, Shanley was a trim, athletic New Jersey lawyer who had played baseball at Columbia with Lou Gehrig. Perhaps the courtliest, most gentlemanly member of the White House staff, a man eventually done in by Jim Hagerty—whom Shanley had criticized for portraying the President as a golfing chief executive—Shanley had joined the Eisenhower forces only after leading Harold Stassen's 1952 presidential delegate search. Significantly, Shanley was a prominent and ardent Catholic.

Even in the narrative of C. D. Jackson—a hotly engaged participant—one sees that on McCarthy all the conservatives didn't line up on one side, all the liberals on another. One gets more evidence of the scene's complexity from the diary of Shanley, a man at one remove from the fire storm's center, as he described the same meeting chaired by Hagerty:

"The President [had said] . . . he sincerely hoped [Communism] would not be an issue in the 1954 campaign—his primary thought being that we would clean all the Communists out of the government. McCarthy more or less took this up to mean that the Communist issue itself would not be an issue in the '54 campaign. I was particularly concerned about this because I knew how deeply it affected the Catholic people, as well as many of my other friends, who felt it was the most important issue in the world today. . . .

"After [Hagerty] finished, C. D. Jackson spoke up and said, 'I was the one who [leaked to Reston].' It was fine and decent of him to do this because it couldn't have been easy as he was very much on the spot. . . . I had a long talk with Jerry Persons after the staff conference and told him all that had taken place and he indicated that he was anxious to have me go with Jack Martin and Jerry Morgan to a meeting with Lenny Hall, the National Chairman, and . . . part of the National Committee staff over at the [committee] headquarters in the Cafritz Building. We went over and for a good solid hour discussed the problem. . . . The thought that permeated the mind of Jack Martin, something that had been bothering both of us for a long time, was that it was time that the President very affirmatively, very clearly, very distinctly indicate his leadership of the

Party, particularly now that McCarthy had to a certain extent challenged it. . . . I had a long talk after lunch [with Persons] and we discussed at some length [how we could] pick up the leadership of the party and show the President was the boss. . . .

"That afternoon we started drafting statements for the press conference on Wednesday. . . ."

One gets still more detail from a man even farther removed than Shanley from ground zero. Robert Kieve was a staff assistant first to Emmet Hughes, then to Bryce Harlow, a wartime colleague of Emmet's with the OWI in Madrid; a keen-eyed, perceptive, literate, and concerned observer from the outer edge of the circle. "[C. D. Jackson] said McCarthy had clearly indicated that DDE is 'harboring' Communists," Kieve wrote in his diary that same day. "This, he said, is quite clearly a time for action; if the challenge is not met, the American people will have cause to doubt whether they have a leader—or they will feel that McCarthy is that leader. [Jackson] strongly urged that the President—who is leaving for the Bermuda conference on Friday, cancel his press conference this week and, instead, deliver a hard-hitting speech on Wednesday night. He, C.D., would like to try his hand at writing that speech.

"Hagerty said this suggestion raises some difficulties. . . . Such a speech would simply raise McCarthy to Eisenhower's level. C.D. countered that the speech could be so worded as to avoid that possibility, but he was unwilling or unable to elaborate when Hagerty asked him to do so. Hagerty went on to say that the President now has a big enough fight on his hands—the legislative program—and that he shouldn't create sideshow fights while that program is being prepared; the President could, he added, wait until the opening gun of the legislative program on January 1 or 4. . . . At this point, both C.D. and Charlie Willis [a junior personnel assistant to Governor Adams] attacked him with the observation that January 1 was too late. Willis added that, already, the Democrats themselves are taking up the cry that Ike is soft on communists. Jerry Morgan, however, observed that 'our enemy right now isn't McCarthy, it's the Democrats.' To this comment there was a chorus of protests— Hagerty, Willis, Jackson—to the effect that the Democrats were not only *not* our enemies, but that we needed their help in the legislative program, as Morgan himself should know. Morgan countered that McCarthy had a very good Administration voting record, that he could be counted on to help, that this was no time to turn him against the Administration. Homer Gruenther [brother of General

Alfred M. Gruenther, and a junior member of Persons's legislative liaison staff] chimed in with a similar comment, said that there were about eight senators who align themselves with McCarthy, that this would be no time to lose their support, that the record shows they have helped our legislative program almost every step of the way.

"Hagerty said he couldn't see how a man who opposes our foreign policies as McCarthy does could be counted on for any help at all. . . . Ned Beach [Ike's Naval Aide, an outstanding submarine skipper and a prominent author of fiction—*Run Silent, Run Deep*— and nonfiction on the drama of undersea warfare] earlier than this commented that, he felt, McCarthy had delivered a speech which had done him, McCarthy, a great deal of good. Beach had no sooner allowed these words to slither from his lips than others . . . commented on how much harm they thought McCarthy had done himself. . . . Pete Carroll [a brilliant young Army officer who had served Ike at SHAPE and had now become White House Staff Secretary, a devoted and fearless liberal, and, like Shanley, an ardent Catholic] said that the press had given McCarthy pretty shabby treatment over the weekend, and he added . . . that while it is true that much of McCarthy's support comes from Catholic sources, it is significant that, just this weekend, many Catholic publications put on their front pages the picture of the President and the various Cardinals who participated in the recent ceremonies at Catholic University. . . . Martin, who is Taft's former Administrative Assistant and who is consistently the one who gives voice to the most conservative judgments, declared that McCarthy had done himself grave harm, that today he would surely be catching hell from many of his Senatorial friends, that he may very well have killed himself off in this particular sally. He talked long, and with much hyperbole, in this vein, and I wonder how many others shared my feeling that Martin's protestations were a deliberate attempt to take the edge off the argument of those calling for retaliatory action by the President.

"Somewhere halfway all through this, two significant contributions were made: One was C.D.'s answer to Homer Gruenther: 'This whole situation began back in September, 1952, when Eisenhower was talked into deleting reference to Marshall in a speech he made in Wisconsin.' The other—more significant—contribution was Bryce Harlow's suggestion that all this be handled, not in a speech, but at the press conference. His reasoning—or perhaps part of it is mine as I now consider his suggestion—is this: . . . *Whenever* the next press conference is held, the President will either have to face the issue or duck it; in either case, his reaction will be obvious. . . . Harlow [suggested] . . . that a carefully prepared statement candidly anticipating questions on this issue be prepared in advance, that the President read that statement and that he refer all additional questions on the issue back to that statement. This procedure, he felt, would be as effective as a speech. To this I add that it would give the matter just the right amount of importance. It would show the President's willingness to face up to the issue and (we hope) to exert his leadership. But it would avoid his giving a speech on McCarthy on the very eve of the supposedly important Bermuda conference. Nobody—with the possible exception of Bern Shanley—gave any indication of disagreement. Even Morgan thought it was a good idea. . . ."

Thus the staff: liberals and conservatives, pleaders and punchers, Catholics, Protestants, and Jews, practical men and idealistic chameleonlike, mercurial, surprising, unpredictable.

But only one man in the end counted—Dwight Eisenhower. His old wartime comrade in arms Omar Bradley had once uttered a great line to climax a moving address: "Let us steer by the stars and not by the lights of each passing ship." In the midst of a sea battle in the dark of night, with his crew split over what kind of a shot to fire at the foe, the President of the United States was steering by the stars—by stars so distant they at times seemed to vanish from sight. In late September, Emmet Hughes had drafted a talk to a New England Republican audience which captured Eisenhower's enthusiasm and proclaimed his dream for the future of the Republican party: "We have, in our respect for priceless civil and human rights, used the Federal authority, wherever it clearly extends, to erase the stain of racial discrimination and segregation. We are making certain that every government employee is a loyal American. But we have opposed the confusing of loyalty with conformity, and all misguided attempts to convert freedom into a privilege licensed by censors. . . . We must, even in our patriotism, guard against that prideful nationalism which impatiently breaks the bonds binding all free peoples. . . .

"We must, even in our honest political fervor, fear neither partisan criticism nor self-criticism. For the pretense of perfection is not one of the marks of good public servants.

"And we must, even in our zeal to defeat the enemies of freedom, never betray ourselves into seizing their weapons to make our own defense. A people or a party that is young and sober and confident and free has no need of censors to purify its thought or stiffen its will. For the kind of America in which we believe is too strong ever to acknowledge fear—and too wise ever to fear knowledge.

"This is the kind of America—and the kind of Republican Party—in which I believe. . . ."

Two weeks later, on October 8, Eisnhower was saying the same thing in blunter words as he dictated to Ann Whitman a diary entry which fumes with his exasperation over the reactionaries who were trying to block his appointment of Earl Warren as Chief Justice: "If Republicans as a body should try to repudiate him, I shall leave the Republican Party and try to organize an intelligent group of independents, however small."

The pursuit of principle might lead him to imagine forming a new political party. It would never lead him into a direct and individual personal attack.

"As for McCarthy," Eisenhower wrote his brother Milton the next day, "only a short-sighted or completely inexperienced individual would urge the use of office of the Presidency to give an opponent the publicity he so avidly desires. Time and time again, without apology or evasion, I—and many members of this administration—have stood for the right of the individual, for free expression of convictions, even though those convictions might be unpopular, and for uncensored use of our libraries, except as dictated by common decency. . . . Frankly, in a day when we see journalism far more concerned in so-called human interest, dramatic incidents, and bitter quarrels than it is in promoting constructive understanding of the day's problems, I have no intention whatsoever of helping promote the publicity value of anyone who disagrees with me—demagogue or not!"

Dwight Eisenhower idolized his brother—younger by ten years—considered him the man most qualified to be President of the United States (making no exception of himself), and believed his judgment nearly impeccable. But he continued to refuse to yield when Milton, impelled by his long liberal background with its associations with DFR and the OWI, implored the President to tear his enemy to pieces. In a late draft of the McCarthy chapter in his memoir *Mandate for Change*, Eisenhower wrote these words which never appeared in the published book: "My brother, Dr. Milton Eisenhower, appealed to me to announce to the world that I strongly disapproved of all that McCarthy was doing and all that he stood for. . . . [I] pointed out that if I were to attack McCarthy, as every instinct in me prompted me to do, I should greatly enhance his publicity value without achieving any constructive purpose. I was convinced that McCarthy's influence, such as it was, would be gone completely if he lost his headline value. . . . In sheer political terms I was increasingly convinced that I would defeat him by ignoring him. . . . I would not demean myself or the Presidency by getting in the gutter with him."

Eisenhower had erected a wall of principle and strategy. It would now feel the shock of collision.

In his State Department press conference on Tuesday, December 1, in words Eisenhower approved and strengthened in advance, Dulles forthrightly defended the Administration's security program and the retention so far of John Paton Davies. He stiff-armed McCarthy on the China trade. The administration, the Secretary said, did not "propose to throw away" the goodwill of our allies by "blustering and domineering methods." But he confided to C. D. Jackson his fear that the President might not back him up when he faced reporters the next day.

"If he doesn't," Dulles said, "I am finished. I might as well quit."

Jackson also worried: "Bryce Harlow—on President's press conference, and to discuss Hagerty draft of statement (re: McCarthy). Hagerty draft had certain big holes, and other efforts by Jerry Morgan and company very, very weak. . . .

"Harlow again—to discuss press conference problem. Worked up quite a head of steam and offered draft strong statement. Harlow kept urging I should inject myself. . . .

"Everybody getting into quite a lather. Tom Stephens began urging me inject myself. . . .

"[Under Secretary of State] Beedle Smith [Walter Bedell Smith] called to ask if he should get into the act, as Foster probably diffident speak to the President about backing. Urged Beedle telephone President.

"Discovered brush-off group about to descend on President, so rush over with my draft to walk in just as though I belonged there. President left office before they could assemble.

"Big session with Shanley, Harlow, Morgan, Carroll, Martin, Snyder, Persons still sick, although had been pulling strings. Showed them my draft, which though not acceptable did start some spine stiffening. Harlow's inexorable logic also great help. Broke up to convene at staff meeting in the morning."

By the end of the afternoon, Shanley had written in his diary, "I was not satisfied that we were any nearer a solution except that Bryce Harlow said he would work that night and go to the White House reception late. At least he understood exactly what a few of us wanted and was the best equipped to put it together. . . ."

That evening, sitting in his office in white tie and tails and pecking away at his typewriter as he waited for the White House–judiciary reception to commence, Bob Kieve set down what he'd heard through closed doors during the day: "It now appears that the President will indeed hold a press conference tomorrow—and that he will read a prepared statement. At least, one is being prepared for him in at least three different offices. . . . Incredible as it seems, the group which seemed to be in the rider's seat, the group that was drafting *the* statement for the President and which had a four-thirty appointment with him, consisted of Jack Martin, Jerry Morgan and Bern Shanley! C. D. Jackson—as he explains it—is or has been left out of both the drafting and the meeting. Bryce, though he contributed a radically changed version of the original draft (which had been done by Hagerty before Hagerty's departure for Bermuda), was not in the actual session in which the draft for the President was hammered out. Nor was he invited to meet with the President until, speaking to Morgan on another issue, he was invited, casually, to sit in. One draft—a draft supplied by the Morgan-Martin-Shanley group . . . was shown to me by Harlow. It is a truly sad document: a defensive, cringing, cowardly page-and-a-half of purely negative prose. If the President reads this statement or anything approximating it, it's my guess that he'll lose the services of C. D. Jackson. . . . I may learn something from Bryce before the evening is over—if I see him among the eight hundred odd people expected."

Minutes later, as Bern Shanley, escorting in tails his gowned wife, Maureen, "hopped out of the car at the White House steps, all the police—my friends at the White House—greeted me fondly," he wrote in his diary. "We walked in and to the right-hand side of the beautiful entrance hall was the Marine Orchestra and above them on the steps a large group of lady reporters waiting to see what the lovely ladies were wearing. Maureen made a terrific hit with them. . . . In the paper they mentioned her . . . and Bill Rogers's wife, Adele, as the two loveliest ladies at the reception. . . ."

At eight o'clock the next morning Jackson's office phone rang: No staff meeting. He leaped to a conclusion: "They are trying to freeze me out. Rushed over and found them all assembled unofficially in Snyder's office, and we went at it again.

"Morgan had moved up considerably. Shanley," the hypersuspicious Jackson misperceived, "tried to see President alone with Snyder, but we all trooped in with Tom Stephens' assistance and the fight was on.

"Prexy read their current draft with visible irritation, and made some mumbling comments. Jack Martin then pitched in with great courage and said that a vacuum existed in this country, and it was a political vacuum, and unless the President filled it somebody else would fill it. The President twisted and squirmed but Martin stuck to his point. I pitched in as strongly as I could by telling him that so long as Taft was alive he might have been able to get out of the responsibility of leading the Party, but now he could no longer get out of it, and that the people were waiting for a sign, and a simple sign—and now was the time.

"Big hassle over text started. President read my text with great irritation, slammed it back at me and said he would not refer to McCarthy personally—'I will not get in the gutter with that guy.'

"But gradually an interesting thing developed. The needling and the goosing began to take effect, and the President himself began very ably to firm up the text as he reread it again, this time very carefully.

"Everyone's mood began to change from divided snarling into united helping him along, and when Prexy dictated the last paragraph exactly as it finally appeared, which contained the real Republican leadership gimmick, the group almost cheered.

"So what started out as a ghastly mess turned out fine. Problem now is, having zippered the toga of Republican political leadership on the President's shoulders, how to keep that zipper shut."

An hour later, the President faced the assembled reporters at his news conference.

"I am in full accord," he said, "with the statements made yesterday by Secretary Dulles in his press conference. . . . The easiest thing to do with great power is to abuse it—to use it to excess. . . . [If] this most powerful of the free nations . . . should turn impatiently to coercion of other free nations, our brand of coercion, so far as our friends are concerned, would be a mark of the imperialist rather than of the leader. . . . I repeat my previously expressed conviction that fear of communists actively undermining our Government will not be an issue in the 1954 elections. Long before then this administration will have made such progress in routing them out under the security program developed by Attorney General Brownell that this can no longer be considered a serious menace. As you already know, about 1500 persons who were security risks have already been removed. Fair, thorough, and decent investigations . . . are the most effective—and the only efficient—way to get this necessary job done. . . .

"In all that we do to combat subversion, it is imperative that we protect the basic rights of loyal American citizens. I am determined to protect those rights to the limit of the powers of the office with which I have been entrusted by the American people.

"In my judgment, the efficiency and vision with which the Government is administered by this Republican administration, and whether or not the Congress enacts a progressive, dynamic program enhancing the welfare of all the people of our country, will determine the future political complexion of the Congress and the future of the administration. I am convinced that those who fight for the program that I shall soon submit to the Congress will deserve and will receive the respect and support of the American people."

And then the final clinching paragraph, which had been dictated by Eisenhower at the staff meeting and taken down in shorthand by Harlow: "In any event, unless the Republican Party can develop and enact such a program for the American people, it does not deserve to remain in power. But I know that these sentiments are shared by the vast majority of the Republicans in this country, particularly by my close associates both in the Senate and in the House of Representatives. Because of this unity of feeling such a program will be enacted."

With these words the President had brought his staff together cheering. By assertion of principle and fact, he had answered McCarthy without descending to a mention of the hated name. And he had once again affirmed in public the individual citizen's right to fair play.

On the evening of that same Wednesday, Eisenhower demonstrated again his devotion to that right, this time in deepest privacy.

That afternoon he had had a long phone conversation with Defense Secretary Charlie Wilson.

"Have you seen the new report of J. Edgar Hoover on Dr. [J. Robert] Oppenheimer?" Wilson asked. "Well, Lewis Strauss [Chairman of the Atomic Energy Commission] and I have received copies directly from Hoover, and it's the worst one yet. Lewis told me that McCarthy knows about it and might pull it on us."

"I'm not worried about McCarthy," Eisenhower answered. "But I do think Brownell should know about this report, if he doesn't already. We're not going to attack anybody's character without solid evidence."

This news about Oppenheimer—one of the world's most brilliant physicists, one of the architects of the atomic bomb—jolted the President. After he hung up he dictated an entry in his hit-or-miss secret diary: "Charlie Wilson . . . has a report from the FBI that carries the gravest implications that Dr. Robert Oppenheimer is a security risk of the worst kind. . . .

"When I first came to this office some one individual (I cannot now recall who it was) stated that in his opinion Dr. Oppenheimer was not to be trusted. Whoever it was—and I think it was probably Admiral Strauss—later told me that he had reason to revise his opinion. At the same time, all of my other inquiries merely brought out that Dr. Oppenheimer had long been under observation because of the fact that a brother and sister-in-law (or was it his wife?) had been definitely connected with the communist movement some years back. . . .

"The sad fact is that if this charge is true, we have a man who has been right in the middle of our whole atomic development from the very earliest days. . . . Dr. Oppenheimer was, of course, one of the men who has strongly urged the giving of more atomic information to the world."

The next day Eisenhower wrote Brownell: "I have already directed the heads of departments and agencies of the Executive Branch of Government concerned in this connection, while prompt action is being taken to determine the full import of the contents of Mr. Hoover's communication, to place a blank wall between the subject of the communication and all areas of our government operations. . . ." And he continued in his diary: "[I instructed the Attorney General] to procure from the Director of the FBI an entire file in the case of Dr. Oppenheimer and to make of it a thorough study. I assured him that I did not intend in any way to prejudge the case; but I did want a thorough and prompt recommendation from him as to what further action should be taken. . . .

"It is reported to me that this same information, or at least the vast bulk of it, has been constantly reviewed and reexamined over a number of years, and that the overall conclusion has always been that there is no evidence that implies disloyalty on the part of Dr. Oppenheimer. However, this does not mean that he might not be a security risk.

"Actually, of course, the truth is that no matter now what could or should be done, if this man is really a disloyal citizen, then the damage he can do now as compared to what he has done in the past is like comparing a grain of sand to an ocean beach. It would not be a case of merely locking the stable door after the horse is gone; it would be more like trying to find a door for a burned-down stable."

Eisenhower had set in motion a process of fact and judgment—a process that would entail long days of hearings before an impartial board, with Oppenheimer having the right to representation by counsel; some forty witnesses; thousands of pages of documentary evidence; and testimony—a process that prompted Franklin D. Roosevelt's brilliant amanuensis and biographer, the playwright Robert E. Sherwood, to write to Eisenhower on April 13, 1954, after the news became public: "The announcement of the manner in which you are handling the case of Dr. Robert Oppenheimer came like a breath of clear, fresh air on the front pages this morning.

"I do not know Dr. Oppenheimer . . . , and it was dreadful to contemplate that the enormous contribution of these distinguished American scientists should provide a series of field days for the McCarthy carnival merely because, apparently, Dr. Oppenheimer had been guilty of political naïveté in some phase of his career.

"The way you are directing this matter is precisely the way it should be done; with dignity, with fairness, with respect for the rights of the individual and with the great authority which is constitutionally yours. . . ."

Though Eisenhower's response was correct, nothing could permanently solve the conflicts which the Oppenheimer case exposed, because its dilemmas of loyalty are endemic to human beings, their poignancy made all the more searing by the enormous destructive power of the nuclear age. The mental strain on the individual scientist, mesmerized by the awesome might for good or evil, was matched by the mental strain on the average citizen, frozen by his lack of might to control his destiny. Even in the phenomenon of McCarthyism itself one recognizes a lashing out at random of the man incapable of mastering his own fate. And everyman was now afraid of the scientist and the scientist's knowledge. The average citizen did not understand the simplest scientific propositions, but he understood that a wizard physicist who was a traitor could hand him over, lock, stock, and barrel, to the Soviets.

If the citizen was frightened, so was the scientist. He knew he was distrusted. Yet he felt pity for the masses of innocent, ignorant, and threatened humanity. It is no happenstance that, as Oppenheimer was a dissenter in the United States, so also Sakharov was a dissenter in the Soviet Union. The pressures on top scientists were almost unbearable. Scientists were worshipped, and they were suspect. They were treated like gods, and they were watched.

Events were now, at last, giving reason for bold hope, for renewed confidence in the President's leadership. At the Eisenhower press conference the toga had been zippered. The next day McCarthy backed off: he wasn't, he assured the reporters, dreaming of challenging the President. The European press had responded with ebullience to Dulles's and Eisenhower's declarations against McCarthy. Then on December 8, on the President's return from the Bermuda conference, came his announcement at the U.N. General Assembly of his Atoms for Peace plan—a proposal for beginning the peaceful international use of atomic energy, for turning mankind away from the chamber of nuclear horrors toward the sunny uplands of peace, a proposal which C. D. Jackson had for weeks upon weeks been fighting through to a triumphant conclusion, over the dead bodies of Dulles and the Joint Chiefs of Staff and assorted Pentagon recalcitrants. For all these reasons, for an enthusiast like Jackson, things were looking up.

So he imagined.

Secretary of the Army Stevens was backing down on the removal of General Lawton. "Jim," he told Congressman Auchincloss just minutes after the President's December 2 news conference, "I haven't yet really quite gotten to the point where I can make the change I want to make. In various ways I have sort of tagged base with the Senator, and he would be very unhappy about it if it were done right now. Of course, I have to run my own business and intend to do so, but on the other hand, I don't want to stir up the animals unnecessarily."

"I think you are dead right," Auchincloss came back. ". . . The damn thing is packed with dynamite, and you have to be awfully careful."

The Monmouth hearings were still smoldering. And John Adams was encountering static in his attempt to get Brownell to agree in writing about the refusal of loyalty-security information to congressional committees. The Army didn't have an answer to the Stevens-Brownell letter of November 4, soliciting such an agreement. Adams had drafted that letter. Hensel had cleared it. Even before Stevens signed, Adams had verbal assurance from Assistant Attorney General J. Lee Rankin that his Department would back the Army on refusal. Brownell had discussed the policy on November 10 with the President himself, and Eisenhower had concurred. But three days later, by chance at a lawyers' lunch at the Willard Hotel, Adams learned from Rankin that Justice had run into a bind: Brownell's revelation of security data in the Harry Dexter White case was making it difficult to write a letter apparently endorsing a contrary policy toward McCarthy.

Time was getting short.

On December 4, Adams wrote Brownell, trying to rouse Justice off its chair: "Present indications are that the Senate Subcommittee will probably begin to call members of loyalty screening, hearing and appeal boards to appear before it during the next week or ten days." Adams sent a copy of his letter to his friend Bill Rogers, asking for help in speeding things up and adding: "Roy Cohn thinks we're going to collide on this issue this week." Two days later the *New York Times* recounted the suit of two Monmouth employees—one past, one present—to enjoin McCarthy from forcing them to produce records on their suspension and reinstatement. The court had denied their motion. Adams sent the clipping to Rogers: it "points up," he said, "the problem which we face with Joe McCarthy. Specifically, we are going to have serious difficulty in controlling all of the people who sit on all of the hearing boards, all of the screening boards, and all of the review boards, unless we have some sort of blanket authority to instruct them.

"It is this subject which will be under discussion with the Attorney General when Hensel and I come over there on Saturday morning at 11:30."

Finally, Schine was still languishing at Fort Dix. With Cohn's help in urging the press of committee business, he had gone off on pass for four weekends and five week nights in his first near-month of service. The Commanding General had then tightened up, declaring on December 4 that weekends would now start Saturday noon, not Friday night, and, on December 8, ruling out week night passes altogether. Cohn violently protested to Adams. Adams made an end run to McCarthy.

On December 9 at 2:43 in the afternoon, Adams phoned Stevens from the Capitol. The Monmouth hearings had moved there because of a New York newspaper strike. "Apparently," he told his boss, "Joe is now kind of reversing himself on Dave, and what he wants to talk about is some sort of an assignment for Dave, and at this moment I don't think we are in any position to say what is going to happen to him."

Stevens stiffened: "That is correct."

"But," Adams went on, "Roy said to me this morning, 'The Army has doublecrossed me for the last time. . . . The Army is going to find out what it means to go over my head.' I said, 'Is this a threat?' He said, 'It is a promise, and I always deliver on my promises. . . . I have had nothing but doublecrosses from the Army. You don't keep your word, and Stevens has not kept his word.' And I said, 'Give us times and places where Mr. Stevens has not kept his word.' 'On that press conference,' he said. 'He has taken Dave and kept him from working with us evenings. I guarantee you we are going to run this hearing; we are going to get your witnesses; and we are going to get this Screening Board up here; and the Army is going to pay for this.'"

Stevens became ironical. "There is a splendid, constructive attitude!"

"This morning," Adams continued, "they had a surprise witness they pulled in, a civilian employee from Monmouth. . . . And I refused to permit him to tell about loyalty or individuals, or anything like that. And Joe teed off, and Joe said, 'This hiding behind Truman directives is silly. . . . Ask the Secretary of the Army to speak to the President about this, and get this directive changed.'

"It is the very subject I told you I was talking to Hensel about; . . . a directive, executive order abolishing all old Truman orders. . . . It would substitute a good, workable order which would guarantee the protection of the loyalty boards. . . . Hensel has an appointment with Brownell for Monday, and I am to go with him; and I personally don't think that is soon enough. . . .

"Joe has the Administration on the defensive again. If we publish an order on this . . . , it will be because Joe forced us again. Each time we drag our feet, then Joe has got the ball. . . . Roy says, 'We are never going to stop this. Joe will deliver, and I can make Joe do what I want.'"

Thus a watershed in the contemporaneous record—the record

written at the time of the event, unencumbered or unimproved or unvitiated by hindsight. Up to this moment in the Pentagon, it had been the record of practical men, in the midst of routine events. Not one word of moral outrage, not one deviation from their determination to cooperate: "He's getting headlines and is entitled to them"; "If you would like to get a hold of me, [Dave,] call this office"; "You've done a magnificent job"; "He's an interesting fellow"; "We have been very clubby here the past few days, [with] every night in some saloon"; "I feel Joe is very strong for the Army"; "Half the battle is having good relations."

Now, for the first time in the contemporaneous record one sees blood. Cohn had lashed out at Adams. There was only one thing for Bob Stevens to do: have lunch with Joe McCarthy as soon as possible. He set an appointment for one P.M. the next day, December 10, at the Carroll Arms, near the Capitol. To get him ready, John Adams put together a little briefing paper that included a warning on Schine:

"The bargain they are attempting to drive for is a guarantee that Dave will go directly to New York City at the conclusion of . . . [the first] eight weeks [of basic]. . . . McCarthy was talking about Dave being assigned to study the textbooks at West Point or something similar. This, of course, is the sort of assignment which we ordinarily would give to a panel of educators instead of a private soldier. If I had one recommendation to make with reference to Schine, it would be that we should exercise care to see that he does not end up in the sort of assignment which would have him working [close] to classified material. . . . I have a personal feeling that he would have no compunction about compromising such material, and then starting a Congressional investigation."

In the event, four sat down to lunch the next day, December 10—McCarthy, Stevens, Adams, and Frank Carr. The reason for Cohn's absence would later become a subject of hot dispute. From the evidence of the record written at the time, one must conclude that all went well. Immediately afterward, Stevens talked with Congressman Jerry Ford of Michigan, who'd been reading about McCarthy's confrontation with the Army in the paper. "I thought your handling of that was damn good," Ford told the Secretary.

"I want to work with the Congress in every way and at the same time I have to be fair to all these people," Stevens replied. "It is difficult, but so far I have gotten along reasonably well. . . ."

He spoke too soon. For Schine, and against the Army, Cohn continued to persevere with unremitting zeal. McCarthy continued to zigzag. Exactly seven days later, on December 17, in a sequence devoid of any contemporaneous record, McCarthy, Cohn, Carr, and Adams—all the principals except Stevens—would go to lunch at Gasner's Restaurant near the Courthouse in New York; Cohn would become extremely angry and abusive toward the Army; John Adams, riding uptown afterward with the others, the car driven by Cohn, would find himself suddenly and unceremoniously standing in the midst of four lanes of Park Avenue traffic; and the participants—unfettered by any record written at the time—would radically disagree about what had happened: the content of the luncheon discussion, the cause of Cohn's rage, the reason for Adams's sudden departure (or ejection) from the auto.

Five days later, on December 22, McCarthy would write Stevens, at last, a "Dear Bob" letter setting down in black and white his unequivocal insistence on no special favors for the private: "I have heard rumors to the effect that some of the members of my staff have intervened with your Department in behalf of a former staff consultant, David Schine. This they, of course, have a right to do as individuals. However, as I have told you a number of times, I have an unbreakable rule that neither I nor anyone in my behalf shall ever attempt to interfere with or influence the Army in its assignments, promotion, etc."

Though shamefully less than candid ("I have heard rumors," "I have an unbreakable rule") about either Cohn's entreaties or his own, the Senator had gone on record.

Meanwhile on December 12, Adams and Hensel had finally met with Brownell and Rogers. Adams laid out the whole problem of the employee security program, underscoring the imperative of protecting security board members (hearing, review, screening) from congressional interrogation. After a long discussion, Brownell concurred. He would support the Army in refusing to permit the interrogation of its security people. Because at the moment Rogers was negotiating with some of the congressional leaders on proposals to curb some of the abuses in congressional investigations, he and Brownell thought they should hold up action on any new executive order and keep it as a bargaining chip. And they agreed, doubtless with a glance at Brownell's disclosures on Harry Dexter White and at Rogers's congressional negotiations, that the Army would not tell McCarthy the Department of Justice had been consulted.

• •

Christmas was coming. Nineteen fifty-three was drawing to a close. The administration surveyed its accomplishments. Its first year, though on some counts rough, had on the whole been heartening: the Korean War had ended; the budget was coming under control; inflation was cooling down; wartime controls on wages and prices had become a memory; emergency immigration legislation had passed, over the dead bodies of some diehard reactionaries. The men in the White House looked eagerly toward more good things and more good days ahead, including good relations with Republican senators and congressmen, one and all.

"Our margin—in the Senate at least—" Jerry Persons told a euphoric staff meeting on December 21, "is so small that we dare not lose the support of a single Republican or Democrat inclined to vote with us. We shouldn't consider any Congressman or Senator against us until he has so indicated by vote. Even the most reactionary Republicans can be swayed to our side." As an example he mentioned Homer Capehart, a stodgy Republican who had told him he would support the President's 1954 legislative program. "That just proves we've come a hell of a long way since this time last year."

That evening everyone took a little time out for fun. Bern and Maureen Shanley hosted a Christmas party for President and Mrs. Eisenhower and the staff. Bobby Cutler, master raconteur, told clean stories. Tom Stephens and Jim Hagerty dressed up like a couple of rag dolls, went through chorus after chorus of "Tell Me a Story," Tom bouncing up and down on Jim's knee. C. D. Jackson, made up as Eartha Kitt with fake bust and wig, gave the roaring audience "C'est Si Bon."

Back in their offices, of course, some of these same people fumed and writhed over Oppenheimer: "The foolishness and/or knavery of past Administration . . . unbelievable," Jackson wrote in his diary December 17. And meeting the next day with Nixon and others on the problem, he declared: "Appalled to hear Rogers propose same procedure as Truman with Harry Dexter White. We all jumped on that, and Rogers smilingly withdrew suggestion."

Meanwhile the Monmouth hearings ground on, with names of loyalty board members starting to leak out.

And G. David Schine continued to undergo basic training. His first eight weeks would soon end, and on December 29 Stevens and Adams surveyed the prospect.

"We have scrupulously kept our hands off the Schine situation,"

Adams wrote Stevens that day, "so that his treatment would be exactly in accord with that received by other soldiers." But now a problem had arisen: Schine had taken some tests at Fort Dix, his records had thereupon gone to Washington, and the Army had concluded that Schine should become a specialist—a criminal investigator. "It is therefore contemplated that he will be ordered from Fort Dix to report about one February to the Provost Marshal [General] School at Camp Gordon, Georgia for eight weeks of training. . . .

"As you know, Schine, Cohn (and, subtly, Joe McCarthy, too) have been struggling insistently to get Schine a New York City assignment. They have gone so far as to say that the Camp Gordon assignment is absolutely unacceptable because of the distance from New York it will take him."

So Adams summed up the alternatives. First, they could offer to cancel Schine's proposed assignment for training as a criminal investigator and thus keep him at Fort Dix for the second eight weeks of basic infantry training—in effect, keep him near New York. "If this alternative is accepted," Adams emphasized, "it will have to be made crystal clear that chances are 99 to 1 that Schine will be ordered overseas as an infantry replacement in April."

Second, Stevens and Adams could tell McCarthy that "Schine must go on to the school at Camp Gordon and then take his chances on assignment at [its] conclusion. . . . From Schine's point of view," Adams continued, "the advantages to this type of duty are many: he would become a Criminal Investigations Division Agent (CID). As a CID agent, wherever he is stationed he would pass as a civilian, would wear civilian clothes, would usually eat in officers' messes if he were on post, and would have a freedom of movement which is completely denied the average enlisted man. Additionally, chances of assignment in or near a large metropolitan area (perhaps even in New York) are much enhanced because of the concentration of CID in our larger areas.

"Additionally, if he goes overseas, to Tokyo, Vienna, Paris or Frankfort, he would be able to live as a civilian so long as he discharged his duties satisfactorily. And with his private income, off duty he probably would live quite happily and handsomely." He could live as a man boasting the world's largest collection of cigars.

Of course, Adams observed, "I do not believe that this will satisfy the McCarthy group (Cohn particularly) because it leaves in abeyance the location of Schine's duties subsequent to his basic, but I believe that we have to face up to it this week and tell them that we just refuse to intercede in the manner they propose.

"The best thing about the foregoing solution is that it has been done as a result of scientific testing and absolutely without interference from outside or from within the Army. I am satisfied that the newspaper men who have been most critical of McCarthy and of the Army-Schine relationship will believe me (they are friends of mine) when I assure them that this has been done honestly."

The Secretary and Counsel of the Army would play it straight. Their honesty, they thought, would convince the skeptics.

Meanwhile, far to the south, in sunny Key Biscayne, Florida, Richard Nixon, the Vice President of the United States, was enjoying a brief holiday. He had brought with him a couple of longtime friends from Senate days, Deputy Attorney General Bill Rogers and Joe McCarthy.

Nixon and Rogers, as political figures of long experience, had an ulterior purpose. They wanted to patch up differences and close the unseemly divisions within the Republican ranks. They reasoned with Joe: "This is your Administration." They urged him to diversify—ease up a bit on the Army, move into some new areas of investigation.

And sitting there in the sunshine, a drink in his hand, Joe seemed to agree with them—seemed to give them reason to hope that in the New Year he would play on the team; be a good boy.

V

THE FRIED CHICKEN LUNCH

"Now that the McCarthy investigation of Fort Monmouth seems to have abated somewhat," John Adams wrote his friend Deputy Attorney General Bill Rogers on January 7, 1954, "wouldn't the time be propitious to attempt to get promulgated the new Executive Order with reference to loyalty programs? . . . Fred Seaton indicated to me yesterday that he was going to talk about it in the White House because he feels that it would be better to attempt to get something done now, rather than when the pressure is on. . . ."

For the moment, the McCarthy theater was quiet. The country was looking elsewhere, at other problems, other diversions. The New Year's Day *New York Times,* for example, featured: a photo of Adlai Stevenson trying out a shotgun on his Illinois farm; a declaration by Senate Minority Leader Lyndon Johnson opposing those Democrats who urged an all-out partisan fight against the Eisenhower administration (". . . we will be ready to fight, and plenty, when and if the occasion comes for it"); advertisements for the Broadway shows *Dial M for Murder* with Maurice Evans, *Kind Sir* with Mary Martin and Charles Boyer, *Tea and Sympathy* with Deborah Kerr, and *The King and I* with Yul Brynner; the announcement that the Supreme Court would view two movies: *M,* banned in Ohio, and *La Ronde,* banned in New York; and James Reston's predictions for 1954—less tension abroad, more economic tension at home, no war and no peace, no depression and no full employment, and the likelihood that Eisenhower would get most of his legislative program passed by the Congress, still under Republican control. "Americans are singing a tune called 'Rags to Riches,'" the year's first issue of *Newsweek* summarized, "learning a British dance named 'The Creep,' reading *Lord Vanity, The Power of Positive Thinking,* and *Life Is Worth Living,* playing a game called Scrabble, living better, eating more, yet probably worrying more than ever before." That week CBS would broadcast Bing Crosby's first TV show, with Jack Benny.

But many problems loomed at home and abroad: a continuing crisis in the city of Trieste, under claims by both Italy and Yugoslavia, which threatened World War III; a Communist beachhead in Guatemala; a failure in Western Europe to agree on a means for its defense against possible Soviet attack; and a losing war in France's Indochina empire outpost.

In his State of the Union Message on January 7, Eisenhower outlined his most sweeping legislative program ever, including proposals for the building of a Saint Lawrence Seaway, tax reform, a new agricultural policy, an amendment to the Taft-Hartley Labor-Management Act, an extension of Social Security, a new health insurance program, provisions for more federal housing, and statehood for Hawaii. The next day former President Harry Truman would hail Eisenhower's "New Deal" proposals.

"Under the standard established for the new employee security program," Eisenhower declared to the joint session of Congress, "more than 2200 employees have been separated from the federal government." And he announced that he would call for additional measures to preserve internal security. These measures would include "immunity bath" legislation, which would compel a witness to give self-incriminating testimony in return for a grant of immunity. When the cabinet had discussed such a proposal on December 15, the Vice President pointed out that although liberals would object to the new rule, Canada and Britain both had similar laws. And the Attorney General added that the distinguished Supreme Court Justice Benjamin Cardozo had favored it.

Over in the Pentagon the Secretary of the Army doubtless enjoyed contemplating this picture. But by Friday, January 8, his attention was forcefully drawn back to G. David Schine. At twelve thirty-seven Stevens returned a call from Fred Seaton.

"Based on [John Adams's] conversation with me last night," Seaton said, "I told him, for whatever my judgment was worth, I was afraid we would get our neck in the noose if that Shine boy was sent to a special training course for investigation. Now John assures me that the boy has the qualifications and that the IBM cards fell that way; but I told John that because of charges that had already been made . . . by some of the columnists that Schine was the beneficiary of a deal with the Army, which I am sure you didn't make, but that when he was taken out of this basic training for eight weeks and sent to the other course, we never would be able to prove there was not a deal."

Stevens, however, was determined to proceed wide-eyed, to play it straight. "Since it came the way the cards fell," he countered, "we would be in an equally bad situation if we tried to change the rules in the middle of the game with a guy who already knows, with his classmates, what schools they will be sent to. . . . I was utterly amazed when the cards fell the way they did. . . . I wouldn't want to do anything for Mr. Schine. On the other hand, neither do I think it would be prudent to discriminate against him . . . , particularly being of the faith . . . that he is."

Seaton persisted: "I told John that I didn't believe that Schine should be kicked around. He is still an American boy. I don't want to have this be something to make you angry, but are you certain that the boy's record in the service stands up, that somebody didn't slip a gear on those cards?"

Stevens became almost indignant: "I have no more reason to doubt what the Army would tell me on a thing like that than when they tell me how many troops they have in Korea. I know the commanding general at Fort Dix very well. . . . General Ryan wouldn't any more be a party to a deal than I would."

To Stevens, the decision had already been made. But Seaton demurred: "When [Adams] talked to me . . . , I didn't understand from him . . . that it was yet an accomplished fact."

"It has been accomplished as far as I know," Stevens replied. "In other words, Schine has been advised that he will be relieved there as of the end of the eighth week, and he will be sent to this school . . . and if you now went back and said, 'This has been changed and you can't do it,' there really would be some talk. I am letting the chips fall the way they may. I know the winds are going to blow, Fred, and I don't relish it, and I don't know what I am going to do about it."

"In my judgment, for whatever it is worth," Seaton diplomatically replied, "if this thing has to go through, I think it is probably very smart to face up to it because you can't hide it. A kid like that is probably being watched by 20 different informers. . . . He is, of course, sort of a Dreyfus in reverse. . . ."

"You're damned if you do, and damned if you don't," Stevens said. "I personally was sorry that the cards fell the way they did;

but now that they have fallen that way, I don't know how to change them. . . ."

Seaton continued to scrutinize the implications: "The unfortunate point is that, through no fault of your own, I am afraid this will turn out to be an unfortunate assignment not only for the Army but for Senator McCarthy and the White House because of what has taken place between the President and the Senator. I, again, am not recommending that this kid be given a dirty deal, but I am a half-hearted second because how the hell you explain it, I don't know."

"Of course, the kid was taken at the very last minute before he would have been ineligible for age," Stevens said. "He is 26, you know. My guess would be that if he hadn't been working for Mc-Carthy, he probably never would have been drafted. . . . I knew this was a hot potato the moment I first heard about it, but now the way the thing has worked, I don't know what I could do at this moment other than to let the thing go the way it is. . . ."

Seaton had an idea: "Another thing you might want to consider— you might want to consider looking into this thing yourself. You say you have all the confidence in the Commanding General, and you should have, but it might be a good thing to be able to say that you have looked into this thing yourself, and that you are sure of the facts." And he added, characteristically: "I am not sure of them."

"I think that is very good, Fred," Stevens concurred. "I will be guided accordingly, and I will talk with you further when the storm develops. I have been telling Adams right along that this one is going to be hotter than a firecracker. . . ."

Whatever Stevens's trouble, he continued to exculpate McCarthy. The "Fort Monmouth thing," he told New Jersey Republican Senator H. Alexander Smith on January 12, "has kind of cooled down."

"Is Joe behaving?" Smith asked.

"I would say so. I have never had any trouble myself at all with Joe. His general counsel there is not the easiest fellow to deal with. I guess you know Roy Cohn."

"Yes," Smith said. "He is terrible."

"Joe has been reasonable all the way through," Stevens concluded.

McCarthy had indeed. "I want to thank you first of all for that marvelous cheese," Stevens told the junior Senator from the Dairy State a couple of days later. "Joe, I am going to the Far East on Sunday, and I would like, if you can, to have you work me in somewhere on your schedule. . . . I would like to have a little visit. . . .

[Would it] be in or out of order to buy you a cocktail that you might name?"

"I would favor that very much. . . . Why don't you drop over here about 5:00 and we will go across the street and have a drink."

They met that afternoon at the Carroll Arms. No one wrote down what they said. Three days later, on Sunday, January 17, Stevens left for the Far Pacific. And two days later the enemy struck.

On Tuesday, January 19, Frank Carr of the McCarthy committee phoned John Adams: By two o'clock that same afternoon, he said, he wanted five people—all members of the Army loyalty boards—brought before Senator McCarthy for interrogation. Adams protested: Stevens had left for the Orient only two days before, and it was unfair to make such a demand with the Secretary out of town. This request, Carr answered, came to him from Senator McCarthy. And, Adams wrote in a memorandum for the record, Carr "inferred . . . that Senator McCarthy was generated by urgings from Roy Cohn, who was very angry . . . about the assignment status of David Schine."

At two that afternoon Adams went to see McCarthy to try to negotiate a withdrawal of the request. McCarthy would not budge. He'd been negotiating with the Army long enough, he said, and he was no longer willing that the Army refuse to let members of Hearing Boards, Screening Boards, or Appeals or Review Boards appear before his committee. He told Adams he would give him until Friday, January 22, to find a means to produce those witnesses. If by that date the Army still resisted, he would have his staff issue subpoenas for five of them—one doing duty in Europe, a second living in North Carolina, and three in Washington. Suddenly, as an afterthought, he told Adams that he wanted to interrogate the board members not only on their participation in the loyalty program but also on alleged graft and misconduct. He would not let them be accompanied by counsel representing the Army. And if he were not satisfied with their reasons for refusing to answer loyalty program questions, he would have them cited by the Senate for contempt.

John Adams now had an ultimatum—a 2½ day ultimatum. He called for help across the river. "[McCarthy] was friendly but very firm" Adams wrote Rogers, sending along a copy of his memorandum for the record of the meeting. "He is going to find a means to interrogate our Loyalty-Security Appeals Board members, come what may . . . ; I do feel that I could not succeed in bending him on this matter. It may be that others would have better luck, particularly if he became aware of the fact that the collision would be government-wide, and would be backed by the Attorney General and the President."

Adams himself wanted a meeting with Attorney General Brownell. Rogers agreed to set it up. Meanwhile, he suggested, Adams should go see John McClellan of Arkansas, the McCarthy's subcommittee's ranking Democrat. McClellan had joined the other Democrats in walking off the committee during the J. B. Matthews ("Reds in Our Churches") tangle back in July. Adams went to McClellan's office at 6 P.M. the next day. For a half hour he laid out the whole story— the Monmouth problem, the Cohn-Schine problem, the loyalty board subpoena problem. McClellan listened. And he played it cagey. Put everything in writing, the wily, respected Establishment politician told the young lawyer, before I'll consider any of it.

Late in the afternoon the next day, January 21, Adams drove across the Potomac for his meeting in the office of Attorney General Herbert Brownell. There, to his complete surprise, he found an impressive group assembled.

Herbert Brownell himself was a politician, razor-sharp and long-experienced. But Brownell was also a lawyer—a Nebraska-born barefoot boy who'd gone to Wall Street and risen to the top. Now, as Attorney General of the United States, Brownell saw himself in a legal role. "I didn't try to act as an assistant president, to explain the administration's views," he observed years later in an interview. "I had responsibility for the legal area. In that area, I was supposed to take initiatives. And if I made a mistake, I could be fired. That's the way government should be run." He did of course have his own private view of McCarthy: "I hated him. We never had a good relationship of any sort." But he'd stayed out of the McCarthy problem. He knew "the President didn't want cabinet officers getting into one another's fields."

But on January 21, 1954, Brownell got in, once and for all. He did so partly because the McCarthy problem had become a problem in constitutional law—in the relationship between the executive and legislative branches; and partly because he doubted the legal horsepower of John Adams, a man who, Brownell said many years later, "didn't see the implications of what he was doing." Brownell belonged to that group which would "eventually," in his words, "take the McCarthy issue and strategy away from the Army people."

A second participant in the meeting, Brownell's Deputy Attorney

General, William Pierce Rogers, shared his boss's view that the Army didn't have the guns for this battle. Bob Stevens, to Rogers, was the salt of the earth but not very smart. John Adams, whom Rogers had known on the Hill, was a nice fellow but without an extensive background in the practice of law. Rogers himself had come up over a tough route. After getting his law degree from Cornell in 1937, he'd gone to gangbuster Tom Dewey in New York and, with thousands of people applying for a handful of jobs, offered to work for Dewey for nothing. "Why?" Dewey asked. "Because if you give me a job," Rogers replied, "everybody will know I'm smart, honorable, and hardworking." So Dewey hired him as an Assistant District Attorney for New York County. After this stint Rogers spent four years in the Navy. Then he went to Washington, first as Chief Counsel for the Senate War Investigating Committee (the old Truman committee) and then as Chief Counsel for the Senate Investigations Subcommittee of the Committee on Executive Expenditures—the predecessor of the McCarthy subcommittee, and the job that Roy Cohn now held. In these jobs Rogers took part in investigations of corruption in the administration—investigations which eventually sent Truman's Appointments Secretary Mathew Connelly and Truman's Assistant Attorney General in charge of the Tax Division, T. Lamar Caudle, to jail. Rogers also got into the subject of Communists in the federal government, hearing testimony from Elizabeth Bentley, focusing on William Remington (the Commerce official she accused of subversion), and helping his committee establish a reputation for fairness and accuracy that contrasted sharply with the buccaneering barnstorming tactics of the House Un-American Activities Committee under the Chairmanship of J. Parnell Thomas. Throughout, Rogers believed in the genuineness of the national security problem—in the threat posed by Communist infiltration into the government. To him, as to Chip Bohlen of the State Department, the tragedy of McCarthyism lay not merely in the fact that it hurt people but also in the fact that it made any form of anticommunism appear disreputable.

Personally, Rogers always liked Joe (in contrast to Roy Cohn, whom Rogers saw as an unfortunate influence on his boss, and whom, after one particularly difficult phone conversation, Rogers refused to communicate with except in writing). Rogers and McCarthy had first met when both served on the investigations subcommittee, and the General Counsel found McCarthy an attractive Irishman, engaging, likable, and capable of charming waiters and customers alike—a man with "a lot of malarky" and appeal. ("Who's that girl?" McCarthy whispered to Rogers one day during a hearing as a new committee staff member entered the room. "Her name is Jean Kerr," Rogers replied; she later became Mrs. McCarthy.) The two men got along fine even though McCarthy didn't like the committee's strictures: he'd leak things to the press ("You couldn't trust either him or Karl Mundt," Rogers observed years later). McCarthy just couldn't help leaking, despite the fact that under the committee's rules all members had to stand up and swear on the Bible, "I will not leak . . ."

When the Tydings Committee in 1950 undertook to investigate McCarthy's Communists-in-government charges, McCarthy asked Rogers, by then in private practice, to represent him and help him out: "I don't have much basis for the accusations I've made," he told him. Rogers refused. But after McCarthy had engineered Tydings's defeat in the 1950 election, Rogers pleaded with him: "Joe, you've been irresponsible. You have a lot of charm and a lot of power. Why don't you change your ways?"

McCarthy agreed—he would always agree: "Bill, you're right. I'll be different from now on."

It was thus that in 1953, as Deputy Attorney General, Rogers (one of the few men in the administration with experience on the Senate side of the Hill and, especially, experience with McCarthy) became a go-between. Brownell kept his distance. With Nixon down at Key Biscayne Rogers once again extracted a pledge of reform from McCarthy. But this pledge, like all the others, would never last more than a few days, sometimes never more than a few hours.

"Joe, why did you lie to me?" Rogers would plead.

"Bill, you're right. I shouldn't lie. I won't lie any more. You have good judgment." Rogers could never trust his old friend.

Rogers would always urge the President not to attack McCarthy. To Rogers, the man who had done more than anyone else to build McCarthy up was Harry Truman, who had carried on a running battle with the Senator in the headlines for three long years and left him stronger at the end than at the start. The only way to bring McCarthy down, Rogers felt, was to let him self-destruct. McCarthy, Rogers realized, always preferred an impediment to an olive branch: out of an impediment he could make something. At the same time, Rogers also advocated trying to undermine and hurt McCarthy in every way possible. He had gladly participated in the waylaying of the Senator, with Richard Nixon, in order to give Eisenhower's denunciation of J. B. Matthews a chance to get onto the news ticker ahead of McCarthy's announcement of Matthews's firing. And he gladly worked hand in glove with John Adams on strategy.

A third man in the January 21 meeting in Brownell's office was Henry Cabot Lodge, Jr. He held Cabinet rank as the United States Ambassador to the United Nations. But he joined the meeting not in this capacity but under another that Eisenhower had given him, that of a special advisor to the President on political strategy. A tall, handsome, articulate, aggressive Brahmin from Boston and Harvard College, a former newspaperman and popular Senator from Massachusetts until his upset defeat by Jack Kennedy in the 1952 election, Cabot Lodge had no respect whatsoever for McCarthy, or indeed for the far right in the Republican party. Lodge as much as anyone else had helped persuade Eisenhower to run for office; and he as much as anyone else had become a symbol of the resurgence of the 1912 Bull Moose Republicans, determined not to be done in by the conservatives in the party. He was a liberal. He saw McCarthy as a threat. He resented the Senator's savaging the careers of such public servants as John Carter Vincent and John Stewart Service. But like Rogers, he was no soft-liner on subversion. Like Rogers, Lodge believed a small number of Communists had in fact penetrated the federal government during the war and been blanketed into permanent jobs afterward. When he took on the U.N. job in January 1953, he had ordered full FBI investigation of all employees of the U.S. Mission. Ten months later he was appalled that not one senior advisor had yet been cleared, and he had kept pushing Brownell to speed up the process. And like Rogers, finally, Lodge consistently urged against an Eisenhower-McCarthy confrontation, which could only equalize the two men, giving them parallel front-page news columns.

A fourth participant in the meeting in Brownell's office—Eisenhower's Chief of Staff, Sherman Adams—also detested McCarthy. Like Lodge, Adams also became a target of reactionaries on the Republican right. And as assistant to the President, Sherman Adams wielded great power. Like another leading Eisenhower lieutenant, Press Secretary Jim Hagerty, Adams had missed the searing White House debates in early December. And like Hagerty—but unlike C. D. Jackson—Adams used his great power to try to establish some kind of middle ground; he tried to respond to Eisenhower's wishes rather than to the flarings of his own liberal conscience. He thus stood between a liberal like Jackson and the fifth participant in the January 21 meeting, Gerald Morgan, who in the December debates had identified the enemy not as McCarthy but as the Democrats, and who, like his boss Jerry Persons, always tried to go the last mile toward accommodation, "spending a lot of time" Morgan once told me, "trying to calm down Joe."

In retrospect, this crucial January 21 meeting at the Justice Department of these six men—Brownell, Rogers, Cabot Lodge, Sherman Adams, Jerry Morgan, and John Adams—became many things. To Roy Cohn it became the place where a club was fashioned to force Cohn's resignation as committee counsel. To Dwight Eisenhower, as we worked on his memoir *Mandate for Change*, it became one of the nitty-gritty too-detailed particularizations of the whole McCarthy episode, and therefore something to be eliminated completely from Eisenhower's book. To Sherman Adams it became the forum that triggered the Army's bill of particulars against McCarthy and thus led to the hearings and thus to McCarthy's downfall. But the most accurate description of the meeting—the only one written soon after the event—comes from John Adams himself, in a memordandum for the record which he dictated on February 12.

The meeting, Adams said, began at four o'clock. Brownell at once turned it over to Adams, who "described in detail the running fight we had had with the McCarthy staff on the subject of interrogating Loyalty Board members over the past few months as a result of the Fort Monmouth investigation." At Rogers's request, Adams pointed out how, "in each instance where McCarthy made a demand on us for loyalty board members, it was almost immediately preceded by a flareup between us and Roy Cohn over the New York assignment requests for David Schine."

In the course of the meeting, Brownell agreed that the success of the loyalty program required that board members be protected from the dangers inherent in congressional review of their actions. In this particular instance, however, Brownell said that he felt that inasmuch as McCarthy wanted to question the loyalty board members about fraud and misconduct, "he had effectively cornered us, and, if McCarthy did issue subpoenas, we probably would have to permit the individuals to respond, although we could instruct them to refuse to answer any question [on] their participation in the loyalty program."

Brownell agreed to take Adams's suggested draft reply to McCarthy in defiance of the Senator's ultimatum and to have the Justice Department lawyers rewrite it, turning it into a state document "so that [if] a blanket refusal to respond to subpoena had to be given to

McCarthy, we would have a document which cited historic prece-dent in some detail." Thus a long fuse was laid.

Finally the conferees agreed "that it would be better to attempt not to collide with McCarthy at this time." Instead they would go to the other Republican members of the committee, "pointing out to them our recent experience, and emphasizing the abuse we had re-ceived on the matter of Private Schine." In the margin of one of his copies of this memorandum, Adams penned in later: "We should surround McCarthy—" i.e., get to the other Republican senators on his committee.

To this end, when the meeting broke up at five-thirty, it was agreed that Morgan and John Adams would interview Everett Dirk-sen of Illinois. They did so that very evening at six o'clock for about twenty minutes. (After delivering Morgan back to the White House, Adams's sergeant-driver from the Pentagon pool reminded Adams that he'd worked through dinner and demanded supper money.) The next morning at eleven forty-five Adams talked to Karl Mundt of South Dakota for a half hour. John Adams's Deputy, Lewis Berry, talked with Charles Potter of Michigan on the evening of January 21, and at noon on Friday, January 22, Rogers spoke to Potter in greater detail. At two that afternoon, McCarthy met with the above Senators. And after the meeting McCarthy announced that he was backing down: it was not urgent that his committee hear loyalty board members; he would defer action until Stevens returned from the Far East.

That evening, January 22, John Adams met with McCarthy him-self, at McCarthy's request. At eight-thirty he rang the doorbell at McCarthy's apartment at the Woodner, far out Sixteenth Street near Rock Creek Park, and McCarthy welcomed him in. Joe and Jean were getting ready to move into an old three-story eight-room three-bath frame house on Third Street Northeast, on Capitol Hill, owned by Jean's mother, who lived in one half and rented the McCarthys the other half. The apartment was piled high with wedding and Christmas presents. As the two men talked, Jean McCarthy sat on the far side of the room writing letters or, Adams suspiciously sur-mised, taking notes.

Adams had hardly entered the room when the phone rang. George Sokolsky, the right-wing columnist, was calling long-distance. Joe chatted with him a few minutes, then told him that Adams was right there, and he might as well talk to him directly. Adams took the phone, and Sokolsky at once began grilling him on the reason for the "flareup" between Adams and Cohn. Adams denied any flareup. Sokolsky then went into an interrogation on the reason for "difficulty" over an assignment for Private Schine. Adams replied that the Army had never changed from its original position—that Schine would be treated exactly the same as any other enlisted man, no better and no worse. Before long Adams decided he should probably not talk to Sokolsky any further; who knows who is listening with him on the other end of the line, or why he's asking these questions, he reasoned.

After Sokolsky hung up, McCarthy said he didn't see why the Army couldn't give Schine "some obscure assignment in New York and forget about it." Three times in the evening he tried to extract a commitment from Adams on this. The Army, McCarthy said, was "walking into large scale 'vendetta' attacks [by] Cohn, and . . . even if Cohn resigned or was fired from the Committee staff (which [McCarthy] inferred was a distinct possibility because of opposition from other committee members) [Cohn] would carry on his campaign of vilification against the Army thereafter from outside Washington." Cohn, McCarthy went on, might resign over this issue. Adams said he couldn't see what worry that was of McCarthy's; he'd got along without Cohn for years.

McCarthy dropped his voice: "The walls," he said, "have ears, and maybe my room is tapped." He had to be very careful about how Cohn left the committee, if he ever did, McCarthy confided, "because [I] might be accused of being anti-Semitic." He said he couldn't understand why the Army worried about where it sent Schine—"useless, no good, just a miserable little Jew, who will never be of any help to [the] Army wherever assigned."

McCarthy tried intimidation, suggesting that Cohn had "very powerful connections with various of the . . . 'right wing' newspaper elements including Sokolsky [and syndicated columnist Westbrook] Pegler . . . and that he would begin getting those people to publish articles alleging great favoritism which the Army had shown in numerous other cases." "I know of no such favoritism," Adams replied. The Army, he said, was accustomed to being criticized and certainly had no objection to being attacked merely for discharging its obligations to Private Schine and to all other draftees.

Once or twice during the evening McCarthy cited what he called the "original agreement" on Schine—a promise which Cohn says was given to him by Stevens that after sixteen weeks of basic, Schine would be assigned to the New York area. Adams categorically denied any such agreement. Schine, he said, would be "handled according to the standard workings of the system[;] there would be no interference and no special assigning."

Next, McCarthy tried flattery. He praised Adams for his integrity in refusing to convey one particular Army double-crossing decision to the committee. Adams bridled: he had never, he said, been anything but "an instrumentality of the Secretary of the Army . . . , and . . . there had never been anything even remotely resembling a 'doublecross.' . . ." McCarthy lauded Adams for his forbearance, instancing the explosive December 17 luncheon at Gasner's Restaurant in New York, which had ended with Cohn's car driving away and Adams standing in the middle of Park Avenue.

"I would not have blamed you that day," McCarthy said, "in view of the abuse Cohn heaped on you, had you walked out and refused ever to speak to him again."

But Adams refused to budge. McCarthy went on to other subjects. He reported the result of the meeting he'd had that afternoon with Dirksen, Potter, and Mundt. The committee Republicans, he said, had talked over the possibility of firing Cohn. They had also discussed the current investigation of the Army. Cohn, McCarthy told Adams, had "accidentally done the Army a great favor by interfering with the Army so much in its attempts to administer the enlistment of Private Schine that it was now necessary for the McCarthy committee to call off its investigation. . . . The committee's position had become untenable because of the accusations which could be made . . . that the committee was using its investigative powers . . . to get better treatment for Private Schine."

For him, McCarthy went on, the investigation of the Army had ended. "He must now," he added, "find a means of saving face . . . a means of not appearing before the press to be backing down on his ultimatum to the Army that we must produce our Appeals Board members for interrogation.

"For this reason," he said, "it was absolutely mandatory that he interrogate these Loyalty Board people." If he interrogated them, he went on, he would not interrogate them on the loyalty-security program. He had received allegations that some of these board members had been "corrupted by bribes [and] promises of promotion . . . if they would agree to make favorable findings [on] certain of the so-called 'accused Communists.' "

The two men had reached the crunch. Adams parried: Can't we

wait until Stevens comes back from the Far East? By that time, newspaper interest in the subject might abate and it might never become necessary for McCarthy to do the interrogations to save face. "At no time," Adams wrote, "did I make any sort of commitment . . . that the Army would in any way agree to the interrogation of [anyone who] participated in our loyalty security program."

It was now eleven-fifteen. The discussion had gone on nearly three hours. "McCarthy drank three highballs, Mrs. McCarthy had one drink, I was offered drinks during the evening, accepted no liquor, but drank about five cups of tea."

Adams dictated this long memorandum at eight o'clock the next morning. As he spoke, he was doing something he had not done before: he was consciously building a record. At the January 21 meeting in Brownell's office—the minutes of which John Adams did not write up until February 12, three weeks after the event, and at least one paragraph of which he revised as late as February 20—something had happened that at the moment John Adams did not even consider significant enough to include in his summary: Governor Sherman Adams, hearing of the long train of efforts by Cohn and McCarthy to jockey special favors for Schine, suggested to John Adams that he go back to his office and set down on paper a detailed chronology of all these attempted interventions. Thus was conceived that document that would become almost as famous as the Watergate tapes.

Adams collected not only all the contemporaneous records he could lay his hands on but added to them his recollections and his interpretations, colored and shaped by his lawyer's drive to win points in the debate he saw looming ahead, by his own emotions, and by his hindsight. Moreover, from now on each contemporaneous record he set down, starting with the account of the meeting in McCarthy's apartment, would be written with awareness that it would become another entry in the chronology, hooked on like a caboose. Adams's account, for example, of Frank Carr's January 19 phone call delivering McCarthy's ultimatum—an account that Adams did not write up until February 12—would contain an "inference" that the ultimatum flowed from Cohn's anger over Schine's plight.

Adams wasted no time in putting the record together. Even before he visited the McCarthys, he had phoned the office of the commanding general at Fort Dix requesting a full chronology of Private Schine's activities. Back it came at once.

On November 10, it revealed, Schine arrived at Fort Dix. On November 11, Carr and Cohn called on the Commanding General—Cornelius Ryan—and asked to see Schine at the reception station. The next day, November 12, a member of the committee called requesting Schine be given a weekend pass. November 13–15 Schine was away for the weekend. On November 17, Schine received a pass to visit with Joe and Jean McCarthy, Carr, and Cohn when Stevens's plane brought them to the nearby McGuire Air Force Base. On November 18, another McCarthy staff member, Thomas LaVenia, requested a pass for Schine until the beginning of his formal training on November 23. On November 19 Schine left Dix for another weekend.

The chronology continued into December: Schine on pass after duty hours to visit members of the committee in Trenton, Schine on pass after duty hours to go to New York City, Schine on pass over the weekend, Schine on pass for the Christmas holidays, Schine on pass over New Year's. The memo also toted up the approximate number of phone calls Schine received from members of the committee—16; the estimated numbers of visits to the post by committee associates—8; the number of weekdays off (after duty hours) before General Ryan called a halt to these—4. The memo concluded with the observation that despite all this time off, Private Schine did not get out of any scheduled training. Some of this story was already leaking out, with embellishments. In late January the *New York Post* reported that Fort Dix recruits, in press interviews, were complaining that Schine was living among them "like a visiting dignitary."

By February 3, Adams had finished his first pass at a chronology. This, the Army's first attempt to write the history of its relations with McCarthy, is a jumble, a loose collection of memoranda, some pulled out of Adams's files, some written by him in retrospection. To the history revealed by the contemporaneous documents, these memoranda now add new detail, dredged out of John Adams's inquiries and memory.

The memoranda in the chronology fall under thirteen Roman numerals.

I. Adams begins with a summary of the efforts to get Schine a direct commission: "In mid July-1953 in his office in the Senate Office Building, Senator McCarthy requested Major General Miles Reber, the Chief of Army Legislative Liaison, to attempt to get a direct commission for Mr. G. David Schine, a consultant to the Senate Permanent Subcommittee on Investigations on the basis of his education, business experience, and prior service in the U.S. Maritime Service. At that time, expeditious action was requested both by Senator McCarthy and by Mr. Roy Cohn, Chief Counsel of the Subcommittee, since it appeared that Schine might very shortly be inducted into the Army, by Selective Service.

"On 15 July 1953, Mr. Schine called the Office of the Chief of Legislative Liaison (OCLL) on the telephone and asked if he could come to the Pentagon that afternoon and 'hold up his hand.' After Mr. Schine was advised that it would be necessary to submit an application for a commission, he came to OCLL where he was assisted in completing the necessary application blanks. . . . On 23 July 1953 Mr. Schine's application for a commission had been processed through the Chief of Transportation and through the Provost Marshal General . . . and each had returned the application stating the applicant was not qualified. On 23 July the Adjutant General referred Mr. Schine's application . . . to the Commanding General, First Army, Governors Island, New York. . . . [He] processed Mr. Schine's application, determined that he was not qualified for appointment and so notified Mr. Schine by letter dated 30 July 1953.

"Throughout this period . . . both Senator McCarthy and Mr. Cohn telephoned OCLL numerous times to inquire as to the status of the application. About 1 August 1953, after it had become obvious that Schine would not be given a direct commission in the Army, Mr. Cohn requested OCLL to explore the possibility of obtaining a reserve commission for Schine in either the Air Force or the Navy. These explorations were undertaken, the results were negative and Mr. Cohn was so advised. . . ."

II. Next in the chronology comes Adams's recollection of an event in mid-October: "One day in New York, about 16 October 1953, Senator McCarthy became irritated with Schine. Schine had managed to get himself into practically every picture the newspaper men had taken, including pictures which were intended to include only Senator McCarthy and General [Kirke] Lawton of Fort Monmouth, or Senator McCarthy and General [George I.] Back [Chief Signal Officer], and numerous other group photographs. The subject had become a matter of amusement to most of the members of the staff, and with them I stood back from time to time and watched Schine in his efforts to be photographed. It was either on this day or the following day that Senator McCarthy spoke to me about it. Mrs. McCarthy was present. I do not remember whether it was in the hotel, or in a taxi, or in the subway. My recollection is that it was in the subway as we rode uptown one evening following the hearings.

". . . Senator McCarthy spoke out quite freely about his irritation over Schine. He told me that the individual is of absolutely no help to the committee, was interested in nothing but the photographers and getting his picture in the papers and that things had reached the point where he was a complete pest. McCarthy stated to me quite emphatically that he was anxious to see this individual drafted, and . . . he hoped . . . we would send him as far away as possible 'to get him out of my hair. . . . Send him wherever you can, as far away as possible. Korea is too close.' . . . I asked him if I could tell . . . the Secretary of the Army. I told him that I wished to because Mr. Stevens was quite concerned over the pressures which were being put on us by members of his staff to get Schine deferred, or to get him immediately assigned to New York if inducted. McCarthy repeated to me that he hoped I would tell it to Mr. Stevens, and soon . . .

"On the very next occasion when Mr. Stevens and Senator McCarthy were together when I was present . . . I brought up the subject again. . . . Senator McCarthy repeated to Secretary Stevens . . . the statements he had previously made to me in almost exactly the same words, and with considerable emphasis.

"On both of these occasions McCarthy particularly requested that Cohn not be made aware of his attitude on Schine."

III. In this section Adams again wrote a narrative out of recollection, of Schine's induction as a private: "The Selective Service system finally determined that Mr. Schine was to be inducted into the Army on 3 November 1953. During the middle part of October . . . a request was made by Mr. Cohn on Secretary Stevens that Private Schine be given 15 days after induction on temporary duty in New York for the purpose of concluding certain important committee work. To this Secretary Stevens agreed. . . . Almost immediately [after Schine's induction on November 3], it became obvious that members of the press were aware of the fact that Schine was supposed to have been inducted but was still around New York in a civilian status. Senator McCarthy thereupon decided to request that this temporary duty be cancelled. . . .

"In the first week of November, after Schine had been inducted, there were numerous conversations . . . when Cohn pointed out that it was necessary that the committee go to Fort Dix quite regularly to conclude certain work which Schine had been doing. Mr. Stevens at that time made one concession. He agreed that, if needed to complete pending committee work, Private Schine could be made available to the Committee on weekends after his training was concluded, and he stated further that if the Committee found it was necessary to consult with Schine during the week about committee matters, he would not object if they went down to Fort Dix and consulted with the soldier on post at the conclusion of the soldier's training in the evening, after first clearing with General Ryan. He also conceded that if the matter was of real importance and urgency, the soldier might be permitted to leave the post on an evening. . . .

"On 8 December General Ryan . . . called me on the telephone. He stated to me that the matter of the handling of Private Schine was completely out of hand, that the soldier was leaving the post nearly every night, that he had been seen in Trenton on business which was obviously social and in no way connected with Committee business, and he advised me that unless we objected he had intended immediately to terminate that activity altogether. I advised him that he could consider that the Secretary of the Army concurred in the action, and that from that moment forward . . . Private Schine was no longer available for Committee business during the evenings of weekdays. . . .

"On the first Friday following this decision . . . Private Schine became aware of the fact that his training would include Saturday morning duty. He apparently got hold of Mr. Cohn, and I had extensive telephone conversations with Cohn throughout that afternoon. These were long-distance calls from New York, all of them initiated by Cohn, one of them lasting an hour and fifteen minutes, and during the entire time I was subjected to a great deal of violent abuse on the fact that the Army had committed another doublecross. . . . The first doublecross, according to Cohn, was when we had not given a commission to Schine after promising it to him. The second doublecross, according to Cohn, was that we had not assigned him immediately to New York. [The Army] doublecrossed him, [he said,] on availability during evenings, and this requirement that he stay Saturday morning was another doublecross.

"The sustained violence of telephone abuse which I took on this occasion is hard to describe. The obscenities and vituperative remarks which Cohn used to describe the Secretary of the Army, the Army itself, and our treatment of McCarthy, Schine and Cohn, cannot be recorded or publicly repeated. The most consistent remark which he made was that the Army was 'requiring Schine to eat "obscenity"' because he worked for the McCarthy committee. He repeated this at least 30 times during this telephone conversation and at least a hundred times during the eight weeks during which we were discussing the Schine situation. . . ."

IV. Next Adams backtracked from December 11 to November 6, to give his recollections of the luncheon in the Pentagon office of Secretary Stevens to which he invited McCarthy, Carr, Cohn, and Adams and—after lunch—the new Army Chief of Staff, General Matthew Ridgway, the new G-2, General Trudeau, and the new Chief of Information, General G. C. Mudgett. "The entire luncheon was taken up with the discussion of means by which the continuing investigation of Fort Monmouth could be brought to a close. Mr. Stevens attempted to point out to McCarthy that the investigation was doing great damage to the Army, that its continuation was having the effect of injuring morale at Fort Monmouth, and that the Army and the FBI jointly were engaged in a large-scale investigation of allegations of Communism at Fort Monmouth and had been for many months." McCarthy agreed, Adams went on, that he would attempt to divert the course of the hearings from Monmouth and the Army.

"Schine's name came up here on two or three occasions, usually raised by Cohn, asking . . . when we would settle on the New York assignment. . . . McCarthy for the first time joined with Cohn in urging us to give Schine a New York assignment. He proposed that we send Schine to New York with an assignment to study and report to the Secretary on the evidence of pro-Red leanings in the West Point textbooks. I did not take McCarthy seriously because he privately continued to tell me that he wished to be rid of Schine."

Adams then moves back to October—to conversations he had with Cohn during the two weeks that preceded Schine's November 3 induction:

"It was on these occasions prior to the Pentagon luncheon that I first referred to the national interest and tried to persuade Cohn that I was fifteen years older than he and could speak from a wealth of experience as a Senate employee and in the Pentagon on this very subject. Cohn replied that if national interest was what we wanted, he'd give us a little and then proceeded to outline how they would expose the Army in its worst light and show the country how shabbily it is being run. He made reference to some officers and civil servants by name whom he said they would ruin," including the hapless General Partridge.

V. Adams now jumped forward from October and November to December 8, to describe a private talk he'd had with McCarthy about Schine: "During the morning of 8 December while the [Fort Monmouth] hearings were in progress, Cohn continued to press me relentlessly with reference to Schine and Schine's assignment. Again on this occasion I attempted to point out to Cohn that the Army had a responsibility to some 300,000 other men who were being drafted annually. . . . On the following day Cohn's pressure became so intense that at the conclusion of the morning hearing I decided that it would be necessary for me to go and see Senator McCarthy. . . . At about 12:30 I followed Senator McCarthy to his office and asked if I could speak to him privately. I . . . told him first that the Army had carefully avoided telling Cohn that he, McCarthy, wanted Schine out of the way. . . . I then asked McCarthy if it would not be possible for him to some way get Cohn to quit abusing me, General Ryan, the people at Fort Dix, and the Army generally about Schine's assignment.

"Senator McCarthy promised that he would write the Army a letter in which he would state that the Committee had no further interest in Schine and that he hoped that Schine would be treated exactly as all other soldiers are. . . . I returned to the Pentagon, and in the middle of the afternoon, I received a telephone call from Cohn. He attacked me with unusual violence even for Cohn, and told me that he would teach me what it means to go over his head. . . . 'That's not a threat, that's a promise.'

"Later in the afternoon . . . Secretary Stevens advised me that he had received a call from Senator McCarthy inviting him to lunch the following day." The next morning, December 10, McCarthy invited Adams to join them, and at one o'clock the three of them, plus Frank Carr, sat down in the dining room of the Carroll Arms. The whole luncheon was taken up with McCarthy's discussion of the possibility of an immediate New York assignment for Schine. In response, "Stevens stated specifically and categorically that there was nothing to which he would agree other than that Private Schine must complete his sixteen weeks of training before anything else could be even considered [and] that he was not even willing to discuss Private Schine until he had assurances from Senator McCarthy that Schine and Cohn would accept that as a requirement instead of insisting that Schine be immediately transferred to

New York. If that sort of acceptance were forthcoming . . . Stevens stated that at some other day he would be willing to talk about the future. Not even in the wildest flight of fancy," Adams interpolates, "could his statement be interpreted as an assurance that the acceptance of this 16 weeks would mean that there would be an assignment in New York. . . ."

In a snide aside to Stevens and Adams, McCarthy said that while he had no proof, he was "quite sure that Schine paid all of Cohn's expenses in addition to certain fees, which he thought might explain Cohn's interest in Schine." Adams ends the memorandum laconically: "The luncheon lasted about two hours, the bill was about $12.00; I paid it."

VI. Adams now jumps ahead a week, to December 17 and the lunch at New York's Gasner's Restaurant:

"On the morning of 17 December, when I entered the United States Court House [in New York's Foley Square] at about 10:30 A.M. I met Senator McCarthy, also entering the building. He advised me that, on the previous evening he had attempted to telephone to tell me that he had learned of the extent of his staff's interference with the Commanding General at Fort Dix with reference to Schine, and that he wished to instruct me thereafter to discontinue anything which was being done in the Committee's behalf [for] Schine. And he wished to tell me that he was advising the staff that they must thereafter do nothing with reference to Schine."

The hearing lasted about two hours. Afterward a group went to nearby Gasner's for lunch: McCarthy, Carr, Cohn, and Adams, along with Patricia Kennedy—Jack and Bob's sister—and her escort, "a movie actor named Peter Lawford." After lunch Adams suggested they discuss Schine; he wanted to get McCarthy on record in front of Carr and Cohn. "This caused the discussion to get rather heated and Cohn restated all of the arguments which he had stated so many times before. . . . Instead of holding his position against Cohn, as McCarthy had assured me he would, he began to withdraw." About this time Lawford and Miss Kennedy left, and McCarthy, Carr, Cohn and Adams stayed at the table.

They argued for about two hours, getting more and more violent all the time. "Cohn was particularly abusive both to me, to the Army, to Secretary Stevens, and to McCarthy. The more he abused Senator McCarthy, the more McCarthy receded from the position he had taken" at 10:30 that morning.

Adams had to catch a train for Washington. Cohn drove his car uptown, McCarthy sat beside him, and Carr and Adams rode in the rear. Cohn continued to rail. McCarthy began suggesting "that certainly the Secretary of the Army ought to be able to find a way to assign Schine in New York at once. . . . During all of this time Cohn's abuse had consisted of a great many obscene insults, and he repeated the one which he had cast at me . . . at least a hundred times . . . that Secretary Stevens was deliberately 'trying to make Schine eat *obscenity* at Fort Dix.' When we got to 34th Street [and Park Avenue], Cohn was unable to make a left turn and was required to go under the tunnel, which put us out at 46th Street and Park Avenue. I objected to Cohn that I would miss the train if we continued to go up Park Avenue. . . . In another fit of violence he stopped the car and said, 'Get out and get to the station however you wish.'

"I got out of the car in the center of about five lanes of Park Avenue traffic. . . ."

VII. Adams now recalled the history of Schine's possible assignment to the Provost Marshal General School for training as a criminal investigator:

"During the early part of December I consulted with the Deputy Adjutant General, General Kline. I advised him that I wished to know what assignment was scheduled for Private Schine. I emphasized that I did not wish to interfere with it, nor did the Secretary. . . ." General Kline said that at the conclusion of his eight weeks' basic at Fort Dix, Schine would probably be transferred to the Provost Marshal General School and trained as an investigator in a course running another eight weeks."

Adams went to see Stevens. "This might be construed by the press," Adams said, "and by enemies of McCarthy as interference on our part, but it was clearly the way the classification testing had come out. . . ."

On December 31, Adams phoned Cohn to tell him that he understood Schine would have eight weeks at Camp Gordon, Georgia, and then be eligible for reassignment. "Cohn repeatedly asked if it would be New York. I repeatedly told him that I did not know. . . . Cohn seemed eminently pleased with this interim assignment. . . ." He called Adams on January 11 and asked him detailed questions about Camp Gordon and the exact number of days Schine would be serving there. Would it be necessary for Schine to live on the post? Because the committee needed Schine regularly, whom should Cohn call for the purpose of "getting Schine off?"

Adams decided to phone the Provost Marshal General, General Maglin, to find out exactly what kind of school Schine would be going into. It turned out to be a call he wished he'd never made. General Maglin told him that "whoever in the Adjutant General's office had given me the information that Schine needed to stay only eight weeks at Camp Gordon had given me inaccurate information": The eight weeks at Gordon, he said, were merely the second eight weeks of Schine's basic training; Schine would have to finish those before he could qualify for training as a criminal investigator. If he did qualify for the CID school, he would then have to stay there another ten weeks—a grand total of nearly five months at Camp Gordon down in Georgia.

Adams immediately phoned Cohn about the snafu.

"He reacted with an explosive violence which exceeded all previous reactions. . . . During the midst of our discussion he hung up the telephone after telling me, " 'This is just another dirty stinking Army doublecross of the sort I have been getting from that doublecrosser Stevens all the time. I am sick of it, and I will not stand it any more.' "

Adams decided to recheck his information. He went this time to the Adjutant General, General Bergin. After some inquiries, Bergin told Adams he was sure Maglin was wrong—that Adams could call the McCarthy committee back and assure them Schine's duty at Camp Gordon would last only eight weeks. Adams did so. A day or so afterward (about January 13), Adams went up to the Hill and talked with Cohn and Carr. "Knowing full well that 90 percent of all our inductees get overseas duty . . . I had a conversation with Cohn which I remember exactly." In Adams's chronology memo, it reads as though it comes straight out of a transcript: "Roy, what will happen if Dave [Schine] gets an overseas assignment?"

"Stevens is through as Secretary of the Army."

"Oh come on now, Roy. Can that stuff. Really, what's going to happen if Schine gets an overseas assignment?"

"We'll wreck the Army. We've got enough stuff on the Army to have an investigation run indefinitely. We'll smear you all over every newspaper in the country. The Army will be ruined. Dave gets out of Camp Dix tomorrow. The day he's gone we're going to start in on [Commanding General] Ryan. . . . He'll be ruined before you know it for the lousy rotten unfair way he's let Dave be treated. We are not going to do it ourselves, but we've got another Committee interested in it. We are going to ruin him, and then we are going to wreck the Army if you pull a dirty, lousy stinking filthy [obscenity] doublecross like that. I wouldn't put it past that lousy doublecrossing Stevens."

John Adams went back to the Pentagon. He reported Cohn's threats to Stevens. He also confessed to having fouled up the information he'd given to Cohn and urged they go directly to McCarthy about it.

Stevens did what he always did: he at once set up a meeting with McCarthy at the Carroll Arms at five o'clock that afternoon. He also called yet another officer to check Adams's information—Major General Robert N. Young, the G-1 of the Army. Within an hour Young reported back with the Army's second reversal: General Bergin was wrong; General Maglin had been right the first time: Schine would have to go through eight more weeks of basic and then, if he qualified, take another ten or eleven weeks to become a criminal investigator.

The next morning, Friday, January 15, Stevens told Adams about his cocktail hour with McCarthy. The two of them had been joined almost immediately by one Al McCarthy (no relation, but a friend of Joe's), a Washington real estate man and songwriter. Al had stayed with them through the whole two hours of their conversation, frequently chipping in.

It was the same old conversation all over again: McCarthy trying to get a commitment for a New York assignment after Schine's tour at Gordon, Stevens insisting on playing by the rules. All of it, in Stevens's view, "completely amicable."

Stevens left for Korea on January 17. Cohn was vacationing in Florida. The next day Carr phoned Adams. "Did McCarthy tell you about his conversation with the Secretary?" Adams asked. Carr answered with a blank. So now it was up to Adams once again to break the news of the latest about-face in the Army's information: he had to tell Carr the full length of time Schine was going to have to put in at Gordon.

Ten minutes later the phone rang: it was Cohn, calling long distance from Boca Raton, beside himself with violence about this "new Army doublecross."

The next morning, Tuesday, January 19, Carr phoned Adams with McCarthy's demand that the committee interrogate members of the Army's Loyalty Security Appeals Board. "Carr made it quite clear that Roy had come back with blood in his eyes from Florida and that this was the beginning of war. . . ." Adams went up on the

Hill at two that afternoon. There he received McCarthy's ultimatum: It was necessary that the committee interrogate "these bastards who have been clearing Communists."

VIII. Adams now recalled, in two short paragraphs, an earlier crisis: the assigning of Schine to KP: "On 9 January I was at Amherst, Massachusetts, filling a speaking engagement at Amherst College when I received a long-distance call from Frank Carr." He'd been trying to reach Adams since the preceding evening, he said; it was now the middle of Saturday afternoon. Cohn, Carr reported, had been desperately trying to reach Adams from New York to get Adams to intervene with the Commanding General at Fort Dix: Schine was scheduled for KP the next day, Sunday.

"To gain time and . . . to avoid talking with Cohn," Adams wrote, "I told Carr that it was absolutely impossible for me to do anything from Amherst, and that I could not successfully deal with anybody at any Army installation unless I was at the Pentagon." As soon as Adams hung up he told the switchboard operator at Amherst's Lord Jeffrey Inn that if anybody called him long-distance from New York, the operator should say that he couldn't find Adams. Instantly the phone rang again. Somehow Cohn had got through the net. Adams said hello, heard Cohn's voice on the other end, and quickly downed the receiver. "I did not talk to him that day."

So there, February 2, 1954, stood eight new pieces in Adams's record of recollections. Among these he interspersed such contemporaneous documents as his briefing memo to Stevens of December 10, McCarthy's no-favors-for-Schine letter to Stevens of December 22, Adams's memo to Stevens of December 29 on Schine's possible entry into the Provost Marshal General School, Adams's memorandum for the record of his conference at McCarthy's apartment on the night of January 22, and the Fort Dix chronology of Schine's activities. In the weeks ahead Adams would add other diarylike documents to the record as events unfolded and he hastened to write them down. But in its present form, the Adams chronology was not only emotional in its remembrance of conflicts past; it was also spotty and incomplete.

It contained no trace of a record on several crucial meetings that would later come under sharp public scrutiny. It contained not one phone call monitored in Adams's office: when he entered his job, he had discontinued the monitoring practice of his predecessor. And it contained not one of the voluminous phone calls monitored in Stevens's office: all these still rested in the notebooks of Jack Lucas and the others in untranscribed Gregg shorthand. Adams knew of their existence, but he had no access to them.

When John Adams finished this chronology, he sent it first not to Governor Adams, who at the January 21 meeting in Brownell's office, had asked him to compile it, but to his closest acquaintance and working associate at that meeting, Deputy Attorney General Bill Rogers: "Pursuant our telephone conversation of today (and also as suggested by Sherman Adams last week) I forward herewith a copy of the full record of the Army's problems with the McCarthy committee over Private Schine. . . . This is the only copy which is leaving my possession."

As this red-hot sheaf of papers was covertly being hand-carried by special messenger across the Potomac to the Justice Department building on Constitution Avenue, a second inconsequential draftee in the U.S. Army suddenly found himself on page one—Major Irving Peress, an alleged pink dentist stationed at Camp Kilmer, New Jersey. Back in early January, Cohn had phoned Adams to let him know the Committee had derogatory information on a doctor or dentist—Cohn didn't know which—at Kilmer. Adams checked, found the physician was headed for discharge, and did nothing further. But on January 30, McCarthy, in executive session, had grilled Peress—still in the Army—on his Communist connections. Afterward the Senator had gone out and told a throng of reporters all the questions Peress had refused to answer. On February 1, Peress requested that his discharge take effect at once. That same day McCarthy wrote Stevens a letter, soon released to the press, respectfully "suggesting" the Army immediately start court-martial proceedings against the Major. The Army—in Stevens's absence—refused. The next day Peress received an honorable discharge. And McCarthy blew his stack. He flayed the Army for "highly improper" conduct.

At this precise moment the Secretary of the Army returned from the comparative calm of Korea. A special emissary flew to San Francisco to give him a full breakfast briefing on Peress after his arrival in the middle of the night. When he touched down in Washington, Stevens second-guessed the decision. No, he told reporters, he himself would not have let Peress go.

At two fifty-five on the afternoon of February 4, Adams was bringing Stevens up to date: "I was on the phone talking to Frank Carr about Major Peress, our Communist major. Joe is still hot under the collar. He wanted all sorts of investigations on it. I thought I would go to his house. . . ."

McCarthy refused to calm down. The next day Adams was writing to General Matthew Ridgway, Army Chief of Staff, for a full Inspector General's report on all the facts. Why, Adams wanted to know, had Peress been ordered on active duty on January 7, 1953, when it was known on October 28, 1952, that he had invoked constitutional privilege as a reason for failing to complete his loyalty certificate. Why did the Surgeon General's office promote Peress from captain to major on November 3, 1953, when it was known that as early as April 28, 1953 Peress was undergoing loyalty investigations? Who arranged for the cancellation of Peress' orders to duty in the Far East? In view of the derogatory information against Peress, when the Army decided to separate him, why did it let him complete twleve months of active service and give him the option of ninety days' notice before discharge? Was surveillance undertaken on Peress at Kilmer to find out whether he was participating in communist activities?

A frenzied and exhaustive investigation ensued. After many weeks, back came an elaborate chronology, bristling with names. It revealed that Peress, born in the Bronx in 1917, was now thirty-six. He'd become a dentist at NYU, and under the Doctors Draft Act of 1950 he had entered active duty in the Army as a captain on January 1, 1953 even though on October 28, 1952 in filling out forms he had claimed federal constitutional privilege in answering questions on his membership in Communist organizations. On March 13, 1953, the Army, responding to a problem in Peress's family, had revoked the orders that would have sent him overseas and had assigned him to dental duty at Camp Kilmer. By April 15, 1953, an investigation of his refusal to answer questions about his Communist associations had been completed, and on April 24 the Counter Intelligence Division of the First Army reported to both the Intelligence Division and the Office of the Surgeon General in Washington that sufficient evidence of subversive and disloyal tendencies existed to warrant Peress's removal from the service.

Months of paperwork and bureaucratic inertia followed. By August 25, Peress, completing yet another questionnaire, claimed federal constitutional privilege once again. Meanwhile, on June 29, the Congress had passed an amendment to the Doctors Draft Act that required the Army to reappoint all persons ordered to active duty under the Act to a rank commensurate with their professional education and experience. Accordingly, on October 23, Peress was promoted to major. Finally the two independent bureaucratic streams—promotional and subversive—came together, and on November 6 the Commanding General of the First Army wrote to the Vice Chief of Staff in Washington that Peress's promotion should be revoked if at all possible and that he should be separated from the service forthwith.

Two and a half months later Peress received notice of his release; he set the date for March 31. On January 30 he appeared before McCarthy. On February 1 he requested discharge at once, and McCarthy wrote his "court-martial Peress" letter to Stevens. To get Peress out the door soonest, the Army had decided to let the discharge be an honorable one. And in an eleventh-hour two-man huddle the night of February 1, in which the decision was made to rebuff McCarthy and let the honorable discharge go through the next day as planned, the civilian official approving that decision—Stevens being away—was John G. Adams.

The Pentagon was becoming a three-ring circus. While Peress held the central glare of attention for the moment, other acts swirled and danced in the half-light. McCarthy continued to probe a nefarious alleged War Department order dating back to 1944 that all files containing evidence of Communist membership be destroyed—an allegation Stevens effectively scuttled on February 16 by citing a letter written by Secretary of War Stimson in 1944 and testimony given by Assistant Secretary of War John McCloy in 1945. Frank Carr spent some time looking into the alarming possibility that the Army had hired the ever-suspect Ford Foundation to write up an orientation pamphlet on citizenship. The Fort Monmouth front produced letters from Senator Herbert Lehman of New York on suspended employees and scuttlebutt from the Hill that Joe McCarthy was continuing to claim that espionage was still going on there. Above all, the future of Private G. David Schine awaited resolution.

On February 5, John Adams took yet another phone call from columnist George Sokolsky. Schine, Sokolsky said, had applied to enter course 95 in the CID School at Camp Gordon, Georgia, a course which would start on February 17. It would be wise, Sokolsky said, for the Army to let him into this course and not make him go through his second eight weeks of basic training, which would take him past the course's starting day.

Adams talked to Stevens. Stevens refused to bend. And at two o'clock that afternoon Adams phoned General Young, Assistant Chief of Staff, G-1, and told him by no means to permit Private Schine to enter the February 17 school. Adams went even further; he told Young to give this instruction by word of mouth only: "I stressed the desirability that there be no written communications, that he handle it by telephone." The record was becoming a weapon. Don't make any replies to any inquiries about preferential treatment for Schine, Adams wrote the Adjutant General on February 10, without first coordinating with this office.

Two days later, February 12, Adams again talked with Sokolsky by phone. Had the Army, Sokolsky asked, cleared the way for Schine's entry into the course on February 17? Adams tried to dodge: assigning Schine to the school before he finished basic went counter to what Stevens had decided. Sokolsky held out some bait: If the Army would assign Schine to the school, "he would be able to move in on McCarthy and Cohn and persuade them to drop the investigations of the Army. . . ." Adams mentioned the Peress case. Sokolsky covered this too: "If you will arrange for this assignment, . . . I'll . . . get them to drop all this stuff they are planning for the Army." (A handwritten note, on Adams's memorandum for the record, reveals that Adams called Sokolsky long-distance to New York—"Pentagon records can prove"—and that they talked about 50 minutes. So Adams had yet another page for his chronology.)

On the morning of February 10, Stevens, at his own request, had gone to the White House to report to Eisenhower on his trip to the Far East. No contemporaneous record exists of their conversation, but one may surmise that in that half hour, Eisenhower gave Stevens some advice on the Peress problem. Six days later, February 16, Stevens wrote McCarthy a long confidential letter: "The developments of this case have made it obvious to me and to the Army staff that there were defects in the Army procedures for handling men called to duty under the provision of the Doctors Draft Act. . . . As a result of these disclosures I have already issued instructions for corrective changes in current practices. . . . We are all cognizant of the extent to which our system fell down in this case. We do not defend this shortcoming, and intend that such cases shall not recur."

But McCarthy wasn't backing off. The same afternoon Frank Carr was telling Adams by phone (Adams summarized the conversation for his chronology) that in just two days, on Thursday, February 18, the committee would hold an open hearing on Peress in New York City; it wanted three witnesses, including the commanding general at Camp Kilmer. Adams told Carr "quite emphatically" that the Army was "seriously concerned" by the way events were going. It "was similar to the Fort Monmouth situation wherein they took our Commanding General and in effect drew the blood of the Army in large bucketfuls for all of the country to see, making it look as though there is another espionage situation at Camp Kilmer." Carr came back with a surprising answer: this was just reciprocation; if the Army would "be reasonable probably the committee would be reasonable."

"What do you mean by reasonable?" Adams asked.

"You should be reasonable about 'hostages,' " Carr replied, using a word McCarthy had recently used in talking about Schine.

"All the Army has to do," Carr said jokingly, "is capitulate, and all its problems would be over." McCarthy, he went on, was still fuming about Stevens's press conference assertion last November that no espionage was going on at Monmouth.

Adams asked Carr when he thought McCarthy was going to lay off the Army and go after another target.

"As far as I can estimate," Frank Carr replied, "there is no end to the present Committee program of attack on the Army."

Adams immediately phoned Stevens. "[McCarthy] wants to get different people onto [the stand and] ask them, 'Did you make a personal recommendation that these people be fired? On what date in April?' And Joe will say, 'Think of it! Eight months transpired, and they didn't take them off.' We have no choice. It looks like it will come into a first class go-round."

"What is your recommendation, John?"

"We have got to make the fellows available. I thought I would go up tomorrow afternoon and stop at Kilmer and talk to [the Commanding General, Brigadier General Ralph W. Zwicker] and his G-2 and brief them on the limitations as to what they can discuss because of the Executive Orders. . . ."

"I hope you told Carr we don't like this at all," Stevens remarked. "Did he have my letter yet?"

"I don't think so, but I read it over the telephone. Joe is actually in Mexico. I read it to Frank, and he thought that was a pretty good letter. He said, 'That is quite an admission . . . why don't you call up George Sokolsky and read it over the phone?' "

"Suppose you do that," Stevens replied, "unbeknownst to me."

Adams did. Sokolsky took it all in. Then he switched subjects. "What are you going to do about Schine?"

Adams told him: Schine's request to get out of basic training and go straight into the CID school had been turned down.

"The Army is being very foolish," Sokolsky shot back. It should use some common sense. "All you're asking for is an unending fight which will last for two years, or as long as Schine is in the service." That same day—two weeks after he'd sent it to Rogers—John Adams sent a copy of his continuing chronology to the White House, to Sherman Adams, at Governor Adams's request.

On Wednesday morning, February 17, with the public hearing in the Foley Square Courthouse now just twenty-four hours away, John Adams got ready to head to New York. He had already written a letter to General Zwicker, which he would carry by hand to their meeting, formally informing him of the hearing. Adams had also taken a few minutes that morning to search his memory and add to the chronology his recollection of a phone call two weeks earlier from Frank Carr: "On either Thursday or Friday the 4th or 5th of February, . . . Frank Carr . . . pointed out to me that Senator McCarthy was bitterly angry with the Army over the release from active duty of Major Peress, and had reached the point where he was no longer willing to discuss matters with the Secretary or with me.

"Carr . . . recommended . . . that I should talk to George Sokolsky. He stated that Sokolsky has a capacity for pacifying McCarthy, and that Sokolsky [with McCarthy's knowledge] had moved in in place of Cohn . . . as the individual who was to attempt to negotiate with the Army . . . [over] the assignment of David Schine. . . . Carr warned me that I had better talk to Sokolsky because Sokolsky had a capacity for getting very angry if he were not consulted when he thought he should be. . . . 'George is the only means you have got of getting back in good with Joe. . . .' "

That evening, February 17, in New York City, the taxi in which Joe and Jean McCarthy were riding was rammed by a reckless driver. Joe was momentarily knocked unconscious. He stayed up with Jean all night. The next morning he sent her to the hospital.

A couple of hours later he was opening the hearing at Foley Square. The klieg lights flooded the room. The television cameras began to turn. Two hundred spectators watched. As Peress testified, John Adams sat with General Zwicker.

At eleven forty-five Adams ducked out, found a phone, and put in a call to Stevens back in Washington: "McCarthy's hearing is in progress now, and he has just upbraided me . . . in a long speech— 15 minutes—with reference to your letter. [He says] he can't conceive that the Secretary of the Army would write this letter, this stupid doubletalk. [He said:] 'I am sick of this coddling of communists . . . ; and I intend to subpoena every officer in the United States, . . . every officer and civilian who had anything to do with [Peress's] commissioning, transfer, etc.' "

It would be a good idea, Adams went on, to release Stevens's letter.

Stevens glanced over his shoulder: "Do you think I need any coordination with Defense in any way?"

Adams was looking at the clock. "I don't know. This has been strictly an Army matter. . . . We are either going to catch these newspaper men before Joe gets his hearing over in the next two or three minutes, or the guys who are writing . . ."

Stevens broke in: "I think the letter speaks for itself. I think it is a good letter. Do you see anything we need to apologize for about that letter?"

Adams did not. He released the letter. Stevens immediately put in a call to Fred Seaton: out of town until Monday.

McCarthy skipped lunch. He spent the whole noon hour visiting Jean at the Flower–Fifth Avenue Hospital, where he learned she had suffered a broken ankle. He returned to the executive session hearing that afternoon hungry and depressed, with a splitting headache. And now he faced the Commanding General of Camp Kilmer, General Zwicker.

Fifty years old, tall, trim, and handsome, every inch an officer and gentleman, Zwicker had grown up in Madison, Wisconsin, graduated from West Point in 1927, and served with great gallantry in Normandy, Northern France, the Ardennes, the Rhineland, and Central Europe. He wore a great garden of decorations, including the Silver Star, the Legion of Merit with an Oak Leaf Cluster, the Bronze Star with two Oak Leaf Clusters, the British Arrowhead for distinguished service. After the war he had received the personal commendation of General Dwight D. Eisenhower. He was given his first star in March of 1953 and four months later was assigned to Kilmer.

Ironically, it was Zwicker who had blown the whistle on Peress. On October 21 he had written to the Commanding General of the

First Army, Lieutenant General W. A. Burress, summarizing derogatory information on the dentist, citing all the previous recommendations for getting him out of the service, and adding a concurring recommendation of his own. On November 3, when General Burress visited Kilmer, Zwicker informed him of Peress's reappointment as a major and voiced his outrage. An unnamed member of McCarthy's staff has claimed that Zwicker early in December had clandestinely tipped off the subcommittee about the whole train of events. Perhaps. But the action seems out of character, and surely improbable, particularly in the light of the certain fact that a month later Cohn, talking with Adams, did not know whether the Kilmer suspect was a dentist or a doctor; and the further fact that as late as January 21 or 22, another McCarthy staff member, George Anastos, had to phone Zwicker to request Major Peress's name.

Zwicker had no use for Peress. But that morning of the hearing, Zwicker had had to tell McCarthy privately that Adams had forbidden him to talk about the Peress history—to tell exactly who had done what all along the way—on the grounds of the existing Executive Orders. McCarthy for the moment had seemed indifferent. But when Zwicker had taken the stand late in the morning and balked at answering several questions, McCarthy gave him a clear warning: "You will be asked that question this afternoon. You will be ordered" to answer.

The hearing resumed after lunch. Taut and frazzled, McCarthy the brawler tore into his quarry. When Lieutenant Colonel Brown, Zwicker's G-2, refused to answer a question, McCarthy ordered Adams, the man who, he believed, was muzzling these witnesses, to take the stand. Adams refused. McCarthy ordered the Army Counselor out of the room. Then he went after Zwicker. "Don't be coy with me, General"; "Don't you give me that doubletalk"; "General, let's try and be truthful"; "I am going to keep you here as long as you keep hedging and hemming"; "I mean exactly what I asked you, General, nothing else. And anyone with the brains of a five-year-old child can understand that question"; "General, you should be removed from any command. Any man who has been given the honor of being promoted to general and who says, 'I will protect another general who protected Communists,' is not fit to wear that uniform"; "You will be back here, General."

Adams at once phoned Cohn. How, he wanted to know, could he get McCarthy to withdraw the order barring him from representing the Army in the hearing room?

"I am no longer authorized to discuss the matter with you," Cohn answered. "The only way to negotiate is to talk to Carr or Sokolsky."

A few hours later McCarthy was driving still more nails into the Army in an after-dinner speech to New York's Traffic Club: "That was a disgraceful performance today. . . . Secretary Stevens should take a new look at the top of the team to see whether this type of coddling of Communists will continue."

Stevens was not taking this advice. By nine thirty-eight the next morning he had already talked with a livid Chief of Staff, General Matthew Ridgway, and he was phoning Zwicker at the First Army Headquarters on Governors Island, in the office of the First Army's commanding general.

"I was having a little meeting this morning with John Adams," the Secretary began, "getting up to date on this business. I put in a call to you to tell you I am thoroughly familiar with this thing . . . and have no intention of leaving you out in left field. I wanted to give you a vote of confidence and tell you I am giving serious thought to what we do next.

"I deeply resent such comments as Senator McCarthy made to you yesterday. I understand he has called you for one of his T.V. shows on Tuesday. Whether or not that will take place, we don't know. We will have to assume it will. I am not sure that it will because there may be something I can do in the meanwhile. The object of this call was to give you a vote of confidence and tell you how much I think of you and say we will have to work this out together and to make some sense out of a serious situation."

Diplomatically but pointedly Zwicker put it to him: "Mr. Secretary, I feel that if that is not done, it is going to make a great deal of difference to the Army because if any other officer's . . . character is impugned as mine was yesterday and the officers in our Army even get an inkling of the fact that . . . higher authority [is] doing nothing to refute those statements, I feel that the loyalty of officers to the Department of the Army is going to vanish. And furthermore, Mr. Secretary, some of the statements [McCarthy] made and the things that he called me . . . yesterday, . . . I do not intend for anyone to stand still until to the best of my ability he [gets] those remarks denied by Mr. McCarthy himself, if possible, because he called me everything you can imagine in the book."

Zwicker was seething. Stevens focused on a technicality: "Was that taken down by the recorder? . . . [Is it] all a matter of record?"

"It should be unless he destroys the record. Of course, you are aware, I am sure, that although so-called Communists were permitted counsel, Army officers called were not permitted counsel."

"I know Adams was thrown out. . . . That, of course, was utterly unfair too. I am very pleased to have this chance to chat with you." Stevens now turned gently diplomatic: "I hope you don't mind that I do know that you haven't been feeling too well."

Zwicker didn't miss a beat: "That is exaggerated too. I am feeling fine, and I will feel a whole lot better if I can wrap this rascal up."

Stevens still floundered: "If you have any further thoughts on it, please don't hesitate to call me or Adams because we want to move on this thing."

General Burress, the First Army commander, came on the line: "Good morning, Mr. Secretary. . . . I am a little bit disturbed."

"We all are. That was a terrible thing General Zwicker went through. Now we have to get out and fight."

"It comes to that because, as General Zwicker said, he has borne the thing for the whole Army; and, as I read it, [McCarthy] was attacking you also this morning."

"That doesn't bother me at all. If he has just attacked me and leaves the Army alone, that is okay. . . . If you have any ideas today or over the weekend, please let us down here know, because I want to get something before the Tuesday television show comes up."

"If they call on me for a statement to the press," Burress replied, "I am going to say I have every confidence in General Zwicker as an officer, in his combat record, and his record after the war against the Bolsheviks is the best I know of. . . . That is all I am going to say. I am in the same fix he is in. Our policy has been never to show a divided front between ourselves and the War Department."

"That is a fine statement," Stevens interjected.

"Anybody who [has been derelict in his] duty, we get them. But I can't say anything about whose fault it was. . . ."

At eleven o'clock at Stevens's request, Adams met with Hensel. Shortly after noon New Jersey Republican Congressman Jim Auchincloss phoned his fellow New Jerseyan Bob Stevens with words of encouragement: "You're getting stronger every day; McCarthy is trying to get you to answer him. . . . You have a lot of friends around here." Simultaneously, at the request of Stevens and Hensel, Adams was phoning Bill Rogers. Adams went over all that had happened the day before—the abuse of Zwicker, the ejection of Adams himself. Secretary Stevens, Adams continued, "has just about reached the point where he . . . [is] not going to permit [either officers or civilians] to appear . . . and put up with this sort of treatment." Rogers didn't hesitate: "That's okay with Justice."

That afternoon, February 19, Stevens and Adams together conferred with the other members of McCarthy's subcommittee—all the members this time, not just the Republicans. And significantly, they began with the Democrats. These men had resigned during the uproar over J. B. Matthews, objecting to McCarthy's self-declared unilateral right to hire and fire the subcommittee staff. The junior counsel Robert Kennedy had resigned shortly afterward. But by now they'd all agreed to return. On January 25, McCarthy had consented to relinquish that exclusive hiring and firing right. He had agreed the minority members would be able to choose their own counsel (they chose Kennedy) and also that whenever the minority members unanimously opposed the holding of a public hearing, the issue should go to the subcommittee's parent committee, the Committee on Government Operations, to umpire. So now Senators McClellan, Symington, and Jackson had rejoined the fold. They would play a curious game. In the words of Struve Hensel, "They opposed McCarthy. But they also wanted Republican blood on the floor."

Adams and Stevens went first to the office of twangy-voiced John McClellan of Arkansas, slender, balding, respected, sharp, conservative, a member of the Senate Establishment. Stevens and Adams filled McClellan in on what had happened at Foley Square. Especially Stevens read what McCarthy had said about Zwicker. After about fifteen minutes a second Democratic committee member joined them. Senator W. Stuart Symington of Missouri had known Bob Stevens at Yale and liked him. He was tall, suave, and handsome, a liberal Presidential hopeful, the son-in-law of the distinguished Senator James Wadsworth of New York, a St. Louis executive who once headed the Emerson Electric Company. Symington, an authority on national defense, had served as Harry Truman's Air Force Secretary and had enjoyed a personal friendship with Dwight Eisenhower before 1952: Ike had put him up for membership at Augusta National and invited the Symingtons as house guests for Eisenhower's inauguration as President of Columbia University, before practical politics drove them apart.

In the upshot of this conference, McClellan and Symington decided Symington should write a letter to McCarthy urging that no hearing be held on the following Tuesday, in accordance with the subcommittee's rules. On this, Symington said he had the support of the committee's third Democrat, Henry M. Jackson of Washington.

Stevens, Adams, and Symington repaired to Symington's office. Symington put in a call to one of the wisest lawyers he knew—Clark Clifford, former Assistant to President Harry Truman, and now a knowledgeable and urbane Washington fixer and mover and shaker— "the beautiful Clark Clifford," snide Missourians called this onetime boy wonder who could now charge thousands of dollars a minute for his services, for his knowledge of whom to call in the bureaucracy or on the Hill. Symington wanted Clifford's advice. Clifford gave it: In no circumstances should the Army permit any subordinate officer to be taken on by McCarthy in any sort of contest; any engagement must be top level. Symington then called Republican Margaret Chase Smith—another stalwart of the Senate military affairs establishment. She assured him she would vote with the Democratic members of the Committee against McCarthy in opposition to any assault on the Army.

Now Clark Clifford arrived in person. Symington asked Adams to leave the room. Symington, Stevens, and Clifford remained. For twenty minutes the two Democrats urged Stevens to keep his traffic with McCarthy strictly formal; and to make no appearance before the subcommittee until Symington returned from a brief trip to Europe.

John Adams rejoined them. "What's the worse thing Cohn ever said to you about Schine?" Symington asked him.

"When Cohn said if Schine were sent overseas, Stevens would be through as Secretary of the Army, and the McCarthy committee would wreck the Army."

Stevens and Adams left the Democrats and next called on Senator Everett Dirksen (Republican of Illinois). At that moment Dirksen was regarded as a slippery conservative, known far and wide as the Wizard of Ooze, a flannel-voiced orator with a keen mind and the rigidity of a chocolate eclair. He had infuriated Eisenhower Republicans at the 1952 convention when he personally excoriated Eisenhower zealot Tom Dewey: "We followed you before, and you took us down the path of defeat." One never knew exactly where Dirksen stood. Seven months earlier, just before the death of Robert Taft, in July of 1953, Eisenhower had invited Dirksen to breakfast and urged him to become the Administration's unofficial knight on a white horse in the Senate (the official knight, the about-to-become Majority Leader, was the "cumbersome" conservative Bill Knowland of California); at this breakfast conference Ike still had some hope that Dirksen might shape up (he had fought, for example, on the side of the angels for the Eisenhower Refugee Relief Bill, over the dead bodies of McCarran and McCarthy and Welker and Jenner), but trying to pin him down was, to use Teddy Roosevelt's phrase, at times like trying to nail a custard pie to the wall. For 20 minutes Stevens and Adams told Ev the story. Dirksen, Adams recorded in his memorandum on the conference, was "disturbed." He asked them to go see other committee members.

On they went to the office of Karl Mundt (Republican of South Dakota). This round-faced senator with horn-rim glasses was remembered by one of his boyhood teachers as "a good C student, nothing more." In Washington he became one of those with "feet stuck in concrete," an unreliable conservative whom Eisenhower would have loved to extirpate from the Senate. Adams and Stevens once again went through their routine. "I just can't understand why McCarthy has it in for the Army," Mundt commented.

Then on to the office of Senator Charles Potter (Republican of Michigan), a limping war veteran, a man with his heart in the right place but weak, who could not avoid flip-flopping, but who in occasional instances would do the right thing. They spent thirty minutes with him. He was genuinely concerned. He would, he said, phone Dirksen and Mundt and try to get something done to head off the hearings for Tuesday.

The *New York Times* the next morning carried the word that the Army had rejected McCarthy's demand for the names of the perpetrators of the Peress foul-up. It was now Saturday of the Washington's Birthday weekend. At nine-forty Stevens reached McCarthy by phone at the Ten Eyck Hotel in Albany. Stevens forthrightly told McCarthy of his visits with the other subcommittee members, Republicans and Democrats, "because I was so upset by the reports I had on the executive appearance of General Zwicker . . . that I just felt in fairness to the officer corps of the Army I had to do something about it."

McCarthy became intransigent. "I think the best thing you can do is not to follow in the old tradition of the previous administration. I think you have got a wonderful opportunity here, Robert, to either set the course for a housecleaning [or] to try to cover up, as

has gone on before. That will be impossible, I will guarantee you.
. . . Let me ask you this: is it your position that you are going to
try to keep from us the names of the officers who protected these
men?"

"I am going to try to prevent my officers from going before your
committee until you and I have an understanding as to the abuse
they are going to get. . . ."

"You are not going to order them not to appear before my committee. Just go ahead and try it, Robert. I am going to kick the
brains out of anyone who protects Communists. If that is [your] policy . . . , you just go ahead and do it. I will guarantee you that you
will live to regret it. . . . I don't give a damn whether an officer is
a general or what he is, when he comes before us with the ignorant,
stupid, insulting aspect of those who appeared, I will guarantee
you that the American people will know all about it."

Stevens protested he wasn't covering up Communists. McCarthy
repeated his question: Are you refusing to let your officers testify?
Did you tell the other committee members that?

"Yes."

". . . Consider yourself subpoenaed for ten o'clock Tuesday
morning. . . ." McCarthy slammed down the phone.

Once again Stevens began making the rounds of the other committee members to tell his story, starting with Dirksen, who listened
and said little, and then John McClellan.

Announce to the press you're requesting an opportunity to appear
before the committee, McClellan advised Stevens. "Beat him to the
punch."

At ten o'clock Stevens phoned Potter, who agreed to confer with
Ev Dirksen and Karl Mundt. Five minutes later Stevens phoned
Symington.

"[McCarthy]," Stevens reported, "really started to beat my brains
out. . . . I am a coddler of Reds, you see."

"Did you have anybody on the phone?" Symington shrewdly
asked, wise in the ways of the Pentagon.

"Yes, I did."

"That's good. Keep the recording."

Symington had some good news: McCarthy's man had just
phoned; because of Symington's prospective absence next Tuesday,
the appearance of General Zwicker would be postponed. Symington
conferred once again with Clark Clifford. At ten twenty-five he
phoned Stevens again:

"I talked to our legal friend. He thinks it was a mistake for you to call Mac." Symington read Stevens the letter he was writing McCarthy thanking him for the postponement of Zwicker's appearance and requesting also a postponement of any hearing on Stevens or the Army.

"I would suggest two things to you, old fellow," the Senator cozied up to the Secretary, "1) Let's counterpunch this stuff and not lead; 2) I think your people over there are pretty harassed and I don't blame them, but maybe some of them can't see the forest for the trees. This boy gets awfully rough. I would use those telephone numbers I gave you yesterday. He [the mystery man] has deep, it could not be deeper, dislike for your opponent. . . ." From across the political aisle Stevens was getting names of possible liberal legal helpers. One was Abe Fortas, New Deal luminary now in private Washington practice. Another was Morris Ernst, veteran counsel of the American Civil Liberties Union.

"It isn't a question of politics at all," Symington concluded. "It is a question of the integrity and fighting morale of the Army, and therefore everybody, in my opinion, who has a concept of what is decent will break their back to help you . . . I would never get near him if I could help it."

At eleven o'clock Stevens spoke with Mundt. "I don't feel you can ignore a subpoena," Mundt concluded.

"I don't intend to," Stevens answered, "but I don't believe I can be subpoenaed over the telephone." Mundt had to agree.

At two-thirty that afternoon Symington phoned again. "This guy got any steel in him?" a friend of Symington's had asked the Senator about Stevens, and Symington told Stevens he had told his friend, "[Damn] right." "If he has steel," Symington's friend concluded, "he can do a great service. [But] he has got to be careful of each move he makes." Symington agreed, and he went on to give the Secretary some warnings: "I think you may have put this fellow on the run a little bit, but he is terrifically agile in getting around something. . . . I think you are in shape to protect your Army, provided you . . . stay tough, I don't mean silly tough. I mean firm. . . ."

"I've got to do that, Stu," Stevens resolved.

"One other fellow that is on your side, and I know he is absolutely tops, . . . is Bill Rogers. I mean, you can't go wrong with Bill." As an afterthought Symington mused, "[McCarthy] might be sick, you know. . . ."

Stevens set up an appointment that afternoon with Jerry Persons at the White House. Afterward, back in his office in the Pentagon at four-thirty, Stevens returned a call from the dean of Washington's reporters—James Reston, a top man in the Washington bureau of the *New York Times.*

"I want to get one or two things straight," Reston began. "I know you don't want to be quoted on this. As I said to John [Adams], this guy is so slippery that I want to be sure about my facts. . . . John told me . . . that you had been in touch with McCarthy. . . . I wondered what kind of reaction you got from him. . . ."

"I would say, Mr. Reston, and, of course, I talk to you perfectly frankly, because that is the way you deal and won't quote me, he was quite put out about the whole business. . . . What I am talking about is this Zwicker case, . . . a case of real abuse to this officer, who is one of our outstanding combat generals and a highly decorated fellow, you know, and we cannot maintain the morale of this Army, or the prestige of the armed services of this country as a whole, if we are going on with this kind of thing. . . ."

"I think you are entirely right. I have seen what has happened to my friends in the Foreign Service and we have got to the point now where we are not reporting accurately, people are not sticking their necks out. A guy like myself, who has talked to them for many years, I know it is affecting the service in a very serious way."

"That is correct."

"And it is certainly true of our propaganda agency [USIA]; it has been riddled from top to bottom, and that's what will happen to your officer corps, if they are going to get beat on the head by this character. . . .

"Has [McCarthy] indicated at all . . . to you that he would ask you to come before his committee . . . on Tuesday?"

"I would say that I got the impression that I will probably be given that opportunity pretty soon. In fact, I would like to ask you, if I may, . . . if he calls me definitely, and there is some indication that he is going to, . . . I had in mind sending him a letter in which I would say that I would come and appear, provided it was an open hearing; in other words, I have nothing to cover up, and if I was going to appear, I would like to appear in an open hearing with all the press there and get all the facts before the American people. Would you think that would be a good thing to do?"

"I don't think that the head of an executive agency can refuse to appear in executive session . . . but I think you can add that you think this thing has been discussed in private long enough and you certainly hope and assume that the senator would wish that this thing should be threshed out in public. . . ."

Finally Stevens put in a call to his superior in the Department of Defense—Deputy Secretary Roger Kyes, out in Bloomfield Hills, Michigan, where he was weekending at his imposing home, to which he would soon go back for good, when he returned to the upper rarefied reaches of General Motors. Kyes was tall, tough, raunchy, arrogant, a no-nonsense auto man, tunnel-visioned, with an ordered hierarchy of objects of regard: (1) his GM and Pentagon boss, Defense Secretary Charlie Wilson; (2) Charlie Wilson; (3) God; (4) Charlie Wilson. He was an abrasive gut-cutter and hatchet man. Early in 1953 Bryce Harlow, a White House staff member responsible for getting Pentagon programs through on the Hill, had gone to see Kyes about a difficulty.

"Don't tell me *what's* the problem," Kyes briskly cut in. "Tell me *who's* the problem."

Bryce mentioned the name of the highly respected, longtime Chairman of the House Armed Services Committee, Carl Vinson.

"Where's he from?" Kyes demanded.

"Milledgeville, Georgia."

Kyes made a note on his legal pad. "GM has a plant down there. We'll take care of him. Who's your next problem?"

Later that year when C. D. Jackson was trying—against almost overwhelming State and Defense opposition—to ram through Eisenhower's U.N. atoms-for-peace proposal, which entailed contributions from the U.S. nuclear stockpile to an international agency for nonmilitary humane purposes—Kyes was one of his most vociferous—and unscrupulous—opponents. "Red lights started blinking all over the place," Jackson wrote in his diary after one brawling session. And among the most recalcitrant was Kyes, with his below-the-belt asseveration if the President offered to contribute to a UN atomic pool, somebody should hand him an umbrella. Jackson had ultimately beaten Kyes and the others back, but the battle had left its scars.

For all his impeccable credentials as an alley brawler, Kyes somehow always sidestepped any bespattering by Joe McCarthy. So far he had stayed out of the Army's particular fight. When Stevens phoned him at five forty-five on that Saturday afternoon, Kyes continued to sidestep. Stevens told him about the Zwicker beating and about his visits to the committee members. And then, he said, "This morning . . . I decided the fair and right and sportsmanlike thing to do was to call [McCarthy]. . . . I . . . told him on the phone that I had visited the members of the committee and what I had said. . . . He blew his lid, which I expected, but I think it was the right thing to do. He had a hearing scheduled for Tuesday morning in New York to . . . put General Zwicker on public display and abuse him some more before the television cameras."

"What was his name?"

"Zwicker, z-w-i-c-k-e-r. . . . He has a very fine war record and all kinds of decorations. . . . What Joe is trying to do is what he always does, and that is to try to get a list of Army officers and get them up before him and abuse them and make somebody the goat. . . . Here is the kind of thing that Zwicker says Mac said to him in this executive session: 'You're shielding traitors,' 'You are shielding Communist conspirators,' 'You are a disgrace to the uniform. . . .' 'How did they ever select one like you to be a general officer?' . . . I made up my mind he wasn't going on public display next Tuesday. When I got through talking with Mac, he said, 'Well you can consider yourself subpoenaed for 10:00 Tuesday morning. . . .' I started to ask him where the committee would meet . . . , and he hung up the phone. Well, anyway, I will tell you what I did today. I saw Bill Knowland, because I thought it was so important that the top of the Administration leadership ought to know all about this, Roger. . . . Knowland reached Nixon while I was there and went all over the thing with him. This afternoon I went over to the White House and went over it with Jerry Persons and Sherman Adams. . . ."

"I am glad to [know about it]," Kyes replied, "because there is apparently something in the wind. The *Times* and *Free Press* . . . are trying to get a hold of me. . . ."

"Roger, the way it was left late this afternoon . . . with Sherman Adams and Jerry Persons is that we would sort of play it by ear for the next day or so. . . . I think Jerry is toying with the idea of getting Everett Dirksen to call up Joe and get him down to earth. . . . I have been spending the time in between calls on the Hill and [the] White House getting together a basic brief statement of the facts involved, so that if I do go up there on Tuesday, I know exactly what I am going to say. . . . In the meanwhile, between Knowland, Nixon, Persons and [Sherman] Adams, I feel any decision[s] at a high level that [need] to be made will be made and told to me sometime tomorrow and, of course, whatever they are, I will follow them meticulously. . . ."

Kyes registered indignation: "It is certainly a crime when the fellow throws everybody out of the place so nobody knows whether it is an honest show and then crucifies the fellow."

"He wouldn't even let John Adams stay in there. Every lousy witness that pleads the Fifth Amendment can have an attorney, but General Zwicker couldn't. I don't think Mac will get away with that one, but I want you to know that everything is very stable. Nobody is getting mad or losing their heads or anything of that kind. . . ."

Stevens had at the moment tossed his problem upstairs. Kyes now disposed of *his* immediate problem: "I think I will simply say [to the reporters] that the Secretary of the Army has been handling all those matters, and I am not thoroughly familiar with this case . . . ; so I would rather make no comment about it. . . . If you get two balls going, you can't quarterback."

Reston's story hit page one of the *Times* the next morning: no more appearances by Zwicker. A cheer went up: from anti-McCarthyites within the administration itself, from editorial writers far and wide, from liberals coast to coast. At last a hero to battle the monster; at last a man with guts enough to tell him off. Stevens went to work on a forthright declaration for his possible appearance: "I am here today to defend an officer of the United States Army, Brigadier General Ralph W. Zwicker, . . . who was humiliated . . . before this committee on February 18, 1954. . . ."

That Sunday morning at ten-fifty Symington phoned Stevens again, this time a bit disconcerted: "The *Washington Post* says you are going to volunteer to appear."

"They must have dreamed that up," Stevens replied. He'd said nothing of the sort. Symington remained uneasy. "If you and I are going to work together, we have got to be on the table with each other." And he warned: "If you are going to play with McCarthy, you have got to forget about any of these Marquis of Queensberry rules. . . ."

That evening at five thirty-five Stevens phoned a young friend, Arthur Hadley of the Washington Bureau of *Newsweek*, an alumnus of Groton and Yale and service as an Army officer in the war. After reading the morning's papers, Stevens told Hadley, he'd thought he'd better get the facts straight. So that afternoon he'd put out a press release denouncing McCarthy's attack on Zwicker and adding that if the subcommittee wanted Stevens himself to appear, he would. Hadley cheered; Stevens, he said, should have backing from the President.

"It so happens I am Acting Secretary of Defense," Stevens told him, "and [I] determined it was time for me, Stevens, to make a statement; do the job myself; couch [it] in my own language; [I] haven't asked anybody's approval or clearance."

Hadley offered to help on the statement for Tuesday. Stevens accepted. He would, he said, come over to Hadley's house in Georgetown at nine o'clock; they could have something to eat and go over the text.

The next day, Monday, February 22—Washington's Birthday—the unedited transcript of the Zwicker testimony was released. The *New York Times* published it verbatim. The country was stunned, including Republican Committee member Charles Potter. At once he fired Robert L. Jones, a staff man Potter had sent to the hearings, for unauthorized pro-McCarthy remarks. Jones thereupon announced his candidacy for the Senate seat of liberal Republican Margaret Chase Smith of Maine. At twelve-forty Potter called Adams: the hearing had been postponed.

Stevens and Karl Mundt flew together that holiday to Valley Forge; the Secretary got an ovation for pledging to defend "the loyal men and women in our Army." He continued to look toward his eventual testimony. He had received help not only from Arthur Hadley but also from Morris Ernst, who had sent in a suggested draft. And now, in a crucial move, Stevens reached for the General Counsel of the Department of Defense, Struve Hensel.

For some time a distance and a coolness had separated the two men. Many weeks earlier in casual cocktail party conversation, Stevens had mentioned to Hensel that he was having difficulty with Wilfred McNeil, the Pentagon's able budget chief. Hensel had defended McNeil's high professional competence: "Don't ever question him," he told Stevens, "on any facts." This remark, Hensel always felt, had left Stevens angry. Hensel suspected, though he could never prove it, that Stevens had told Hensel's former deputy John Adams to stay away from his old boss. Stevens and Hensel had of course seen one another on social occasions, including one conciliatory dinner to which the Hensels invited the Secretary of the Army; in the Pentagon, however, they had gone separately about their work.

But now, on Monday, February 22, Stevens's holiday assistant Ted Rhodes was trying to reach Hensel. He found him at the Nassau Inn in Princeton, New Jersey. Stevens and Hensel agreed to get together Wednesday morning, on Hensel's return to Washington.

Meanwhile, the phone continued to ring off the hook in Stevens's office. Democratic Senator Allen Ellender of Louisiana called in from New Orleans to voice his "full support." Congressman [Leroy] Johnson of California phoned to congratulate the Secretary on his handling of the McCarthy problem. Richard Harkness, Irwin Safchik of INS, and Martin Agronsky called. The media dearly desired—they were clamoring after—a new hero.

Lay liberals were also rushing in with enthusiastic applause. Harvard's treasurer Paul Cabot phoned repeatedly. A Mr. Belmont called demanding to know: "What's happening? Why doesn't the President back the Army?" Senator Matthew Neely of West Virginia phoned leaving a message of congratulations on Stevens's courage in a battle that should have been started long ago, declaring himself "one Democrat the Secretary can count on a hundred percent," and voicing a hope that the Secretary had the guts to defend his rights and those of all Americans against this dictator. And liberal Republican Paul Hoffman—anathema to the radical right—phoned from faraway Palm Springs, California, telling Stevens's assistant to convey Hoffman's congratulations on Stevens's courage; he was delighted to see the Secretary go into battle. To some in Stevens's office, Hoffman's message seemed to carry the imprimatur of President Dwight Eisenhower, at the moment Hoffman's vacation guest out in the California desert.

But as Stevens had told Kyes, he was not master of his own fate; he was not even master of his next move. A decision would be made higher up; he would follow it meticulously. And at that very moment a decision was being made—made by the peacemakers. Pragmatic strategists all, these men submerged their varied moral convictions and confronted the practical problem they saw before them. That problem was how to still the guns; end division within the Republican party; salvage the wayward. Even the President from time to time would get off a comment to Jim Hagerty suggesting that—in the face of all contrary evidence—somehow the most outrageous might return to the fold. On January 20 he had said to Hagerty, without mentioning McCarthy or anyone else, "[I] see no reason getting anyone elected who is trying to doublecross us." If a man changes and becomes a prodigal son, Ike went on, he'd "kill the fatted calf for him; . . . if not, I have need for my own beef."

Of all Eisenhower's lieutenants who never lost hope in the power of conversion and redemption, his Legislative Liaison Chief, Jerry Persons, headed the list: "Don't write off a single Republican Senator," he had told the White House Staff late in December as they surveyed the prospects for the enactment of Eisenhower's 1954 legislative program. And at nine o'clock on the morning of Tuesday, February 23, as Washington went back to work, Jerry Persons was phoning Stevens on the White House line. Persons had recruited a powerful ally—the Vice President of the United States. The two of them were setting up a strategy meeting that afternoon in Nixon's Capitol office.

Driving to the Hill, Stevens and John Adams stopped at the White House to pick up Persons and Jack Martin. Persons mused on the Schine history—the worst example of improper pressure he'd seen in all his years in Washington. Then Persons looked up toward the Capitol dome: "If the bones of all the crow I have eaten . . . were piled together, that . . . dome wouldn't be high enough to cover them. But I always took the attitude . . . that I was doing it for the Army. And so I just ate crow. Jerry Persons as a man didn't count, but what was good for the Army did."

Arrived at the Capitol, the four men sat down in the Nixon hideaway with the Vice President, Bill Knowland, Bill Rogers, and Everett Dirksen. Stevens outlined what he planned to say at the hearing. He was warned that McCarthy would "tear him to pieces" not only because of the Peress record but because of his stand against the subpoena power of the Senate. The group urged conciliation. In the course of the discussion Dirksen said he would go see McCarthy and tell him he had to fire Cohn.

That solution didn't work. But ultimately the negotiators arrived at an idea for a move toward resolution acceptable to both sides. Late that afternoon Karl Mundt phoned Stevens to convey an urgent message. Steven's aide, Colonel BeLieu, took the call. "Tell the Secretary," Mundt told BeLieu, "that tomorrow we are setting up a lunch at the Capitol for him and the Republican members of the committee—McCarthy, Dirksen, Potter, and me. And no one else is to know."

It would be a fried chicken lunch.

The Secretary of the Army's calendar for Wednesday February 24, 1954, indicated a relatively quiet day ahead: at eight-thirty a meeting of the Army Policy Council, at ten a meeting with his old friend George Montgomery from California, at twelve-thirty lunch with his son Bob Stevens, Jr., and at four a meeting of the Joint

Secretaries in the office of Charlie Wilson. It would not so turn out. Through the morning he had a bizarre parade of callers: at nine-thirty Francis Simmons, the Washington, D.C., manager of American Viscose, phoned to see whether he might set up a luncheon that day with Harry Dalton of Philadelphia, an old friend of Stevens, or, failing that, an afternoon appointment. At ten forty-three Bob Harris, of the *State and Union Labor* newspaper in Indianapolis, phoned with an original observation on the effects of McCarthyism on the Army (what will kids think when they are ordered to go into battle?). And a little request: ask Bob to drop me a line.

The front page of the *New York Times* that morning had carried a story by Bill Lawrence headlined: "McCarthy Says Red Decodes Secrets, but Army Denies It." By ten-thirty the McCarthy subcommittee was focusing on this menace: one Annie Lee Moss, a middle-aged black woman who moved slowly into the hearing room leaning on the arm of her attorney and wearing a fur-collared coat with a dark beret which she pulled down to cover the tops of her ears. She appeared ill, and she trembled as she took the witness stand. From time to time she would remove her glasses and wipe her eyes. Finally McCarthy excused her; she could come back and testify later when she felt better. But he refused to drop the issue he was focusing on: "Who in the military, knowing that lady was a Communist, promoted her from waitress to coding clerk?" (After considerable bickering over her exact identity, Mrs. Moss would eventually be reinstated in her Defense Department job by Secretary Wilson.)

As all this was going on, back in the Pentagon the Secretary of the Army continued to polish his opening salvo for the next day. As far as he—and the *New York Times*—knew at that moment, the confrontation was still on. Harvard University Treasurer Paul Cabot of Boston had been trying to talk with him, and at eleven fifty-four, Stevens finally returned the call.

"I hope I haven't hounded the hell out of you," Cabot began diplomatically, "but . . . on the Harvard front we have been having difficulty with the same man. I don't know whether this would do you any good, but I have had to go around making some speeches about it, and I had prepared for me by the Harvard news office what Joe said—put down on one side of the paper . . . and then what the truth was on the other side of the paper. So I have got fifteen pages of lies. It occurred to me maybe you would like to see them."

Stevens jumped at the prospect. "Can you send them air-mail, special delivery . . . ? I would sure like to see it. . . . Send it to my house, 2852 McGill Terrace, Washington, D.C."

"I will send it right along. What time are you coming on?"

"Ten-thirty tomorrow morning."

"If I have time, I will go out to look at you."

"The Treasurer of Harvard," Stevens quipped pleasantly, "will go look at TV."

At twelve forty-five Drew Pearson's office phoned. Pearson would like to speak with Stevens—only Stevens—personally. He had something, his office informed Stevens's office, that might help against McCarthy. No sale. Administration officials did not trust the sensational "Washington Merry-Go-Round" columnist's accuracy or integrity.

All this while Hensel and Adams were still working with Stevens on his draft. Suddenly the Secretary got up and left the room.

"Where's he gone?" Hensel asked.

BeLieu, believing that Adams should accompany Stevens, had told the secret to the Army Counselor. Adams smiled a wan smile. "He's going to a secret lunch on the Hill."

Adams made an unspoken attempt to have Stevens invite an ally along. Stevens didn't bite. As he headed for his car, Adams reminded him, "Peace with honor."

The Republican members of the subcommittee (except Potter), the grilling of Mrs. Moss having ended, walked to the office of Senator Dirksen in Room P54 of the Capitol, just off the rotunda, an office immediately adjacent to Vice President Nixon's. Stevens's limousine let him off at the portico on the Senate side of the Capitol, and he took the elevator upstairs. As he approached the door to this by-agreement "secret" meeting, he saw reporters milling about outside. Then and there, White House Special Counsel Bern Shanley observed in his secret diary the next day, Stevens should have turned on his heel and gone home. But he didn't. He opened the door and walked in alone: without a lawyer, without even an accompanying aide as a witness.

Republicans McCarthy, Mundt, Dirksen, and Stevens—Potter had yet to arrive—sat down to lunch, served by waiters from the Senate dining room. The menu featured fried chicken, peas, french fries, and hearts of lettuce salad. The exchange quickly became stormy.

McCarthy and Stevens went at each other's throats.

"I'm not going to sit there and see a supercilious bastard . . .

smirk." McCarthy let it all out—his fury over Peress, his fury over Stevens's end-running him by going to the other committee members before phoning the committee chairman. When Stevens demanded public assurance against any further abuse of witnesses, McCarthy adamantly refused.

For two hours the argument raged. But finally an agreement began to emerge—an agreement pecked out on a typewriter by round-faced Karl Mundt. One smudgy editing followed another. And at last a final typed text appeared. It spelled out, in full, Stevens's retreat: he would permit Zwicker to testify and give the committee the names of all who had promoted and honorably discharged Peress. But it omitted without a trace any mention of courtesy to witnesses. And it had the approval of everyone, including Senator Potter, who at long last arrived, and, with misgivings, an acquiescent Bob Stevens.

The paneled doors of Room P54 swung open. Fifty reporters and photographers swarmed into the room, where dessert plates and coffee cups were still in place. Flashbulbs popped; they caught Senator McCarthy ("all smiles") and Secretary Stevens seated side by side on an old green leather sofa, cordially chatting and shaking hands. When the reporters asked whether Army witnesses would be beaten up in the future, Stevens, sworn to say not a word beyond the written agreement, faithfully responded: "No comment."

"Dirksen and Mundt," Struve Hensel to this day fumes, "those guys made McCarthy. If a tough directive had come down from the White House against playing the soft-shoe game, Dirksen and Mundt would have stopped. Neither one of them was a man of great principle or fortitude."

But no such directive had come. Strategy had emanated from men who believed the Republican party could still salvage McCarthy and his ilk; get their votes, see them as SOBs, all right, but *our* SOBs.

Stevens climbed into his long limousine and rode back to the Pentagon. He carried with him no text. He phoned Nixon on his arrival, reporting himself "fairly pleased" with the result.

Next Stevens met with Pentagon newspapermen for a few minutes. Once again they asked: Would Army witnesses be abused in the future? And this time Stevens waffled: He had, he said, "every reason to believe" they would not. Then, at four-thirty, he called together twenty-one of his top Army officers and Pentagon associates to announce: Mission accomplished.

We assured the protection of our people, he said. The thing he had been trying to do was to create a climate by which Army personnel of any rank could go before McCarthy's committee and receive fair treatment. And now he was satisfied that that had been achieved.

Stevens's audience included Chief of Staff General Matthew B. Ridgway, fifty-eight, a 1917 graduate of West Point; Commander of the Eighty-second Infantry Division in 1942; a Commanding General of the Eighty-second Airborne Division in Sicily, Italy, and Normandy in 1942–44; Commander of the Eighteenth Airborne Corps in Belgium, France, and Germany in 1944–45; Commanding General of the Eighth Army in Korea in 1950–51; Supreme Commander of the Allied Powers in Korea in 1951–52; and Supreme Allied Commander in Europe, succeeding Eisenhower, in 1952–53. "I'd hate to meet him alone in an alley in the middle of the night," one admiring GI once said of this tall, steel-muscled, combat-hardened officer. Ridgway, though Ike's Chief of Staff, was a man Eisenhower didn't particularly like (in *Mandate for Change* he called him, with reserve, "an unusually competent combat commander," specifying that he would have preferred to have been succeeded as SACEUR [Supreme Army Commander Europe] by his longtime admired friend General Alfred Gruenther).

Ridgway hated—to this day hates—McCarthy: "I was there," he would always recall, "while Bob Stevens, an honorable man, suffered abuse from that skunk."

Ridgway listened to his boss, the Secretary of the Army, and then broke into an impassioned seconding speech: the Secretary had done battle like a champion, the General declared; he had victoriously upheld the honor of the officers of the United States Army.

Sitting near Ridgway amid the array of Army brass was Fred Seaton, a short, balding, somewhat rotund civilian. A wire-service copy of the memorandum of understanding lay on the table. Struve Hensel picked it up and handed it to Seaton—then Assistant Secretary of Defense for Legislative and Public Affairs. Seaton, forty-four, educated in journalism at Kansas State, where he did some sports broadcasting, was a Nebraska publisher who had built up a family empire of newspapers and radio stations in the Middle West. He was a liberal Republican, a man soft-spoken and unflappable, with a politician's shrewdness honed since he had traveled the country as a personal assistant to Alf Landon in the 1936 campaign, but also with a newspaperman's suspicion of what might lie in the fine print or around the next corner. As a teenager he'd made a brief excursion into barnstorm boxing; as a member of the Nebraska State Legislature years later he had ended an altercation by knocking a six-foot-three adversary across a coffee shop. He always loved to quote, pointedly, Percy Crosby's comic strip character Skippy, a little boy saying his bedside prayers: "Dear God, please make me a good boy." Pause. "But please don't make me too good a boy." Pause. "Because you know better than anybody else what a tough neighborhood this is."

For months Seaton had counseled Stevens at arm's length from the Department of Defense. He had insisted on looking beneath the surface and seeing the inevitable implications when Stevens and John Adams insisted on proceeding wide-eyed with Schine's appointment to the CID School as a result of the fallout of an IBM card lottery. And now at the meeting in Stevens's office Seaton read the text of the agreement with the McCarthy committee. He read it with care, as years later, when he became Secretary of the Interior, he would read with care every document that passed across his desk, realizing that half the problems of his predecessors came from a too great readiness to sign what landed before them. (Looking at a stack of documents, he once remarked, "Any one of these things may contain a bomb that could blow us sky-high.") Now he read and reread that memorandum of understanding in the room with the twenty-one Pentagon officers. He listened to Stevens's and Ridgway's euphoria. And again he read the text, in utter disbelief at the 180-degree discrepancy.

The meeting broke up. The twenty-one disbanded. Seaton approached Stevens as he walked out the door.

"Bob," he said quietly, "you've been had."

Stevens refused to see. At five-ten he returned a call from U.N. Ambassador Cabot Lodge in New York. Lodge was calling in with some suggestions for toughening up Stevens's statement on the morrow: "I had a few thoughts, based on my 13 years in the United States Senate, that might be helpful to you. . . ."

Stevens quickly straightened him out. ". . . Cabot, the hearing is off. Did you know that?"

Lodge was incredulous: "No."

"I . . . went up and had lunch at their request . . . with the Republican members of the committee."

"All of them?"

"Yes. We were there a long time, and finally worked out a memorandum of agreement which involves three things: 1) If there are Communists in the Armed Services, we want to get them out. 2) On the Peress case, . . . we had already instructed the Inspector General to make a report and when the report [is] finished, the fellows that . . . were connected with the promotion and honorable discharge . . . would be available for questioning by the committee. 3) With respect to Zwicker, . . . when Symington got back [from Europe], if the committee—not Senator McCarthy— . . . decided they wanted Zwicker to appear, he would be available."

Stevens was talking from memory. He had returned to the Pentagon without one scrap of paper on the understanding reached in the Capitol. And he still refused to realize what he had done.

"The net of all of it," Stevens continued, drawing a unique conclusion, "[is] that I fought the good fight, Cabot, for one thing, and that was to have the people from the Army and the Navy and the Air Force, when they go before that committee, to be treated decently. That is all I was fighting for. . . ."

And then Stevens looked back wistfully at the hearing that had now been scrubbed: "I personally . . . would like nothing better than to have gone on . . . and I have got some damn good material, let me tell you. On the other hand, the Republican leadership was very concerned about it. I wouldn't say they put any pressure on me, but they didn't want the hearing, if it could be avoided."

Lodge reminisced: "The underlying thing in all of this, between you and me, [is that] that is all preliminary to an attempt to destroy the President politically. There is no doubt about it. He is picking on the Army because Eisenhower was in the Army, and it is not the end of this. You have got to be prepared to live with it, you know."

"I have got to be prepared to live with it," Stevens answered. "And when the top leadership, and you know who that would be, were so anxious for me in any way possible to get this hearing called off at this time, I cooperated with them fully."

"I don't take any issue with this decision today," Lodge said, acquiescing. "In fact, it may be a good thing."

Stevens justified himself: "I showed these men I was dealing with at the top of the party there I was not taking an arbitrary stand. I was willing to listen to reason. I went along. And it will break out again, and I will say, 'We did it your way last time. This time we will do it mine.'"

"I know these guys," Lodge said, "and I know how their minds work. And the same crowd that supported Senator Taft at the convention in 1952 are all now revolving around Joe. And this is basically an attempt to destroy Eisenhower. . . ."

Stevens ventured into forbidden territory: "I had no knowledge at any time during this as to what the President thought about it, and I didn't want it. I thought this is one I had better handle myself. . . ."

Lodge had some information on the subject. "I sent the President this long memorandum last night about it, and he called me this morning . . . and asked me if I could talk to you on the phone."

"How did he feel about it?" Stevens asked anxiously.

"Pretty good."

Stevens was of course confused. "But [it] was his top legislative leaders who were talking to me." He couldn't understand the divergence—Eisenhower's encouraging Lodge's aggressiveness, Eisenhower's lieutenant, Persons, preaching accommodation.

Lodge knew about Persons and company: "They are inclined to appease this guy, you know." Then for the first time he revealed his knowledge of the John Adams chronology: "You have that documentation there on Boy S, and I think you ought to get that in shape . . . for publication."

"We are doing that."

"That would be a devastating thing."

At five thirty-three Stevens talked with Karl Mundt. "Dirksen said you wanted a copy of this memorandum of understanding," Mundt said. "I wonder if you would have an officer come to pick it up."

The copy arrived—an authentic text.

Stevens still refused to believe the obvious. He had a scattering of calls on the White House line and a call from McCarthy stalwart Senator Herman Welker of Idaho ("I can't have two friends like you fighting"). At six-thirty he phoned General Zwicker and went through his set piece once again: I have kept the faith; if you are called, you will not be abused, I guarantee you.

Then at six thirty-eight he got a call from Fred Seaton: "I wanted to tip you off to this. This gang of reporters caught up with Roger, Struve, and me in the hall. Roger went in his office, and we covered the front. The fellows who were talking to us were fellows like [Charlie] Corddry [of United Press] and boys like that. Our problem was this: . . . They said one of them was over at the Senate, apparently, and said they asked Mundt the question, if the treatment of officers was discussed, and he denied it categorically. Then they said when you came into your office, you said no comment on that. Then in the third of the press conferences, they quoted you . . . as having [said] you had every personal reason to believe that the military would be treated all right. They sighed over that; they said that does not add up. . . ."

Stevens turned defensive: "I gave a personal opinion because that is something outside those four walls I was in. But as to what happened inside those four walls I was in, I couldn't discuss that. I certainly did tell Joe McCarthy in no uncertain terms I thought he had abused General Zwicker very badly. I don't know what Mundt means. . . ."

"I am not trying to imply any criticism for what you said," Seaton replied. But, he went on, "there was the AP, UP, INS, *Washington Post* and the *Washington Star,* and they all seemed to have a unanimity about it. I would surmise that the story on it would not be too satisfactory."

Stevens writhed about in self-justification: "I . . . have told Nixon and Persons. . . . I expected an adverse press on it . . . I have played it out 100 percent. I have been stopped from something. . . . I think we would have given an excellent account of ourselves tomorrow, and I explained to you the reasons why we were stopped, and I did it as a cooperator because I believe in cooperation and playing on a team. But if it turns out I am a yellow-belly and McCarthy is a hero, I will have to go back to Dirksen and Mundt and Potter and McCarthy too, and tell them this is more than we in the Army can take, and I will have to issue a statement, and see what kind of a statement I could get them to approve."

Seaton once again soothed Stevens: "I wouldn't want to say it was going to be that bad"; then Seaton reverted to cold reality: "But on judgment, you might just as well get your statement prepared as to what you are going to try to get those Senators to agree to because I don't believe you have any choice in the matter if you want to avoid that sort of public opinion."

Stevens temporized: "I think we will wait and see how bad it is . . ."

"If up to now what is coming over the tape is bad, any corrective measures would have to be taken before tomorrow," Seaton added.

The addendum was unnecessary. It was, in fact, all over. At home and abroad reporters were already typing up their stories of Stevens's capitulation and surrender. He had gone into the luncheon a national hero; he had come out a national joke.

The icy truth at last dawned. That evening Ken BeLieu and Art Hadley met as Stevens's home. The Secretary had already downed several scotch-and-sodas. An old friend of his, a general in the Quartermaster Corps, was sitting on the stairs trying to console the Secretary: in a day or so it will all blow over.

"Can't you get him to eat something?" a shaken Mrs. Stevens implored Hadley and BeLieu. The two men got to work. They rewrote and toughened the statement Stevens had planned to use in his testimony before the committee. Mrs. Stevens carried it upstairs. The Secretary, only partially aware, approved. Hadley got on the phone and dictated from it to a group of top reporters. All went with it except one—John Finney, Pentagon correspondent for the United Press and a friend of one of Stevens's sons. He insisted on confirming it with the Secretary. Ken BeLieu handed Stevens the phone: "It's your old friend John Finney."

"Hi, John, I'm going to fight. I didn't eat chicken. I'm going to fight."

"Is the statement accurate, Mr. Secretary?"

"I'm going to fight, John."

That was corroboration enough: in the UP office the news was already clattering out on the AP ticker.

As the evening wore on, Stevens put in one phone call after another. He tried to reach Sherman Adams and failed. He did get through to Dick Nixon, who remembers the caller as "highly emotional," a man who had made up his mind to issue a statement the next day and then submit his resignation. And Stevens called Eisenhower's press secretary, Jim Hagerty, the man who had brought Ike the first word of the fried chicken lunch as it poured out over the White House news ticker—in this period, before later elegant White House redecoration, housed in Jim's office bathroom. And Hagerty recorded in his secret diary: Stevens called "me . . . at 10 P.M. to say he wanted to release his statement and then resign. [I] told him to cool off overnight. But we were sure dumb. Someone let Stevens walk right into a bear trap, and now I'll have to work like hell to get him out of it. What a job!"

The roof fell in. Over a front-page photo of Stevens and McCarthy sitting side by side, McCarthy smiling, whispering into Stevens's ear, the *New York Times* the next morning ran a three-column headline: "Stevens Bows to McCarthy at Administration Behest; Will Yield Data on Peress . . . Officers to Testify." Every major paper in London would include in its headline the key word "surrender," the London *Times* announcing: "Senator McCarthy this afternoon achieved what General Burgoyne and General Cornwallis never achieved—the surrender of the American Army." McCarthy would be credited with a gleeful quote: "He couldn't have given in more abjectly if he had gotten down on his knees." The brave words of Stevens's planned statement in defense of Zwicker only raised the height from which Stevens had fallen.

At eight-thirty that morning, February 25, Stevens phoned Dirksen. "It worked just about like I told you it would, and I can't buy it. I am going to have to do something. It may get drastic. I don't want to do anything until all you fine fellows that are working on these big problems tell me what you think, but I am not going to leave it where it is.

"I think I have been absolutely crucified and the Services along with me. . . . Just what the right thing to do is, I don't know. My present thinking on this, Everett, since I feel bound by the fact that I can't comment on what went on yesterday, . . . I feel I have to ask that group . . . to reassemble and go back up there and say . . . that the whole thing is so misunderstood by the press that I will have to make a statement. . . ."

"Let me call Karl," Dirksen replied.

An hour and a half later he phoned back. "I had a hell of a time rounding them up," he told Stevens. "[Be] in my office at 1:00, 204 Senate Office Building. . . . Now Bob, not a soul knows about this. . . ."

No one ever would. The meeting never took place. Other strategies outside Stevens's control overrode it. And for the moment, as twenty-five reporters milled about in the hall, all he could do was sit in his office and wait, as he'd been instructed from higher up, for a possible call from "over there."

A few minutes after Dirksen hung up, Stevens called J. Edgar Hoover. The FBI Director was upset at a Roy Cohn allegation that John Adams had said he paid no attention to FBI reports.

"Anybody in the entire Army who said he wouldn't pay attention to FBI reports," Stevens reassured Hoover, "would be instantly relieved by me."

Within hours John Adams himself would beg ex-FBI man Frank Carr to tell him "[Have I] ever done anything to indicate . . . that I thought the FBI had no capacity in the field of security?" He would implore Carr ("Are you close to the Director?") to vouch for Adams's fealty to "what the FBI [is] trying to do for all of us in this field."

At twelve twenty-three Stevens talked with Hensel.

"Don't let this damn thing get you down," Hensel counseled.

"It is hard not to. . . ." Stevens reviewed his defenses: "I was all ready to appear with a magnificent statement, . . . and I was not a bit afraid of McCarthy's bullying. Then some of the high political advisors of the Administration—I don't mean the President—got worried about it, and a number of them put a lot of pressure on me that there must not be a hearing: there must be an agreement. . . . I knew they were wrong."

Hensel, a man ever inclined to do battle and now gifted with hindsight, agreed: "They were absolutely wrong."

"It really was put on the basis that I had to cooperate. . . . The fact is that they gave the President a bad steer. There was no reason for it to get to the President at all; and now, by reason of the advice that was given and the course of action I was embarked upon, the President through no fault of his own or mine, really, he is right in the middle of it." Loyalty to the organization had been replaced with loyalty to the leader.

Hensel had some memories of his own: "As I have known for many months, they have got some very timid souls in the White House. . . ."

"They gave [the President] a very bum steer on this . . . ," Stevens reasoned, "and now there is no way he can stay out of it. . . ."

What did the President think? That was Stevens's—and everybody else's—question. At two-thirteen Stevens got a call from one of the few men in the world who could give Eisenhower unvarnished advice—General Lucius Clay, phoning from New York. "I was his 'no' man," Clay declared years later in an interview. Clay—a courtly officer from Georgia with a steel-trap mind—had succeeded Ike in Germany at the end of the war and had on the ground responded to the Russians' Berlin blockade by immediately ordering the breaking of it by the airlift. Lucius Clay was a civilized George Patton. When Eisenhower was pulling and hauling over whether to run in 1952, it had been Clay who had finally secured Eisenhower's assent. Clay was devoted to the United States Army and he was devoted to Eisenhower. Now he phoned the Army's civilian Secretary.

"I got the dope," Clay began, "that Sherman Adams and the group were all set to battle, and then I read the papers. Have they let you down from up above?"

"Yes, but not the Boss. . . . About 48 hours ago some of the top political advisors got into the act and they said that the Republicans shouldn't be squabbling among themselves. . . . I had everything in great shape, the flag at the mast. The President wasn't in it in any way, shape or form. They pulled the carpet completely from under me; and they dropped it right in the President's lap. . . ."

"He is accredited all over the country with having run out on you."

Clay asked about his old friend of campaign days, Herb Brownell: "Did Herb advise that they compromise this thing?"

"I never had any contact with him on it at all."

"Mainly the Senate people?"

"Yes, plus Jerry [Persons]."

Clay had known Persons for years, and they had high respect for each other: "Oh well, he is always for armistice. I personally think this has hurt the party one hell of a lot. . . . I have a right to go to the Boss and tell him what I think at least once, and I have never used it yet; and this is an issue on which I am prepared to use it."

Clay didn't miss a beat. He at once phoned the White House.

"I heard about this fracas just this morning," Eisenhower told him. "I feel the Army must go down and admit [an] administrative error. . . . [And then stand its] ground and [not] give an inch. . . . [Stevens] is now in a state of shock and near hysteria. He made an error in agreeing too quickly."

"They were just too smart for him," Clay answered.

"He is too honorable," Eisenhower continued. "I personally have done this time and again—I have stood for straightforward Americanism. I have never mentioned a name. I don't intend to advertise [McCarthy]."

Clay touched a nerve: "This thing [gave an] initial impression that you instructed Stevens to settle this thing."

Eisenhower bridled: "Nothing could be further from the truth!"

Clay raised a specter: "This fellow [has] got too powerful—people [are] scared to do anything about him. I'm willing to bet he has information on honorable discharges while you were Chief of Staff."

Eisenhower brushed off the threat: "Never in my life has any Communist been brought to my attention in any organization except at Columbia where . . . [a] man was fired. [McCarthy] could never be able to prove there was anything where I authorized [a subversive's honorable] . . . discharge." But he discerned Mc-Carthy's political vision: "[He has] made speeches calling all Demo-crats traitors, knowing that that will defeat us in the long run be-cause we must have Democrats to win. Consequently he will go around and pick up the pieces. He's crazy if he believes that."

Finally Clay returned to the practical question: "[I] don't think you can lock horns on this one—[Stevens] has made [a] fight im-possible. . . ."

The Secretary, Clay reflected years later in an interview, had "cut Eisenhower's feet off at the ankles."

Meanwhile, behind the curtain that separated Stevens from the White House, in the words of the diary of Eisenhower's press secre-tary, Jim Hagerty, "[The] Stevens-McCarthy row really kicked up a mess. Staff meeting broke early so Adams, self, Persons, Martin, Morgan could have meeting with Nixon and Bill Rogers. Later moved meeting to East Wing where Sen. Dirksen joined us. Piec-ing together yesterday's news seems that the senators really jobbed up on Stevens, or else he didn't realize what he was doing. May have good results in long run, however.

"1) Dirksen agreed to get Republican members of committee to-gether and see if they could issue additional statement saying com-mittee had complete confidence in Stevens's 'integrity and ability.' 2) That he was pursuing proper course of action in dealing with problems arising from Peress case. 3) Action to be taken by Ste-vens after completion of Inspector General's report made it evident may not be necessary to call any officers involved and 4) If called would be treated with 'proper respect.'

"Also Dirksen will work on Republican members and Democrats on committee to get Cohn fired, to stop one-man committee from meeting, and to strip McCarthy of some of his powers by saying subpoena could be issued by only majority vote. Dirksen couldn't deliver." As the senator implied in a press conference late that after-noon after hours of deliberation, McCarthy adamantly rejected any wording that suggested criticism of his past conduct.

"President very mad and getting fed up. It is his Army and he doesn't like McCarthy's tactics at all. . . . Ike on subject: 'This guy McCarthy is going to get into trouble over this. I am not going to take this one lying down. . . . My friends [Clay?] tell me it won't be long in this Army stuff before McCarthy starts using my name instead of Stevens's. He's ambitious. He wants to be President. He's the last guy in the world who will ever get there, if I have any thing to say.'"

At four o'clock, Hagerty recorded, Stevens and Roger Kyes came to the White House to meet with the President and "all of us . . . worked 'til 5:30 on a statement. Cleared it with President, who made it stronger, and then released it in press conference in my office."

"I shall never accede to the abuse of Army personnel under any circumstances, including committee hearings," Stevens told the assembled reporters. "I shall never accede to them being browbeaten or humiliated. I do not intend them to be deprived of counsel when the matter under consideration is one of essential interest to me as Secretary, as was the case with General Zwicker.

"From assurances which I have received from members of the subcommittee, I am confident that they will not permit such conditions to develop in the future."

When Stevens finished reading his statement, Hagerty came forward. The President, he told the reporters, endorses Stevens's words "one hundred percent."

Stevens returned to his office at the Department of the Army. His staff burst into applause as he entered. "We've certainly got a commander-in-chief," Stevens told them. "He stepped right up and hit a home run."

Within minutes, Stevens was phoning General Ridgway. Once again, euphoria. Ridgway was jubilant over the ringing declaration, backed by both the President and the Secretary of Defense. "I can't tell you how proud we are of it," Ridgway rejoiced. "And Penny is right here, too."

Stevens phoned Art Hadley, and the two congratulated each other on the way they had, the night before when the clouds looked darkest, got things moving, had their say in the morning headlines, and begun to "save the situation."

The next morning Stevens talked with Clay: "Thanks for getting in when the going was tough."

"That is the only time I am worth a damn." No elation here; Clay was already looking ahead. He, like Cabot Lodge, had learned about John Adams's chronology. "I would let that Adams' [*sic*] story leak out."

"That is being, you might say, staffed carefully now with that thought in mind," Secretary of the Army Stevens replied.

So by this time Rogers, Sherman Adams, Lodge, and Clay knew about the John Adams chronology. So did Vice President Nixon, who that same day, February 26, told the *New York Times*'s Arthur Krock—off the record—about this devastating document "two inches thick," which would ruin Cohn, and about Eisenhower's approval of the plan to get Cohn fired.

In the midst of all this furor Frank Carr was phoning the author of that chronology, John Adams: "What a ruckus, huh?" The two men still spoke cordially. Carr came from the University of Pennsylvania Law School and more than a decade in the FBI. He was amiable of disposition and bulbous of shape, and Adams had watched him down many a piece of pie at working lunches. But now Adams deplored that "the situation has deteriorated since those friendly days." For the first time he had a stenographer on the line, monitoring.

Over at the White House, Eisenhower would confide to his diary: "McCarthy is grabbing the headlines and making the people believe that he is driving the Administration out of Washington." And a few feet away in the privacy of his office, Jim Hagerty recorded the scene: "Everybody jittery around here. Can't beg off when going is tough."

VI

"WITH YOU AT THE HELM"

At the beginning of March 1954, the President had just won a contentious battle against the Bricker Amendment, a constitutional change introduced by conservative Taftite Republican Senator John Bricker of Ohio to cut down the power of the President to make treaties. One of its clauses Eisenhower had found particularly objectionable: the "which clause." In some instances this would have kept a treaty from going into effect until it had undergone action by the United States Senate, the United States House of Representatives, and 48 separate State Legislatures.

Eisenhower did not stonewall all attempts to compromise. But, he told the legislative leaders on January 11, 1954, if the "which clause" stayed in, "I'll go into every state to fight it." In such a fight he would have undoubtedly come up against members of his own party. The Democrats, he informed Hagerty on January 29, were then in the position of saving the Constitution from the Republicans.

In the weeks that followed, Eisenhower had dug into legislative details, had phoned, had twisted arms, determined to block this "stupid, blind violation of the Constitution by stupid, blind isolationists." And in the end he won. On February 17 the Senate killed the "which clause."

In this fight Eisenhower had a simple strategy and a simple desideratum: to persuade the Congress to vote his way. And he looked with scorn and exasperation on the Republican senators who shrank from conflict.

"Senator Bridges, Senator Millikin, and Senator Saltonstall," he wrote in his diary January 18, "are not natural leaders. . . . They do not seem to realize when there arrives that moment at which soft speaking should be abandoned and a fight to the end undertaken. . . ."

Although Eisenhower's scorn this time hit Saltonstall, a Massa-

224

chusetts liberal, it tended to fall hardest on the party's far right. "Ike never had any concern about taking on a man like Jenner," former Attorney General Bill Rogers recalled years later in an interview, adverting to a time when Jenner wanted an unqualified Indiana candidate appointed as a judge and Eisenhower and Rogers had ridden roughshod over his objections and threats, insisting on a sterling appointment. On March 12, 1954, Eisenhower wrote to his longtime newspaper-executive friend Bill Robinson, attacking the "reactionary fringe of the Republican Party that hates and despises everything for which I stand. . . ." On August 21 he confided to Hagerty that the only right approach on domestic problems was a liberal approach. "Our hidebound reactionaries," he declared, "won't get to first base." And he told Hagerty to hold to this line and pay no attention to anyone else in the White House who was advising the opposite, "particularly the boys working with the Congress," i.e., Jerry Persons, Jerry Morgan, and Jack Martin.

Given a clear-cut issue, Eisenhower did not hold back from battle. He did not lack combativeness. He did not fear the right wing of his party. And he did not fall short in his inner commitment to the root issue—freedom of the mind. In the secret intimacy of his diary in the week of February 7, 1954, he set down the theme for the approaching bicentennial of the university he had headed, Columbia: "Man's right to knowledge and the free use thereof." And then he expatiated on it: "An intriguing phrase—it rings in the ears almost as if we could hear Patrick Henry's immortal call to liberty or death. Merely to claim this resounding slogan as our own gives us a feeling of superiority over the demagogues, the jingoes, the tyrants who thrive [on] the ignorance of others and employ curtains of iron or of oratory to deepen and prolong that ignorance. We thrill ourselves by our own insistence on academic freedom—the teacher's right to knowledge and his privilege of imparting his own interpretations thereof. We point with pride to American schools from primary to graduate level and, comparing them to institutions of learning in Prague, Budapest, and Moscow, we emphasize the extent and scope of our freedoms and the enrichment of human life deriving therefrom.

"We are proud of our guarantees of freedom in thought and speech and worship. Of such value are all these things to us that, unconsciously, we are guilty of one of the greatest errors that ignorance can make—we assume that our standard of values is shared by all other humans in the world." And then he set down, in tantalizing and unelaborated list form: "We are not sufficiently informed. Probable have more need for education than any other. Twenty-one POW's chose Communism. . . ."

The President could set down these abstract convictions. But he still had no effective practical means of enforcing them against McCarthy. No showdown vote was approaching. No constitutional principle had come under challenge. A head-on collision of assertions in the news columns and headlines wouldn't work. In fact, it would backfire, Ike was convinced, as it had backfired for three long years on Truman and Acheson.

So as the month of March began, Eisenhower had no anti-McCarthy blueprint. He had only a determination to do three things: to avoid a personal engagement in the loathsome enemy's gutter; to focus the attention of the country on higher ground, principles of right conduct and the enactment of constructive legislative proposals; and to chip away at the Senator through the instrument of his organization.

But that instrument was defective. It included, for one thing, a shaken and questionable Secretary of the Army. "Ike let Stevens hang alone out there for a long time," a knowledgeable Pentagon correspondent reflected years later. "He should have said, 'I won't let my Secretary of the Army be treated this way.'" Perhaps. But Stevens's evident errors precluded a full presidential stamp of approval. There was at this point little that the President could do. Stevens had one of the most important positions in the world, and the dog with the bone is always in danger. His television audiences were eventually to see him as a good guy but indecisive; the White House already saw him in the same light. To his superiors, the underling necessarily is a man supposed to do his job; he must not expect his superior to do it for him. Ideally, if the organization chart works as it should, the superior never has anything to do. One must of course add as a corollary that no organization has ever worked as it should. Publicly, Eisenhower had backed Stevens's press conference assertions 100 percent.

Ike's organization included, as Stevens's superior, the Secretary of Defense, Engine-Charlie Wilson, with his penchant for foot-in-mouth press conferences (he once antagonized unemployed workers by likening them to "kennel-fed dogs" that instead of hunting "sit on their fanny and yell" and once described a perilous Middle East crisis as "a ripple")—a man who, for all his bluff honesty and managerial strength, lacked the finesse to maneuver through a political morass. "The trouble with you fellows," he would tell a Senate committee, white-haired in a striped suit, a cigarette bouncing on his lips, "is you don't understand the problem."

Ike's organization included also a set of Republican senatorial leaders of dubious reliability; at any given moment you never knew exactly which side they were playing on. And it included a split White House staff—men who, fervently loyal to the President, honestly differed, even at this date, on presidential strategy toward McCarthy and McCarthyism, disagreeing both on the weight they would assign to the McCarthy threat and on the advice they would give the Boss.

So a month of improvisation began. Within the larger Republican organization an operative ad hoc organization began to form. It was an organization never given a chart or charter, never given formal marching orders for day-to-day guidance; yet it was an organization absolutely loyal and responsive to the President and capable of immersing itself in the detail he habitually delegated to men he trusted. This activist organization had at its core four men—Sherman Adams and Jim Hagerty in the White House, Fred Seaton and Struve Hensel in the Pentagon. These four were to do the job.

Sherman Adams was Eisenhower's alter ego. "Here's my conscience after me again," Ike once quipped to fellow golfers as Adams crossed the fairway bearing some papers requiring a presidential decision. "He didn't say *that* very often," Adams reflected years later with pride.

Dour, tough, and liberal—but no ideologue like C. D. Jackson—Adams was a liberal ready to subordinate his liberalism to the exigencies of practical politics and the wishes of the President, to which he remained always exquisitely sensitive.

"The White House Staff," Adams reflected years later, "was an adjunct to the President. Without a commission, it responded to what was going on, and fell together to meet its responsibilities. The President never told the staff to get him out of the McCarthy crossfire. But he obviously hoped the staff would." Equally obviously, if the staff had done something wrong, the President would have objected; Eisenhower therefore exercised a negative control.

The entire White House staff made contributions in the battle, Adams added, but particularly men like Hagerty, who had a press responsibility, and Persons, who had his responsibility for the Congress. Some of the President's most valued advisors, of course, like Gabe Hauge, remained largely "in the cheering section in this struggle." For with the exception of Adams, Persons, and Hagerty, few of the staff were versed in tangling with such a rending practical political problem.

Press Secretary Jim Hagerty, in and out of the President's office hour after hour, day after day, had the President's ear and total confidence. A canny judge of the press, redheaded, with a pungent personality, a hot Irish temper, and aggressive honesty—"I have never lied to a reporter," he proudly proclaimed—Jim had gone through the political fires with Governor Tom Dewey of New York. He served in his White House job from the moment Eisenhower entered the building until the moment he left. Reporters to this day recall his regime as the best, most responsive, most professional in memory.

On New Year's Day 1954, Jim began keeping a diary—the best single record in existence of the behind-the-scenes Eisenhower, his anger, his asides, his fire matched by Jim's own. Jim had known Joe McCarthy since 1948, when the two of them campaigned in the Oregon presidential primary—Jim for Dewey, McCarthy for Harold Stassen. He had seen Joe even then putting out "mystical numbers." But between them through the intervening years there had arisen no personal bitterness.

Jim had met another campaigner in Oregon that year—Fred Seaton of Nebraska, also campaigning for Stassen against Dewey. Years later, after Fred became Secretary of the Interior, in the Washington practice of covering every wall with inscribed photographs of one's political acquaintants, Fred had hung in a prominent place in his office a shot of Jim inscribed: "To Fred Seaton, from his friend and fellow traveler—Jim." In the hot crucible of the McCarthy conflict, their trust and friendship would be refined.

As Assistant Secretary of Defense for Legislative and Public Affairs, Fred Seaton was the Jim Hagerty—and also the Jerry Persons—of the Pentagon, that most mammoth, most powerful of the twentieth century's impersonal bureaucracies, sprawling into every state and onto every continent. Fred always called it "the puzzle palace." Significantly, Fred always saw himself as an Eisenhower staff member, whatever his location, whether on the 1952 campaign train, in the Pentagon, in the White House later as Deputy Assistant to the President under Sherman Adams, or in the Department of the Interior, where, as Secretary, he heightened his effectiveness by never breaking his iron ties with all his pals in the White House Palace Guard.

During the McCarthy crisis Fred became the indispensable link—

the only link—between Pentagon and White House. On one side of the river he worked with John Adams and Stevens on the Army's emerging chronology. On the other side he met constantly with Sherman Adams, Hagerty, Persons, and Morgan. On the death of Nebraska Republican Senator Ken Wherry, in 1951, Fred had been appointed an interim United States Senator. He was thus also a member of the world's most exclusive club—the only one on either the White House or Pentagon staffs. Around the Hill he knew his way. He was an operator, in Sherman Adams's admiring words a "situation man, as I discovered when I first met him during the 1952 campaign out in Eisenhower's headquarters in the Brown Palace Hotel in Denver." Adams had had Seaton organize the campaign train as a "good detail man."

Fred could be blunt without irritating people. As he traveled the country with Vice President Nixon during his 1960 campaign, a young staff member came up with a remark that annoyed Fred. "Any more comments like that, my friend," Fred said with a smile, "and you'll find yourself spending the rest of the campaign either back in your office in Washington or here on the train with the candidate—wherever you want to be least." The message got through; no feelings were bruised. "Fred had a lot of good qualities," Sherman Adams once reflected, "and one of them was that he was not afraid to work hard."

In the McCarthy combat, Adams well remembers, "Fred took on the responsibility for calling the shots. In fact, he fell into it. We knew the President would neither be the spokesman nor delegate formal responsibility for solving the McCarthy problem. He remained a bystander, absenting himself from the core of the problem." So Fred became the point man. "I gave him," Adams added, "the nominal support of the President's office." Adams and Seaton didn't go to the President for suggestions: "We'd make those decisions." It was as simple as that.

Fred was a politician through and through, circumspect and surefooted about whom he could trust. "He was a smoothie," a Pentagon reporter who knew him well recalled admiringly. "*He* would never have gone to a fried chicken lunch." And Seaton had long since lost confidence—along with the White House staff—in Robert Ten Broeck Stevens. "I think [in this chapter the boss] is being a little overly kind to Bob Stevens," Fred wrote me about an early draft of the Eisenhower *Mandate for Change* chapter. "Wittingly or not, [Bob] got the Administration in one hell of a lot of unnecessary trouble."

But there was one man in the Pentagon whom, above everybody else in those electric days, Fred Seaton trusted to the core—Struve Hensel. On the Pentagon organization chart Hensel occupied a new position—Assistant Secretary of Defense for International Security Affairs. But through the McCarthy fracas he continued to wear his old hat as the Defense Department's General Counsel, its chief lawyer. Hensel shared Seaton's lack of confidence in Stevens. Moreover, he had had his personal run-in with the Secretary of the Army over W. J. McNeil, Pentagon Comptroller, and had considered himself almost *persona non grata* in the Office of the Secretary of the Army until the day of the fried chicken lunch.

Hensel had an office next door to Seaton's. "Fred was a westerner," Hensel once recalled with an amused smile, "who tried to make believe he didn't like eastern ways." (Hensel himself was born in Hoboken, went to Princeton and Columbia Law School, and practiced law on Wall Street before and after his Washington years in the Navy Department during the war.) "But if you looked carefully, you could see his raincoat came from Brooks Brothers." The McCarthy problem threw the two men more and more together. "They worked hand in glove," Seaton's trusted aide Phil Mullin recalls, "with great respect and trust on both sides." Again and again one could hear Fred say with amused resignation, "I've got to go hassle with Hensel."

Fifty-two-year-old Struve Hensel, an observant reporter remarked, "was kind of a big woof-woof"—huge, well over six feet, and heavy, well over two hundred pounds. Fred, eight years younger, was relatively short and stocky, though with a onetime boxer's cockiness. Gladys Seaton, his wife, recalls that seeing the two of them walking together reminded her of a great shaggy dog with a small terrier trotting alongside. Both Gladys Seaton and Isabel Hensel were—and are—attractive, bright, articulate, sparkling, and informed. They became fast friends. And they and their husbands loved to drive up Connecticut Avenue and relax over an abundance of Chinese cooking.

Both Struve and Isabel Hensel were people of force and outspokenness. As the Pentagon's top legal officer, he radically changed the practice of his predecessor, a legalistic-minded lawyer who kept seeing the presence of gray areas wherein nobody could move. Hensel took the stand that no gray areas existed; that he should enunciate clearly the prerogatives of the Secretary and make those prerogatives stick. And Isabel Hensel, at an elegant party at the home of

Edward R. Murrow in Pawling, New York, upon hearing Murrow make a disparaging toast to President Eisenhower, turned on her heel and walked out, forcing his later apology.

The four men—Adams, Hagerty, Seaton, Hensel—did not confer together. Each saw part of the whole. And Fred Seaton, the only man at home in both buildings, saw most.

Secretive, he kept few records. He left no trail. He carried information in his head. He wrote no memoranda of meetings. He almost never had a phone call monitored. If he needed a witness to his end of a phone conversation, he would call in Phil Mullin to listen. Even in talking with Hensel, Seaton confined himself to what Hensel needed to know. Seaton would never tell him, for example, everything that happened in the White House.

Slowly, through the whole month of March, the tight organization solidified in marching order. And one watches with fascination as the fingers of its participants reach out to touch the other players— the Secretary of Defense, the Secretary of the Army and his counselor, the White House congressional liaison staff, the Republicans and Democrats on the subcommittee, and Joe McCarthy himself— all for the advantage of the President.

Out of sight in shrouded secrecy, Hensel and Seaton had started to rework the John Adams chronology to make it unassailable. And time was running out. At eleven forty-four on the morning of March 1, Hensel talked with Stevens. "We made some investigations as to the number of people who knew about [the chronology]," Hensel said, "and there are so many that know about it, that we became very worried that the story would leak out." Both men agreed that the Pentagon should not take the initiative in putting out the Adams chronicle. But, Hensel went on to Stevens, "I am apprehensive to the point that I am not sure we can sit on it. When I talked to the fellow who wrote most of it, I found that a lot of copies had been given out, outside of the department; and every day he thinks of a new one who has seen it; and he made a guess that probably fifty people inside the Department had read it and maybe a hundred heard about it.

"It is a question of time [until] somebody forces it. So [Adams] had better be ready . . . with the documentation, and . . . all of the people who can confirm [it]. . . . Certain telephone calls, and any recordings—let's check them. . . ."

Despite his on-the-record memo to Rogers ("This is the only copy [of the chronology] leaving my possession") and his two-week pause before sending a second copy to Sherman Adams, John Adams had admitted to Hensel what he later admitted under oath: that in the month of February he had been leaking the chronology—in whole or in part—all over Washington. Specifically, he would testify later, he had shown all of it to columnist Joe Alsop and at least parts of it to Phil Potter of the *Baltimore Sun* (a fellow South Dakotan and a close confidant), Homer Bigart of the *New York Herald Tribune*, and Murray Marder of the *Washington Post.* In addition, he had made no particular secret of the pressure Cohn was putting on him, discussing it with at least twenty Army officers, as well as his wife, his family, and occasional guests in his home.

Was this leakage a deliberate Administration stratagem? Did someone higher up—not Stevens, who swore he didn't know about it and in fact disapproved of it—put Adams up to it?

Sherman Adams in his memoir *Firsthand Report* at least seems to leave open the possibility that someone did: "Not entirely by accident," he writes, the Army's document "fell into the hands of a few newspaper correspondents" before the subcommittee saw it. "Their stories built up a backfire against McCarthy, as intended."

But behind this enigmatic sentence lies a curious history. As Sherman Adams in 1959 was writing *Firsthand Report*, with the under-the-table help of then Interior Secretary Fred Seaton, he would make occasional notes of questions to ask Fred. One such question reads: "Ask—who did we leak Adams notes to?" And an answer to this question—doubtless from Seaton—also recorded in Sherman Adams's notes, reads: "[John] Adams past [*sic*] transcript to Alsop."

If John Adams in 1954 leaked to the press in accordance with an administration master plan, the inquiring Sherman Adams in 1959 had, on this evidence, forgotten its details.

If John Adams leaked in accordance with an administration master plan, Fred Seaton's answer to Sherman Adams says nothing about such a strategy.

If John Adams leaked in accordance with an administration master plan, one must assume that Seaton knew about it—indeed controlled it—in total detail. But an undated, unsigned one-page sheet in Seaton's handwriting—without a caption but doubtless on the chronology—reveals that Seaton had only a limited knowledge of exactly where, and how far, it had gone. In one column Seaton lists the men who, to his knowledge, had *read* it, whether they got it from John Adams, Sherman Adams, Bill Rogers, or someone else: Nixon, Rogers, S. Adams, Persons, Hensel, Lodge, Seaton, Clay,

Morris Ernst, J. Edgar Hoover, Alsop. Fred also lists four men who *knew* about the document—Dirksen, Art Hadley, Reston, and "[Jack] Anderson." The last three have question marks after their names. But John Adams, as he admitted in his testimony, had gone far beyond the limits of Seaton's list.

Finally, if John Adams leaked in accordance with an administration master plan, Fred Seaton's closest Pentagon confidant, Struve Hensel, knew nothing about it. In fact, to him the leakage was just making life tougher: inquiries might start coming any minute, and the Pentagon was unready for them. Nobody had yet climbed on top of all the facts, and Hensel was scrambling trying to assemble them.

As Hensel talked on the phone to Stevens that March 1, he sized up the demands of this job. First, who should do the nitty-gritty work? "I talked to John about that," Hensel remarked, "and he said he has a fellow in his office who could make that kind of investigation . . . ; and I think we ought to use that fellow as legwork. But I would like to have somebody from this office do it too because I want somebody [on] a little different level to be critical about [the] proof. . . . If an assistant of John's does all of it, he may not be so critical."

Next, Hensel reflected on how the evidence should be sorted out. "We probably want to make up . . . an outline of the facts and substance that can be confirmed by at least two people," Hensel told Stevens. "We have got some [talks] where we . . . had only one fellow present and he [McCarthy] had three. I would say destroy that because we don't want the document in this shape to get out. Does that make sense?"

Stevens concurred. Then Hensel turned to a shortcoming in Stevens's organization. "I think one thing you need there is an investigative section, probably in John Adams's office, so that when one of these things breaks, somebody just goes to work twenty-four hours and gets all of the facts—something I recommended back in April for Roger [Kyes] to do up here. We have got it in the [Department of the] Air Force. . . . When Zwicker was up there testifying about Peress, . . . somebody could have gotten up at the back of the room and said, 'Mr. Senator, we don't object to your talking about this with General Zwicker, but we have all of the papers and information on this matter. . . .' [That way we'd] make sure we get a full story right away, rather than a piecemeal story which enables [McCarthy] to get the [first news] story, and then the full facts are never read. I would check back like the devil and try to get on top of all of the facts in the Peress case. . . ."

Stevens bridled. "Listen, Struve, that has all been taken care of. Hell, I published it in the newspaper. I wrote [McCarthy] a letter which appeared in the newspaper. If we have any more Peress cases, the discharge will go to a Board of Officers. . . . We have changed all those things."

"Has [the change] been made public . . . ?"

"I saved a lot of that material to use in the hearing. I don't want you to think that we sat here . . ."

"I am not thinking. I am asking questions. . . . Maybe we ought to start thinking [about] our next move . . . because I am sure the Peress case is going to come up again. I think two things: that we ought to have a release that will promptly go out as to what the new procedure is . . . , and that we ought to be grooming a witness who can testify, . . . someone who knows all the facts. . . ."

Stevens bridled again. "I will be that fellow. . . ."

"Have you got all the facts?"

"Sure, I have got all the facts."

"I think you ought to check the fellow you want to advise you. Let me have the facts. Let's run through some skull practice as to what the questions are to be at your convenience."

Hensel, characteristically, was anticipating evil. Stevens, characteristically, wasn't.

"We will have some notice for the meetings," the Secretary of the Army replied. "So I don't think we ought to do that right now."

Hensel pressed him: "You might let me see what you have got, so we can get ready. . . ."

Stevens at last acquiesced: "I don't think it is good enough just to sit back and do nothing. But what it is, that is what I need some help on."

Hensel cast about for a diversion: "Is there something else we can start talking about that takes [people's] minds off . . . McCarthy . . . ? Are there some releases we can give on what the Army is doing or has done?"

"I think there are; but I have been under the impression that the thinking at your level and other levels up there was that we ought to do nothing."

"Let me grab hold of Seaton and see what his view is."

As this crucial conversation reveals, even at that late moment the Army's strategy remained defensive. The raw Adams chronology was leaking; the Army policy was to stand ready, fully armed with facts, if it had to respond. The Peress case remained a threat; the

Army was to get itself organized to answer. Meanwhile, they thought it might help to try to divert public attention from McCarthy altogether.

Work went full speed ahead turning the Adams chronology into a new document. "It included some obscenities," Hensel recalled later in an interview. "So Fred and I cleaned it up." At this period there was still leisure to sanitize a text. "Stevens and Adams went through it for about three days," Hensel continued. "If they disagreed on something, we'd drop it out. If they agreed, we'd leave it in. A career man on my staff, Frank Brown—he's dead now—did a lot of the revision. He was very reliable and thorough. And that's how we produced an expurgated version. . . ."

On page one, while the Army was limping along, the nation's press was yelling for action. The March 1 *Washington Post* had carried a column by Walter Lippmann denouncing McCarthy's "totalitarianism . . . his cold, calculated, sustained and ruthless effort to make himself feared. . . ." In Lippmann's view McCarthy had become a "candidate for . . . the dictatorship of the Republican Party." Two days later Joseph and Stewart Alsop would write: "If the President permits just one more appeasement of Senator McCarthy, he can say goodbye to his own authority in his administration, in his party and in the Congress." And *Time* magazine would declare that "no one but the President can get McCarthy out of his dominant position in the headlines—a position from which he gives the false impression of dominating the government."

Eisenhower met alone with Stevens on Sunday, February 28, and Tuesday, March 2. In these extended conferences he made his instructions crystal clear to the Army Secretary. As Eisenhower remembered the talks in a diary entry dated May 11: "I gave him one piece of advice, which to my mind is still sound. I told him, 'Admit that the handling of the Peress case was bungled in the Army. Tell the entire truth in connection with the affair and hold back no information unless the security of the country might be involved in some way. Along with these two things stand upon your rights; demand the treatment that should be accorded to an American in a responsible position, and if you are not accorded this kind of courtesy and respectful treatment, do not attend the hearings until you are guaranteed this kind of treatment.'"

On Monday morning March 1, as Hensel was talking with Stevens, Eisenhower was trying to make some things clear to the Republican legislative leaders. In doing so he had his problems. He would never, he said, challenge the right of Congress to investigate the executive branch.

"But," he went on, "we can't defeat Communism in the United States by destroying things in which we believe."

"The President was tough," Hagerty recorded, "and said he was going to speak his mind." Senator Saltonstall broke in with the irrelevance that the Army should have admitted its mistake. Eisenhower sharply reminded him that the Army had. Eisenhower deplored the fact that "under some sort of pressure [Stevens] agreed to a statement that was just terrible." Representative Charlie Halleck outright chastised Dirksen, Mundt, and Potter for not having protected Stevens. ("How Halleck stands out," Hagerty once wrote admiringly of the gutsy majority leader from Indiana.) Knowland protested. The three senators, he contended, had tried to protect the Republican Party from an open hearing on TV. The Army's conduct, in his view, had been inexcusable. He rambled on about Army red tape, coming up with the suggestion that all refusals to sign loyalty statements should be put onto IBM cards. As he spoke, he tore off sheets from a notepad in emphasis.

As this exasperating exchange went on, back at the Pentagon Stevens was talking to Michigan's Charles Potter—the subcommittee Republican who had missed most of the fried chicken lunch. Stevens fell all over himself with praise: "If it would have been possible for you to attend that luncheon meeting, things would not have come out as they did."

At ten forty-seven John Adams phoned Stevens from the Hill: "I am in the hearing. . . . Joe has agreed that I can be present as an observer at any time. . . . I told him I will always be here as the representative of the Secretary of the Army and will never be here representing an individual who is a Communist. . . ."

Almost wistfully, Stevens grasped at a straw: "John, I don't know whether you will get a chance . . . but if it happened that you were talking with Dirksen as you walk out and told him what a bad situation your boss was in, that might work out."

"I will try, sir."

Some small comfort had come from the Democratic side, and at eleven-ten Stevens phoned Wyoming's Senator Lester Hunt his heartfelt thanks: "That letter I got from you—it has kind of done something to me. It really has, because, after the battering and beating around I have taken the last few days, to have a friend come in to put it on the line like you did with that quotation from

Lincoln, it has given me new courage. . . . You know what I have been going through. . . . They murdered me."

Hunt replied, "I just wish that some of us had been able to talk to you a minute before you got engaged in that luncheon, because you were dealing . . . with some mighty high-powered gentlemen . . . you couldn't have gotten into the hands of two more high-powered men than Dirksen and Mundt. You were trying to do the right thing, and they took advantage of you. . . . Keep in there pitching. . . ."

"Stay in there and pitch," Republican liberal Senator Prescott Bush of Connecticut—who himself had bravely outlined to a pro-McCarthy campaign crowd in Bridgeport his disagreement with McCarthy's methods—echoed a half hour later. Stevens needed such bucking up. McCarthy was already making noises about summoning him back for an appearance before the subcommittee within the next few days. But that Monday the Secretary of the Army had a more immediate concern: what would the President of the United States say about him at his Wednesday news conference?

"You remember we talked about being sure that the President answered some of those questions?" Stevens asked Bush. "Will you [follow up on] that? . . . He is going to have a press conference, and I just . . . think in view of the fact that I received some very bad advice, I hope nobody is going to talk him into the proposition of ducking or evading some of the questions. . . ."

"I am going to talk to Nixon today," Bush answered, "and I will [also] talk to Shanley about it."

Lester Hunt had stuck his neck out. But the streetwise establishment Democrats were still playing a cagey game. John McClellan of Arkansas, for example. "I never was so surprised when you got off over there in that gang without anybody with you," he told Stevens that afternoon. . . . We were left out of it. I just had to take the position it was a Republican quarrel."

"Uh huh," Stevens replied.

As Stevens turned and twisted, the administration racked up two anti-McCarthy victories elsewhere. Secretary of State John Foster Dulles announced that McCarthyite Scott McLeod was losing his jurisdiction over State Department personnel though he would continue to conduct the department's security activities. And that evening McCarthy's longtime apologist H. V. Kaltenborn of NBC fell off the bandwagon. He had enjoyed defending McCarthy these many months, he said, but now he believed McCarthyism was no longer necessary, given the administration's vigorous anti-Communist efforts. Furthermore, he went on, McCarthy had hit too often below the belt.

Most of the next day Hagerty spent working on a statement on McCarthy for Eisenhower's Wednesday, March 3, press conference. He found the President in an angry mood, ready to fire back.

"What's the use of trying to work with guys that aren't for you and are never going to be for you?" Ike repeatedly bemoaned. "You know, what we ought to do is get a word to put ahead of Republicans—something like 'new' or 'modern' or something. We just can't work with fellows like McCarthy, Bricker, Jenner and that bunch."

By noon Hagerty was lunching with the President, Nixon, Sherman Adams, and Jerry Persons. Jim submitted his preliminary draft on McCarthy. The President made some suggestions. Hagerty spent the afternoon revising, and at six-twenty he and Jerry Morgan went over to the Mansion to continue the editing process. They carried with them a memorandum from Nixon. The Vice President had been working to tone down the Hagerty draft. They had all heard Ike declare that at the Wednesday press conference he wanted to equate the methods of McCarthy with the methods of the Communists. To Nixon, "such a statement . . . would cause Eisenhower and the party more trouble than he or his White House staff and liberal friends . . . could imagine." So Nixon soft-pedaled a bit, and he submitted some good wording on the browbeating of witnesses.

Back at the Pentagon, Bob Stevens knew none of this. He phoned his friend Arthur Hadley of *Newsweek* at the White House Press Room: After the President's press conference tomorrow, can you give me a rundown on what he said?

In other moves that Tuesday, March 2, Eisenhower discussed at lunch the need to keep the heat on the Republican leaders to back the administration. And he cited once again his perennial prescription for doing battle, instilled in him by his old boxing instructor at West Point: Even if you get knocked clear across the ring, get up with a smile. To Nixon that day, Eisenhower seemed genuinely convinced that some people in the administration were scared to death of McCarthy.

Ike also met that same day with Republican National Chairman Len Hall. And Hall thereafter went out and told reporters, "I don't think anyone would say generals in the Army are not fighting Communism," adding that he couldn't go along with McCarthy when he attacked "persons who are fighting Communism just as conscientiously as he is."

The Senate Republican Policy Committee had launched a study aimed at curbing one-man inquiries by any Senator. The President that day watched closely the senatorial discussion of this reform, which ran up against the tradition that rules for Senate committees remain in the hands of each individual committee. And finally, in a crucial move, Eisenhower spoke by phone, in Brownell's absence, with Deputy Attorney General Bill Rogers:

"One thing people keep talking about," Eisenhower told Rogers, "is [the] authority of the President to protect people against McCarthy. No one has ever even suggested what kind of authority this is. I hear about power of a committee of Congress to subpoena. I suppose the President can [refuse to respond to] this. But when it comes down to people down the line appointed to office, I don't know what the answer is. I would like to have a brief memo on precedent, etc.—just what I can do in this regard. For example: Suppose I made up my mind that McCarthy is abusing someone in a department. What is constitutional for me to do in this regard?"

Since the January 21 meeting in the office of the Attorney General—with Brownell, Rogers, John Adams, Sherman Adams, Jerry Morgan, and Cabot Lodge present—the Justice Department lawyers had been readying just such a document. They had been doing the job Eisenhower expected, foreseeing events. Rogers promised to rush the document over. Before nightfall he had sent the President two memoranda. The first outlined the powers of the President to withhold information from congressional committees. He may do so, the document asserted, "whenever he finds that the information sought is confidential or that its disclosure would be incompatible with the public interest or jeopardize the safety of the nation." The second memorandum—twenty-four double-spaced pages—set forth historical precedents buttressing this assertion of the Presidential power, precedents going back to the time of George Washington. So now in deepest secrecy Eisenhower had at his command a powerful constitutional cannon. The unfolding of events would decide when or where or whether he would fire it off. He would make this decision himself.

As the principals got ready to square off in the headlines, the John Adams–Frank Carr subterranean channel of communication remained open, every word now caught with care on paper.

"Just a moment until I get my [wire recorder] running," Adams quipped to Carr at 5:45 P.M. that Tuesday, March 2, as they discusssed the hearing scheduling.

"I would very much like to get together with you on this," Carr volunteered, "so we could have a private chat some time while we have a quiet moment."

"I will give you a ring tomorrow. . . ."

"I would like to see if we can get together."

"Right, pal."

The next morning, March 3, before the press assembled, Eisenhower was still working over words with Hagerty and Morgan. (Hagerty had also planted a question on Dulles's downgrading of McLeod in order to let the President reply that the responsibility for an executive branch department rested with the Secretary and nobody else.) He also put in a call to Knowland, who reiterated the difficulty of trying to jam rules changes down Senate committees' throats—an effort that could produce a "general revolt."

Finally, at ten-thirty, before a capacity crowd in the Indian Treaty Room of the Executive Office Building, the site of presidential news conferences, Eisenhower faced the reporters and began to read. The audience were sharp-eyed; the mood was tense. But the statement was judicious.

"The Department of the Army," the President began, "made serious errors in handling the Peress case, and the Secretary of the Army so stated publicly, almost a month ago. The Army is correcting its procedures to avoid such mistakes in the future. I am completely confident that Secretary Stevens will be successful in this effort.

"Neither in this case, nor in any other, has any person in the Executive Branch been authorized to suggest that any subordinate, for any reason whatsoever, violate his convictions or principles or submit to any kind of personal humiliation when testifying before Congressional committees. . . .

"We must be unceasingly vigilant in every phase of governmental activity to make certain that there is no subversive penetration.

". . . In opposing Communism, we are defeating ourselves if either by design or through carelessness we use methods that do not conform to the American sense of justice and fair play.

". . . The conscience of America will clearly discern when we are exercising proper vigilance without being unfair. That conscience is reflected in the body of the United States Congress. We can be certain that its members will respond to America's convictions and beliefs in this regard. . . ."

"The ultimate responsibility for the conduct of all parts of the executive branch of the Government rests with the President of the United States. That responsibility cannot be delegated to another branch of government. It is of course likewise the responsibility of the President and his associates to account for their stewardship of public affairs. All of us recognize . . . the congressional right to inquire and investigate into every phase of our public operations. . . .

"I spent many years in the Army, during the course of which I sometimes appeared before committees of the Congress. . . . In all that time, I never saw any individual of the Army fail to render due and complete respect to every member of Congress with whom duty brought him in contact. In all that time, I never saw any member of the Congress guilty of disrespect toward the public servants who were appearing before him. . . . It is that tradition that I intend that the executive branch will observe and apply as long as I hold my present office. . . .

"All of us know that our military services and their leaders have always been completely loyal and dedicated public servants. . . . I am certain that no one in any governmental position wants to have his own utterances interpreted as questioning the lasting debt that all of us as Americans owe to the officers and enlisted men and women of the armed services. In this tribute to the services, I mean to include General Zwicker, who was decorated for gallantry in the field.

". . . Except where the interests of the nation demand otherwise, every governmental employee in the executive branch . . . is expected to respond cheerfully and completely to the requests of the Congress and its several committees. In doing so, it is, of course, assumed that they will be accorded the same respect and courtesy that I require that they show to the members of the legislative body. . . .

". . . Obviously it is the responsibility of the Congress to see to it that its procedures are proper and fair. Of course, I expect the Republican membership of the Congress to assume the primary responsibility in this respect, since they are the majority party and, therefore, control the committees. I am glad to state that Senator Knowland has reported to me that effective steps are already being taken by the Republican leadership to set up codes of fair procedure.

". . . There are problems facing this nation of vital importance. . . . The views of myself and my associates on these matters have been outlined in the proposals for legislation we have submitted to the Congress. They deserve the undivided and incessant attention of the Congress, of the Executive Branch, of the public information media of our nation, of our schools, and even of our churches. I regard it as unfortunate when we are diverted from these grave problems—of which one is vigilance against any kind of internal subversion—through disregard of the standards of fair play recognized by the American people. . . ."

The President finished reading. He would say no more on the subject.

Joe Alsop, gleefully expecting a vituperative blast, leaned over to Willard Edwards of the *Chicago Tribune:* "Why, the yellow son of a bitch!"

Edwards, a McCarthy confidant who likewise expected a slashing presidential denunciation, knew that McCarthy had readied a mean counterattack. And immediately he saw that McCarthy was now heading straight for trouble.

Edwards hailed a cab and sped toward the Senate Office Building. As he arrived at McCarthy's office, McCarthy's secretary, Mary Driscoll, was typing up the President's statement, which she had taken down in shorthand over the phone. The reporters were waiting. McCarthy was hot to go. Edwards tried to hold him back. McCarthy struck out one sentence ("Far too much wind has been blowing from high places in defense of this fifth-amendment Communist"). But he was determined to hang tough. Before the TV cameras he plunged ahead with his gut-cutting answer to Eisenhower: "If a stupid, arrogant, or witless man in a position of power appears before our committee and is found aiding the Communist party, he will be exposed. . . . Apparently the President and I now agree on the necessity of getting rid of Communists." On Edwards's advice McCarthy ostentatiously did send a later "correction" to the wire services deleting that poisonous word "now." But the American people had seen the kick in the groin, and they would not forget it. To Willard Edwards, this was "the day McCarthy died."

No sooner had the President's news conference ended than Arthur Hadley was phoning Stevens with reassuring word. And Hagerty was assessing the reporters' reaction: "Went well with some reporters. New Dealers and fuzzy boys disappointed—wanted President to call McCarthy names, crack him over head, etc.—typical of reaction from these quarters was Reston in *New York Times*—'turning the other cheek'—and [columnist] Doris Fleeson—'McCarthy can say President didn't lay a glove on him'—Nuts. All these people want is to have President get down in gutter with Joe—personally think President's statement strong and dignified.

"Particularly in light of Joe's intemperate rejoinder when he said in effect he'd go right on bullying etc.—now it's up to our leaders in Congress—if they take the ball and run with it—if they force change in rules, then they can come out ahead—if they haven't got the guts, then, with Senator Potter, we'll have to do it with Democratic votes on Joe's committee and let Democrats take the credit—[Homer] Ferguson [Republican of Michigan] walking all around on this and so [are] Knowland, Millikin and Saltonstall—they have a chance now to make it good—my bet is they'll kick it over."

The next morning Hagerty read the press accounts flailing the President's performance and saw Herblock's *Washington Post* cartoon showing a glum down-in-the-mouth Eisenhower confronting a gleaming-eyed McCarthy, a bloody meat cleaver in his hand, the President drawing a white feather from his scabbard and warning the butcher: "Have a care, sir." Understandably, Eisenhower resented this press reaction. And Hagerty's wrath continued to boil. The stories in both the *Washington Post* and the *New York Times*, he wrote in his diary, "really hit below the belt and were deliberately needled up by [*Washington Post* reporter Ed] Foliard and Reston, both of whom know better but can't forget to play their favorite side of the record—straight New Deal in thinking and in writing—other papers praised President for stand, for temperate language and for dignity—believe as President's statement sinks in . . . real reaction will be favorable. That's why I'm glad we released tape of statement to radio, TV and newsreels—

"To hell with slanted reporters, we'll go directly to the people who can hear exactly what President said without reading warped and slanted stories."

Meanwhile the distance between the White House and the Office of the Secretary of the Army widened. One of Stevens's assistants, John F. Kane, resigned after the Eisenhower news conference: in his view Stevens had not received "fighting support." And back at the White House Hagerty was looking askance: "Secretary Stevens developing persecution complex—highly emotional—trying to talk himself into position where he actually thinks he is big hero, did

the right thing and was only following orders from someone above—
who I'll never know."

Through the President's organization the counterattack next
picked up some speed. On the morning of March 4, Ike breakfasted
with Everett Dirksen. Dirksen agreed to try to influence Republican
members of the subcommittee to observe proper procedures. That
same day Karl Mundt asked that a majority vote be required for
calling unscheduled out-of-town committee meetings. Len Hall gave
an interview to the *New York Times*—to Jim Hagerty's father, a
veteran political reporter—in which he branded "nonsense" the allegation that McCarthy had split the Republican party and cited
chapter and verse on the administration's efforts to stamp out Communism. Charlie Wilson put down as "damned tommyrot" Mc-
Carthy's claim that the Army lacked vigilance against Communist
infiltration. And the next day Eisenhower wrote a personal memorandum to all department and agency heads sternly reminding them
of their responsibility to protect subordinates against unjust congressional attack.

Meanwhile that March 4, John Adams and Frank Carr had their
nice quiet lunch, at the unpretentious, decorous, dry Methodist
Building restaurant, noted for its lemon meringue pie, on Capitol
Hill. And the next day they talked again on the phone.

"Where the hell have you been all day?" Adams began jovially.

". . . Went downtown with Joe . . . ," Carr replied.

On the forthcoming hearing, Carr told him, "We are giving you
ample time."

"In a very amicable manner," Adams contributed.

"We are giving you adequate time," Carr said once again.

The repetition triggered Adams's question: "Are you recording
this conversation?"

"There is no sense of both doing it," Carr agreed, and the two
men chatted cordially on, their words taken down by Adams's Secretary, Eleanor Glancy.

Adams had some news for Carr—a cheery report on Private Schine,
now continuing his basic training down in Georgia at Camp Gordon:
"Something has happened to Dave. Everybody is very pleased with
him. He is behaving in [a] circumspect manner. Is very interested,
is damned good soldier.

"For God's sake don't tell Roy what I am going to tell you. They
are considering him for leadership course. . . . Apparently [he] got
rid of [his] Cadillac [and] went into Augusta and got [a] second-

hand Chevy. . . . [But] I don't want . . . Roy . . . to think he has a commitment to leadership school. . . . He would start calling me. . . ."

As Adams and Carr were enjoying this good report card, Stevens had gone to New York to mend fences with masters of public opinion—Clare Luce, Cardinal Spellman, Julius Ochs Adler of the *New York Times*, Charles Collingwood of CBS. Stevens's aides spent much of Friday, March 5, trying to set up an appointment with the top man at *Time* magazine, Allen Grover (Henry Luce being out of the country).

Meanwhile, John Adams was doing his best to refresh Stevens's memory.

That day he sent the Secretary a detailed recounting of the happenings over the Washington Birthday weekend that preceded the fried chicken lunch. "On Sunday the 21st," Adams wrote, "I telephoned Hensel at his home in the morning and read him an early version of your proposed statement to be given to the committee. He suggested the insertion of the paragraph which said: '*I issue orders to the U.S. Army.* . . .' This I know was his suggestion; and I know that it was in the text which you showed to Art Hadley on Sunday night, because on Monday I had before me Hadley's suggested changes, and he referred to 'that magnificent paragraph.' Thus I am certain that a draft of your statement had been read to Hensel—and not objected to by him—as early as Sunday. . . .

"On Monday, the 22nd, I telephoned Hensel at the Nassau Inn [in Princeton, New Jersey] at 9:30 A.M., read him the revised section of the text which included his especially favored paragraph. . . . We talked first about the publicity your [brief] press statement [issued Sunday] had received. I don't know that he was too happy about this turn of events, but I certainly left the telephone with the impression that insofar as your statement was concerned, it was still all right with him. . . ."

The next morning, March 6, gloom: the *Washington Times-Herald* carried a report that Stevens was going to resign. Instantly Stevens phoned Seaton—he reached him at the White House—to deny it.

That evening, euphoria: At the White House Correspondents Association's annual dinner, Eisenhower suggested that the head of the association call on Stevens to stand and take a bow. Hagerty, sitting next to the Secretary of the Army, recorded his reaction: "Sat next to Bob Stevens at head table—is he jittery—and is he talking—talks about 'Jim's the only one who stuck with me'—and stuff like that in front of anyone and everyone—very unstable and excited—says 'he's all alone in this fight'—'matter of principle'—President had [Bob] Donovan introduce him and he got standing ovation—made him almost drunk with delight—kept muttering to himself 'they're for me—they're my friends'—quite a case—someone better ride herd on him but good."

Years later Sherman Adams, who took many a Stevens unmonitored phone call, recalled Stevens exactly the same way: "He had considerable ability, and he was pretty reliable. But in the McCarthy episode he seemed to go into a trance. He'd come in at his wits' end (Allen Dulles used to do the same thing) and almost cry, as he released impounded emotions.

"In the White House we didn't consider him a social nuisance, but we knew he couldn't solve the McCarthy problem (a man like Tom Dewey would just have laughed it off instead of moaning). Though Stevens kept at arm's length, he was in the White House offices a good deal. He wanted self-assurance, and he felt the lack of support from the White House and the Cabinet. He conferred with the White House Staff only in times of extreme emotion."

Meanwhile, in a speech down in Miami that same Saturday evening, Adlai Stevenson at last was taking off the gloves. Like Lyndon Johnson, who said he didn't want to take the affirmative in an anti-McCarthy debate and argue "Communism is good for you," Stevenson had remained quiet. As John McClellan had sagely observed, this was a Republican quarrel. But now the Democrats saw an opening, and Stevenson headed for it.

"A group of political plungers," he said, "has persuaded the [Republican] Party McCarthyism is the best Republican formula for political success. . . . A political party divided against itself, half McCarthy and half Eisenhower, cannot produce national unity. . . ." By chance vacationing in Miami, McCarthy immediately announced he would ask the networks that had carried the Stevenson broadcast—CBS and NBC—for equal time to reply.

Eisenhower would have none of it. Stevenson, he told the legislative leaders first thing Monday morning, March 8, had attacked the Republican party. Therefore the networks should ask the Republican National Chairman to designate a spokesman. Then he looked straight at his Vice President. In his opinion, he said, Nixon should take on the assignment. Dick could make a more political speech than Eisenhower himself; and he ran no risk of being called a pink.

When the meeting broke up, Eisenhower phoned Len Hall. The

Republican National Chairman should call the networks and designate the party's spokesman, and if the networks gave him any trouble the President would personally "get in touch with [Bill] Paley
[of CBS] and [Dave] Sarnoff [of NBC]," both good friends of his.

"Get busy right away," Ike told Hall. "This is a good job for you."

Nixon wasn't leaping at the hazardous opportunity before him.
So at three-twenty the President called and twisted his arm. He
shouldn't, Eisenhower told the Vice President, think of this talk as
an answer to anybody: "Our own publicity shouldn't mention Stevenson and McCarthy." The talk should be "positive, forward marching . . . , and it would be a knockout!"

Touching down from Miami, McCarthy learned that Hall's request for network time had been accepted and his own turned
down. Furious, he told the reporters that the networks "will grant
me time or learn what the law is."

That same day McCarthy got another turndown, this time from
Ted Streibert, the new head of the embattled United States Information Agency, who informed McCarthy sniffily that the pro-
McCarthy books the Senator had submitted for the use of U.S. overseas libraries were "not well adapted to the special purposes served"
by those repositories. The President, Hagerty noted in his diary, is
"dead set [on] stopping McCarthy—a pimple on the path of progress." Ike was determined "to fight him from now on in."

Meanwhile, walled off not only from the White House but also
from the upper reaches of the Pentagon, Stevens tried to find out
what was going on. At eight forty-eight on the morning of March
8, for example, he phoned Assistant Secretary of Defense Dr. John
Hannah on a post-Peress effort underway in the Defense Department to reformulate its procedures for coping with Communists in
the Army.

"If someone gets in to the Secretary of Defense," Stevens warned,
"some hasty decision might be made. I want to be sure the Army is
heard." An hour later Stevens called Hannah again: "I have learned
that Charlie Wilson has an appointment to see the President this
morning, and apparently he has a paper from Hensel on the subject
of Communists." Things were happening; he was being shut out.

Stevens spent most of the rest of the day fencing with the press.
He told Seaton that at the White House correspondents' dinner Marshall McNeil of the Scripps-Howard papers had asked him, in Hagerty's presence, to meet with a small group of reporters. Fred said

he'd check with Jim. Having got his guidance from the White House, Stevens phoned McNeil to say that he'd meet, but not with more than three or four reporters. McNeil wanted eight to ten. Impasse.

Aware that he might have to release the Adams chronology at any minute, Hensel was continuing to work flat out to transform it. Adams was still filling in details of the record. On March 8, for example, he wrote up a detailed account of how on February 18, in the presence of a witness, he had repaid Roy Cohn $42.00—a twenty, two tens, and two ones—for a ticket to the Olson-Turpin middle-weight championship fight, which Adams, Cohn, and Carr had attended together, and for three theater tickets that Cohn had got for him. Whatever Cohn might allege, Adams was no deadbeat.

Subcommittee Democrat Stu Symington—previously helpful—was trying to get hold of the now notorious Army document. At six o'clock on March 8 he phoned Stevens: "Sorry to bother you. I wonder if it would be possible for me to see something. I have heard about it, and somebody has been leaking about it, but I would like to see the report on Schine sometime, if the Army is willing to release it."

Stevens dodged. "Stuart, I doubt very much that they are. Whatever they have got on that would have to be pulled together. . . ."

"I understand it has been pulled together," Symington replied, "and I don't want to see it pulled apart before we get a chance to look at it. . . ."

"I don't have anything at all, myself," Stevens equivocated, "because Adams has been handling the contact with the committee. . . ."

"Have you seen the report, Bob?"

Stevens again dodged: "I would know of certain things that Adams has transported to me that have transpired. . . . I personally think that anything in that line would prove to be very much exaggerated. . . . I think there has been some talk around that has been very much exaggerated over anything that is there."

He now tried to get Symington off the trail: "I am the Secretary, and I have had some talks with the committee and the chairman . . . , and by and large as far as the treatment of me is concerned, I have no personal complaints. . . ."

Symington refused to follow the bait: "I would appreciate this being private between you and me. I have heard that the Army is pulling back a bit on the report because it is not good for the Army."

"I don't know anything in it that is not good for the Army. . . . It is a hell of a lot of stuff. . . . I have more important things to do in my opinion than that particular thing. So I don't feel I have any particular knowledge of it, and I don't think there is too much to it. . . . However, I can talk to Adams and find out what I can see. . . ."

Symington was not the only Democratic senator wanting to get his hands on the document. Both senators from Florida—George Smathers and Spessard Holland—had heard reports on favors for Schine, and in late February they asked to know more. Even more significantly, the ranking Democrat on the Armed Services Committee, the powerful and respected Senator Richard Russell of Georgia, had written in three weeks before them at the instigation of *Baltimore Sun* reporter Phil Potter, John Adams's close friend and confidant, Russell's letter—to Chief of Staff Matthew Ridgway—had received an interim acknowledgment on February 5. A month passed. Then, on March 8, Russell wrote Ridgway once again, with courtly ominousness: "It would seem to me that ample time has elapsed for a matter of this nature to be investigated, and I should like very much to be informed as to the findings of the Department of the Army after this investigation."

Time had run out. In a move Hensel always believed Fred Seaton engineered, on the evening of March 8 Secretary of Defense Charles Wilson phoned his Michigan friend, Senator Charles Potter.

Potter was the one Republican member of the subcommittee who, in Stevens's opinion, had his heart in the right place—a World War II veteran who in fighting in France had lost his left leg at the hip and his right leg below the knee; a man physically and personally courageous, with decent instincts. But he was no political infighter like McCarthy, Mundt, and Dirksen.

Charlie Wilson was a man of great managerial force, head-knocking skill, and blunt, outspoken honesty. But he was a man whom Struve Hensel always considered somewhat soft on McCarthy, particularly when under the influence of his fellow citizen from Michigan and fellow cabinet officer Arthur Summerfield, Postmaster General and former Republican National Chairman, who through the 1952 campaign had repeatedly shilled for McCarthy and who even now desperately clung to the hope that McCarthy could produce Republican votes in future elections. In any event, Wilson was a man who, in the view of Sherman Adams, was "so damned tickled" to confront a problem that wasn't going to get him into trouble that he resolutely kept his distance. "He would have sent over the hearse to pick up any bodies, but he was determined himself this time not to contribute to the carnage."

Wilson told Potter about the now-revised Army chronology; told him that a Democratic posse, headed by the powerful Russell of Georgia, was hot on the trail, demanding copies; and urged Potter to make a formal request for one, to get it soonest into friendly Republican hands.

Before business closed that night, Potter wrote to the Secretary of Defense requesting "all of the facts" about "any effort whatsoever . . . made by any source affiliated with the . . . subcommittee to exert pressure for the purpose of gaining preferential treatment for Private Schine"—facts "upon which the committee may base immediate action."

The next day, March 9, in his diary Hagerty succinctly summed up the strategy: Sherman Adams had told him, he wrote, that Potter would ask the Defense Department for the Schine record. "That ought to kick up fuss and start ball rolling to get rid of Roy Cohn." And he added the laconic comment: "Joe getting reckless."

Early that morning Potter met with Mundt and Dirksen in the Senate cloakroom. He summarized the Army's charges. And all agreed that Cohn must go. Then Potter bearded McCarthy. And Joe flared up in anger. Not only would he not fire Cohn; he would loose the dogs of the right-wing press on Potter himself.

On one front McCarthy was digging in. But other fronts were crumbling. After the networks refused him equal time to answer Stevenson, he had appealed to the Federal Communications Commission. They had upheld the networks' decision. And if they had not, Hagerty wrote in his diary, Governor Adams stood ready to phone the commission's chairman and get things "nailed down." Moreover, that same Tuesday, March 9, another old friend of the Governor's, Senator Ralph Flanders of Vermont, who had lunched with Adams at the White House just a week before, took to the Senate floor to denounce his Senate colleague from Wisconsin: In this Armageddon of the ages, Flanders asserted, McCarthy "dons his war paint[,] goes into his war dance[,] emits his war whoops[,] goes forth to battle and proudly returns the scalp of a pink Army dentist." Before nightfall Eisenhower was writing Flanders a personal letter: "America needs to hear from more Republican voices like yours."

In the anti-McCarthy strategy the President was pursuing, those voices were still not to include Eisenhower's own. As he wrote to his friend Paul Helms in California that day: "For the past thirteen years, I have occupied posts around which there focused sufficient public interest that they were considered news sources of greater or lesser importance. . . . Out of all those experiences, I developed a practice which, so far as I know, I have never violated. That practice is to avoid public mention of any name *unless it can be done with favorable intent and connotation;* reserve all criticism for the private conference; speak only good in public.

"This is not namby-pamby. It certainly is not pollyannaish. It is just sheer common sense. A leader's job is to get others to go along with him in the promotion of something. To do this he needs their good will. To destroy good will, it is only necessary to criticize publicly. This creates in the criticized one a subconscious desire to 'get even.' Such effects can last for a very long period. . . .

"I by [no] means approve the methods that McCarthy uses. . . . I despise them. . . . Nevertheless, I am quite sure that the people who want me to stand up and publicly label McCarthy with derogatory titles are the most mistaken people that are dealing with this whole problem. . . ."

Eisenhower deplored the space given by the press to McCarthy's "completely unwarranted and despicable insinuations" in preference to space on "a statement of a code of procedures, law and ethics that should govern the relations among the several departments of government."

But he welcomed the raising of other anti-McCarthy voices that March day, not only Flanders's but the voice of one of the most powerful in the broadcast media—Edward R. Murrow's.

Dean of the Establishment reporters, a man who had undergone his baptism of fire broadcasting from London during the blitz, a stylist who seemed to confine himself to hard, clipped fact, an unshakable civil libertarian, Murrow for a half hour that night, to an audience in thirty-six cities coast to coast, devoted his entire "See It Now" program to the Wisconsin junior Senator.

Murrow began with an offer to McCarthy of equal time; displayed the uncouth Senator in distortions of fact, giggles, and boorish humor ("Alger . . . I mean Adlai"), and wrapped up his message in understated editorializing: "Upon what meat does Senator McCarthy feed? Two of the staples of his diet are the investigation (protected by immunity) and the half-truth. . . . We cannot defend freedom abroad by deserting it at home. The actions of the junior Senator from Wisconsin have caused alarm and dismay among our Allies abroad and given considerable comfort to our enemies. And whose fault is that? Not really his. He didn't create the situation of fear; he merely exploited it, and rather successfully. Cassius was right: 'The fault, dear Brutus, is not in our stars but in ourselves.' "

Murrow was not the first to denounce the demagogue. Elmer Davis had long and eloquently preceded him. But Murrow's broadcast produced a torrent of phone calls and telegrams—the heaviest in CBS's history. Murrow at last had brought not only the word but the picture of McCarthy into the American living room in prime time.

At his news conference the next morning the President got no questions on Murrow. But he did get a question on Flanders, and he gave the distinguished elderly Senator a pat on the back: "When Senator Flanders points up the danger of us engaging in internecine warfare . . . he is doing a service. . . ." That same day up on the Senate floor, McCarthy, in his damned-fool playful way, was giving Flanders a mock stranglehold from behind.

After the morning news conference, Hagerty reported: "President in fighting mood, has had it as far as Joe is concerned—'if he wants to get recognized anymore,' President told Persons, 'only way he can do it is to stand up and publicly say, "I was wrong in browbeating witnesses, wrong in saying the Army is coddling Communists, and wrong in my attack on Stevens. I apologize—" That's only way [I'll] ever welcome him back into fold.' "

The President had a good morning. Just before his news conference he'd had a call from Senator Knowland about the Republican Policy Committee's suggested revisions of the committee rules—revisions that would turn up the heat on Dirksen, Potter, and Mundt to prevent the humiliation of witnesses by McCarthy. And Eisenhower had concluded his long phone conversation with the majority leader by beating the drum one more great bang: "There is nothing wrong with us (the Republican Party) that a hell of a good enactment of legislation won't cure."

Then he crossed the street to his press conference and took the reporters' questions in stride, occasionally interjecting humor. But he lost his equanimity when he learned a couple of hours later that Charlie Wilson had invited Joe McCarthy, once again without telling anyone, to lunch.

"C. E. Wilson threw monkey wrench in carefully prepared plans,"

Hagerty wrote in his diary, "by sending his car to Senate today and picking up Joe for lunch at Pentagon—Wilson didn't tell anyone in W.H. about luncheon—just let it happen—when I told President he leaned back in chair, muttered a few 'goddams' and then said, 'You know, Jim, I believe Cabot Lodge is dead right when he says we need acute politicians in those positions. They are the only ones who know enough to stay out of traps. The only ones who can play the same kind of game as those guys on the Hill.' Pres. greatly disturbed at Wilson luncheon and called me back several times to see if any announcement had been made from luncheon—'If they are cooking up another statement, then, by God, someone is going to hear from me—but good.'"

Hagerty at once phoned Seaton: What's going on over there? The next morning he had his answer: "Finally caught up with Seaton on Wilson luncheon—seems McCarthy called Wilson after Wilson press conference where he said 'damn tommyrot' Army coddling reds—Joe wanted to tell Wilson he wasn't against Army—Wilson asked him to lunch but didn't tell anyone over here—went on his own—bawled Seaton out mildly. [Seaton] said, 'Listen, if you think you have troubles, come over to the Pentagon'—and I guess he's right—doing good job."

Seaton and Hensel indeed had their hands full. As the President held his March 10 news conference, Hensel was frantically trying to get Stevens to give his final O.K. to the revised chronology. Time was running out; Adams had signed off on it. Hensel had checked with Rogers, Brownell, and Charlie Wilson.

"Struve Hensel has a very important matter to see you about," Seaton urgently phoned Stevens at eleven o'clock, "and we are getting great pressure from the Hill."

Stevens became testy: "I told him this morning I would see him anytime, [if] he called me and gave me just a few minutes' notice . . . I just finished awarding two Medals of Honor."

At last the document—all approved—was ready to go to Senator Potter. But Secretary Wilson couldn't sign the covering letter; he was having lunch with McCarthy.

"You sign it," Seaton adroitly suggested to Hensel. Hensel did. And he regretted it ever after. "This chronological statement," Hensel wrote Potter, "has been compiled under my supervision by examination of various files of the Army and after oral examination of the individuals mentioned who were available to the men assigned by me to prepare the document itself."

That night, document in hand, Potter met with the Republican members of the subcommitte plus Knowland and John Bricker. The next morning at ten-forty, John Adams phoned Stevens: "Berry [an Adams assistant] has a report from Charlie Potter on the meeting which the Republicans held with Joe in secret last night. . . . They laid it on pretty violently and one of the recommendations was the termination of one of the staff members and to get off the Army's neck. There will be more developments today. [Berry] is up reporting to Seaton and Hensel now."

"What are they going to do with the paper?" Stevens asked.

"I don't know."

"[It] may or may not come out," Stevens speculated.

"We can sit on pins over the weekend," Adams replied. For the moment he was planning to go up on the Hill: "I told Seaton so he wouldn't be afraid I was up with McCarthy."

Stevens had a question: "Would you say that the publication of this paper, if it takes place, would probably not be before Monday?"

"It depends on whether McClellan or Potter decides to tell the press they have it, and whether they press Seaton and Hensel enough to get the release here. . . . I have a personal feeling that it will never see the light of day."

McCarthy was getting the same message from one and all: Fire Cohn. He could buckle. Or he could counterattack. He counterattacked. At one-thirty that afternoon he phoned Fred Seaton.

In making this call McCarthy was dredging for himself a channel of communication. An old one, between Frank Carr and John Adams, was closing up. "I take it you are not interested in getting together with me," Carr had complained to Adams the afternoon of March 9.

Adams had demurred and dodged and pleaded the press of business. He had loaded the guns of war, and he knew the shelling could begin any moment.

"I am serious, John," Carr persisted. "I have gone to great lengths. . . . I am a little disturbed. . . ."

"I have not been able to get away from my desk. . . ."

"I did want to talk to you. It is up to you, boy. . . . This is my last offer, friend." And so it ended.

The new back-channel opened between McCarthy and Seaton, however, still permitted two-way communication with the enemy.

"McCarthy had known Fred for a long time," Seaton's assistant

Phil Mullin recalled years later. "And he felt he could trust him." Fred at times talked to McCarthy by phone without any third-person witness. At times he would ask Mullin to stay in the room to listen in. But in one rare instance, on March 11, he put his trusted personal secretary, Violet Bryan, on the line to monitor.

"The Secretary [Wilson] should get the full story," McCarthy opened.

"You have no argument with me on [that]," Seaton replied evenly.

"I have stuff available if they want to incorporate [it in the Army's] report. . . . I have a memo which I am pulling out of the files on the Adams incident. My staff have had strict instructions to keep written notations on any dealings with the Army."

There are two sides to the story, McCarthy was saying. I have my side down in black and white documentary evidence. The charges in the Army's report could backfire. Better hold it up.

Was McCarthy lying? Was he bluffing? Seaton had no way to know.

Fred took a chance. "The Army," he said, "has been bombarded on all sides from Senators and Congressmen." It had to move.

McCarthy remained insistent: "The Army should not make its report without checking with me. I am offering to supply the information I have on this incident. And my information can be made available [to you] by tonight or tomorrow morning."

Seaton made McCarthy a promise: "I personally guarantee to give this information to the Army: that you request your material be included in the report; that your people are working on pulling material from the files; and that you believe it will be ready for inclusion by tomorrow." Within a half hour McCarthy's office called again: the first memo the Senator wanted Seaton to see was on its way by riding page.

Through a foul-up in the government's mail system, it would take more than twenty-four hours to travel the few miles between Senate Office Building and Pentagon. But the delay didn't matter. Events were toboganning downhill, out of control. At three-eighteen that afternoon Secretary Stevens phoned Army press aide Lloyd Lehrbas: "I just wanted to alert you that I am afraid this whole business is going to break. This is subject to a final check; . . . but . . . [the report] will probably be sent up there around five o'clock to all the Senators that have asked for a copy. . . . Therefore it will probably all break in the morning papers.

"I wanted to tell you I think it is going to take that turn and maybe, all things considered, it is the best thing to get it over with. . . . So, while I am reluctant, I have agreed . . . that is probably what is going to happen. . . . [Colonel C. J.] Hauck [in Legislative Liaison] can tell you when it is finally released by Seaton, who is really carrying the ball on it now. And I am going to try to slip out to get a good night's sleep. . . ."

Fifty minutes later Stevens phoned Seaton: "Did you decide on [the release] finally yet? Or is it subject to further telephoning?

"No, I think it is going to go all right. . . . Senator McCarthy sent me a message a short time ago by riding page, a document that he thought I would be extremely interested in. His office then called me a few minutes ago to say that the Senator went to the floor for a vote on Alaska-Hawaii statehood and was trying to reach me. I told them I would be right here. I thought at that time that I would tell him that the Army feels it could do nothing but make the material available. . . . I shall do my best not to discuss particulars or individuals. . . ."

Twenty minutes later Seaton phoned Stevens: "I have just informed Senator McCarthy's office that [the chronology] would be delivered to the Hill this afternoon. . . ."

"We will ride it out," Stevens replied, "and with you at the helm, I think we will ride it out, Fred. This is nothing you had anything to do with, but [I] have complete confidence in your judgment on the thing. We will see where we go from here, but the right and the truth will prevail."

"I assured John [Adams] he is not in this alone," Seaton answered. We will stay with him through thick and thin."

Stevens was resigned—a sad, decent, trusting man facing he knew not what. But over in the White House, Jim Hagerty was exuberant: "Army report on Schine-Cohn-McCarthy going up on Hill today. It's a pip—shows constant pressure by Cohn to get Schine soft Army job, with Joe in and out of threats. . . . Should bust this thing wide open. . . ."

Through the feverish, probing, skeptical labors of Struve Hensel and his assistant Frank Brown, the original John Adams chrolonogy had undergone a transmutation. It was no longer a loose magpie-mass of copies of memoranda and dictations of hit-or-miss top-of-the-head recollections, all in helter-skelter time sequence. It was now a crisp rat-a-tat-tat factual rundown, expurgated of obscenities, freed of some unprovable charges rooted in one man's uncorroborated recollection. It was ordered, and it was devoid of extraneous coloring detail. Of its distribution, Seaton was at the helm.

Now a "Stevens-Adams chronology," it started at the beginning and included these flat assertions of fact, date by date:

"1. Mid July, 1953: Major General Miles Reber, then Chief of Army Legislative Liaison, received a phone call stating that Senator McCarthy desired to see him. He went to the Senator's office, and Senator McCarthy there informed General Reber that he was very interested in securing a direct commission for Mr. G. David Schine. . . .

"2. July 15, 1953: Mr. Schine called the Office of the Chief of Legislative Liaison (OCLL), Department of the Army, on the telephone and asked whether he could come to the Pentagon that afternoon and 'hold up his hand. . . .'

"8. Mid-October 1953: During the course of hearings in the courthouse in Foley Square in New York . . . at one time Senator McCarthy, Mrs. McCarthy, and Mr. John G. Adams were together. Senator McCarthy at this time told Mr. Adams that Mr. Schine was of no help to the committee but was interested in photographers and getting his pictures in the paper, and that things had reached the point where Mr. Schine was a pest. . . .

"10. October 18–November 3, 1953: During this two week period, Mr. Cohn and Mr. Adams spoke in person or on the telephone almost every day concerning an assignment for Private Schine to the New York City area. On these occasions Mr. Adams suggested to Mr. Cohn that the Army had an obligation to 300,000 other men being drafted every year and that Mr. Schine wasn't the only college graduate to serve as a private. It was on these occasions that Mr. Adams first stated that the national interest required that no preferential treatment be given to Schine and explained to Mr. Cohn that he was fifteen years older than Mr. Cohn and could speak from a wealth of experience as a Senate employee and in the Pentagon on this very subject. Mr. Cohn replied that if [the] national interest was what the Army wanted, he'd give it a little and then proceeded to outline how he would expose the Army in its worst light and show the country how shabbily it is being run. . . .

"13. November 6, 1953: At the invitation of the Secretary of the Army, a luncheon, attended by the Secretary, Mr. Adams, Senator McCarthy, Mr. Francis Carr, and Mr. Cohn was held in the Pentagon. The principal subject of discussion at the luncheon was the Fort Monmouth investigation. During the course of the luncheon, however, Mr. Cohn asked when the Army would be able to arrange for a New York City assignment for Private Schine. Senator McCarthy also stated that he was interested in Private Schine's receiving a New York City assignment and suggested that Schine might be sent to New York with the assignment of studying and reporting to the Secretary on evidence of pro-Communist leanings in West Point textbooks. . . .

"17. November 17, 1953: Secretary Stevens and Mr. Adams lunched with Senator McCarthy [at the Merchants Club] in New York. The Secretary, enroute back to Washington, gave Senator McCarthy and members of the committee staff a ride in his plane to McGuire Air Force Base which adjoins Fort Dix, New Jersey. Private Schine was given a pass that evening to see Senator McCarthy and members of the committee staff. . . .

"24. December 8, 1953: The Committee began open hearings in Washington with Aaron Coleman as principal witness.

"25. December 9, 1953: Just before the hearings opened in the morning, Mr. Cohn spoke to Mr. Adams concerning the Army's prospective assignment of Private Schine, and Mr. Adams explained, as he had many times before, that Private Schine was going to be handled the same as any other private soldier. Mr. Cohn broke off this conversation in the middle, turning his back on Mr. Adams in the Senate Caucus Room.

"At about 12:30 P.M., at the conclusion of the morning hearing, Mr. Adams followed Senator McCarthy to his office and conferred with him concerning the inquiries of Mr. Cohn about Private Schine.

"As a result of Mr. Adams' request, Senator McCarthy told Mr. Adams that he would write the Secretary of the Army a letter [saying] that the committee had no further interest in Private Schine. . . .

"Mr. Adams returned to the Pentagon and in the middle of the afternoon received a telephone call from Mr. Cohn. Mr. Cohn stated to Mr. Adams that he would teach Mr. Adams what it meant to go over his head. . . .

"26. December 10, 1953: . . . At Senator McCarthy's request, Secretary Stevens and Mr. Adams lunched with Senator McCarthy and Mr. Francis Carr at the Carroll Arms. . . . At this luncheon there were extensive discussions led by Senator McCarthy as to the possibility of an immediate New York assignment for Private Schine.

The Secretary stated that Private Schine must complete his basic 16 weeks' training before his further assignment could even be discussed. . . .

"27. December 11, 1953: On this day Private Schine was informed that thereafter training would be expanded to include Saturday morning duty. . . . During the afternoon Mr. Adams had extensive long-distance conversations with Mr. Cohn from New York, all of them initiated by Mr. Cohn, and one of which lasted nearly an hour. During these conversations Mr. Cohn, using extremely vituperative language, told Mr. Adams that the Army had again 'doublecrossed' Mr. Cohn, Private Schine, and Senator McCarthy. . . .

"29. December 17, 1953: On the morning of December 17, Senator McCarthy spoke to Mr. Adams at 10:30 A.M. at the entrance to the United States Court House in New York. He stated to Mr. Adams . . . that he had learned of the extent of his staff's interference with the Army with reference to Schine, and that he wished to advise Adams thereafter to see that nothing was done on the committee's behalf with reference to Schine. After the hearings, Senator McCarthy, Mr. Cohn, Mr. Francis Carr, and Mr. Adams were present together [at Gasner's Restaurant]. Mr. Adams, in order to have Senator McCarthy state his views in front of Messrs. Carr and Cohn, suggested discussing the Private Schine situation. The discussion became heated, and Mr. Cohn restated all the arguments which he had used before and referred to a so-called commitment that Private Schine be assigned to the New York City area immediately upon finishing basic training. Mr. Cohn was vituperative in his language. During this discussion, Senator McCarthy remained silent.

"The party rode uptown in Mr. Cohn's car. . . . Twice during the ride uptown and as Mr. Adams was getting out of the car, Senator McCarthy asked Mr. Adams to ask Secretary Stevens if the Secretary could find a way to assign Private Schine to New York. . . .

"34. January 9, 1954: Mr. Adams was at Amherst, Mass., filling a speaking engagement at Amherst College. In the middle of the afternoon Mr. Adams received a long-distance call from Mr. Francis Carr, who said he had been trying to reach him since the previous evening. Mr. Carr stated that Mr. Cohn had been trying to reach Mr. Adams from New York and that the purpose of Mr. Cohn's call was to have Mr. Adams intervene with the Commanding General at Fort Dix because Private Schine was scheduled for K.P. duty on the following day, a Sunday. . . .

"37. January 13–14, 1954: . . . Mr. Adams went to the Capitol and called on Mr. Cohn and Mr. Carr. . . . Knowing that 90 percent of all inductees get overseas duty and that . . . Private Schine would [therefore probably face] overseas duty when he concluded his tour at Camp Gordon, Mr. Adams informed Mr. Cohn of this situation. Mr. Cohn upon hearing this said this would 'wreck the Army' and cause Mr. Stevens to be 'through as Secretary of the Army.' . . .

"42. January 22, 1954: On Friday evening at Senator McCarthy's request, Mr. Adams went to the Senator's apartment. . . . Mrs. McCarthy was present. . . . On many occasions during the evening, Senator McCarthy said he did not see why it would not be possible for the Army to give Private Schine some assignment in New York and forget about the whole matter. . . .

"44. February 16, 1954: Mr. Carr telephoned Mr. Adams and requested the Army to produce as [a witness] . . . in New York City on February 18, the Commanding General of Camp Kilmer [General Zwicker]. . . . Mr. Carr stated that if the Army would be reasonable, probably the committee would be reasonable. Mr. Adams inquired how Mr. Carr thought that the Army should be 'reasonable,' and Mr. Carr answered rather facetiously that if the Army would only do all that had been requested of it, the Army's problems would be at an end."

So there, drained of most of its original juice, stood the Adams-Stevens bare-bones outline.

The next morning, Friday, March 12, led by John Adams's friend Phil Potter of the *Baltimore Sun,* who got hold of the copy sent to Senator Symington, the nation's newspapers blared the contents to the world. Republican Majority Leader William F. Knowland read the news in the despised *Washington Post.* And he hit the roof. Nobody had sent *him* a copy. By mistake he had been omitted from the first-run deliveries the day before and scheduled for the second run, which that very morning would speed a copy his way. He got on the phone to Nixon's office. The Vice President, he was informed, was in seclusion, holed up at the Statler Hotel working on his reply to Adlai Stevenson scheduled for the following evening; he'd left instructions not to be disturbed. No matter. The furious Majority Leader bulled his way through. Not only had he been left off the delivery list, he told Nixon; someone in the White House had dropped an unflattering story about him to some columnist. He'd made up his mind; he was going to call together all Senate Republicans and submit his resignation as their leader.

Nixon told him to take it easy: don't make a move until after my speech tomorrow. But Knowland didn't simmer down. He got on the phone to the White House, straight to the President.

"According to the papers this morning," Knowland thundered, "this report from the Defense Department was circulated to some eighteen Senators over here. . . . As Majority Leader, I did not get a copy. . . . I don't know who the eighteen Senators could have been unless they were on the Democratic side of the aisle."

Ike bristled: "Someone just said there is a report about a man named Cohn. I don't know a damn thing about it. . . ."

"I don't think you could operate a team this way," Knowland went on.

Eisenhower repeated: "I know nothing about that. Errors do occur, and somebody has made a blunder."

Knowland threatened to resign all over again.

Eisenhower refused to fall all over himself: "I can't talk about your operations down [there]. I can only say I will check up and find out what happened and get somebody in touch with you. I think we have got to realize that blunders do occur and," he added pointedly, "not all on the Executive side. . . . I know nothing about [this]. . . . There has been a blunder, and I am sorry."

Eisenhower immediately commissioned Deputy Defense Secretary Roger Kyes to placate Knowland. Kyes, rough and tough as he was, did his best by phone to comply: "I personally don't know about this Schine document. I have not read its contents. I don't know who specifically handled it, but I will find out right now. . . . Someone," he added ominously, "will be in trouble. . . ." Kyes then passed the baton to Fred Seaton: "Roger quite considerately gave me the job of going up on the Hill to see the very irate Senator," Fred recalled years afterward.

Later in the day the President sounded off to Hagerty: "If those [Republican] Leaders had seen the report, it would never have gotten out in the papers. . . . They always want to play everything the hard way—compromise, compromise—nuts." This contretemps only reinforced an observation Eisenhower had made a few days earlier to his Press Secretary: "I used to think Knowland was a good candidate for President, and now I know he isn't."

Eisenhower having reminded Knowland that the White House

had had no part in distributing the chronology, Hagerty now warned the staff members on the same thing: they should give no sign or hint of any inside knowledge of the devastating report.

McCarthy had refused to fire Cohn. But he had agreed to meet with the Republican committee members that day to talk further. Cohn had to go, Charlie Wilson told Senator Potter. Stevens couldn't get rid of him, Wilson said; Stevens would gladly hand over his wallet to a gunman and therefore the committee had to do the job. As Potter sat through that morning's hearing on Annie Lee Moss with McCarthy, he thought the meeting was still on. But when he got back to his office, the phone rang.

"I am postponing the meeting," McCarthy told him. "I have to go to Wisconsin to make a speech."

Once again Potter implored Joe to get rid of Cohn. Potter felt sure, from his conversations with Charlie Wilson, that the Army in turn would get rid of John Adams, and the whole hysteria would come to an end. McCarthy giggled his curious giggle and hung up. He and Cohn were scheduling a news conference at one o'clock.

At twelve-two Stevens phoned Hensel: "The blast will be coming over at lunch."

"I have to go to a Stassen luncheon," Hensel replied. "So I will see that Fred has that covered. . . ." Fifteen minutes later he changed his mind: "I got Fred; and after talking it over, I am not going to that Stassen lunch. We will be staying right here. . . . We will have lunch in the Secretary's mess here. I asked Fred whether we ought to try to have the conference [covered]. He said no; we would get it fast enough."

They did. McCarthy, in a fighting mood, praised Cohn to the skies and announced that he would battle to the end to save his neck: "There is only one man the Communists hate more than Roy Cohn. That is J. Edgar Hoover."

McCarthy was refusing, he said, to knuckle under to the Army's attempt to blackmail him into stopping his investigations of the Army. Cohn asserted his innocence of any attempt to get special favors for Schine: "The statements . . . that improper pressure was exerted by us are a lie. . . . I didn't say I would wreck the Army. I never threatened anyone or did any other such absurd thing."

Then they exploded a mushroom cloud—not just the single memorandum that McCarthy had sent to Seaton to dissuade the Pentagon from its attack; but eleven such memoranda, all of them reporting on the months-long traffic by phone and in person between the agents of the Army and the agents of the committee. McCarthy's memoranda were designed to establish the nefarious machinations— up to and including attempted blackmail—of Robert Ten Broeck Stevens and John Gibbons Adams.

First came a memo from Frank Carr to McCarthy dated October 2, 1953. It portrayed Stevens as making a commitment on Schine:

"Mr. Cohn and I met with Secretary Stevens at the Pentagon to discuss General Lawton of Fort Monmouth and his blackout order re Fort Monmouth personnel speaking with our staff. . . . Mr. Stevens was very helpful. He called Lawton and had the order immediately rescinded stating that it was his policy to cooperate with the congressional committees. During the course of the conversation, David Schine's pending induction into the Army came up. Mr. Stevens stated that he thought Schine should take his initial basic training and that after he had completed his basic, that he, Stevens, would be able to use Schine to his own advantage in the Army. He stated . . . that he could envision that Dave could be of great assistance to him if, after basic, he could attend some security-type school with the Army and report to Stevens his observations, based on his own experience as an investigator in the Communist field. . . ."

Next came an unsigned Memorandum for the File on the Pentagon lunch with Stevens on Friday, November 6, 1953. It portrayed Stevens and Adams as trying to get McCarthy to leave the Army alone and go after the Navy and Air Force:

"At the request of Mr. Stevens, Senator McCarthy, Frank Carr, and Roy Cohn went to Stevens' office at the Pentagon for lunch. John Adams was present. Stevens asked us to outline what evidence would be produced at our scheduled public hearings on the Army Signal Corps, which we did.

"Stevens said that if we brought out everything, he would have to resign. . . . He said that they were particularly worried about us seeking to identify those who were responsible for not acting to get rid of Communists and security risks in the Army, and who had ordered their reinstatement.

"Mr. Stevens asked that we hold up our public hearings on the Army. He suggested we go after the Navy, Air Force and the Defense Department instead. We said first of all we had no evidence warranting an investigation of these other departments.

"Adams said not to worry about that, because there was plenty of dirt there, and they would furnish us with leads. Mr. Stevens thought this was the answer to his problem.

"We said this was not possible because we have already planned our next investigation which was one of subversion in defense plants handling government and military contracts.

"He asked why we did not start on that, and we told him we were jammed up . . . and that David Schine was about to enter the Army and had much information . . . on the . . . investigations that we could not get along without.

"Mr. Stevens said that he would arrange for Dave to complete the work over weekends and after training hours. We said this would be satisfactory. . . .

"After lunch General Ridgway, General Trudeau and General Mudgett came in. . . . McCarthy reiterated in their presence that he would cooperate as much as possible, but that under no circumstance would there [be] a whitewash of the Army situation. . . ."

Another unsigned Memorandum for the File follows, on the November 17 lunch at the Merchants Club in New York. It portrays, once again, an Army attempt at diversion:

"[At his own request,] Stevens came to New York and asked Senator McCarthy to have lunch with him at the Merchants Club. The Secretary was accompanied by John Adams. Frank Carr and Roy Cohn were present throughout. A friend of the Senator's with whom he had a prior engagement also joined the luncheon a bit later.

"The discussion centered about Secretary Stevens' press conference in which he said there had been no espionage at Fort Monmouth. Mr. Stevens produced the correct transcript of the conference and said he had been badly misquoted. . . .

"At this meeting Stevens again said he wished we could get onto the Air Force and the Navy and the personnel employed directly by the Defense Establishment instead of continuing with the Army hearings."

Roy Cohn wrote the next memorandum, dated December 9, 1953, to Senator McCarthy. It portrays Adams as making good on his offer to supply dirt:

"John Adams said today that following up the idea about investigating the Air Force he had gotten specific information for us about an Air Force base where there were a large number of homosexuals. He said that he would trade us the information if we would tell him what the next Army project was that we would investigate."

The next memorandum, under the same date, bears the signature of Frank Carr, writing to McCarthy. It self-righteously portrays Adams as using Schine to twist the committee's arm:

"I couldn't get you on the telephone. What I want to tell you is that I am getting fed up with the way the Army is trying to use Schine as a hostage to pressure us to stop our hearings on the Army.

"Again today, John Adams came down here after the hearings, and, using clever phrases, tried to find out, 'what's there in it for us' if he and Stevens did something for Schine.

"He refers to Schine as our hostage or the hostage whenever his name came up. I made it clear that as far as I was concerned, I don't personally care what treatment they gave Schine, and that as far as I was concerned, he was in the Army.

"I did say that I thought that it wasn't fair of them to take it out on Schine, because we were [investigating] the Army or to keep using it to try to stop our investigations. . . .

"My telling him this does no real good, as he constantly lumps together all his talk about Schine with suggestions that we stop holding hearings on the Army.

"I am convinced that they will keep right on trying to blackmail us as long as Schine is in the Army. Even though they said he deserved the commission, they didn't give it to him because of the left wing press and they keep trying to dangle proposed small favors to him in front of us.

"Adams, by his attitude, makes it clear that the Army will do nothing to see that Schine gets into any kind of an assignment to which he is qualified, unless we stop investigating the Army. When he brought up the 'what's there in it for us' this morning, I told [him] that I saw no chance of stopping the hearings. . . .

"This hostage business is getting to be a real thorn in my side and I wish that they would either give Schine what he deserves or leave him in the rear ranks forever without bothering me about it."

The lone memo bearing McCarthy's name follows, dated December 17, 1953, and addressed to Cohn and Carr. It portrays the Army's vengeance against General Lawton for his helpfulness toward McCarthy:

"In talking to John Adams today, I learned that General Lawton, who as you recall, cooperated fully with the Committee in the exposure of subversives at Fort Monmouth, is about to be relieved of his command.

"I questioned Adams very closely on this in a friendly manner, and find that the only reason that he can give is that Lawson embarrassed the military by helping to make it possible for us to expose the incredibly bad security setup which has existed at Fort Monmouth.

"Apparently they were particularly incensed about Lawton's statement in executive session that it was impossible to get the necessary cooperation for the cleanup until our Committee hearings commenced.

"I don't know what we can do in this matter. Certainly we are not in the position to tell the Army who [*sic*] to promote and who [*sic*] to demote. However, if we are to get cooperation from officers in the future we must take some steps to protect those from retribution when they cooperate.

"This proposed revenge against Lawton is difficult to understand in view of the fact that you will recall Stevens personally called him and told him to fully cooperate with us."

The next memo, over Carr's name, is addressed to McCarthy, December 21, 1953.

"Following my conversation with you on last Thursday in New York, I think you should know that the staff of the Subcommittee has not called upon Dave Schine's time or services except when necessary to the Committee work. . . .

"So far as I have been able to ascertain there has been no instance where he has missed training because of Committee work. . . .

"I think you should also know that during the past months since we have been closely associated with John Adams, I have on numerous occasions talked with him on the subject of Dave Schine. In all instances that I can remember the topic either came into the conversation as a natural result of some other subject we were discussing, or Adams in a facetious vein made some statement concerning the 'hostage.'

"I have always taken the position that I personally had no particular interest in Dave Schine's Army career. . . . On a number of these occasions, I have stated that it was my opinion that Schine should get an assignment for which he was qualified and in which he could actually be useful to the Army in an investigatory position. I have never, however, suggested that his assignment should be other than one which he is entitled to by all Army standards of fair play."

Next, Frank Carr to Roy Cohn, January 9, 1954. This one portrays Adams's malevolence in keeping Schine on KP:

"I called John Adams about the question of the insert for the [Subcommittee's] Annual Report re the change of the Army Security Program. Also told him that you had been trying to reach him about Dave not being free Sunday to help with the report.

"He was up in Amherst, Massachusetts, stated that he was snowbound and that he couldn't do a thing about it from Massachusetts.

"I am sure that he doesn't want to do anything. . . . I think he will duck you. It is obvious that he doesn't want the part about Army laxity in the report, so don't expect Dave to get off to help."

The next memorandum went from Cohn to McCarthy on January 14, 1954. It portrays Adams as angling for a big law-firm job:

"John Adams has been in the office again. He said that if we keep on with the hearings on the Army, and particularly if we call in those on the Loyalty Board, who cleared Communists, he will fight us in every way he can.

"As you know, Adams's present assistant, [Charles] Haskins, was one of those on the Board. His last assistant was eased out after we advised Adams of his record.

"Adams said this was the last chance for me to arrange that law partnership in New York which he wanted. One would think he was kidding, but his persistence on this subject makes it clear he is serious. He said he had turned down a job in industry at $17,500 and needed a guarantee of $25,000 from a law firm."

A short memo from Carr to McCarthy dated January 15, 1954, portrays Adams as a free-loader:

"Maybe one of these days you should speak to John Adams in a friendly way. I have tried. He is baiting Roy pretty much lately on the 'hostage' situation. They get pretty heated before Roy buys the lunch, but it's going to lead to trouble."

The eleventh memorandum, written for the file by Frank Carr and dated March 11, reports the McCarthy-Seaton phone conversation just before the Army let fly its allegations:

"This is to record that on the afternoon of this date in my presence and that of Roy Cohn, Senator McCarthy advised Assistant Secretary of Defense Fred Seaton that he had heard that a report supposedly prepared by the Department of the Army Counsellor John Adams concerning alleged pressure by the committee upon the Department of the Army and Mr. Adams to obtain preferential treatment for Private G. David Schine was to be sent to several Democratic Senators the same afternoon.

"Senator McCarthy advised Mr. Seaton that the writer was searching the files for memoranda dictated concerning Schine. The Senator distinctly stated that he was not suggesting to Mr. Seaton what he could or should do with the report as far as the distribution was concerned, but that he was offering to Mr. Seaton some of the memoranda prepared by the Subcommittee concerning Schine. . . ."

So there they were: on one side the Army's recitation of dry facts; on the other side these eleven clumsily written memos, purportedly contemporaneous, often oleaginously self-serving—a tight collection of file-cabinet evidence that, incredibly, just happened to answer every one of the Army's main contentions one by one. It seemed a documentary refutation almost too fortuitous to be true.

McCarthy flew off to Wisconsin for his weekend speaking-trip, where he would tell an Appleton audience that he had a "secret witness" to back one of his charges against the Army.

Roy Cohn, about to appear on the cover of *Time* magazine, got ready to go on Sunday's "Meet the Press," during which he would embellish on one charge by describing a map, drawn by John Adams, of the Air Force bases which sported homosexuals.

Everett Dirksen, infuriated by McCarthy's run-out on the planned meeting, told reporters that Roy Cohn would have been questioned under oath at that meeting of the four Republican members. All those Republicans, not just McCarthy, he said, had to take responsibility for the conduct of staff members.

"I do mean to meet it," Dirksen thundered. "There will be no fooling about it. The matter has gone far enough."

Robert Stevens immediately issued an indignant retort against McCarthy's allegation that he had urged the committee to go after the Navy and Air Force and lay off the Army.

Given these deafening assertions and counterassertions, some committee of the United States Senate would have to investigate them. Under the public eye, the senators had no choice. The only question was which committee. Karl Mundt, while demanding an immediate showdown, didn't want the investigation to come within the McCarthy committee itself. Let another committee take it, he urged—a committee impartial. Charles Potter agreed.

Nothing could stop the carnage now.

Whatever the venue, readiness was all. Memo by memo, the Army stood attacked by McCarthy. It had to find its rebuttals. At ten-ten the next morning, Saturday, March 13, Hensel phoned Secretary Stevens: "I think we are doing all right. Fred hasn't shown up yet. He is over at the White House. . . . We have got to take those memos of Mac's and go over them carefully.

"For instance, I have gotten through the [first] memo. . . . There has been no mention of this General Lawton in any of our conversations before, but I suppose that is correct, I don't know. . . . Then comes the story of Schine's induction. They make it seem you could use Schine on this . . . stuff. I would run through those [memos] and search my recollection and then I hope we can talk to you later today. . . ."

"Maybe I could join you and Fred for lunch," Stevens suggested. "I will come up there about one. One other item; this will amuse you I think. It solves the missing link to the releases yesterday. I couldn't understand why they didn't give out the self-serving letter [of December 22, in which McCarthy ruled out any favors for Schine]. We had a call a few minutes ago from Mrs. Driscoll over at Joe's office, and they have lost it. She [called] up with fear and trembling and asked whether she could have a copy, and I think it is all right, but I am not making a move without you knowing it."

"I think that's all right. . . ."

"One other thing. . . . I was [wondering] whether we should try to check up through the telephone company to see if we could get the telephone calls to John by Cohn over a period of time. . . ."

"I think that would be a good stunt, Bob. I think if you can show a large number of calls initiated by Cohn, it just backs up the story."

Up in Massachusetts, Dean Eugene Wilson of Amherst College wrote Adams a longhand note: "Your friends in Amherst wish they could help you win this battle with McCarthy. We remember your January remarks—'half my time is spent answering phone calls from McCarthy and his men.'"

Over at the White House, C. D. Jackson eyed the conflict and the presidential staff:

"Conversations [March 13] with [Sherman] Adams, Persons on McCarthy situation and [the] essentiality [of] realizing gravity [of the] situation rather than just taking it as routine political nuisance. Persons quite wishy-washy. Adams much firmer. . . . Decided get in touch with Seaton, who seems to be stage-managing the affair."

It was Saturday, March 13; Nixon was still getting ready to go on the air that night. The President had invited him to the White House to give him some advice on his telecast: emphasize the administration's positive program; smile; laugh off Stevenson's attacks;

mention Nixon's experience against Hiss and Eisenhower's experience in World War II command.

Before a huge Saturday night audience of 10 million, Nixon put on a brilliant performance. He savaged not only Stevenson, for whom he had little or no political respect, but also McCarthy, about whom, he admitted years later in his memoirs, he had ambivalent feelings.

In an analogy deftly designed to split away moderate anti-Communists from the Senator's train, the Vice President of the United States called up a graphic and loathsome image: Some people, he said, think Communist traitors should be shot like rats. "Well, I'll agree they're a bunch of rats, but just remember this: When you go out to shoot rats, you have to shoot straight, because when you shoot wildly it not only means that the rat may get away more easily, you make it easier on the rat, but you might hit someone else who's trying to shoot rats, too. . . . Men who have in the past done effective work exposing Communists in this country have, by reckless talk and questionable methods, made themselves the issue rather than the cause they believe in so deeply." As Eisenhower had suggested, Dick Nixon smiled.

In his own manner, which made some Eisenhower loyalists wince, if not retch, Nixon had gone public against McCarthy. He had also made a major contribution to the Eisenhower strategy. As he told the President, he had not pleased the extreme McCarthy zealots or the extreme McCarthy haters. But Eisenhower was not aiming at these tiny fringes. These people, he told Nixon, wanted only all-out war. The Vice President, Ike declared, had reached the people who counted—the 85 percent in the middle. Against McCarthy, as against the entire extreme Republican right, Eisenhower was implacably pursuing his centrist strategy—a strategy that entailed severance and isolation. The day before the broadcast he had written his close friend Bill Robinson: "There is a certain reactionary fringe of the Republican Party that hates and despises everything for which I stand or which is advanced by this Administration. In many cases, you will find that McCarthy's voting record does not align him very precisely with this group. However, the members of that gang are so anxious to seize on every possible embarrassment for the Administration that they support him. . . . There seems to be a gradually dawning realization that the Republican Party has to get itself squared away in the public mind even if this means the complete loss of the fringe of Old Guarders. . . ."

In consonance with such a strategy, the Vice President had appealed to the centrist citizen, the anti-Communist man or woman whom he could persuade to desert the McCarthy formula (chemically pure anticommunism diluted by disreputable methods) for the Eisenhower formula (chemically pure anticommunism compounded with fair play and decency). After this TV address McCarthy spoke more and more of "that prick Nixon."

The Army side hoped that other attendees at the November 6 Pentagon luncheon could help refute McCarthy's charge that at that meeting Stevens had tried to sic the McCarthy sleuths onto the Navy and Air Force. Accordingly, one attendee, Major General G. C. Mudgett, spent the next day, Sunday, writing up in laborious longhand what he remembered about that conference. What he recalled didn't help Stevens very much. He remembered "the atmosphere appeared very friendly." He remembered he was amused at a McCarthy story which terminated with McCarthy's requesting a drink of bourbon. The General remembered Cohn's mentioning a "new witness or new evidence that would give the committee its strongest case of active espionage."

But then, unhappily for Stevens, Mudgett remembered how the Secretary had voiced "his concern over the effects of the investigation on Army morale. . . . He restated his previous position to cooperate fully with the committee but felt that the American public were beginning to believe that the Army was the only agency in the United States that did not have this [Communist] problem under complete control. He inquired if McCarthy had plans to work in other areas."

After thus stepping on the Army's indignant denial of any diversionary designs, Mudgett went on to remember a couple of intriguing things that also happened at the gathering:

"Mr. Stevens and McCarthy left the room alone. Mr. Cohn was upset and stated every time McCarthy got away from him he made concessions that were harmful to the committee. . . . McCarthy approached Mr. Stevens and reached into his (Mr. Stevens') breast coat pocket and pulled out the handkerchief. When Mr. Stevens questioned this action, McCarthy stated that he was looking for his 'eye teeth' that Mr. Stevens had just stolen."

At Hensel's prodding, Stevens systematically explored *his* memories. Looking at three long lists of phone calls and appointments stretching from September to March, he dictated his reflections. They were somewhat better than Mudgett's, but not much. They ran just eleven single-spaced pages; they contained a quantity of extraneous detail—a lot of dirt with each potato—and they revealed few new nuggets.

For example, Stevens described September 8, 1953, this way: "Following General Wainright's funeral at Arlington National Cemetery, at which I represented the Secretary of Defense, I proceeded directly to the Senate Office Building. I had a luncheon engagement with Senator McCarthy and Senator Dirksen. When I arrived in Senator McCarthy's office, Senator Dirksen was there and half a dozen photographers. Senator McCarthy suggested that a few photographs be taken before we had any discussion. Senator Dirksen, Senator McCarthy and I stood behind Senator McCarthy's desk and pictures were taken. . . .

"I do not definitely recall just where Senator McCarthy, Senator Dirksen and I lunched. I am inclined to believe it was at the Carroll Arms Hotel. We discussed three or four cases of possible subversion in the first Army area. . . ."

Not very incisive.

"Late on the afternoon of 15 September," Stevens further remembered, "I flew to New York with Secretary Wilson and Secretary Humphrey. . . . The next morning I was to meet Senator McCarthy at 10:00 in suite 30A of the Waldorf-Astoria Towers. On arrival at 10:00 I was ushered into an attractive apartment by a maid who informed me Senator McCarthy had not yet appeared. Shortly thereafter the Senator showed up, as did David Schine. We went into the dining room for breakfast. . . . Upon this occasion, Senation McCarthy raised the question of a commission for David Schine. I refreshed his memory on the fact that the application had been turned down by the Army, and that I had been informed that neither the Navy nor the Air Force had commissions available for the qualifications of David Schine. There were then questions about whether or not Schine might serve as a special assistant to me on matters of Communist infiltration. I indicated that such an arrangement was not possible and that Schine, if inducted, must take the same training and treatment as any other boy.

"Aside from the question of Schine's forthcoming induction, it was a very pleasant breakfast. . . ."

On September 29, Stevens recalled, he was "personally urged by Senator McCarthy and Jean Kerr to attend their wedding, I did so [at] the Catholic Cathedral. The church was packed. . . ."

On October 13 "I took off from Washington at 8:00 in the morning and spent the day at the Federal Court House, Room 1402, Foley Square, New York, where Senator McCarthy was conducting hearings. As the Federal Court House is only two blocks from the Merchants Club in the textile district, a club of which I have been a member for 30 years, I invited Senator McCarthy and members of his staff to lunch with me at the club. I arranged for a private dining room and in addition to myself, the following were present at the luncheon (according to my best memory): Senator McCarthy, John Adams, Roy Cohn, Frank Carr, David Schine, and the pilot of a private plane . . . for a Texas man, I believe Mr. [H. L.] Hunt, who from time to time provided air transportation for Senator McCarthy.

"The luncheon was very pleasant and the main subject of discussion was the Fort Monmouth situation. . . . I told Senator McCarthy that I had arranged for the private dining room to be available throughout the week for his use if the hearings continued.

"The evening of 13 October I was invited to a dinner party in a private dining room at the Waldorf-Astoria Hotel. I believe the dinner was given by Mr. and Mrs. Schine, Sr. There were about fourteen people in attendance, including in addition to Mr. and Mrs. Schine, the following: David Schine, Judge Cohn [Roy's father], Mrs. Cohn, Roy Cohn . . . , Senator McCarthy, Mrs. McCarthy. . . .

"I spent the night at the Union League Club and the next morning by arrangement David Schine picked me up at the corner of 37th Street and Park Avenue about 9:30 in order to reach the court house in plenty of time for the day's hearings. David arrived alone in his Cadillac car which carries a big siren on the left front fender. We had quite a visit on the way downtown. He said that I was in position to be the biggest man in the United States by continuing to do a good job in getting rid of commies from the Army. He thought he could be of much more value helping me in this work as a special assistant rather than going into the Army. I told Schine that if he did not go into the Army and take the regular GI treatment for the next two years that he would regret it all his life. I said that people would ask him to his dying day why he did not do his part in the military. . . ."

Six days later, on October 20, "at 10:07 A.M., after waiting 15 minutes because Roy Cohn was late, we left for [the Military Air Transport Service terminal at Washington National Airport to fly to] Monmouth. Members of the party were: Secretary of the Army,

Senator McCarthy, General Back . . . [Stevens' aide] Colonel Be-
Lieu, Roy Cohn, and John Adams. Landing near Spring Lake, New
Jersey, we were met by [Commanding] General Lawton . . . who
took us directly to Fort Monmouth. We were joined there by Senator H. Alexander Smith and later by Congressman Auchincloss. . . .
We had a meeting with General Lawton and his staff and there were
many questions by Senator McCarthy and Roy Cohn. . . . [Their]
intent was to show laxity in security procedures and to prove, if
possible, that classified documents had been removed from the
premises. . . ."

For the first time, Stevens now dredged up a crucial cogent happening: "One particular incident stands out in my mind. We came
to one laboratory where work of a very highly classified nature was
underway. The security personnel stopped the whole party at the
door, indicating that the Secretary of the Army could enter, but no
one else was wearing a security clearance button of the right color.
I was faced with making a quick decision. I decided that anybody
elected by the voters of the United States could join me in a tour
of inspection. This included Senator McCarthy, Senator Smith, and
Congressman Auchincloss. The rest remained outside during the
ten-minute inspection trip. . . . Rejoining the group outside, I
found that Roy Cohn had blown his lid. He considered himself
highly insulted because I had not invited him into the laboratory
and he had already intimated to Colonel BeLieu and John Adams
(who, though having a pass to enter the building, had stayed outside with Roy Cohn in an effort to placate him) that this was the
last straw, that he would now really take out after the Army. . . ."

Stevens next recalled the November 6 luncheon in his Pentagon
office: "This was the luncheon at which I'd invited Senator Mc-
Carthy as well as Roy Cohn, Frank Carr, and John Adams. . . . I
pointed out that it was damaging to the Army to be hit over the
head every day in the newspaper headlines. I commented on my
efforts and the efforts of the Army to cooperate with Senator Mc-
Carthy and his committee to the end of routing out Communists and
fellow travelers. . . . It seemed to me, however, that the Executive
Branch of government was entitled to an opportunity to follow up
the suggestions and the leads of the Legislative Branch. . . .

"At no point did I suggest that I would resign, although I did indicate that, in my opinion, we in the Army were very capable of
handling our internal affairs to the best interest of the country, including the elimination of security risks. But if continued day-to-day

publicity of the type emanating from the current committee activities pertaining to Monmouth gave the country the opinion that I could not manage the Army, then perhaps I might be forced to resign. . . . [McCarthy] turned the attention of the discussion to some industrial concerns where he said there were communist problems on classified work. I said that this had been a real problem not only to the Army, but also to the Navy and the Air Force. . . . Perhaps this phase of the discussion is the basis on which Senator McCarthy's fantastic charge of my diverting him to the Navy and Air Force was based. . . .

"Senator McCarthy indicated in one of his recently released memoranda that I had said, 'if the truth comes out about Fort Monmouth, I would have to resign.' I never made any such statement. . . . In fact, a week later, on 13 November, I stated at a press conference that thus far no evidence of current espionage at Fort Monmouth had been developed. . . ."

For the first time in the written record Stevens then recounted the events between his no-current-espionage-at-Monmouth press conference on November 12 and his Merchants Club lunch with McCarthy on November 16: "Roy Cohn and John Adams came to my [Pentagon] office. Cohn said McCarthy was very mad, that I had doublecrossed him, and that my statement about [no current espionage at] Fort Monmouth was not true. Cohn was pretty mad himself. . . . I said that if Senator McCarthy (who was in New York) was so mad, I would go up to New York and see him next day. I flew up in the morning. . . .

"We had arranged for another luncheon at the Merchants Club. Senator McCarthy was late in arriving but came in either with or about the same time as George Sokolsky. In addition, there was Roy Cohn, Frank Carr, [Stevens aide] Tom Cleary, and John Adams. Jean McCarthy arrived just before we adjourned late in the afternoon. . . . Senator McCarthy was obviously provoked at my remarks at the press conference of 13 November.

"When the discussion began, I said in effect, 'Why are you so mad at me, Joe?' He replied in substance, 'No, you haven't done anything, you just called me a liar before the press.' He and I argued quite a bit about the matter and George Sokolsky attempted, upon occasion, to act as peacemaker.

"As this was the day upon which Attorney General Brownell was making his TV statement with respect to the White case, I arranged for a TV to be put in the next room, and we all moved in to have a look. Sokolsky, Cohn, and Adams were all writing out a suggested press release while the balance of the group viewed TV. . . . [The release] finally boiled down to the proposition that I could speak for the Army but not the McCarthy committee. Accordingly, as the press had started to overrun the Merchants Club, Senator McCarthy and I agreed we would make a press appearance. . . .

"[Afterward] an Army car took Colonel Cleary, John Adams and myself to Newark Airport. David Schine's car carried Senator McCarthy, Mrs. McCarthy, Roy Cohn, and Frank Carr. The Senator drove the car and frequently blew the siren mounted on the left front fender. . . .

"We flew from Newark to McGuire Air Base, adjacent to Fort Dix. . . . General Ryan and members of his staff, plus Private Schine, met us on arrival. . . ."

Next Stevens recalled why he had wanted to fire Commanding General Lawton:

"[On November 24] at his request, I called upon Congressman Auchincloss, an old friend from New Jersey. . . . I spent about an hour with him. He was somewhat worried about what seemed to him and to me, some possibly indiscreet remarks by General Lawton at recent off-the-record meetings of the personnel at the post. Apparently the general attacked some of our colleges and universities as being hot beds for fellow travellers. . . .

"[The next day] I met with General Back, Chief of the Signal Corps . . . regarding General Lawton. . . . I was thinking of asking General Back to relieve General Lawton. I knew General Lawton once before in his military career had received an official reprimand for poor judgment. . . . However, as General Lawton seemed to be getting along fine with the McCarthy investigators, I withheld decision for the moment. . . ."

Stevens then skipped ahead seven weeks to the January 14 cocktail session at the Carroll Arms with Joe and Joe's friend Al McCarthy:

". . . I can remember saying that if Schine qualified for CID school and successfully finished the course that he might be assigned to any one of one hundred places. I said, 'Honolulu wouldn't be so bad, would it, Joe?' During this conversation with Senator McCarthy concerning Mr. Schine I said in substance to Senator McCarthy, 'You know, Joe, I have a letter from you dated 22 December saying you wanted no more favors for Schine. You have brought up the possibility of assigning Schine to the New York area four or five times during this conversation.' Then turning to Al McCarthy . . . I said in substance, 'Would you consider this pressure, Al?' . . ."

Stevens was not only searching his memory, such as it was, but also he was sending out for more information—in fact, going all the way to Tokyo for data on one Army private. To the Commander-in-Chief in the Far East, General Hull, he cabled March 15: "General Bedell Smith informs me that you were contacted by him concerning possibility of commission for G. David Schine in early part of August 1953. Would appreciate your informing me by return cable of your knowledge of this subject." Meanwhile, having written to General Back, the Signal Corps chief, about General Lawton, of whom Hensel was hearing for the first time, Hensel received a memorandum recounting Back's November conference with Stevens: "Secretary Stevens appeared to be most disturbed about . . . [a] report . . . that [General Lawton] had . . . left the impression that the graduates of [several leading universities] had been indoctrinated with leftist ideas. He further stated that if General Lawton had made such statements, he felt that General Lawton had used exceedingly poor judgment. . . . Upon returning to my office I telephoned General Lawton . . . [and] suggested that he visit my office the following morning in order that I might obtain a statement from him as to what had been said at the meetings. . . .

"After conferring with General Lawton, I visited the office of the Secretary of the Army for the purpose of rendering a verbal report. . . . After listening . . . the Secretary again . . . [said that Lawton's] remarks could not but reflect unfavorably upon the Army and that he seriously questioned General Lawton's judgment as a commander of a large installation. . . ."

At last Joe Alsop broke his silence. John Adams had shown him his original unexpurgated chronology *in toto*. Alsop had sat on it for six weeks. Now he could wait no longer. On Monday morning, March 15, the *Washington Post* carried a frenzied Alsop column starkly contrasting the juiceless bowdlerized revision, now public, with the, in his view, lurid secret original.

"The country and the Congress have been shocked as seldom before by the sordid tale" of McCarthy, Cohn, and Schine, Alsop began. But "the shock would be immensely greater," he went on, "if the Army Department had told the whole story. For policy reasons, Assistant Secretary of Defense Fred Seaton heavily censored the Army's original account. . . ."

Alsop went on to specify exactly what Seaton had blue-penciled: Cohn's obscenities (". . . the unbounded arrogance, the inflated egotism, the Nazi-like sense of power that Cohn displayed was of course derived from his position as McCarthy's chief counsel."); details on the McCarthy-Cohn-Schine relationship, including an open avowal by McCarthy that he wanted to get rid of Cohn; and the "record of attempts to act as peacemaker by at least one well-known member of the McCarthyite press," Alsop's fellow syndicated columnist Sokolsky. Having nicked Seaton as censor, Alsop offered a palliative: "As to the censorship, the aim was understandable. It was desired to tell the story, soberly, plainly, and unsensationally. Nonetheless, the full facts deserve to be published. . . ."

At 12:31 P.M., Hensel talked with Stevens: "Did you read Alsop? . . . Either Joe's memory is awful damned good, or Joe has a copy— no matter what John Adams says."

Already Hensel had had a caller: "Symington sent young [Bobby] Kennedy, who's counsel for the three Democratic senators, over to try to pump me; and I told him we were not in any position to talk. . . . He wants the original document mentioned in the Alsop column. . . ." The "young Kennedy" hadn't impressed Hensel. "He tried to pretend he was on my side," Hensel recalled when interviewed years later. "Really he wanted Republican blood on the floor."

Hensel for the moment had his plate full with something else he told Stevens about: the Inspector General's report on the impact of Cohn and Schine on Fort Dix—a 241-page document of undigested testimony, "a bad story," in Hensel's words, "the story of [the] demoralization of at least one company by these two brash kids." The day before, in a long interview with Lieutenant John B. Blount, aide to Commanding General Ryan at Dix, Hensel had got a rundown of particulars: Schine's intimating to his fellow soldiers that he was not an ordinary GI but an important figure on a secret mission; his wearing special boots and a special fur hood, and sleeping on a special mattress with special covers; his staying out all night on his special passes, once showing up five minutes before reveille, and thus posing a possible threat during target practice; Cohn's telling Blount that, with his "long memory," he would never forget the names of the officers at Dix who were giving Schine a hard time; Schine's frequent running off during training hours to take important phone calls.

Hensel told Stevens in their March 15 phone conversation that he didn't think much of the Inspector General's report—a dump of the raw words of witnesses. And he didn't think much of the incisiveness of the inquiry. For example, Schine spent a lot of time on the phone during his basic training, "and he has got a telephone credit card. That means they have got a record of every damn call he made—but nobody thinks to [check] that." Likewise, on Schine's trips into Trenton, ostensibly on committee business, the I G sleuths report only that he took a hotel room. "And I say, 'Well, have you been around to see that he did?' . . . I think there is an awful lot of baloney on [Schine's alleged] committee work. . . ."

Bob Kennedy's name reminded Stevens of something: "Struve, there was some talk about Kennedy's sister in one of these situations. Do you know anything about that?"

"She is supposed to have been there. I didn't want to ask this kid anything. I didn't want to be in the position of where he was telling me something. . . ."

"Didn't anybody tell you that Patricia Kennedy was present and heard a fair amount? Are we doing anything to try to doublecheck that?

"Haven't yet."

"I think we ought to."

At that precise moment, back in his office, John Adams was also scrutinizing the eleven McCarthy memos. Unlike Stevens, he was not just going into mild-mannered reverie. He was burrowing into the memos' accuracy and even authenticity. And he began firing off to Hensel a volley of rebuttals, seriatim, and of additions to the record.

On the unsigned McCarthy memorandum of November 6 about the lunch in Stevens's Pentagon office, Adams parried the allegation that he offered to supply leads into Navy and Air Force dirt by affirming that "the discussions were not about investigations of the other services but [about the committee's plans to go] after labor unions and Communists in plants which had defense business. There was a suggestion made, by Cohn I think, that we should furnish them leads on this. . . ."

On the unsigned memorandum of November 17 about the luncheon at the Merchants Club in New York, Adams revealed that the McCarthy friend present was George Sokolsky, possibly the "secret witness" McCarthy was harboring; reported that Lieutenant Colonel Tom Cleary, also present, had no recollection whatsoever of Stevens's saying "he wished [McCarthy] could get on to the Air Force and the Navy . . ."; disclosed that McCarthy had ordered "the most expensive steak on the menu," saying he wanted to make Stevens "pay plenty for the lunch"; described Sokolsky as a peacemaker, urging McCarthy and the Army to find a common meeting ground; denied any discussion of investigations of other armed services; and gave a vivid description of McCarthy en route to the airport at the wheel of Schine's Cadillac—a siren on its left front fender—which he took over from the chauffeur after going one block:

"At intersections, in the [Holland] tunnel, and at various places along the highway where there was intercepting or approaching traffic, McCarthy sounded the siren of the Cadillac. He sounded it also as we approached the airplane at Newark Field. . . ."

In an addition to the record, Adams revealed that on a train ride with Frank Carr from Newark to Washington on November 25, Carr had volunteered to Adams that he was spending two thirds of his time on Schine. He recognized that nothing could be done for Schine but predicted that as long as Cohn was dissatisfied with what the Army was doing to his friend, the Army could expect the investigation to continue.

On the Cohn memorandum of December 9 to Senator McCarthy and Cohn's follow-up remarks on "Meet the Press," Adams flatly denied Cohn's allegation that he had offered to trade information about a homosexual ring at an Air Force base in return for information on the committee's next investigation of the Army. He had not drawn a map of the country to show Cohn and Carr the Air Force base's location.

Here's what really happened, Adams said: Cohn had been boasting that the committee had another big Army investigation about to break. This boast bothered Adams because his office had underway an extensive study of allegations about the existence of a large homosexual ring at Fort Bragg, North Carolina. Moreover, Adams knew that a disgruntled employee who had been spreading these allegations was at that very moment walking the corridors of Washington. Had he been talking to the McCarthy committee?

To find out, Adams had drawn a map of the country for Cohn and

Carr, split it up into nine numbered sections, and invited them to check the section they were zeroing in on. They refused. Then he asked them whether they were looking in the North or in the South. They clammed up again. But then, through an offhand remark, they dropped the hint that they were focusing not on any place in Dixie but on a spot in the New York–New England area.

On Frank Carr's memorandum of December 9 in which Carr attributed to Adams the word "hostage," Adams asserted he never heard the word used for Schine before January 22, when Senator McCarthy had used it—Carr himself had confirmed the fact to Adams—in his stormy meeting with his fellow Republican Committee members.

On McCarthy's memorandum of December 17 to Cohn and Carr, Adams for the first time raised the question of authenticity. He frankly didn't believe McCarthy wrote that memo on that date. McCarthy, Adams remembered, had no stenographic help in New York.

Moreover, Adams added, the sequence of events went like this: On December 16, Adams flew to New York and checked in at the Commodore Hotel. That afternoon he went downtown to Cohn's office. Cohn telephoned a friend and set up theater tickets for Adams and two aunts of his for that evening. The next morning Adams met McCarthy going into the Foley Square Courthouse at ten-thirty; McCarthy told him he had become angered with his staff over their interference for Schine. When they got to the room McCarthy was using as an office, they met Frank Carr. McCarthy began to chew Carr out, and Adams left.

When the hearings ended that morning, they all walked together to Gasner's restaurant for a luncheon that all would long remember, and that Adams now described for the first time in the written record. Leaving the courthouse, Adams recalls, he himself walked alongside Peter Lawford. Patricia Kennedy walked with Joe. When they got to the restaurant she asked Joe at length about "these fifth amendment people"; Joe explained to her how they were carrying on before his committee. For some reason, Adams went on, Cohn became "rather ugly and . . . made a nasty remark . . . that the Army was relieving Lawton just because he was friendly to Joe." Both Peter Lawford and Pat Kennedy heard Adams's reply: "Roy, you ought to be ashamed of yourself. You know that is not so."

At about one-fifteen, Adams continued, Lawford and Miss Kennedy left, having planned to stay only for a cup of coffee. And then for the next two hours a "magnificent argument," raged. "Cohn violently [abused Adams] and McCarthy" about Schine. Cohn ejected Adams from his car in the middle of four lanes of traffic at Forty-sixth Street and Park Avenue. A few minutes later he did the same thing to McCarthy in front of the Waldorf, where McCarthy was staying.

All this narrative, Adams concluded, would establish "that all of us were together during much of the two preceding days, and also would indicate that we had a discussion . . . in the presence of both Cohn and Carr which would" obviate the necessity for the purported December 17 memorandum of McCarthy. Moreover, in order to write that memorandum, sometime after three-thirty in the afternoon, McCarthy would have had to get a Waldorf-Astoria public stenographer to type it up and it was improbable that at that moment McCarthy would be writing Cohn about Lawton. At Gasner's he and Cohn had just participated in an extensive and heated discussion about the General in front of Bob Kennedy's sister and her escort. And the violence of the Park Avenue car ride would have pushed the subject out of the forefront of McCarthy's mind.

"It is just possible," Adams wrote Hensel, "that Peter Lawford and Patricia Kennedy . . . might remember . . . our argument at Gasner's Restaurant. . . . If they do, it would make the necessity for a memorandum from McCarthy to the effect that he had questioned me in a friendly manner appear . . . very doubtful. Is it worth suggesting to Bob Kennedy that he check with his sister?"

On Carr's memorandum to Cohn on January 9 and Cohn's embellishment on "Meet the Press," Adams questioned Cohn's assertion that on January 9, when Schine was scheduled for Sunday KP, the committee urgently needed him in order to get out its annual report. Adams suggested checking with the Government Printing Office, which probably by January 9 had had the report in page proof, beyond the need for Schine's emendations.

On Cohn's memorandum to McCarthy on January 14, in which Cohn suggested that Adams was trying to wangle a law partnership, Adams said Cohn was twisting a standing joke between the two of them. They had three such standing jokes, Adams said: (1) Paulette Ames, "a pretty young girl" about whom Adams would quip to Roy: "Why don't you take her out to the Stork Club tonight?"; (2) the idea of throwing a birthday party for Adams—a knee-slapper that somebody would suggest nearly every evening; and (3) the high-priced law job.

"I often suggested to Cohn that we ought to chuck the whole thing, get away from the hurly-burly of government business, find somebody with more money than sense who would pay us twice what we were worth for working twenty or twenty-five hours a week, and thus lower our blood pressure and extend our lives." Adams had already had some feelers from industry, where he'd probably head if he ever left government because, as he told Cohn, he'd "never tried a case, had never drawn a complaint, had never been in a courtroom, and . . . would therefore be useless to a New York law factory." Anyway, with a boss like Stevens, head of a great textile company, with lots of blue-chip connections, why would Adams need help from Roy Cohn?

On the January 15 memorandum from Carr to McCarthy containing Carr's "nasty crack" that Cohn always "bought the lunch," Adams went into great detail to establish that he had insisted on paying for: (1) a room at the Drake Hotel in New York, originally charged to Cohn; (2) the Turpin-Olson fight ticket ($20.00 at ringside), which Cohn alleged he had got free; and (3) three tickets to *Wonderful Town* with Rosalind Russell. Adams acknowledged he had accepted one invitation from Cohn to lunch with Carr and a newspaperwoman named Shirley Eder at the Stork Club. And when four of them went to the Stork Club after the Olson-Turpin fight, Adams didn't reach for the tab: all the others had had hard liquor; he had had orangeade. Moreover, when one looked at the comparative amounts spent by the Army and the committee, Adams went on, the Army laid out considerably more, given Stevens's expenditures for McCarthy and his staff at the Merchants Club, plus parties thrown by McCarthy at the Merchants Club, using Stevens's membership, for groups of five, six or eight.

So there at the moment the Great Debate rested: the Army's meticulously expurgated list of facts, in chronological order; the eleven McCarthy memos—self-serving, crudely written, questionably dated rejoinders; Stevens's innocuous, wordy, always amiable, frequently irrelevant recollections; Adams's fact-engaged, detailed retorts, descending at times into niggling quibbles over who paid the bills and why a single private should do Sunday KP. The controversy often turned on the Army's undocumented word against McCarthy's purportedly contemporaneous written evidence. Small wonder that when C. D. Jackson lunched with Fred Seaton on that Monday, March 15, he found Fred not happy with either of the

Army's first firing-line witnesses: ". . . appalled to discover how badly Army had handled a) keeping a record, b) how personally shaky both Stevens and Adams are."

The subcommittee's moment of truth had arrived. The next day, March 16, they met in a showdown executive session. They agreed that they couldn't dodge, couldn't buck the problem to another committee—for example, the Armed Services Committee under Republican Chairman Leverett Saltonstall, or even to the full parent Committee on Government Operations.

From the start the ranking Democrat, John MClellan, and his fellow Democrat Stu Symington insisted on open hearings, on spreading the facts—all the facts—before the public, not arousing suspicion through closed-door sessions.

"I am not here, brother," McClellan declared, "to defend the Army." If it had dirty linen, he wanted it displayed and cleaned up—*now*.

For a while Everett Dirksen questioned the desirability of a public spectacle. The committee's inquiry into the charges and countercharges, he said, could have only two possible outcomes—the termination of Roy Cohn or the suggestion to Charlie Wilson that he terminate John Adams; and the committee needed no nationwide ventilation to accomplish either. Dirksen expatiated on the merits of screening witness testimony in secret session before going out on stage; such pre-screening, he argued, would prevent "caterwauling and chopping."

But Charles Potter agreed with McClellan: "Somebody has committed perjury, and I don't know who." The committee could not sweep that under the rug. McCarthy himself lined up with McClellan and Symington and Potter: "I am accused of interfering for Private Schine. I want the evidence on that in a public session." So finally Dirksen acquiesced, and the vote to go public became unanimous.

Throughout the meeting the senators danced around the specification of the suspect. Adams and Cohn were principals for sure; on that much all agreed. But Stu Symington, no longer proffering helpful advice in the Army's corner, now contended: "There are more principals than that. Secretary Stevens is in it, and he is in it deep; and the feeling in the United States today is that the Secretary of the Army may have committed perjury." Karl Mundt tentatively took a further step: "This is a controversy," he declared, "between a staff member of the committee, and perhaps the chairman of the committee, and Mr. Adams and Mr. Stevens. . . ." And although Senators McClellan and Dirksen in the unanimously approved formal motion removed the name of McCarthy from the list of those proclaimed to be the targets of the investigation, the wording stretched far enough to cover him. At the end of this meeting the players were engaged. No one could turn back.

The conferees on the committee agreed they should bring in a temporary special counsel; Mundt mentioned that he had thought of the possibility of asking Deputy Attorney General Bill Rogers or Justice Bob Morris, formerly of the Senate Internal Security Subcommittee; both were skilled and seasoned in anti-Communist investigations on the Hill. And the committee members displayed an eagerness to get the whole thing over with as expeditiously as possible, although Mundt farsightedly warned it would take some time— at least ten days or two weeks. They at once publicly announced several unanimous decisions. The subcommittee would hold public hearings. It would take up no other inquiry in the meantime. Mundt would serve as temporary chairman. A special counsel would be appointed.

In public view at his news conference the next morning, March 17, the President defended Stevens: "When you ask me whether I believe Secretary Stevens, of course I do. If I didn't believe him, if I didn't have faith and confidence in him, he wouldn't be where he is. . . . I don't say he can't be mistaken . . . there may be something that he has been misinformed on; but so far as his integrity and honesty are concerned I stand by him."

Behind the scenes the President the next day conferred with C. D. Jackson and Bobby Cutler after a meeting of the National Security Council, got the advice of the two and zeroed in on his main target—not Roy Cohn, McCarthy. In C.D.'s at times condescending words: "Got hot and bothered about McCarthy, and conferred with Cutler. We decided to explain gravity of the situation to the President. . . . He called Mundt in our presence to make two points— 1) speed; 2) McCarthy could not be both investigator and investigated."

Listening in the outer office, Eisenhower's personal secretary, Ann Whitman, also monitored the phone call and wrote it up in the third person. The President asked Mundt, she wrote, "how rapidly he can drive through the job. . . . Mundt said less than a week, once they get a staff. D.D.E. can't think of anything that's hurting our position more, and looks to Mundt to settle it. Mundt looking for high-ranking counsel that the country will accept—in stature, objectivity and competence. Right now, he has call in for Earl Warren to see if he will lend a District Judge. D.D.E. mentioned he'd like John W. Davis [Calvin Coolidge's presidential opponent in 1924, and a former Solicitor General], one of the rudest and [most] dedicated old patriots he's ever known . . . D.D.E.'s next question, confidentially and as a Republican: what would reaction be to having on Committee [a] man involved as deeply as [McCarthy]? Mundt replied that McCarthy insists upon staying on as a member of the subcommittee, but that they will insist that Army have right to cross-examine him. D.D.E. advised that . . . Mundt and Dirksen and Charlie Potter must not let anything be put over on them. . . . D.D.E.'s two points: Push, and remember that there's honor and decency at stake right now."

Hanging up the phone, the President agreed, Jackson wrote in his diary, "to let us draft follow-up letter to Mundt, which we did. Showed to Brownell, at President's request. He glommed on [to the] idea. Seaton all for it.

"Showed Pres. the draft on Saturday morning. He had pretty well made up his mind not to send it and got very angry when I told him that this time he was morally involved. He reacted so quickly I didn't have a chance to get the extra clause out: 'in the eyes of the American people.' However, stood my guns. . . ."

Ike didn't send the letter to Mundt. (As he remarked a few days later to Jim Hagerty: "If I could trust him, I'd have sent the letter. But you can't trust that fellow. He plays everything against the middle.") But after Jackson left the Oval Office, the President did phone Bill Knowland. The Majority Leader reported that he had stressed to Mundt and Potter that McCarthy should be barred from voting or from questioning witnesses.

"Everybody in the United States," the President replied, "will approve what you said." He phoned the news to C. D. Jackson. Better than nothing, Jackson concluded, adding disconsolately in his diary: "However, the way it has developed is Symington, the Democrat, took the initiative, was endorsed by Knowland not too enthusiastically, and later the Pres. will do a me-too. Not pretty."

Meanwhile, up on the Hill, Symington was pursuing another trail. The perennial liberal Democratic Presidential candidate picked up the phone and called Fred Seaton.

Like Jackson, who had talked with Symington and found him "very plausible, but somehow don't quite trust him," Fred neared

Symington as he would an adder fanged. As Struve Hensel had remarked, the Democrats would pretend to help—and in fact would help—but they would also revel in Republican blood on the floor. So now two smoothies fenced.

"I don't know whether to call you Secretary, Senator or Mister," Symington amiably began.

"Make it Fred."

"All right, you say Stuart or Stu." Then he came to the point. He'd read the Joe Alsop column about the bowdlerization of the Adams chronology, he said, and he was concerned. "You and I both know that what hurts the Army hurts the D.O.D., the President, the country. . . . I would like very much to get a copy of the unabridged text of the report. . . . The article says, 'For policy reasons Assistant Secretary of Defense Fred Seaton heavily censored [it]. . . .' Since that time, we have set up this special [inquiry] here. The Republicans are anxious to have your participation. . . . I think the American people are entitled to the truth. . . ."

Seaton dodged: "In the first place, Joe's information is incorrect. I did not go over a report and censor it; in fact, there actually was not a report. There was a collection of memoranda and papers—some totally unrelated to the subject."

"And tapes, I understand."

"No sir, not to my knowledge. . . . Some of the lawyers from Hensel's shop went over it and assembled the material in chronological form. I told the reporters at the White House there was some unpleasant language taken out—words which we would not want to send to the Hill—I would not want my children seeing or hearing it."

Symington reviewed some of his own credentials: "I was Secretary to the Air Force . . . when this [Major General] Benny Meyers [procurement scandal] busted in my face. I blew everything—I just shoveled it out. In two weeks we were out of it. Bill Rogers, now Deputy Attorney General, was of great assistance to me. . . . Having spent four and a half years in the Pentagon and having been, for a little time, in the field artillery; having been to college with Bob Stevens, I have to be neutral. But I want to tell you there is going to be no holds barred with respect to this situation. I think it would be terribly wrong if any information of any kind—except that which would be beneficial to a foreign enemy—was not completely disclosed. . . ."

Seaton took the high ground: "Let me assure you, I only took one oath of office and I swore allegiance to one thing. As far as I am concerned, anything the committee asks for that is within my power to get, the committee gets."

Symington backed off: "I would know that—knowing you and of you . . . I think an ounce of prevention may be worthwhile. I would like to get it all."

Seaton continued to stand on his rock: "You can pay your money and take your choice with reference to these miscellaneous items being included in that report which went to you men. If the committee asks for [them], the committee gets them."

Symington closed with a compliment: "Telling you how to act on the Hill is like trying to tell a grandmother how to suck eggs. If they ask you something and you don't know the answer, tell them you don't know. . . ." But before he hung up, he assured Fred: "Incidentally, I have no recorder down here. I just wanted to get in touch with you and bring this up respectfully for your consideration. . . ."

At this particular moment Fred could not be equally candid. Uncharacteristically, he had his secretary, Violet Bryan, on the line, and after she finished the monitoring she wrote him a cryptic one-liner: "I ran off two copies—I destroyed my notes."

Symington would also by chance find himself at a dinner party with Milton Eisenhower, whom he didn't know, and would bend his ear with advice.

The next morning Milton picked up a piece of stationery at the hotel where he was staying in Washington, the Mayflower, and wrote his brother down the street a longhand letter: "Senator Symington had these things to say to me at Willard [Cox's] dinner last evening . . . :

a) "Since the President has backed Stevens, the real contest is between McCarthy and the President. In the actual hearing, the contest will be between Stevens and McCarthy. Cohn and Adams will be mere incidentals. Stevens must not make the mistake of backing Adams. Let him (Adams) stand on his own feet. Adams is a carryover from the previous administration, may not be too smart, might be caught with a damaging admission such as 'I *did* say to McCarthy that he ought to shift his attentions from the Army to the Navy.' This is all that would be required to have McCarthy win his case.

b) "Since possibly McCarthy will have the right to cross-examine (otherwise he would be a martyr), Stevens should by all means have with him the best lawyer in the United States—such as Thurmond Arnold. The reason: McCarthy is the shrewdest man on the Hill, but Stevens, while honest and filled with good intentions and integrity, is slow-witted. He also can be tripped. But a really good lawyer to do Stevens' cross-examining for him can devastate McCarthy.

"*The larger McCarthy issue.* Symington said that he is convinced and has some documents which he says could prove that McCarthy in good time will directly attack you. First he will go after CIA and try to discredit the two Dulles brothers. Then he will go after many who served under you in the German occupation. . . . Symington says there is bad stuff in the files on both.

"So he urges you, after the Stevens affair is over and possibly earlier, to get rid of McCarthy simply by insisting that the Republican leadership in the Senate take McCarthy off the present committee. . . .

"Finally, Symington says that the greatest political myth of our time is the political strength of McCarthy. He pointed out that you carried Wisconsin with 150,000 lead over McCarthy. He, Symington, carried Missouri over the bitter opposition of McCarthy and in the face of an Eisenhower landslide. The same, he said, happened many places. . . ."

Milton was reporting Symington's opinions, not urging them. "Naturally I cannot endorse any of the foregoing," he added. "I give it to you for what it is worth."

Schine had departed Fort Dix, New Jersey, and left in his wake the shocking 241-page Inspector General's report Hensel was plowing through. He'd gone to Camp Gordon in Georgia, and a report on his doings there had come to John Adams. No dirt this time. Adams told Hensel, as he'd earlier told Carr: at Gordon, Schine "has behaved very well."

McCarthy flew to Chicago for a March 17 roof-raising St. Patrick's Day address. On the plane he told a couple of reporters that he blamed his troubles on "Pentagon politicians, holdovers from the old Truman-Acheson regime." And when he landed, he laid it on before a huge Palmer House audience, taking off his coat to their cheering clamor: "You're in your own ball park now, Joe!" John Chadwick, an AP reporter, filed a story that made McCarthy appear violently anti-Eisenhower. But McCarthy had carefully tempered his attack on the President. In fact, in the interview on the plane he had alleged that the Communists were doing their best to egg on a fight between President and Senator. McCarthy at once wired the AP, copying the White House, denying he had challenged the President to name any Communists *he* had exposed. And he personally chewed out Chadwick.

On March 19 in a speech to five hundred Young Republiacns in Milwaukee, McCarthy, suffering from laryngitis, fever, and exhaustion, attacked "Ad-lie" Stevenson, twenty counts of treason by the Democrats, and the American news media. If the American people want the true story on the Army-McCarthy dispute, he said, they should write directly to his office.

The next day in Oklahoma City he patted Eisenhower on the head: "[He's] doing the best job he can, but I don't think he is a Superman."

"The enemy's ranks are closing . . . they strive to hamstring our investigations," he had declared in Milwaukee. Despite the bravado of the speeches in his own midwestern ball park, even McCarthy might have sensed he was sliding. On Sunday, March 21, two towering pulpits on the Eastern Seaboard had turned political. Exchanging churches, Dean James A. Pike of New York and Francis B. Sayre, Jr., the grandson of Woodrow Wilson and Dean of Washington's National Cathedral, attacked McCarthy in simultaneous sermons, one for his "new tyranny," one for his reality as "another of the devil's disguises."

Newspapers and magazines large and small, including the formerly steadfast *Arizona Republic* and *Time*, were turning against him. Not only Majority Leader Knowland but Senator Homer Ferguson, Chairman of the Republican Policy Committee, and Republican National Chairman Len Hall announced their agreement with Symington's insistence that McCarthy drop his membership on the subcommittee during the investigation. McCarthy himself, though digging in his heels on membership, had to announce that "days ago" he had agreed with Karl Mundt that he couldn't vote on the committee's findings.

Both Mundt and Hall confided to Richard Nixon that they thought McCarthy was starting to "blow up," Mundt recalling how Joe had kept him up until two in the morning in fear that his political future was imperiled; Hall recalling how, on ringing Joe's home doorbell one recent evening, he suddenly found himself face to face with the Senator, a gun in his hand.

Behind these happenings, McCarthy's public approval had, in the weeks since the fried chicken lunch, plunged. The news columns were peeling away his followers. A Gallup Poll completed March 2 had reported 46 percent favorable to McCarthy, 36 unfavorable. A poll completed just three weeks later, on March 24, showed the two groups had sharply switched: only 38 percent favorable, 46 percent unfavorable. He'd come a long way downward since February 2, when the Senate of the United States had voted its approval of his committee's investigatory appropriation 85 to 1.

Perhaps McCarthy was tumbling. Who really knew? And who knew when another updraft would send him soaring again? All Struve Hensel knew for sure was that a tough ordeal lay ahead for the Army. He continued to trudge forward, getting the facts together. He had a long way to go. On March 18, Hensel wrote Seaton: "The time has come, I think, for you to blast Beetle Smith [Undersecretary of State and Ike's Chief of Staff during the war] loose [on the attempts made through him to keep Schine from becoming a draftee]. I tried three times to reach him on Wednesday, March 17, and each time was told he was in a meeting. . . . I called again at 11:15 today and was again told that he was in a meeting. . . . I will keep trying if you want me to, but I think it is time for you to apply the pressure."

The next day Hensel wrote Seaton again, this time about Roy Cohn's March 14 "Meet the Press" assertion that "never, directly or indirectly, has my law firm or anyone with whom I am associated profited by one cent from any dealings with Mr. Schine or any member of his family." Hensel thought he saw an opening: "While I think any reasonably honest man would consider Cohn to have lied if the Schine Hotel Corporation has retained Roy Cohn's firm on any basis whatsoever, there is perhaps a weasel in the answer. . . . Technically, I suppose the Schine Hotel Corporation is a separate entity and is neither Mr. Schine nor any member of his family. Nevertheless, if it should come out that the Schine Hotel Corporation does retain the Cohn law firm, I would charge that he lied, and I think it will stick publicly." (On March 22, Adams sent Hensel his further speculation that McCarthy, Cohn, and Carr had probably paid nothing to stay at the Schine hotel in Boca Raton.)

Hensel continued to drive for details—more, more, more. By now he had learned of the monitored phone calls, and on March 22 he put them at the top of a list of subjects for inquiry: check the legality of these calls; ask Jack Lucas about the monitoring and transcribing process; make a second review of all Lucas's notes, however trivial; get Army Intelligence to find out exactly where Schine went while stationed at Dix; question his chauffeur; check up on those witnesses who allegedly had to be interviewed by Schine in Trenton;

find out whether phone operators listened in on Schine's conversations—a total of twenty-three avenues to explore.

Two days later, March 24, John Adams sent him his recollections—to add to Stevens's—of Cohn's rage at being kept out of the too-sensitive Fort Monmouth building because he lacked an adequate security clearance. The same day Adams informed him that his phone calls to Fort Dix about Schine stretched from November 10, 1953, to March 12, 1954.

John Adams moreover recalled in the same memorandum, now that he searched his memory, a different genesis for his original chronology. Sherman Adams had without question suggested the compilation at the 4:30 P.M. meeting January 21 in Brownell's office. But even earlier that same day, John Adams now remembered, Bill Rogers had told Adams that a record of the Army's problems with Schine should be made; and at three o'clock that same afternoon Adams had phoned Lieutenant Blount at Fort Dix to start pulling together information about Schine's passes.

In reply to another Hensel inquiry, Sherman Adams phoned Hensel a few days later that General Persons's notes confirmed that Roy Cohn came to see the White House Legislative Liaison Chief in August of 1953 about getting Schine a commission in the Navy. And pursuing still another avenue, Hensel urged Stevens to get out a sharp pencil and estimate the total number of hours he had spent discussing Schine and his needs.

By Monday, March 22, Hensel had written up his preliminary analysis of the facts in hand. He boiled them down to three:

"a) Stevens decided that he would cooperate to the utmost in facilitating the investigating work of the McCarthy subcommittee.

"b) When Schine was inducted into the Army and sent to Fort Dix, many requests were made for passes for him in order to do subcommittee work. . . .

"c) As a result of this practice of giving Schine time off, plus the stories he spread at Fort Dix about his work, Schine received special treatment and caused a certain demoralization of discipline at Fort Dix. . . ."

In Hensel's shrewd view only those facts counted. "Stevens," he wrote, "decided . . . that he would cooperate fully with [the] Subcommittee. . . . To that end, he went to see McCarthy; visited with McCarthy at Schine's apartment; had dinner with Schine and his family and their friends; and told the McCarthy group that he would make Schine available to the Subcommittee whenever the

Subcommittee needed Schine's work. . . . There is nothing wrong in the position taken by Stevens to that effect. . . . There was no reason for anyone to apply any pressure on Secretary Stevens. No pressure was needed. Stevens had decided to cooperate, and the policy of cooperation is certainly not one which either the Senate or the American people will condemn.

"The treatment of Schine in the Army falls into two phases—first his treatment while receiving his basic training at Fort Dix and second, his ultimate assignment. . . . [On] the second phase of Schine's career as a soldier . . . there is not any indication that Stevens made any promises to McCarthy or anyone else. If he seems to have listened too long and too kindly to McCarthy's suggestion that Schine be made an investigator, sent to New York and assigned the job of reading textbooks used at West Point, there is no evidence that Stevens ever agreed to any such proposition. . . .

"The only arrangement made by Stevens related to Schine's basic training at Fort Dix. . . . Stevens did make a promise to McCarthy and Cohn, i.e., that when requested and needed for Subcommittee work Schine would be made available on weekends and in the evenings when there was no training. . . .

"There is likewise no doubt that many requests were made for passes for Schine . . . based on the necessity of Schine doing work for the Subcommittee. . . . Neither General Ryan nor Lieutenant Blount had any means of checking the truth of the statement that Schine was needed for Subcommittee work and the position can well be taken that in that respect Stevens and all the rest relied upon the truthfulness of the McCarthy subcommittee. . . .

"The work of the Subcommittee not only interfered with Schine's training at Fort Dix, but when thrown against the background of the stories spread around the camp by him, it damaged discipline at Fort Dix and obviously had an adverse effect upon the morale of the trainees in Company K of the 47th Regiment.

"This situation is probably completely unknown to McCarthy, Cohn and the others. It is likewise doubtful whether it was ever intended or contemplated by them. Cohn may know of the stories spread around the camp by Schine as to Schine's importance and secret mission, but it is doubtful whether Senator McCarthy ever did know. At the same time . . . the fact that these two youngsters were brash and irresponsible is to be laid at McCarthy's door and not at Stevens' door. . . .

"The only wrong which can be charged against Stevens is that he should have known that excessive demands would be made for Schine's absence from Fort Dix and that such absences would result in special treatment for Schine. If Stevens must plead guilty to that sin, it is a very small sin and doubtful in its establishment. . . . Stevens had every right to assume that McCarthy and Schine would not abuse the arrangement which he made with them. . . . It is far more reasonable to assume that Major General Ryan and Colonel Ringler [at Dix] should have seen that the frequent absences by Schine . . . were bringing about a situation whereby Schine escaped all of the unpleasant duties such as cleaning the barracks, cleaning weapons and KP. . . .

"Viewed in this framework, the Cohn-Adams go-around fades substantially in importance. They may have been extremely annoying to the participants and they may attract a certain amount of public interest. They had, however, no effect on Senator McCarthy or Stevens, and they were not productive of any changes in the arrangement which Stevens made at the very beginning of Schine's induction training, i.e., that Schine would be made available to the Subcommittee. . . .

"Viewed in that perspective, a number of the charges are reduced in importance. . . . The statement by Senator McCarthy that his Subcommittee was blackmailed by Stevens and Adams becomes a little ridiculous. As to Schine's training at Fort Dix, Stevens was delivering all he had been asked to deliver . . . delivering it in abundance. Certainly McCarthy cannot complain about Schine's treatment at Fort Dix, nor can McCarthy point to a single indication . . . where it was ever threatened to change the arrangement Stevens had made with him. . . . Consequently, the charge of blackmail has to be shifted entirely to the future assignment of Schine. It cannot be considered blackmail to have refused McCarthy's rather ridiculous request that Schine be set to work at studying West Point textbooks. Furthermore, it cannot be called blackmail if Stevens threatened to make Schine go through his training period and face his future assignment just as other trainees faced it. The whole blackmail charge becomes rather ridiculous as it is analyzed."

"A damned good analysis," Hensel remarked years later as he looked at it once again. "That should have been the whole thing." But then he added thoughtfully: "The analysis was good on the McCarthy-Army dispute. But it didn't include the people McCarthy hurt—little people."

• •

The day before his March 24 news conference, perhaps still goaded by C. D. Jackson's imputation that he was "morally involved," the President told Hagerty he was "set to blast" as "inconceivable" the proposition that McCarthy should serve on the committee investigating his row with the Army. At the staff meeting the next morning, in a "bitter session," C. D. came out, expectedly, for a "straight statement" on the inadmissibility of McCarthy's simultaneously being investigator and investigated. Morgan and Martin, backed by their underlings Earle Chesney and Homer Gruenther, opposed it. Former congressional liaison staff member Bryce Harlow "pitched in" on Jackson's aide. A few minutes later in the Oval Office, Persons and Morgan again tried to hold the President back. Eisenhower rode roughshod over them: "He can't sit as a judge. . . . I've made up my mind you can't do business with Joe and to hell with any attempt to compromise."

The two Jerrys, the President chuckled to Hagerty later, "didn't look very happy." Hagerty diplomatically made no comment.

"Listen, I'm not going to compromise my ideals and personal beliefs for a few stinking votes. To hell with it."

"Mr. President," Jim burst out, "I'm *proud* of you."

Hagerty happiness didn't last long. "In at eight and boiling mad," he started his diary the next day, March 25. "Army kicked over their own case by giving story to Washington *Post* that they had promoted Schine to Army Criminal Investigators School at Camp Gordon—waived two out of three requirements—1) two years service in Army, 2) physical disability—how dumb can they get. McCarthy can now blow Army report claiming Cohn and Joe had urged preferential treatment for Schine out of the water by saying Army did it themselves.

"Called Seaton, he's checking and didn't know about it. 'It's deliberate sabotage, and if I can find out Pentagon source of story, he won't be with us any longer.' "

At the Pentagon, irate reporters were clamoring for a comment; the Army was refusing to talk. Seaton got to work. He phoned Major General Maglin, the Provost Major General, and took down information in his own hand. "Seaton called by [later]," Hagerty wrote, "to tell me Army was flatly denying . . . story—turned down Schine's original application—they still have one pending. Good job by Fred—lots of guts."

That same day Hagerty "went to lunch at [Secretary of the Senate] Mark Trice's office [at the Capitol] with Persons, Martin and Morgan—They said they didn't know who was going to be there—when I walked in there was Joe McCarthy, [Senator Herman] Welker [Idaho Republican], Mundt [South Dakota Republican], [George "Mollie"] Malone [Nevada Republican], [Bourke] Hickenlooper [Iowa Republican], [John Marshall] Butler [Maryland Republican], [Dwight] Griswold [Nebraska Republican], and [William] Purtell [Connecticut Republican]. Welker started in on me on McCarthy area—Knowland dropped in for handshake—McCarthy, Mundt and Malone left right after social luncheon—then Welker and Hickenlooper started in—proposed both Cohn and Adams resign and case be dropped—I kept quiet and just listened, as did other three from W.H.—feel being jobbed by McCarthy boys—Hickenlooper criticized 'those who advised Pres. to get into row'—said 'he should have kept out'—arrived at 12:45, left at 2:20—on return to [White] House heard that rumors floating around Capitol of 'compromise luncheon'—called in Persons and Morgan and told them I was going to tell wire services entire story—they agreed and told wires what happened—no W.H. approval of luncheon—only 'social'—still think it was a put-up job and don't know whether our boys in on it."

For a month now, Hensel and Seaton had been putting the Army's argument together, trying to get a grounding of fact. They had probed the memories of Adams and Stevens. They had called on adjunct witnesses—for example, stern-faced General Matthew Ridgway, who pronounced McCarthy's St. Peter joke at the November 6 Pentagon luncheon not funny—and Lieutenant Colonel Tom Cleary, one of Stevens's multiple aides, who remembered that on the flight up to New York for the November 17 Merchants Club lunch, Stevens scanned the *New York Times*, and Adams and Cleary analyzed the Washington Redskins; and that at the Club Stevens asked the waiter to have a double Manhattan ready for McCarthy on his arrival. Hensel had continued to revise his analysis of the attempts to get favors for Schine—through Cohn's ill-tempered pressurings and (in Stevens's felicitous phrase) McCarthy's "continuous smiling nagging."

Behind Hensel and Seaton, John Adams and his staff of departmental lawyers also combed through the evidence with organized thoroughness. Prompted by Hensel's proddings, lists—more than sixty subjects to be looked into—from Annie Lee Moss to Zwicker to Adams's repayment of the forty-two dollars—were drawn up. Assignments were handed out; status reports were written and received. Long memos of possible questions were prepared—for example, Why didn't you, Roy Cohn, serve in the armed forces? How did you try to help David Schine avoid the draft?

But Seaton and Hensel didn't want to lean too heavily on Adams as the Army's lead lawyer. After the fried chicken lunch, Adams wrote years later, Seaton had testily warned the Army Counselor: "Don't let this happen again. Don't get into these things and wait until there is a mess and expect us to get you out." Increasingly thereafter, Adams had felt himself squeezed out, shut off from Seaton and his powerful friends "over there" at the White House. When Adams complained about this isolation and lack of help from across the river, he would get from Seaton not sympathy but a sharp retort: "Now don't try to threaten me, boy. I just don't go for that at all." And after the Army released its attack on McCarthy, Seaton himself appeared in Adams's office to demand—under White House orders—all copies of Adams's original chronology.

By April 1, Seaton and Hensel had effectively grounded Adams as head of the Army's legal forces. Not only was he demonstrably implicated in the McCarthy controversy; he was deficient in litigation experience: neither Sherman Adams in the White House nor Herbert Brownell in Justice thought he had the legal muscle to extricate the Army from its mess. And to more than one person Adams also appeared weak—like Stevens, a potentially wobbly witness. One close-in observer recalls John Adams as "wringing his hands, a man who was not where he wanted to be, who knew something was going to happen to him, a very nervous person." To those who hoped for a strong Army showing, it was "disconcerting" to find Adams a man of so little visible strength, a man subservient to the subservient Stevens, a man whom McCarthy had evidently taken advnatage of for his willingness to come to an accommodation. Therefore in the Army's armament, one key piece was still missing.

"How are you coming on a lawyer?" Stevens asked Seaton on the morning of April 1.

"Ours?" Seaton replied. "There's no need to worry."

They had not had an easy time. A distinguished lawyer from the distinguished firm of Shearman and Sterling in New York, Frederick Eaton, had come down at Stevens's urgent telephoned request, stayed at the Shoreham Hotel, and given Stevens—and only Stevens—advice. But he had come in as a personal friend and counselor; he would not conduct the litigation in the public hearing.

So the search for the Army's lead lawyer continued. Finally a candidate turned up. Colonel Ken BeLieu and Colonel Jean Wood of Stevens's office were dispatched to the airport to meet him.

"Don't let him leave town," BeLieu was instructed. "He's reluctant to take the job." On the gentleman's arrival BeLieu discovered one of his nonnegotiable demands was that the Army provide him an apartment during his stay in Washington. BeLieu, knowing that the Army had budgeted nothing for such a need, fished into his pocket and put down $325 of his own money to meet the attorney's request. Then BeLieu looked at the results of a background check on him. And it turned out that the man had some kind of unsavory association with racetracks. So he returned to the airport and went home. BeLieu never got back his $325.

The search continued. Then one day up in Boston the phone rang in the office of Joseph N. Welch, a partner in the firm of Hale and Dorr. Welch was busily talking to a widow about a will. The caller, an old friend, asked Welch to excuse himself. "I'm calling from a pay phone," he said, "on an extremely sensitive subject." The caller asked Welch to go to New York, to a particular club, and to a particular room, where a gentleman would be waiting to talk with the two of them. Welch agreed, flew to New York, walked through the door, and found himself face to face with Thomas E. Dewey.

The name of Thomas E. Dewey never got into the thousands of news columns on the McCarthy-Army controversy. Dewey, fifty-two, was Governor of New York—a popular, liberal, smart Republican. He was short and dapper and urbane and cocky, and he wore a little mustache. FDR had once condescendingly put him down as "Buster Brown" and Alice Roosevelt Longworth devastatingly compared him to the "groom on the wedding cake." He had had a luminous career. In his thirties in the 1930s he had hit the nation's front pages as a fighting, incorruptible, racket-busting New York County District Attorney. In his forties, he had won the New York governorship and had twice become the Republican party's presidential nominee, running in 1944 against Roosevelt and 1948 against Truman, so confident of winning the second time that he began announcing his cabinet before the voting started.

Now in his fifties he was through with national politics and about to be through with New York State politics, having chosen voluntary retirement in a lucrative Wall Street law practice. But he was still a powerful force in the party, the supreme symbol of its liberal Eastern Establishment. In 1950—long before most Republicans—he had announced for Ike. He had helped head up the group of powerful Republican governors and senators who worked to persuade the General to run. He had given Ike his own former national campaign manager, Herb Brownell, to lead the crucial search for delegate votes in the 1952 convention. As Lucius Clay, who worked with Brownell, would later observe, "without Tom Dewey we couldn't have got the nomination."

When the election was all over, Dewey gave Ike not only Brownell as his attorney general but also Bill Rogers as his deputy attorney general, Tom Stephens as his top political advisor and appointments secretary, and Jim Hagerty, Dewey's longtime press secretary, as Ike's intermediary with the reporters.

Personally, Ike at times found Dewey abrasive. He didn't look forward to even a short motorcade ride with the brisk, take-charge little Governor. Dewey was never invited into the Eisenhower Cabinet, either because (as Cabinet recruiter Lucius Clay said) he didn't want to be, or because Ike didn't want to antagonize Dewey's "choicest bunch of bitter political enemies." But from the sidelines he made contributions. The administration now solicited his expert advice on litigation against McCarthy. One member of the White House staff—Bern Shanley—even wanted Dewey to head the Army's legal team himself. But the feisty New York Governor did a far far better thing: he contributed the name of Joe Welch.

Dewey hadn't known Welch. But Dewey knew Welch's caller, Bruce Bromley, a former Dewey appointee to the New York State Court of Appeals, and now a formidable curmudgeon courtroom infighter in one of New York's most prestigious law firms, Cravath, Swaine and Moore. Bromley had recommended Welch to Dewey. And Dewey recommended him to Sherman Adams.

"I've been talking with Tom Dewey," Struve Hensel recalls Fred Seaton's saying one day. "He recommends a lawyer in Boston named Welch. Do you know him?"

"He'd be a natural," Struve enthusiastically replied. "I should have thought of it myself."

Hensel phoned Boston. Welch came down to Washington, talked with Charlie Wilson. "The problem," Seaton recalled later, "was to get Wilson to agree." But after this boggling—not uncharacteristic of Engine Charlie—Welch became the Special Counsel of the United States Army.

Joseph Nye Welch, sixty-three, an enormously successful partner in Boston's elegant Hale and Dorr, was courtly and unflappable and old-fashioned. He wore bow ties, button-down oxford shirts, and custom-made three-piece suits with—his hallmark—two welts on each sleeve. He was tall—over six feet—but he kept a modestly low profile. Gladys Seaton remembers him fondly to this day as "that dear little man." He was witty and crisp, with abundant common sense. Everybody instantly liked him. He had a twinkle in his eye for a pretty pair of legs, and he was something of a puckish prankster. Joe Welch, for example, enjoyed binoculars. He liked to peer out of his high office window scanning the Boston skyline. One morning his gaze fell on a fellow lawyer in a nearby building closeted in his office with his secretary on his lap. Welch reached for the phone. The philandering gentleman heard the ring and answered. "Stop what you're doing immediately," Welch commanded. The startled lawyer blurted: "Who is this calling?"

"God," Welch told him, and slammed down the phone with a chuckle.

Often Welch seemed to live in the nineteenth century. He worked at a stand-up desk, his head resting on his palm, writing everything out in longhand. He habitually spoke in old-world phrases: "I'm weary"; "That's delicious." He was a man of amused and mild exterior. But underneath he was a worrier. And underneath everything else he had, as Roy Cohn later admiringly wrote, "an unerring instinct for the jugular."

Welch brought with him a thirty-three-year-old junior partner, with whom he'd worked for the past five years, James St. Clair, a gap-toothed, short, muscular, streetwise attorney, a native of Ohio and, like Welch, a graduate of the Harvard Law School, who would return to Washington twenty years later to represent the embattled Richard Nixon in his death throes during Watergate.

Welch and St. Clair represented the Army—specifically Stevens and Adams. But from the start they reported in to Seaton. He secured their hotel accommodations. He discussed with them whether they should be paid (they were not). He didn't tell them how to try the case; he was a newspaperman, not a lawyer. But they talked strategy with him and kept him informed. And he in turn—as their only link to the beyond, they themselves having no access to the President or any of his other advisors—informed those up the ladder, like Charlie Wilson and higher. They never knew exactly whom.

Welch had come originally from Iowa. He had grown up on a

farm and had gone to Grinnell College (Phi Beta Kappa) before winning a six hundred dollar scholarship to the Harvard Law School. Seaton had come from Nebraska. They therefore had, as St. Clair later observed, "something in common." And they got along, he also noted, "very cordially—for a while. Fred Seaton was easy to get along with as long as you did what he wanted," St. Clair reflected.

To Welch and St. Clair, Vice President Nixon was an outsider, a man viewed as pro-McCarthy, as "persona non grata" in the White House on this subject at this time. Even the United States Attorney General usually gave advice to the lawyers through Seaton, although presumably Brownell, like Bill Rogers, favored the holding of the hearings. Within the Pentagon, Deputy Defense Secretary Roger Kyes, like Charlie Wilson, was far removed: "Not in it much," as St. Clair recalls. Through Stevens's aide Ken BeLieu, Welch and St. Clair could call on Major Gabby Ivan and the other career Army lawyers in the Judge Advocate General's Corps for law-clerk and stenographic work. And of course they worked in total trust with Welch's friend Hensel, until events forced Hensel to confront another crisis of his own.

At five twenty-one on the afternoon of April 2, Stevens returned a call from Seaton. And as Stevens's aide Jack Lucas dutifully recorded, the Secretary of the Army thereupon went to Seaton's office to see Seaton, Hensel and Mr. Welch.

The announcement at once went out: Welch, assisted by St. Clair and a second young Hale and Dorr lawyer, Frederick G. Fisher, Jr., would represent the Army.

Welch, St. Clair and Fisher went to dinner at the Carlton. Afterward Seaton and Hensel joined them in the cocktail lounge. Welch began inquiring into personal vulnerabilities—openings McCarthy might attack. Fred Fisher spoke up: at Harvard, he revealed, he had joined a far-left organization called the National Lawyers Guild. The group, shaken by the news, went up to Welch's room. Seaton had earlier sent the Bostonians a welcoming bottle of Chivas Regal. Short of chairs, Welch sat on the bed as they agonized over the Fisher problem.

At that instant Jim Hagerty was a few blocks away at the Sulgrave Club, attending a dinner party given by fellow White House staff member Charlie Willis. Suddenly someone slipped Hagerty a message. He had an urgent phone call from Fred Seaton: Could he come immediately to Struve Hensel's house in Georgetown? Emergency.

Hagerty and his wife Marge dashed across northwest Washington to rendezvous with the group from the Carlton. "Marge visited with Mrs. Hensel upstairs," Hagerty wrote, "while I talked to Hensel, Seaton, and Joe Welch—the Army's new counsel in Stevens case." Welch had brought along his two young assistants. "Fisher admitted that he had been a member of the Lawyers Guild (on Attorney General's subversive list) and had helped organize Suffolk County Chapter in Mass. with assistance from a Mr. Greenberg, a Communist organizer." At first Hagerty thought they should not give in on Fisher's membership. But then he had second thoughts: "Greenberg association was different story." As they writhed over the problem, Isabel Hensel recalls, she inadvertently—and fleetingly—walked in on their meeting in her negligee.

Finally they bit the bullet: "It was decided Fisher to drop out . . . too dangerous to give McCarthy opportunity to brand Fisher as Red and smear up Army defense. . . . Tough decision, but necessary." Within hours Fisher was on the midnight sleeper back to Boston.

Three days later, at ten forty-five in the morning, Charlie Wilson's secretary, Mrs. Abbott, phoned the office of the Secretary of the Army. Stevens's presence was requested at a confidential off-the-record meeting the next day at the White House; he should come in by the east entrance to avoid reporters. Stevens had no idea what was afoot. Was this part of Stevens's life-and-death struggle with the chairman of the Permanent Investigations Subcommittee? Or was it just another bizarre interruption, like the request several weeks earlier that he come to the White House to help throw the switch for the new Fort Randall Dam in South Dakota?

These questions remain unanswered, in part because of Fred Seaton's insistence to Defense Secretary Charlie Wilson that the Pentagon's monitoring machine grind to a stop.

The cryptic notations made by Stevens's aides still reveal shadowy sounds and alarms: for example, Hensel to Stevens on April 6, 10:35 A.M.: If Stevens gets a call from the Hill, get the information, say you'll check and call back; note to Secretary of the Army Tuesday, April 6, 11:08 A.M.: Mrs. Abbott phoned to say the President asks the Secretary of the Army to attend the NSC meeting today at 2:15; Tuesday, April 6, 1:53 P.M.: Secretary of the Army tries to phone Hensel, Welch, or Seaton. All out to lunch. Tuesday, April 6, 5:46 P.M.: Henry Cabot Lodge phones Secretary of Army (not monitored).

That night, April 6, McCarthy went on nationwide television. First he warmed up by smearing Edward R. Murrow. And then he veered off on a new course: he had in his hand evidence, he said, of an eighteen-month deliberate delay in U.S. hydrogen bomb research.

Most people didn't know what McCarthy was talking about. But Jim Hagerty knew: "McCarthy . . . seems to be skating pretty close to Oppenheimer case," he wrote in his diary on April 7. "Hope we move fast, before McCarthy breaks it and it then becomes our scandal."

At his news conference that day Eisenhower said he knew nothing of any delay in the H-bomb. He also said that he had always considered Edward R. Murrow, whom he'd known for many years, a friend.

In a letter that same day to Aaron Berg, a lawyer friend from Columbia days, Eisenhower reiterated for the zillionth time his refusal to get into a "newspaper-television brawl with" McCarthy. And he looked ahead to the hearings: "Only the Republicans of the United States Senate, supported by public opinion, can accomplish the result you rightly believe would be a God-send to all of us."

In still another piece of strategy—a follow-on to Nixon's peel-away-the-decent-anti-Communists broadcast—Eisenhower was looking ahead to another nationwide telecast, this one by Brownell on April 9, which would tout the administration's antisubversive successes. Ike told the Republican legislative leaders the Attorney General would "lay out the whole Red set up." And, he reminded them, "The FBI stands in well with the kids, and that means also with poppa and momma."

Up on the Hill the subcommittee had at last found itself a special counsel. On April 1, they had given the job to Samuel Sears of Boston. At once, however, his pro-McCarthy utterances in the past had come to life, and five days later he resigned. Finally, on April 7, the committee announced its selection: Ray H. Jenkins of Knoxville, Tennessee, fifty-seven, six feet two inches, a Taft Republican recommended by Everett Dirksen and then given an energetic investigation (which still passed over the trivial fact—which could have become significant only in those hypersensitive days—that at the end of World War I his father had gone to his congressman and got young Jenkins a speeded-up discharge from the Navy). Jenkins had managed the 1940 unsuccessful senatorial campaign of Tennessee's Republican Congressman Howard Baker, Sr. During the uproar over the selection of a counsel, Dirksen fortuitously had been visiting Huntsville,

Tennessee, for the first birthday of his granddaughter Darek Dirksen Baker, the daughter of his daughter Joy and Howard Henry Baker, Jr.

The lawyers were all in place: Welch for the Army, Jenkins for the committee, Roy Cohn for himself.

Months before, Bern Shanley had realized McCarthy's appeal to America's Catholics. So did Struve Hensel, who saw that McCarthy's attack on Communists pleased some Catholic bishops. But on Friday, April 9, this foundation under McCarthy's feet trembled and shook. Before an audience of 2,500 at a United Auto Workers Educational Conference, Bishop Bernard J. Sheil of Chicago took out after the Senator as a dangerous "man on horseback. . . ." Other men of other faiths across the country were joining in the chase: Republican Paul Hoffman, the honored administrator of the Marshall Plan; Philip M. Klutznick, leader of B'nai B'rith; and Retired Major General Arthur R. Wilson, who offered a hundred dollars to the commanding general at Fort Dix to be awarded to the first noncommissioned officer to punch G. David Schine in the nose.

McCarthy's knowledge of the Oppenheimer episode continued to hang over the White House. Talking to Hagerty April 10, the President insisted that in their every move they "stick carefully to fact and to orderly procedure. . . . We've got to handle this so that all our scientists are not made out to be Reds. That goddamn McCarthy is just likely to try such a thing." Two days later the story broke—the charges and the temporary suspension of the distinguished scientist, the investigation underway. Thus the Senator was headed off at the pass.

Meanwhile, back at the Pentagon, Welch and St. Clair had hit the ground running. From Hensel came more memoranda (on the mysterious disappearance of the actual eleven memos McCarthy had released to the Senate Press Gallery; on information the new subcommittee counsel should be asked to get—*e.g.*, bank records, phone-call records, records from Sardi's, the Stork Club, and the Copacabana).

Skulduggery was also proceeding. On Monday, April 12, Welch received two pieces of cloak-and-dagger intelligence. The first, from Jim St. Clair, described how over the past weekend James Juliana, a McCarthy operative, had dropped by Walter Reed Army Hospital out Sixteenth Street, disclosed he lived in the same neighborhood, and said he wanted to pay a "courtesy call" to inquire after the health of a patient, General Kirke Lawton, the Fort Monmouth commanding general. The "courtesy call" lasted a half hour and turned into a full-scale interview.

"This," St. Clair concluded, "is interesting. . . . It is the first indication we have had as to what the other side is doing and . . . who is doing it."

That same day. in a memo from John Kimball, Jr., the staff lawyer who had replaced Fred Fisher, Welch got another indication of the tack the enemy was taking, indeed, a report on a penetration of the McCarthy organization and its planning. Kimball had heard the report from Stevens's top career military assistant, Colonel Kenneth BeLieu.

Ken BeLieu, a forty-year-old westerner, had joined the Army's Enlisted Reserve in 1937, had fought in Europe from Normandy to Czechoslovakia, and had suffered the loss of a leg in Korea. Stocky, muscular, frank, and outspoken, he had earned the respect and trust of Republicans and Democrats alike on the Hill, and liked to label himself a "militant moderate." He brooked no nonsense. When an FBI agent complained to Stevens that BeLieu had not reported to the FBI a claim of Roy Cohn that he, Cohn, had "access to FBI files," BeLieu cut him dead: "I work for the Secretary of the Army, not for Mr. Hoover." And when, after the Fort Monmouth visit, Roy Cohn instructed the driver of the car in which Cohn, McCarthy, and BeLieu were riding to pull over to an establishment selling whiskey so the Senator could get a drink, BeLieu countermanded the order: "If you do, Sergeant, you're busted out of the Army. You're taking orders from me, not from that character in the back seat." And McCarthy had roared with laughter: "You tell him, Colonel." And when BeLieu was interrogated as part of the pre-hearing process and asked the routine question "Have you ever associated with Communists?" he replied forthrightly "Sure. The last time was in Korea. There were a million of them in front of us and a million of them behind us, and we were shooting like hell at the bastards."

Though a career man in uniform, BeLieu found himself thrust into a wide variety of assignments to help his boss during the battle with McCarthy. The first week in April he met in the office of Secretary of Defense Charlie Wilson with Fred Seaton and Struve Hensel. They had a problem: they needed an emissary of absolute honesty and integrity to go to New York City and meet with a most secret informant. So BeLieu headed for Greenwich Village, in civilian clothes.

On April 7, BeLieu told Kimball, he had gone to the Manhatten

apartment of the informant whom he did not identify by name—
a man who had been conducting an investigation and who had
tapped sources mysteriously described as "derived originally from
Roy Cohn's father."

The informant—his wife was also present—said "the subcommittee
[*sic*]" would try first to sink Secretary Stevens, having made extensive inquiry into his background. They would next go after Adams,
particularly on his alleged offer to supply investigative dirt on the
Navy and Air Force; they most feared that Adams would reply that
he had in fact said: "I bet you would be investigating the Air Force
and the Navy if [Dave Schine] were in one of them rather than in
the Army."

The informant suggested that the Army subpoena Schine's father,
persuade a Democratic subcommittee member or Potter to get hold
of Cohn's income tax records, secure Schine's medical and draft
board records, and question a young lady named Janet Weber—
recently picked up in a New York bar by an acquaintance of the informant—who claimed she had once lived with Schine at the Waldorf, had a falling out with him, and wanted to tell all. Finally the
informant added a warning—that Stevens's, Adams's, and BeLieu's
phones were probably all tapped—and a cloud of suggestions—e.g.,
that Welch should get the White House to obtain the full FBI
files on Schine and Al McCarthy, Joe's real-estate–songwriter friend;
and that Welch should get himself "a good Jewish assistant."

The informant was Morris Ernst, a brilliant and witty sixty-six-
year-old New York lawyer, who for the past quarter century had
served as General Counsel to the American Civil Liberties Union
and more than twenty years earlier had won a landmark decision in
federal court exonerating James Joyce's *Ulysses* from charges of obscenity. A liberal Democrat and friend of Franklin Roosevelt, Harry
Truman, Herbert Lehman and a host of leading liberal figures,
Ernst was a courageous defender of the rights of man and the citizen. He had contributed wording for the aborted Stevens declaration on Zwicker. He had met with BeLieu. He wanted to help. But
he wanted to help in secrecy, not to protect himself but largely to
protect his family against retaliation. This secrecy squared with the
inclination of Robert Stevens, who had told John Adams he didn't
like the idea of getting help from any liberal New Dealer.

That same day, April 12, Welch and Stevens met on procedure
with Ray Jenkins, the three subcommittee Democrats, and Mundt
and Potter. McCarthy, away in Arizona, would meet with the sub-

committee later. They had a largely friendly session. Welch encountered no disagreement when he asserted that the Army, as the "plaintiff," should have its witnesses testify first. He did hesitate to make a blanket promise, as Senator Symington demanded, to turn over to the committee everything in the Army files. He might, Welch said, find out he had violated some presidential directive, and Mundt disclosed to Symington that he had promised Fred Seaton that the committee at this meeting would not force Welch and Stevens into any commitments. But after an hour of wrangling and drafting Welch did agree to a declaration that "the Army advised the Committee that it will cooperate fully in making available to the Committee . . . all information, records, witnesses, and documents bearing upon the pending controversy." Welch carried it back to the Pentagon. Seaton and Hensel concurred.

Two days later, on April 14, the Army unveiled its third and last Cohn-Schine document: not another loose collection of recollections like the still-secret John Adams original chronology of February; not a dry rundown of hard facts like the Stevens-Adams report sent to the Hill in March; but a withering drumfire of prosecuting-attorney accusatory charges—a formal Bill of Particulars.

James St. Clair, Welch's assistant, had drawn them up, and in St. Clair's words years later, "they infuriated McCarthy." The Particulars totaled twenty-nine, and they included:

1. On or about July 8, 1953, Senator McCarthy sought to obtain a direct commission in the U.S. Army for Mr. Schine and informed Major General Miles Reber, Chief of Army Legislative Liaison (OCLL) of his interest. . . .

3. On or about August 1, 1953, Mr. Cohn requested General Reber and others . . . to explore the possibility of obtaining a reserve commission for Mr. Schine in either the United States Air Force or the United States Navy. . . .

8. On or about November 6, 1953, Senator McCarthy, Mr. Cohn, and Mr. Carr sought to induce and persuade Secretary Stevens and Mr. Adams to arrange for the assignment of Private Schine to New York City to study and report evidence, if any, of pro-Communist leanings in West Point textbooks. Mr. Cohn, in the presence of and with the consent of Senator McCarthy and Mr. Carr, sought to induce and persuade Secretary Stevens and Mr. Adams to arrange to make Private Schine available for subcommittee work while he was undergoing basic training at Fort Dix, New Jersey. These requests were coupled with promises reasonably to limit or to terminate subcommittee hearings on Fort Monmouth. . . .

13. On or about November 17, 1953, Senator McCarthy, Mr. Cohn and Mr. Carr made known to Secretary Stevens the importance attached by them to Private Schine's military assignment and there by innuendo and inference indicated that their plans for continuing further investigation of the military installation at Fort Monmouth[,] New Jersey[,] were related to the importance attached by them to Private Schine's military assignment. . . .

16. On or about December 8, 1953, Mr. Cohn, upon learning that special weekday passes for Private Schine had been discontinued, called Mr. Adams and by abusive language and threats to Mr. Adams sought to have this decision reversed. . . .

22. On or about January 9, 1954 Mr. Cohn, in [an] effort to obtain Private Schine's release from KP duty at Fort Dix on January 10, 1954, stated to First Lieutenant John B. Blount that Colonel Earl L. Ringler and First Lieutenant Joseph J. M. Miller, then stationed at Fort Dix, were making things difficult for Private Schine and that Cohn had a very long memory and would never forget their names. . . .

24. On or about January 13, 1954, Mr. Cohn, upon learning that Private Schine might be assigned to overseas duty, threatened to cause the discharge of Secretary Stevens, and [said] he would cause the subcomittee to "wreck the Army." . . .

28. On or about January 22, 1954 Senator McCarthy requested Mr. Adams to obtain a special assignment for Private Schine in New York and suggested that Mr. Cohn would continue to harass the Army unless this demand was acceded to. . . .

Selectively and carefully, this Army document threaded its way among the events of the preceding ten months, omitting, inferring, underscoring. Somehow the Bill of Particulars got out to the press ahead of time. McCarthy threatened to boycott the hearings until the subcommittee plugged the leak. The same day, April 15, Welch confirmed press reports that he had removed Frederick Fisher from the Army legal team as a result of Fisher's admission of his onetime membership in the Lawyers Guild. The story, with Fisher's picture, appeared in the *New York Times* on page 12.

By now Welch was rehearsing Stevens and Adams, getting them ready to testify, trying to buck them up. The next day he left a message for Stevens: John Adams is making as beautiful a start on his prospective interrogation as Stevens himself had made.

For better or worse, Stevens was eager to start talking. On April 17 he had a long discussion with Lieutenant Colonel John Murray of the Judge Advocate General's Corps, which was helping Welch and St. Clair with legwork. Stevens voiced his enthusiasm over his forthcoming opportunity to tell his story to the American people on TV, looking ahead to a skull-session cross-examination by Welch and St. Clair as soon as possible. Stevens was also worried about leaks: any and all future documents, he said, should remain under JAG control at all times.

The question of McCarthy's stepping down from the committee continued to boil. Mundt insisted on it. If the Senator refused, he said, he'd go to the Senate floor for a decision. Finally, on April 19, after a three-hour closed-door session, the subcommittee reached its conclusion. McCarthy agreed to step down temporarily from the committee. And all agreed that McCarthy and his associates—like the Army officials and their counsel—would have the right to cross-examine. McCarthy, given the right to select his temporary replacement on the committee, chose nondescript conservative Henry Dworshak of Idaho.

McCarthy, Cohn, and Carr filed with the committee their denials and countercharges—forty-six points, five thousand words. This document included an attack on (unnamed) Frederick Fisher, described as a partner in the Welch law firm, who "in recent years belonged to" an organization which was the "legal bulwark" of the Communist party—a man discharged from the Army's legal defense group only when his red link became "publicly known."

And it included for the first time a slashing attack on Struve Hensel. What was the motive, McCarthy asked, for the compilation and dissemination of the Army's chronology? It lay, McCarthy implied, in the fact that Hensel—the chronology's supervisor—was himself under investigation by the McCarthy subcommittee. He therefore "had . . . every motivation to act as he did in attempting to discredit the Subcommittee."

The subcommittee's investigation turned on Hensel's wartime activity in "a top procurement post with the Department of the Navy." While in this post Hensel, the report alleged, "helped to organize [a] ship's supply firm for the purpose of selling priority goods to ships." Hensel, while in this procurement post and while General Counsel and later Assistant Secretary of the Navy, McCarthy went on, "drew large sums of money, believed to be far in excess of his government salary, from this ship's supply firm"—in 1943, more than $12,000, in 1944, more than $13,000, in 1945, nearly $31,000—all from a private firm "operating with government sanction and with government priorities." Hensel, McCarthy concluded, had supervised the allegations against the subcommittee in order to stop its investigation of these charges.

Within minutes after McCarthy released his attack, Hensel slammed back his reply. McCarthy's charges, Hensel declared with characteristic bluffness and energy, were "barefaced lies." And if McCarthy would drop his senatorial immunity and make the same charges, "I will guarantee a law suit which he will not be able to drop. Senator McCarthy . . . has . . . reached the high mark of scandalous malice and the low mark of cowardly irresponsibility."

McCarthy knew full well, Hensel went on, that Hensel in no way instigated the Army's charges against the Senator. McCarthy knew full well that Hensel had no awareness that the McCarthy committee was investigating Hensel until March 22, nearly two weeks after the Army issued its report.

McCarthy's smear "that there has been anything illegal or even unethical in my financial or governmental history is both malicious and dishonest." The facts about Hensel's limited partnership in Arthur L. Pierson and Company—a firm that during the war sold corned beef hash (Hensel to this day praises its quality) to private shipping companies—not the Navy—had been known for years. In 1946, Hensel had laid them all out in a letter to the Bureau of Internal Revenue. In 1948–49 the Bureau had looked into an anonymous charge of income tax evasion by the firm's partners and dismissed it as false. The sums McCarthy alleged Hensel had pocketed were profits credited to his account on the company's books. He had actually withdrawn nothing except the amounts needed to pay his taxes on those profits.

"Senator McCarthy," Hensel asserted, "is cornered and is attempting a diversionary move. The attempted smear is his favorite method. . . ." On the night of March 22, Hensel revealed, two unidentified men, self-described agents of McCarthy, had appeared at the Brooklyn home of Arthur Pierson's mother-in-law, given her a phony story that Mrs. Pierson, her daughter, "had just been involved in a hit-and-run accident," and demanded the Piersons' address. Terrified, Pierson's mother-in-law gave it to them. Four days later two McCarthy operatives—Jim Juliana and Don Surine—showed up at Pierson's home, threatened him with a subpoena, and interrogated him for four or five hours, telling him baldly that "they were out to get Hensel." Pierson went over all the facts in detail. "Consequently," Hensel concluded, in making his charges, "Mc-Carthy knew he was lying. . . ."

Hensel had hit back with force. But at that particular moment he felt resentful that Charlie Wilson hadn't come galloping at once to his aid. Wilson did deny McCarthy's accusation. But he had not, in Hensel's view, denied it with sufficient vigor. Wilson knew, Hensel later said, that Hensel had nothing to do with triggering the Army's allegations against McCarthy. In fact, during his supervision of the chronology, Hensel was acting as Wilson's agent, at Wilson's behest. When McCarthy's charges broke, Hensel to this day still believes, Wilson should have issued a "ringing declaration." He didn't. And Hensel was—and still is—"browned off."

Moreover, Hensel felt rueful that at the time when the Pentagon was readying the Stevens-Adams report to go to Senator Potter, he had agreed to sign the letter of transmittal for the absent Wilson, who was lunching with McCarthy. "You sign it," Fred Seaton had told him. And he had.

Hensel always believed that Cohn had recognized the flimsiness of the charges against Hensel and had tried to get McCarthy to back off. But McCarthy hadn't. And now Hensel had to look to his own defense.

He offered the FBI all his records. When he failed to hear from them soon enough, he asked Fred Seaton to inquire; Fred returned with a reassurance: "The FBI doesn't have to investigate you; when you were confirmed, they had a file on you [2½ inches] thick."

Suspicious, speculative, Hensel always wondered whether Mc-Carthy got the information on him from somewhere in the FBI itself, or from Scott McLeod in State. As the hearings approached, he put his Georgetown house under extra surveillance: the District of Columbia Police were asked to "pay close attention to [it] at night"; Georgetown's Precinct Seven was alerted: in the event of any call, they were to get there at once. It was an eerie moment. Even as balanced a man as Jim St. Clair realized that any given hotel switchboard might be monitored by McCarthy minions.

Late in the day on Tuesday, April 20, as the hearings approached, the Secretary of the Army decided he needed a haircut. He had his office telephone for an appointment with his barber at 8 A.M. on Thursday, the day the hearings would start. Thursday turned out to be the barber's day off. Stevens's aide phoned again: would the barbershop make an exception? The Secretary had to go on nationwide television. Sorry, the answer came back, no exceptions. Stevens gave up.

On the evening of April 21 down in Houston, at the base of the San Jacinto Battlefield monument, McCarthy addressed a rousing audience of the Sons of the Republic of Texas. It was the eve of the hearings. The Gallup Poll revealed that 46 percent (Democrats 4 to 1, Republicans 50 to 50) tended to agree with Stevens; 23 percent agreed with McCarthy. But no one at that moment in the White House or Pentagon or on the Hill could foresee the outcome. All that anyone knew for sure was that the sides had been chosen. The match was about to begin.

VII

ACCIDENTS:
Lacrimae Rerum

At ten thirty-five on the morning of April 22, temporary chairman Karl Mundt rapped a glass ashtray on the table before him, and the Army-McCarthy hearings began. In the spacious high-ceilinged Caucus Room on the third floor of the Senate Office Building there are white marble walls and imposing Corinthian columns, and the scene was wild confusion. More than 400 spectators, some of whom had waited in line three hours, jammed into every square inch of space. Messengers pushed and shoved and crawled. Reporters jockied for position—more than 100 writers; 3 TV crews; 12 fixed cameras on scaffolds; 3 roving cameras; 36 still cameramen. Flash bulbs popped, and occasionally a photographer jumped up and down for shots. Heavy brocade curtains shut out the sun. The raucous klieg lights made spectators squint and paled the sedate ornate chandeliers overhead. Outside, in the parks and beside the buildings, flowers were beginning to bloom in every hue of the temperate zone, their perfume scattered in rivers in the warm spring sun; they were even occasionally noticed by the men caught up in their personal and constitutional battles.

There had never been anything like it. Three years earlier home TV viewers had sat through a series of hearings presided over by Senator Estes Kefauver of Tennessee and featuring the Mafia underworld—Greasy Thumb Guzik, Frank Costello and other notables. But that had petered out after a few days. The Army-McCarthy hearings promised to be a far bigger show. It had a coast-to-coast audience of ten million and who knew when it would end?

There, at a twenty-six-foot-long mahogany table, the members of the subcommittee took their places. At the center sat round-faced Mundt, fifty-three, the jovial pipe-smoking temporary chairman of the proceedings, a nonlawyer—a former college teacher and debate

313

coach; a man who on the House Un-American Activities Committee had got into anticommunism before McCarthy. Mundt had personally typed out the devastating memorandum of understanding at the fried chicken lunch. Dwight Eisenhower had entrusted him with the nation's honor and had then, in a turnabout, lashed out to Jim Hagerty: "You can't trust the fellow."

To Mundt's right sat lantern-jawed Ray Jenkins of Tennessee, the committee's Special Counsel, forthright and bulldogged in manner. Jenkins was conservative by instinct and reputation ("at least 18 degrees to the right of Barry Goldwater," one knowledgeable observer placed him). But he was a litigant, an aggressive courtroom infighter. And he had come to Washington to get the facts—all the facts— without fear or favor to either side.

To Jenkins's right sat the committee's Republican senators, beginning with mellifluous Everett Dirksen, fifty-eight. He had been many things: Ike's informal putative champion in armor after the death of Robert Taft, a coarchitect of the fried chicken lunch, a confidant in the White House East Wing meeting the next day, a man infuriated by the McCarthy-Cohn news conference and McCarthy's double cross on his agreement to reason further together before going public. But whatever his turnings and changings, he was a conservative politician ever mindful of the transcendent good of the Republican party, a buttery operator whose profusion of honeyed words cloaked a mind swift and sharp.

Next to Dirksen sat Charles Potter, thirty-seven, good of heart, weak in the clutch, wary of both sides ("Someone has committed perjury, and I don't know who"), a man who had urged the jettisoning of both Cohn and Adams. And there was low-profile white-haired Henry Dworshak of Idaho, fifty-nine, McCarthy's hand-picked substitute, reliable, unlikely to make waves.

To Mundt's left the Democrats lined up, led by wily John McClellan of Arkansas, fifty-eight, wiry and bespectacled, who shunned having his party take the affirmative in a debate on the subject "Resolved: Communism is good for you"; courteous and ostensibly even-handed ("Brother, I'm not here to defend the Army"); out just to get the facts—to go all the way, the whole way, the long way, to the bottom of the barrel.

Next to McClellan in seniority came tall, silver-haired W. Stuart Symington of Missouri, fifty-two, a former Secretary of the Air Force, already deeply enmeshed in trying to help Stevens and the Army, a man who had clandestinely stuck out his neck on McCarthy ("This fellow may be sick"; "You can't play by Marquis of Queensberry rules"); yet a man, like his fellow Democrats, still playing the political game of Republican bloodletting, and perhaps, in the words of one shrewd observer, "trying to pole vault over McCarthy into the Presidency."

Third and last among the Democratic senators came young (forty-one) Scoop Jackson of Washington, a sharp lawyer, keenly following his party leaders.

Farther down the long table, beyond Jackson, sat Army Secretary Stevens, flanked by Lieutenant General Lyman Lemnitzer, Deputy Chief of Staff for Plans, and Major General Robert N. Young, Assistant Chief of Staff for Personnel—both silent, grim-faced symbols, dressed in their winter blouses and pinks, which all Army officers would continue to wear, however uncomfortable in the Washington warmth, because—as Colonel Jean Wood, a bright young Stevens aide with graduate training in communications, pointed out—that way they showed up better on TV. Then came McCarthy, flanked by Cohn and Carr.

By agreement the adversaries would switch places at the table every day to give the television cameras a better shot. And they would answer questions in accordance with agreed-on ground rules. First, they would go through a direct examination by counsel Jenkins. Next, Jenkins would subject the witness to cross-examination. Then the opportunity to question would go around the table, first to Republican Mundt, then to a Democrat, in ten-minute bites, ending with Welch and McCarthy or their surrogates. Jim St. Clair, for one, always thought Karl Mundt set up the ten-minute rule on purpose: "No one could be damaged by any questioner." Only one thing could interrupt this procedure—a point of order, strictly an objection, addressed to the chairman, to the departure of the proceedings from their governing rules.

Nearby sat other principals—Adams and Hensel—and the secondaries. On McCarthy's side there were a bunch of staff men, mostly ex-FBI agents. Serious and disciplined, they sat quick-eyed, tensely awaiting McCarthy's commands. On the Pentagon's side there were a host of decorated generals and colonels—an array that, even so, appeared insufficiently overwhelming that first day to Frederick Eaton, Stevens's temporary personal legal consultant, who phoned Ken BeLieu in the middle of the night, got him out of bed, and demanded the young colonel immediately phone four-star General Matthew Ridgway. Thus there was produced the next day that flurry in the hearing as the bespangled war-hero Chief of Staff and a phalanx of brass strode into the Caucus Room and took their places near their embattled civilian Secretary.

A few feet away from Hensel, smarting under McCarthy's attack and eager for a fight, sat his wife Isabel, loyal and outspoken, among a group of pleasant middle-aged ladies who helped pack the gallery for McCarthy. She wore her blue best dress. "Who are you for?" the woman seated next to her asked. "For?" Isabel replied. "Of course," the woman insisted. "We're for McCarthy. There's a Communist conspiracy in America. All of us are from the DAR." "Well, I'm not for him," Isabel Hensel retorted. She stayed through the session that day and never went back.

The two senior senators, Mundt and McClellan, made their opening declarations of fairness and impartiality. Suddenly, at ten forty-two, just seven minutes into the proceedings, McCarthy raised his first point of order: Don't list Stevens, Adams, and Hensel as the Department of the Army, he demanded; list them as three individuals.

Mundt rode over this objection. The first witness for the Army took the stand—stocky, well-groomed General Miles Reber, Commanding General of the Western Area Command of the United States Army in Europe, and formerly Chief of the Army's Office of Legislative Liaison. He began at the beginning, with a plodding recitation of facts about Schine's initial attempts to get an Army commission. Suddenly McCarthy struck again: "Is Sam Reber your brother?"

"Yes sir."

"Do you know that Mr. Sam Reber was the superior to Mr. Kaghan [when] Mr. Cohn and Mr. Schine were sent to Europe by me to inspect the libraries, that your brother, Mr. Sam Reber, repeatedly made attacks upon them and that your brother, Mr. Sam Reber, appointed a man to shadow them throughout Europe . . . ?"

The hearing had taken its first swerve off course. Jenkins tried to get it back on the rails. McCarthy persisted: "Are you aware of the fact that your brother was allowed to resign when charges that he was a bad security risk were made against him as a result of the investigations of this committee?"

Reber reddened in anger: "I do not know and have never heard that my brother retired as a result of any action of this committee." He pounded his fist into his hand. "The answer is 'positively no' to that question."

Reber, fuming, stepped down. Next General Walter Bedell Smith, Under Secretary of State, having been blasted loose by Hensel and Seaton, took the oath. Smith, who had been Eisenhower's Chief of Staff through the war, Ike's self-described "prat man," was a George Marshall and Dwight Eisenhower loyalist and, at State, an admired confidant of C. D. Jackson. Ravaged by ulcerous pain, driven by duty, his attention consumed for weeks by the imminence of the French forces' collapse in Indochina, Beetle Smith now went through his recitation with crisp efficiency: Cohn had phoned him on July 31, he testified, and complained of the Army's uncooperativeness in helping Schine get a commission. Cohn had come to his office on August 1 to follow up. There the two men had discussed the possibility of a position in the CIA for Schine, but Cohn had asked Smith not to pursue this: the CIA was, in Cohn's words, "too juicy a subject for future investigation," and he didn't want Schine caught in a conflict of interest.

"Did you regard these requests by Mr. Cohn on behalf of Mr. Schine as extraordinary or unusual or improper?" Jenkins asked.

"I did not," Smith replied.

McCarthy sidled up to this no-nonsense military man: he would ask him no questions. "I think he has very many more important things to do than to discuss a private in the Army. . . ." Smith did indeed. The French fortress of Dien Bien Phu was falling to the Communist enemy. And in the Caucus Room, under his factual answering, the stridency of the Army's claim faltered.

Secretary of the Army Robert Ten Broeck Stevens took the stand. Through hour after hour of skull practice he had been briefed and instructed by Welch and St. Clair. Now he faced the fire of unpredictable questions. Nearby sat Major Gabby Ivan, holding the Secretary's appointment books to refresh his memory if necessary. At the end of each day's hearing the Major would return the 1954 appointment book to Jack Lucas in the Secretary's office to let him make the entries for the day; the next morning he'd pick the book up and carry it back to the hearing. And Stevens had a second crutch—a chronology of events which Welch and St. Clair had put together. From time to time Stevens would glance down at it. But on the whole he told his own story in his own way out of his own memory.

Stevens mentioned a phone call from McCarthy on November 7. Knowing from prehearing discussions what Stevens would answer, Jenkins followed up: Do you have your phone calls monitored? Stevens hastened to explain. He did. He had, he said, inherited the process from his predecessor. He also inherited the monitor, Jack Lucas. And he had kept up the practice as an aid to efficiency, a means of letting Lucas follow up on a conversation—make a hotel reservation, for example, or write a memorandum to get a speech draft started. The whole process freed the Secretary up, made his office run better.

A wide-open discussion on the introduction of these phone calls ensued. At the moment it seemed like a diversion. In fact it would prove pivotal, focused on a central question: Exactly what evidence, within what limits, could come into this investigation?

Quite properly—given our later concern over the individual's right to privacy—McCarthy denounced root and branch the practice of monitoring any call without informing the caller. It was, he declared, "indecent and dishonest." But that was not the question, as everyone recognized. The question was simply this: Should the transcripts of the phone calls come into the hearing as evidence? If so, what calls? Beyond that question lay another: What other documentary evidence—for example, memoranda of conferences and intragovernmental memoranda—might one side or the other introduce? McCarthy himself had already introduced his eleven memos. But in its files the Army had reams more. How many of these documents—if any—could Stevens and company introduce; how many—if any—could McCarthy subpoena?

From the outset McCarthy had a clear-cut blanket insistence: no picking and choosing among the monitored calls. Publish all of them or none. From the start he wanted the phone calls not only between the Army and members of the committee, but also between the Army (Stevens and John Adams, for example) and others in the administration, including Hensel.

The subcommittee—Republicans and Democrats alike—agreed. By unanimous vote they approved John McClellan's motion to subpoena all memoranda, documents, and notes of monitored conversations between the parties to the controversy and all others that were relevant, in chronological order. They did so with the understanding that the documents would go to Ray Jenkins; that he would decide on their relevance to the hearing; but that before they could be entered into evidence, each caller would have to consent.

The first day of hearings ended. Stevens got into his black limousine and rode back to the Pentagon. Two phone messages lay on his desk. One came from Secretary of Labor Jim Mitchell, a former Pentagon colleague: I listened to your testimony all day—a masterpiece of presentation and content. The other message came from a Mrs. Roddenberry of Pasadena, California: You did a wonderful job. Fred Seaton's agent Walter Swan, however, who had watched from among the spectators all day, wasn't so delighted. The Democrats, he wrote Seaton, are asking a lot sharper questions than the Republicans except Potter. "I hope the public doesn't get the idea they are protecting McCarthy."

That evening the Republican exception, Charlie Potter, drove in secrecy to the White House. He regaled the President with a rehash of the first day's hearing; recorded Ike's bewilderment at McCarthy's excursion into the history of Sam Reber ("What in the name of God has his brother got to do with it?"); noted Eisenhower's hope that Bob Stevens could dispose of the whole sordid business in a couple of days; and left with the feeling that Eisenhower had remained so aloof from McCarthy's maraudings that "he just didn't understand."

As the President and Senator Potter talked, back at the Pentagon work continued. After each day's hearing Welch, who affected physical laziness, would frequently unwind with a Pentagon rubdown. The transcript of the day's hearing would arrive. And work would then begin on the game plan for the next day. At times Welch and St. Clair would rehearse the Secretary on facts or instruct him on answers at dinner—Welch regularly had two whiskey sours—in a basement room at Fort McNair. Other nighttime sessions would convene in the Pentagon dining room of Defense Secretary Charlie Wilson, with Wilson, Seaton, and Hensel in attendance, sometimes with Welch and Stevens (never with John Adams, who didn't even know about these sessions). Around the sumptuous table they concentrated on what move McCarthy would make next, and they tried to figure out what to do tomorrow.

After these meetings Stevens would go home in his Packard limousine. Welch's sedan would take him back to the Carlton, sometimes stopping at the Lincoln Memorial to let the aging Boston lawyer, ramrod straight, mount the steps with his young aide, Corporal James Franklin, look up at the statue of the Great Emancipator, read his words chiseled in the marble, and descend to the car without the utterance of a single word. And BeLieu and St. Clair would return to their Pentagon offices to work late into the night on the details for the day ahead.

The next morning the routine would begin again, with Welch's 8 A.M. arrival at the Pentagon's River Entrance; ad hoc meetings in various offices; a frequent greeting to Fred Seaton's petite and vibrant secretary: "How is my favorite secretary today? And what kind of shoes are those you're wearing?"; a ride up to the Hill with Welch, next to the driver, draping his arm over the seat and strategizing with St. Clair, seated with Jim Franklin in the back; arrival at the Senate Office Building; the morning session; and—as Stevens, Adams, and St. Clair dashed back to the Pentagon during the noon break—lunch at the Methodist Building, followed frequently by a stroll across the broad Capitol lawns.

At times the Army would engage in clandestine communication with the committee or the enemy. Jean Wood, a classmate of Scoop Jackson's in Washington, would on occasion converse with the Senator in the evening and report observations back to Ken BeLieu. Through a longtime friend, General Anthony Drexel Biddle, BeLieu could when necessary send circuitous messages to Roy Cohn or Bobby Kennedy.

On many a weekend St. Clair would fly back to their Boston area homes in Stevens's Convair. Time did not permit Joe Welch to indulge his passion for travel by train. Even there they would if necessary spend Saturday afternoons on strategy for the coming week.

The second morning of the hearings, at nine fifty-five, Karl Mundt phoned Stevens, about to leave for the Hill. McCarthy had a suggestion: Why not let both sides keep the seats they now had instead of switching? Stevens promised to call back. Five minutes later he did: no deal; stick to the original arrangement; change seats every day.

Thirty minutes later Stevens again faced Jenkins. Then he yielded to a nervous but meticulous Jack Lucas for an extended disquisition on phone call monitoring, and the nation listened in fascination. Meanwhile offstage, Hensel assembled evidence for his own defense. The next morning, Saturday, he went to the office. But suddenly and secretly that afternoon he and Isabel left town.

An hour later they were in the Catoctin Mountains of Maryland, at a country retreat owned by Washington auto dealer Floyd Akers near Camp David, in the company of two strangers who had surprised them with this impromptu invitation—Governor and Mrs. Sherman Adams of the White House. They had a picnic lunch. Adams and Hensel fished. Rachel Adams and Isabel Hensel—lovely and sparkling both—painted. And the friendship between the two couples warmed.

The dour New Hampshire Governor even took to heavy-handed kidding with Isabel about her pets: "What do you call them dogs?"

"A poodle."

"I knew it was some strange breed. I wondered what they have done to a dog."

"When you can kid with Sherman Adams," Isabel Hensel recalled long afterward, "that's something."

To Sherman Adams those two days away from Washington were a "temple of solace," an "act of mercy" to an embattled fighter. And through that entire weekend Sherman Adams never uttered one word about McCarthy. On Sunday night Adams drove Struve and Isabel home. The traffic thickened. They arrived late at Hensel's house. Hensel's lawyer Freddie Bryan was waiting at the door.

"Who's car was that?" Bryan wanted to know.

"Governor Adams's," Hensel replied.

"My God! Suppose you'd had an accident? Suppose a reporter had found out? What a story!"

Ray Jenkins completed his direct examination of Stevens—friendly questions designed to elicit the Secretary's account of the facts. Now, on Monday, April 26, the Counsel reversed his role. He became the prosecutor, almost savagely aggressive as he probed the lacunae in Stevens's story. And under the withering fire Stevens at times stumbled.

"Mr. Secretary," Jenkins demanded, "is it not a fact that you did make concessions to David Schine with reference to leaves of absences, passes, and so on?"

"Mr. Jenkins, we did, and the reason we did it is because, as I said on Friday, we did not want, or I did not want, the Army to be in the position of obstructing the work of a committee of Congress that at that time was engaged in investigating the Army. . . ."

"And he was given an extraordinarily large number of passes and leaves of absence, wasn't he?"

"That is correct, sir."

"I believe that you have already stated that you . . . were vitally interested in cleaning out subversives. . . . And you concede that Senator McCarthy and his staff did that very thing, do you not?"

"I concede that Senator McCarthy and his staff, through the investigation, speeded up to some extent the suspension of some people; but we had information about all of these people and the action would have been taken . . ."

"But the point is that it had not been taken, had it, Mr. Secretary?"

"It was in the process . . ."

"But Senator McCarthy accomplished it before you had the opportunity to do it; is that it?"

"No sir, I do not quite agree that that is it. . . ."

"Let me show you a picture, Mr. Stevens, for the purpose of refreshing your recollection," Jenkins said, trying to substantiate McCarthy's allegation of friendly rapport between Stevens and Schine. "I ask you whether or not that is a photograph of you, the Secretary of the Army, and David Schine, a private in the Army. . . ."

"I do not know whether it is Schine or not. . . . That picture does not look very much like him."

". . . What is your best impression about whether or not that was David Schine?"

"I think it probably is."

The moment passed. No one noticed any particular significance in the exchange. The questioning darted down other alleyways.

"Do you belong to a social club in New York City called the Merchants Club? . . . I will ask you whether or not at the very inception of this matter you, as a member, made arrangements at the Merchants Club for the McCarthy committee to be entertained there . . . [whether] he, investigating you or the Army, and his staff were to eat at your expense, without let, without hindrance, with no limitation [?] Did you think, Mr. Secretary, that it was within the bounds of propriety for you to do that?"

"Completely. . . ."

Hensel, Stevens testified, had supervised the assembling of the Army's Chronological Series of Events. In this process Stevens had conferred with Hensel's man Frank Brown; most of Stevens's own contributions to the chronology, the Secretary went on, came out of his own memory, not out of his records.

Jenkins shifted to the episode in which Cohn had excoriated the Army when he was shut out of the Monmouth laboratory. "You did not tell Senator McCarthy," Jenkins asked Stevens, "what you understood Mr. Cohn had said that day?"

"I didn't personally tell him, no."

". . . Did you convey [Cohn's] threats to [the Secretary of Defense]?"

"I don't think that I did, probably."

"Did you convey them to . . . the [President]?"

"No sir."

Jenkins probed another soft spot. Had Stevens let McCarthy take his plane from New York to Boston the afternoon of the Merchants

Club lunch, November 17, "after these threats had been made by Mr. Cohn . . . ?"

"That is right."

"And after all of this controversy had been going on between you and the committee for weeks and weeks?"

"That is right."

Stevens was becoming weary, but not McCarthy. When Senator McClellan focused on an implication that Stevens was trying to buy off the committee, McCarthy broke in with an angry point of order.

"I just wanted to point out that the implication there is that the chairman could have been bought off, and there is no evidence that this chairman ever could have been bought off any hearing and never will be bought off any hearing." The gallery erupted in applause.

To those of a judicial turn of mind who fixated on the Army's charges and the McCarthy countercharges, Stevens by now was losing points. To them, the name of the game was to cite the evidence, to argue the brief—to prove the Adams-Stevens recall of the facts right and the McCarthy-Cohn recall wrong. But those who had the perspicacity of a Struve Hensel would agree instead with his preliminary analysis of the facts: much of this wrangle was irrelevant. It didn't matter what Cohn said to Adams or Stevens said to McCarthy. For, as the contemporaneous documents made abundantly clear to Hensel before the hearing began, no disagreement whatsoever existed on or could exist on the only two central facts that counted: (1) that Stevens had made up his mind to cooperate in every possible way, shape, and form with the committee; and (2) that to this end the Army awarded Schine special privileges.

Given those facts, all the surrounding contentions—over the plans to fire General Lawton, over Cohn's vituperative words, over Adams's or Cohn's paying for fight tickets, over the offer to get Adams into a lucrative law firm—became hollow. The hearings—their effective thrust and significance—would turn not on these issues but on something different: a series of accidents, unforeseen, unpredicted, fortuitous. And these accidents in the end would make all the difference. They would dominate the hearings and determine their national and international consequences.

To some extent the occurrence of these accidents would reflect McCarthy's habitual day-by-day and night-by-night body-pushing routine, evident from his early years at the poker table. This routine typically began with a breakfast strategy session at his home, followed by the morning hearing, a working lunch at the Carroll Arms, the afternoon hearing, dinner at home or at the Colony Restaurant off Connecticut Avenue, an evening of hard work to get ready for the next day, then often an all-night vodka drinking session. But to an even greater extent the outcome of those accidents would reflect the lightning speed and brilliant improvisatory attack of Joseph Welch.

The first accident had happened that April 26 afternoon, when Jenkins showed Stevens the photograph of the Secretary and Schine. No one in the hearing room had recognized it at the time. But back at McGuire Air Force Base—the site of the photograph of the meeting—an alert public relations man thought he detected something. He had gone to his files of photos and then had put in a call to the Pentagon. His message quickly reached Joseph Welch.

Welch had been sitting through the hearings tweedy and bow-tied, watching Stevens buffeted by unpredictable questions. "We've got to take the offensive," Welch had told his colleagues. And now on the fourth day of the hearing he had his first chance.

His instinct was to hold his fire until the cross-examination. But Frederick Eaton urged attack at once.

Within seconds of the hearing's opening next day, Welch burst in: "Mr. Chairman, I don't know what it is, but it is a point of something . . . My point of order is that Mr. Jenkins yesterday was imposed upon, and so was the Secretary of the Army, by a doctored or altered photograph produced in this courtroom as if it were honest. . . . I show you now a photograph in respect of which I charge that what was offered in evidence yesterday was an altered, shamefully cut-down picture, so that somebody could say to Stevens, 'Were you not photographed alone with David Schine?' when the truth is he was photographed in a group."

Deftly, Welch exculpated Jenkins of any part in the "trick" and then with a flourish entered into evidence "the original undoctored, unaltered piece of evidence," a photograph that included not only Schine and Stevens but a third man and part of a fourth.

McCarthy began flailing. He demanded Welch be put under oath. He demanded the third man be identified. Flashbulbs popped. Then McCarthy threw a haymaker: "I now have before me . . . the picture that was introduced yesterday and the one Mr. Welch puts in today, and he makes the completely false statement that this is a group picture, and it is not." Symington tried to break in. McCarthy:

"Oh be quiet." More uproar. McCarthy bore down on Stevens, still on the stand: "Who is the third man, do you know?"

"Colonel Bradley is his name. . . ."

"Let me ask you this now: if you take off the third man, does that change the setup insofar as you and Mr. Schine are concerned in any way?"

"Yes, sir."

"Aside from cutting off the fourth man, [who was taken off by an Army photographer]," McCarthy said, "and cutting off the third man, who [was] either cut off by Mr. Schine or someone in my committee . . . is the picture of you and Mr. Schine completely accurate, and is there any doctoring in any way?"

". . . I would say," Stevens conceded, "that looking at it quickly, that that is probably true. . . . But I think you overlook the major trouble with this picture, which is that it was introduced on the basis that I had asked for a picture with Dave Schine alone, and I have no recollection of asking for such a picture. . . ."

McCarthy jumped to a recurrent diversionary theme: "Mr. Secretary, . . . with these hearings, you [have] succeeded . . . have you not, . . . in getting the [investigation] on the Communist infiltration in the military suspended[?]" But Ray Jenkins and the committee wanted to know more about the cropped photo. Cohn took the stand and tried to explain. His story made plain sense. Stevens, he said, had asked to have himself photographed with Schine. When Jenkins, in preliminary session, had asked to see that photograph, Cohn had phoned Schine in New York City, and Schine had sent down a photo, framed. One of McCarthy's staff men had cut out the irrelevant third man, had made a blow-up, and had sent the result to Jenkins without Cohn's seeing it.

Welch rode over the plausibility of Cohn's account. He now had an opening and a theme; and he played another virtuoso variation on it, with a light, puckish Scarlatti touch.

"Mr. Cohn," he began, "I assume you would like it understood that although I sit at the same table, I am not your counsel."

Cohn, trying to parry, lapsed into heaviness: "There is not a statement that has been made at this hearing," he said, "with which I am in more complete agreement, Mr. Welch, although I say I am sure you are a lawyer of great ability and maybe I would be fortunate if I had you as my counsel. I have no counsel here. Roy Cohn is here speaking for Roy Cohn, to give the facts. . . ."

Welch showed Cohn the picture. "My question now is this: You have referred to that picture as showing Mr. Secretary Stevens smiling at Dave Schine. . . . Would [you] like to qualify that statement?"

Cohn had earlier confessed to some slight nearsightedness. "Sir, I will accept your characterization of the picture."

"It is a grim smile on Stevens's face," Welch observed.

"I accept it," Cohn answered. "If you want to call Mr. Stevens's smile a grim smile, sir, I fully accept what you say. They are standing next to each other. They are facing each other. Their eyes are meeting. They are looking at each other. If the smile is grim or if it isn't grim, I know not, sir."

"Not too fast, Mr. Cohn," Welch broke in lightly, "not too fast. Stevens is looking to his right, isn't he?"

Cohn hesitated.

"Isn't he?" Welch pursued. "You can answer that one easily. . . . Well, answer it. Mr. Stevens is looking to his right, isn't he?"

"Sir, if you will give me the chance," Cohn came back, "I will try to answer it. . . . The picture, to me, looks as though Mr. Stevens and Private Schine are looking at each other."

"My question was a simple one," Welch repeated politely. "Mr. Stevens is looking to his right, is he not?"

"Yes, I would say he probably is looking to his right, and Private Schine is standing to his right."

"On Mr. Stevens's right are two figures, is that correct?" Welch asked. "One is Private Schine . . . and further to Mr. Stevens's right is Colonel Bradley?"

"Standing sideways."

"It would take someone with clairvoyance to know to whom Secretary Stevens is looking, would it not?"

Cohn dug in. "No sir. I don't think so. It would take somebody with common sense who can look at a picture and see what is in it."

"I think I observe on Colonel Bradley's face a faint little look of pleasure. Do you, sir?"

"I would say I know that Colonel Bradley had a good steak dinner shortly afterward. Maybe he was anticipating it. I do know that Colonel Bradley looks to me as though he, too, is looking at Private Schine."

"If Bradley is feeling good about a steak dinner," Welch followed up, "Schine must be considering a whole haunch of beef." The spectators erupted in laughter.

Subtly, Welch had undermined the smiling Stevens–smiling Schine relationship. Now he turned to ridicule: "Had Mr. Stevens actually said to you that he wanted to fly that big plane over there so he could see a private in the Army? . . . 'yes' or 'no.' . . ."

Cohn was stuck with his absurd contention: "That is one of the things which Mr. Stevens said on that day, yes, sir."

Jenkins had naturally been embarrassed at the alteration of the photo which he had introduced. He insisted on taking the stand to exonerate himself. He had no part, he asserted, in any deception. When Stevens resumed testifying, McCarthy, with heavy hand, tried once again to change the subject; "You know," he badgered the Secretary, "that the hearings were suspended the day you or some-one filed your charges against Mr. Cohn, Mr. Carr, and myself. You know that, don't you? Let's not be coy."

"I am not being coy at all . . . ," Stevens protested.

"Have they not been suspended since you filed your charges? Was not that the way you got them suspended?"

The bludgeoning continued. "Mr. Secretary, did you want the hearings suspended? . . ."

"I wanted the type of hearing that you were conducting sus-pended, yes, sir."

"You wanted our hearings suspended, did you not?" McCarthy charged.

"I wanted to have the type of hearing that you were conducting suspended."

"Now you say the type," retorted McCarthy. "Did you want us to continue holding hearings or a different type of hearing? . . . You did want the hearings we were holding suspended. Is that right?"

"Hearings of that type, yes."

"Did you tell Mr. Adams you wanted those hearings suspended?"

"I don't recall having told him that."

"You kept it a secret from him . . . ?"

McCarthy tried ham-fisted ridicule. Another Army charge, he an-nounced, is that Schine "had special boots with straps and buckles on the side. . . . I understand that Dave has about a size 12 or 13 foot, and he couldn't get a 13 . . . shoe at the usual place, so he went downtown and bought a shoe. . . . You don't think the com-mittee intervened to allow him to buy a special shoe, do you?"

"I wouldn't know."

"Another charge was that he had a furlined hood. . . . Or that he had complained about the cold weather. And do you think that this committee intervened to allow him to complain about the cold weather?"

"I wouldn't think so. . . ."

"Another charge was that instead of walking behind [a] jeep that was parked, he walked in front of the jeep. And do you think that anyone on the committee called and asked permission for him to walk in front of the jeep?"

"I don't have any information on that, Senator."

At times it was Jenkins who backed Stevens into a corner: "I will ask you, Mr. Secretary: Did or not early in November of last year Mr. Adams talk to General Lawton and say in substance, 'General, I hope you see your way clear to withdraw certain cases which you have recommended for removal as bad security risks.' Did you direct Mr. Adams to make such a communication to General Lawton?"

"I can't recall anything about that," Stevens replied, oblivious of the monitored phone call which bore out Jenkins's contention.

"Did Mr. Adams ever adivse you that he had given such a directive or made such a request of General Lawton?"

"I can't recall anything about that."

"That is a tremendously important thing, isn't it, Mr. Secretary . . . ? I ask you now to search your mind. . . ."

At times McCarthy veered off toward a target of opportunity. Seeing the Army officers seated near Hensel, he objected. If they were in the room to help Stevens, he said, they shouldn't be lending dignity to Hensel.

"I think that remark was uncalled for," Hensel retorted, "and Senator McCarthy ought to be asked to apologize. . . ." The gallery applauded.

Despite diversions, Welch kept his eye on that cooked photograph. On Thursday, April 29, when David Schine took the stand, Welch returned to it.

"Were you shocked" he asked the private, "when you saw the picture from your wall published, minus one third of the characters who appeared on your wall?"

"Was I shocked, sir? . . . I was not shocked."

"Were you surprised?"

"I have not been shocked lately at anything the newspapers of the country publish, sir. . . ."

"Were you saddened?" Welch went on with quiet humor.

"Was I saddened, sir, about what?"

"About the missing Colonel Bradley in your picture? . . . Do you know now, Private Schine, how Colonel Bradley, one third of the characters in the play, disappeared from the cast?"

"I have absolutely no idea, sir."

Jenkins joined the attack. McCarthy rose up in reckless wrath against the respected Counsel from Tennessee. "I want to make the very strong point of order that this is the most improper exhibition I have ever seen. You have a lawyer here who brags about being one of the greatest criminal lawyers in the country, badgering this private . . ."

The next day Welch and Jenkins continued their grilling. They pursued the mystery of the photo into the recesses of McCarthy's back room. One by one his operatives faced counsel and cameras and klieg lights.

First came George Anastos, a McCarthy staff member who had come to the subcommittee from the Justice Department, where he had served under attorneys general from McGranery to Brownell, and who had taken the wrapped photograph from the hands of David Schine. And finally came Jim Juliana—engineer, ex-FBI agent under Frank Carr—the man who had taken the photo from Anastos; the man, at last, at the end of the trail, the photo editor in the heart of darkness.

Like Roy Cohn, Juliana told a patently plausible story. When the photo sent down from New York by Schine arrived, he said, Juliana whispered to Cohn in the Caucus Room that it had come. Cohn instructed Juliana to have it enlarged. Juliana thereupon had had another staff member, Don Surine, make two enlargements—one of the three figures, one of Schine and Stevens only. Believing that Jenkins and Cohn wanted the pair only, he had delivered that one alone to Jenkins's office.

Once again, plausibility didn't count. Welch played another variation, seizing on Juliana's innocuous little inadvertent word "whispered."

"When the picture reached the courtroom, you turned to Mr. Cohn and whispered something to him, didn't you?"

"I advised Mr. Cohn of something; yes sir."

"Advised him in a whisper, didn't you?"

"Yes sir."

"What did you advise him in a whisper? . . . When you leaned over to tell this glad, good news to Mr. Cohn, were you under the impression that he was hoping to hear you had a picture of the Secretary and Private Schine alone? . . ."

"I was under the impression that Mr. Cohn knew and was expecting a picture of Mr. Schine and Secretary Stevens to be brought here from New York."

"Which picture Mr. Cohn wished to have placed in evidence? . . . Without any doctoring?"

"I assume that, too; yes sir."

"Why did you doctor it, then. . . ."

". . . I contend I did not doctor it."

"All right, altered. Would you like that word better, sir? . . . Mr. Juliana, you just told us that you were under continuous instructions to furnish a picture of Stevens and Schine; is that right, sir?"

"That is right; yes sir. . . ."

"And like a good hired man, in the end you produced, didn't you?"

"Yes sir." Welch had him. But he didn't stop.

"Another thing: you just told Senator Mundt that you had no malicious intent when you handed in what I shall now call the smaller picture; is that right? . . . Are you intensely sorry that you did it?"

Juliana tried to dodge. "Due to the fact that—"

Welch cut him short: "I don't care due to what fact."

"Due to the fact that it has wasted so much time, I am sorry."

"Only that, sir?"

"Yes sir."

"Your conscience, then, doesn't bother you to this moment; is that right?"

"I did nothing wrong, in my conscience, and it does not bother me." Now Juliana himself said the word: "Do you claim I was involved in a fraud, Mr. Welch?"

"I claim that there was at least a small fraud or else a terrible unfortunate mistake."

The country-store lawyer—the man who made few notes, wrote few memoranda, always had with him a leather envelope case (he called it his "lucky case"), which contained nothing but a few pencils and a half-empty foolscap pad, who kept nearly everything in his head, and who sometimes seemed to have a bad sense of direction around the Pentagon because, as he told Corporal Franklin, "I don't want to think about where I'm going, only what I'm going to say when I get there"—Joe Welch had scored his first triumph.

The vision of the back room would never disappear. The listeners would forever remember—however plausible the excuse, however thinly sliced—the atmospherics magically conjured up by the gentle man from Boston, the smell of skulduggery, of below-decks boys whispering, phonying up the evidence in the dark of night, without remorse.

Clumsy and unperceptive, McCarthy denounced Welch for playing to the gallery for laughs. He denounced this circus which was taking senatorial time away from compelling national problems. In a pique he even lashed out at feckless Henry Dworshak, informing him that he got his place on the subcommittee only because McCarthy's first choice, John Marshall Butler of Maryland, had been sick.

When Stevens resumed the stand, McCarthy resumed his badgering, opening up vague and gaping holes. "I told you, didn't I, Mr. Secretary, that I could not call off the investigation. . . ."

"I remember some general talk along that line, yes, Senator," Stevens acquiesced.

Cohn joined in: "Did you ask us . . . to suspend the type of hearings which were being held?"

"I would say," Stevens again argued, "that would be the clear implication. . . ."

The hammering was taking its toll. In the midst of this interrogation Stevens dashed back to the Pentagon for a farewell luncheon for Roger Kyes. Press Secretary Jim Hagerty also attended, and he didn't like what he saw: "Bob Stevens," Hagerty wrote in his diary, "came in jittery as the dickens. Everyone gave him a pat on the back and tried to bolster his morale. He is almost to the breaking point but [hopes] that two days' rest over the weekend will get him back. He has had a terrible ordeal in the witness chair for a whole week."

Stevens did get some rest over the weekend. But on Monday, May 3, the assault resumed. Under questioning he denied asking for an end of the hearings before the meeting in his office on November 6. He admitted knowing about the existence of Adams's draft of a press release, designed to announce the end of the hearings, on October 20, on the flight from Washington to Monmouth, but denied knowing anything of the contents. He testified that after the fried chicken lunch he spoke to no one except a few members of his staff and then went home.

"Did you discuss with Mr. Adams the preparation of these charges?" McCarthy demanded.

"Which charges do you mean?"

"The ones against Mr. Carr, Mr. Cohn and myself?"

". . . Actually, the charges were prepared by counsel."

"Oh, answer my question," McCarthy rudely demanded, and Jenkins backed him: "You have not answered the question. . . ."

"Did you ever come to me and complain about any alleged misconduct on Mr. Cohn's part?" McCarthy probed in a different direction.

". . . I think you were well aware of what our attitude was with respect to the pressure Mr. Cohn was putting on us."

"Mr. Stevens, you can answer my question; will you? Did you ever complain to me of any misconduct or any pressure on the part of Mr. Cohn?"

Stevens dodged: "Mr. Adams did, repeatedly."

McCarthy was not put off: "I am asking you. Did you, Robert T. Stevens, ever complain to me about any misconduct on the part of my chief counsel?"

"I complained to you about some things when you kept trying to get Schine assigned to New York, for example, Senator."

"I think you should answer the question, Mr. Secretary. . . ."

Stevens at last conceded: "I did not personally do that." Despite his obvious honesty and decency, Stevens was revealing extensive ineptitude. And he was taking a beating. Eisenhower hadn't seen the hearings. But he knew what was happening, and he fumed.

When he met with the Republican Legislative Leaders on April 26, Eisenhower reminded them that the American people shouldn't get the impression that the Congress consists only of McCarthy. "The Army-McCarthy argument, and its reporting," he wrote to his old Abilene boyhood friend and confidant Swede Hazlett the next day, "are close to disgusting. It saddens me that I must feel ashamed for the United States Senate."

On April 29, at his weekly news conference, when a reporter asked him whether Secretary of Defense Wilson had ever talked with him about Schine, Ike bristled: "You mean talking about this private? . . . I never heard of him. I never heard of him." And when a second reporter asked his opinion of "all the excitement at the Capitol over the privilege granted this private," Eisenhower snapped: "The whole business . . . I don't think is something to talk about very much. I just hope it is all concluded very quickly. That's all." And he strode from the room.

On Monday May 3, Eisenhower urged the Leaders to push through legislation with a specific human appeal in order to combat "this shameful inquiry." Unquestionably he wanted it to come to an end.

As Eisenhower was speaking to the Leaders, Joe Welch was coming up with a proposal to accomplish just that. He suggested limiting the testimony to just two witnesses, Stevens and McCarthy. At the most, he would want to call only two others in addition. Ev Dirksen seized on the idea; he knew the hearings were doing the Republican party no good. The committee, he urged, should explore Welch's suggestion.

When the day's hearing ended, the senators and the principals went into executive session. McCarthy agreed on the proposal to truncate. He would, he said, ask no more questions of Stevens, and he would at once take the stand himself. From the start he had ridiculed the whole circus—this nationwide obsession with Schine's shoes. He wanted to get out of that Caucus Room, get back onto the attack, ferreting out suspects, doling out the headlines.

When the closed session ended, McCarthy met privately with Hensel and Hensel's lawyer Freddie Bryan. The Senator offered to withdraw his accusations if he could do so without looking like a "damn fool." Hensel demanded as his price a complete public confession of error. McCarthy refused. Hensel asked him why in the world, given the absence of any evidence, he'd ever made his allegations in the first place. McCarthy replied with a story: Back on the farm he had known an Indian named Charlie, and Charlie had told him that when you get into a fight, there is just one thing to do: kick your opponent in the groin, and kick him and kick him and kick him until there is nothing left of him.

All the Republicans now agreed on truncation, with one exception—the maligned object of their solicitude, Robert Stevens, Secretary of the Army. The worm turned. The most jittery and unstable of all the principals balked. His good name had been smeared. He had been humiliated and abused. He had gone through the fiery furnace. His accusers—all his accusers—should too. Bob Stevens would have none of this proposed escape. He would stand firm.

Fred Seaton, reflecting Eisenhower's disgust and his own awareness of the danger being inflicted on the administration through the grilling of its Secretary of the Army, turned on the heat. No use. Stevens stuck by his refusal. Welch and St. Clair stuck by their client. As the Secretary and his two attorneys drove from the Pentagon to the Capitol the next morning, St. Clair recalled years later in an interview, they believed they were the only three in Washington who wanted the hearings continued. And he recalled Fred Seaton as "more than annoyed" with Welch and St. Clair for not leaning harder on Stevens. "Fred Seaton was very agreeable as long as you were doing things his way." But now they were not doing things his way. He'd done a lot for them; now he found them ungrateful. He never forgave them.

It was Welch who had to backtrack. He met with Ray Jenkins. He withdrew his original offer. And Jenkins concurred. The committee met in open session. Dirksen pleaded his proposal. McCarthy signed on. Potter—the man who had started the whole fracas, he freely admitted, with his letter to Charlie Wilson—now called for truncation; it was disconcerting, he said, taking an Olympian view, to see the Geneva Conference on Indochina pushed off page one by the Army-McCarthy fracas. Of course he believed that the public and the committee should get all the facts, but he thought that after Stevens and McCarthy testified, the others would merely rehash the repetitious.

Welch now weaseled. He contended he had never made the Stevens-and-McCarthy-only suggestion in the first place, citing his having mentioned that the Army might want to call two more witnesses; and those two "would seem to me to be a minimum—Messrs. Cohn and Carr." He and Jenkins, he said, had found no formula for shortening the hearings. And therefore he came out with the only possible conclusion: "to plow the long furrow" to the end.

The Democratic committee members unanimously concurred, urging a carrying-on, a washing of Republican linen, to its bitter-ended conclusion.

Seaton had not called in his biggest gun: he had not got from Eisenhower a direct order to Stevens to cease and desist. Given a man's determination to defend his personal honor to the end, one senses such an order—such a personal intervention in a procedural question—out of character for the President. If Bob Stevens passionately wanted to continue in his self-exoneration, the President would not overrule him. And when the subject came up at Eisenhower's news conference two days later, one senses in his response, along with his loathing for the proceedings, a measure of sympathy for the embattled Secretary's stand. The hearings were costing the nation in international prestige and self-respect, he said; he did want them quickly concluded. But he wanted them concluded with "effective answers" on the "main issues."

• •

On the afternoon of May 4, Stevens once again took the stand. And as former FBI agent Frank Carr looked on aghast, McCarthy, in a brash, unpredictable move, reached into a briefcase and whipped out a letter purportedly from FBI Director J. Edgar Hoover to the head of Army Intelligence, Major General Alexander Bolling, dated January 26, 1951. This letter, McCarthy alleged, should have alerted the Army to espionage at Monmouth. But the Army had ignored it.

Of the FBI Director, Struve Hensel all along had a deep and abiding suspicion. McCarthy had only a small staff, incapable of doing much research; they must, Hensel believed, be getting their information from J. Edgar Hoover. As the hearings unfolded, this suspicion intensified. A mysterious car would follow Isabel Hensel when she went shopping. A mysterious crew calling themselves "telephone people" would show up at the house. Could these, the Hensels wondered, have been FBI agents?

Such suspicions, Welch and St. Clair shared, though less heatedly. They had no traffic whatsoever with Hoover during the hearings. They always assumed that whenever McCarthy got tax information, it came from the Director.

Even to the man on the street, evidence abounded that J. Edgar Hoover and his team stood at ringside behind McCarthy's corner. For years McCarthy and Hoover had made no secret of their warm friendship. They would have dinner regularly together at Harvey's Restaurant. They would go out to the racetrack, where Hoover would let McCarthy use his private box. Moreover, Frank Carr was an ex-FBI agent. So was Don Surine. So was Jim Juliana. Their friends in the Bureau, the suspicion went, were only as far away as the nearest telephone.

In the battle for the heart and mind and allegiance of the average loyal American Main Street anti-Communist citizen, the possession of the backing of J. Edgar Hoover was a prize beyond price. The Gallup Poll revealed that among the generality of U.S. citizens, Hoover enjoyed overwhelming approval; 78 percent had a favorable opinion of him, 2 percent unfavorable. And in one cloying eulogy after another, culminating in his enshrinement of the FBI Director as the only American the Reds feared more than Roy Cohn, McCarthy played on this fact.

So did McCarthy's enemies. In the 1952 campaign Adlai Stevenson had simultaneously—and ineffectually—courted Hoover and slapped McCarthy in a tut-tut assertion that the rooting out of Communists in government was a job for professionals, not for children, "especially noisy ones."

Stevenson's ploy didn't work. Eisenhower, however, did much better. He started off on the right foot with the Director. Having heard of Hoover's estrangement from the Truman people, Eisenhower early in office personally invited the Director to a meeting to assure him of complete White House confidence. And in the Department of Justice that straight-arrow relationship was cultivated and sustained by Eisenhower's Attorney General Brownell, and Brownell's Deputy, Bill Rogers.

When Brownell attacked Truman over Harry Dexter White in November, Hoover took the oath and testified right behind the Attorney General 100 percent. When Brownell went on nationwide television in March of 1954 to display the administration's anti-Communist accomplishments, the FBI—"it stands in well with the kids, and that means also with poppa and momma," Ike told his Cabinet—became his centerpiece.

Bill Rogers, a fair-minded prosecutor whose anticommunism on the Hill went back further than McCarthy's own (in fact, Karl Mundt had initially wanted him for the Ray Jenkins job), worked with the Bureau day by day. He and Hoover got along fine. Early on Rogers shrewdly introduced a rule among his Assistant Attorneys General and U.S. Attorneys: If you ever have any trouble with the FBI, never write it down on paper. Rogers knew Hoover was "one hell of an infighter if he thought you were trying to embarrass him." The Director would fight tooth and claw to "defend his baby." So no one in Justice was to shaft him with memos. Instead, any aggrieved official would report his complaint to Rogers by word of mouth. Rogers would then go to the Director himself and raise the problem, perhaps over lunch, perhaps over dinner at Rogers's house. And the two together would work out any difficulty.

So far, the name of J. Edgar Hoover had come into the Army-McCarthy controversy only fleetingly. But when it had, it chilled the spine of both the Secretary of the Army and his Counselor. On the morning after the fried chicken lunch, Stevens, with everything else he had on his mind that day, had phoned the Director to assure him that John Adams had never, as reported, said anything bad about the Bureau. And in a monitored phone conversation with Frank Carr, Adams had, almost as if in catechism, affirmed the same allegiance, and practically begged Carr to relay his loyalty to the irascible Director.

Now, as McCarthy brandished the alleged letter from Hoover to Bolling, evidence thus existed that the FBI chief had been working both sides. Who could predict how he would now jump?

The moment in the Caucus Room was electric. Even Ray Jenkins was caught by surprise. Perceptively, Scoop Jackson asked the obvious question first. "I am a little confused. This is a copy of a letter that is being introduced. I would like to know how it arrived here to the committee, where it came from, and how it came here. . . . How did it get into the hands of the Committee? . . . I think it ought to be authenticated."

Jenkins offered to put McCarthy, who had just handed him the letter, under oath. Welch leaped at the opportunity: "I respectfully suggest that that be done. I am a lawyer, and . . . the mere fact that we have an impressive-looking purported copy of such a letter doesn't impress an old-time lawyer." Then he took a long gamble: "I would like to have Mr. J. Edgar Hoover say that he wrote the letter and mailed it. . . ."

Welch had bet all his chips on the Director. Then in folksy vernacular, he became the aggressor, addressing McCarthy: "This purported copy did not come from the Army files, and you know I am quite right, sir. And I have an absorbing curiosity to know how in the dickens you got hold of it."

Symington and Mundt, reaffirming their trust in Hoover, urged that the Director merely be asked about the authenticity of the letter, not subpoenaed and forced to testify. Stevens climbed aboard, refusing even to read to himself the purported Hoover letter, marked "personal and confidential," before Hoover himself gave permission.

McCarthy twisted and turned. His strategy—to ally himself with Hoover against the Army—was crumbling. And then with one swift lethal stroke, it collapsed.

The next morning, a staff aide to Jenkins, Robert A. Collier, took the stand. He was young, he was handsome, and—a former ten-year FBI employee—he looked like a cop. He had gone to see the FBI head. And he delivered his verdict. Hoover flatly denied the authenticity of McCarthy's two-and-a-half-page letter. He admitted that on January 26, 1951, he had written General Bolling, then Chief of Army Intelligence, a fifteen-page report on possible espionage at Monmouth by Aaron Coleman and thirty-three others. He admitted that seven paragraphs in McCarthy's purported letter squared identically with this fifteen-page memorandum. But the document submitted by McCarthy, the Director did not write.

Welch, extrapolating, translated the denial: into unforgettable colloquialism: "Mr. Collier, as I understand your testimony, this document that I hold in my hand is a carbon copy of precisely nothing, is that right?"

"I will say that Mr. Hoover informed me that it is not a carbon copy of a memorandum prepared or sent by the FBI."

"Let us have it straight from the shoulder. So far as you know, it is a carbon copy of precisely nothing?"

"So far as I know, it is, yes. . . ."

"So far as you know, this document in this courtroom sprung yesterday by Senator McCarthy is a perfect phony. . . ."

The smell of subterranean skulduggery again filled the Caucus Room.

Then Welch went after the principal. For the first time, McCarthy took the stand.

Welch quietly readied the noose: "Senator McCarthy, when you took the stand of course you understood you were going to be asked about this letter, did you not?"

"I assumed that would be the subject."

"And you, of course, understood you were going to be asked the source from which you got it? . . . Could I have the oath that you took read to us slowly by the reporter?"

Mundt balked. Welch continued: "The oath included a promise, a solemn promise by you to tell the truth, the whole truth, and nothing but the truth. Is that correct, sir?"

"Mr. Welch, you are not the first individual that tried to get me to betray the confidence and give out the names of my informants. You will be no more successful than those who have tried in the past."

Welch remained unruffled: "I am only asking you, sir, did you realize when you took that oath that you were making a solemn promise to tell the whole truth to this committee?"

"I understand the oath, Mr. Welch."

"And when you took it, did you have some mental reservation, some fifth or sixth amendment notion that you could measure what you would tell?"

"I don't take the fifth or sixth amendment."

"Have you some private reservation, when you take the oath, that you will tell the whole truth, that lets you be the judge of what you will testify to?"

"The answer is there is no reservation about telling the whole truth."

Welch had him. And he moved with the speed of light: "Thank you, sir. Then tell us who delivered the document to you."

"The answer is no. You will not get that information."

McCarthy could run. But he couldn't hide.

The next morning, May 6, Brownell compounded McCarthy's confusion. In a letter to Mundt, Brownell declined to declassify the long, fifteen-page authentic Hoover-Bolling letter; he opposed release of the two-and-a-half-page McCarthy boil-down; and he charged McCarthy, in effect, with "unauthorized use" of confidential FBI data. To make things even worse for McCarthy, Stevens came up that same day with a genuine J. Edgar Hoover accolade, made public by explicit permission of the Director, praising the long record of cooperation between the FBI and the Army.

McCarthy flailed. He demanded that Brownell be haled before the committee to testify. He denounced the Truman "blackout order." He declared himself not bound by it. He contended that Brownell himself had disclosed information from FBI reports to the Congress when he testified on Harry Dexter White. When Stuart Symington joined in repudiation of what he called the "fraudulent letter," McCarthy struck at him, accusing him of trying to obstruct the elimination of Communists from government.

But McCarthy's audacious surprise move had backfired. J. Edgar Hoover had come down on the side of Eisenhower and Brownell. The Director knew where power lay. He had tired of Joe McCarthy—tired of McCarthy's antics, which more and more, in his view, were giving antisubversion a bad name, and, indeed, helping the Communist cause by tarring any genuine honest anti-Communist as a McCarthyite. Significantly, Hoover and his top lieutenants in the Bureau had harbored a deep and uneasy suspicion of McCarthy all along.

On March 9, 1953, for example, just six weeks after Eisenhower's administration entered office, Louis B. Nichols, Assistant to the Director, reported on his meeting with Deputy Attorney General Rogers to Associate FBI Director Clyde Tolson. In that meeting Nichols voiced his suspicion of a leading McCarthy staff member who reportedly claimed he could get any FBI information he wanted; congressional committees, Nichols told Rogers, do not require leaks and information from executive branch agencies in order to do their job. By November 9, McCarthy was raising Cain to a top Hoover aide about the FBI's refusal—under a rule imposed by Brownell and Rogers—to give him name-check information, despite the fact that the department was permitting the FBI to give it to the Senate Internal Security Subcommittee. By February 24, Hoover himself was writing in ink on the bottom of a bureau memorandum: "We should indicate to Cohn our concern over the more and more instances wherein they are . . . crossing wires in our current investigations. . . . It is becoming more and more obvious that they are hiring ex-agents solely for the purpose of getting information acquired by such employees while in FBI service. We are not responsible for Cohn acting precipitously—that is his choice but in doing so he is wrecking our internal security coverage and he should recognize it." Nichols immediately relayed this complaint to Cohn and the next day reported back. On the bottom of this report Tolson had scrawled in longhand: "If [Cohn] hires enough ex-agents," he will "get access to our complete security set up, as well as knowledge of individual cases and informants." And Hoover scrawled an echoing concurrence: "That is exactly the point, and that is the reason I originally opposed Carr's appointment both to McCarthy and Cohn. Ex-agents trying to make good on [the] committee job are not going to drop an iron curtain on their past knowledge of Bureau cases, informants, etc." The last thing Hoover wanted was a McCarthy "pipeline into the bureau." He resented Cohn's claim that he had one. And he resented McCarthy's sitting in judgment before witnesses and pretending to read from FBI documents.

McCarthy knew the thrust of all this history. But against long odds he had made his reckless gamble. And he had lost. J. Edgar Hoover and the FBI belonged to the enemy.

The specter of those monitored phone calls—and other contemporaneous documents—still continued to hang over the hearings and over Robert Stevens's testimony under oath. The phone calls had been subpoenaed. But they had not been delivered. Neither Welch nor Jenkins nor anyone on Jenkins's staff had yet read them. The Secretary of the Army had testified that in the afternoon after the fried chicken lunch, he had talked only to his staff and had then gone home. Once delivered, read, and entered into evidence, the monitored phone calls of that afternoon and evening would have torpedoed this recollection. Instead, it was torpedoed from a different direction, by testimony given offstage by a secret witness.

One by one for weeks, a parade of such witnesses had filed by the various representatives of the committee and both contending sides. On April 19, David Schine's father, J. Meyer Schine, had testified that he had given no gifts or payments to either Cohn or McCarthy. On April 23, George Sokolsky had come in and—despite his partiality to McCarthy and Cohn—corroborated Stevens's contention that at the Merchants Club lunch on November 17, Stevens had offered no leads for investigations into the Navy or Air Force. On April 24 a twenty-nine-year-old Miss Iris Flores, who described herself as the inventor of a device for the improvement of brassieres, returned vague and evasive answers on the exact details of her relationship with Schine. On April 28 a man named Caputo, reported to have been ordered by Hensel to eliminate all monitored phone calls unfavorable to the Army, came in and confessed that he'd launched the whole rumor himself out of whole cloth in order to impress his friends. On April 29, General Kirke Lawton testified that he had not been promoted because, among other reasons, he had cooperated too much with McCarthy. On May 5, James Reston of the *New York Times* said he had information that Robert Stevens, despite his testimony, had indeed met with Struve Hensel after the fried chicken lunch and before the issuance of the Army's charges. With this information in hand, the committee called into executive session the next day, May 6, Assistant Secretary of Defense Fred Seaton.

Testifying before Mundt, Ray Jenkins's assistant Tom Prewitt, Jim Juliana of McCarthy's staff, and Roy Cohn, Seaton confirmed Reston's account. He described the meeting in Stevens's office after the fried chicken lunch with twenty-one Pentagon officials, including Struve Hensel, present.

Immediately after Seaton's testimony, Stevens on his own volition hastened to correct his error. He'd misspoken, he admitted, when he said he'd talked with no one that afternoon after the lunch. His records showed he had talked with Kyes, Seaton, Hensel, and the others. And that night at home he'd also conversed with some friends, including *Newsweek*'s Arthur Hadley, and Hadley had thereupon phoned several paragraphs of Stevens's proposed hearing testimony to someone else.

McCarthy lunged. Stevens had committed perjury. He'd changed his story only when Seaton's testimony exposed his lying under oath. Stevens bristled. He had known nothing, he said, of Seaton's testimony.

McCarthy pressed the attack. He reeled off a drumfire of other questions. And Stevens, often seeming to cling to the ropes, returned answers that at least revealed vagueness, and at worst sharply conflicted with the impending contemporaneous written record.

After the day of the fried chicken luncheon, Stevens asserted, he didn't see Hensel for at least ten days and possibly two weeks. He first learned of the anti-McCarthy charges—carefully qualifying "charges" with "in the form of the chronology"—on March 4 or 5, an assertion incompatible with his phone conversation with Cabot Lodge and with Lucius Clay, when he disclosed that the staff work on these charges was underway. He had "heard rumors"—nothing more—to indicate that before Senator Potter wrote to Secretary Wilson the press had its hands on the content of the chronology.

Who decided to prepare the report? Stevens didn't know; he assumed Hensel was getting it ready under orders from the Secretary of Defense.

Did Stevens talk to Adams about the rumors that the report had leaked to the press? Stevens at first waffled, then admitted, after conferring with Adams, that Adams had talked over the information in the chronology with Joe Alsop. What about the phone call from Stevens to McCarthy after the November 6 lunch at the Pentagon in which, McCarthy alleged, Stevens apologized because Adams had told the press that one particular Loyalty Board member had not been discharged, after McCarthy had said he had been? No recollection. Did Stevens believe that Roy Cohn was too upset over Dave Schine's future to attend the December 10 luncheon at the Carroll Arms, as the Army's released chronology alleged? If so, why did the Army omit this assertion from its formal charges?

Did Cohn or Carr ever threaten him? Stevens would have to check the wording in the charges. Mundt repeated the question.

"Mr. Cohn and Mr. Carr," Stevens replied, "were talking about resuming hearings, shall we say, [in] a somewhat unusual way." Mundt repeated McCarthy's question: Did Cohn or Carr issue a threat?

"Well, on the question of resumption of the hearings," Stevens said, taken in conjunction with the discussion, the constant discussion about Private Schine, it was my feeling that they were threatening me."

"Threatening you with what?"

"Threatening to—if I didn't do something, they were going to do something."

"What were they going to do?"

"Well, they were going to—well, as you recall, a declaration of war, and things of that kind. . . . We are going right back to the

Fort Monmouth situation, where Mr. Cohn got so upset because he wasn't allowed in the laboratory . . ."

". . . Did this have anything to do with Schine? Wasn't this a case of Mr. Cohn being excluded from the laboratory after he'd been invited down there?"

"That is right."

"This had nothing to do with Private Schine, did it?"

"It is all part of a pattern in my opinion, Senator. . . ."

"Did [Cohn] talk about the private at that time?"

"Not at that particular time, but on plenty of other times."

"Did [Cohn or Carr ever] tell you that [the investigation] was being continued because of Private Schine?"

"They told me that you were very upset about this press statement I had made, Senator."

"They did not tell you I was upset about Private Schine, did they?"

"But there had been some evidence that you had been."

"Let's stick to the facts, Mr. Secretary. . . ."

The November 16 meeting at the Merchants Club, McCarthy persisted, had nothing to do with getting preferential treatment for Schine, did it?

"All part of a pattern, in my opinion, Senator McCarthy. . . ."

Surveying the carnage, McCarthy summarized his conclusion: Stevens was a tool. Behind him were sinister people—men like Hensel—using him for their own purposes, fearful of being exposed. And down there in the woodwork there were Communists clearing other Communists.

Through all this, Eisenhower remained restless with the hearings' continuation. "When is it going to end, Charlie?" he asked Potter when the Senator once again came to the White House to give him a secret summary, on May 6, and that same day he wrote his friend Harry Bullis, head of General Mills in Minneapolis, agreeing with Bullis that the hearings should be "brought speedily and effectively to an end"—something the Senate so far had failed to accomplish, despite its efforts.

Those efforts were continuing. On Monday, May 10, Senator Everett Dirksen came up with a compromise. When Stevens finished testifying, he urged, the committee would go at once to McCarthy's testimony. After that, they would hold the remaining hearings in executive session, with a summary given out to the press after each one. (This time compromise reportedly came with a new sweetener: Cohn and Adams would simultaneously resign. McCarthy allegedly agreed. And Cohn actually began to write his resignation letter.) Jerry Persons in the White House approved of the plan. So did his friend Fred Seaton, who continued to see no good result—for Stevens or the Army or the Republican party—in a prolongation of the public squabble.

But Stevens once again dug in his heels. It was unfair, he believed, that he should testify fourteen days and others testify not at all. He wanted a probe all the way to the bottom, no matter how long it took. The committee Democrats, once again, wanted exactly the same thing. And at this particular moment they had a new ally— the President of the United States.

On Tuesday, May 11, Hagerty recorded in his diary the "great pressure by Republicans to try to take hearings into executive session after McCarthy's testimony. Legislative people here think it would be a good idea—I think it would be terrible. Discussed it briefly with the President, and he agrees with me. He called Charlie Wilson and told him not to put any pressure at all on Stevens along these lines but to tell Stevens to 'do what you think is right.'"

As a result, Hagerty continued, "Stevens stuck to guns and when Welch objected, on behalf of Stevens in afternoon session, to move, Mundt voted with Democrats and scuttled the plan."

Mundt had announced that he would not vote to end the public hearings over the objection of either Stevens or McCarthy. He would be even-handed. Without question, the South Dakota chairman did want the hearings to end. And given Persons's and Seaton's concurrence with the Dirksen plan, Mundt had good reason to believe Stevens's opposition might crumble. But he had misread the Army Secretary's fortitude.

"Mundt desperately trying to get off hook—tried to get Stevens to say it was unfair," Hagerty continued in his diary. "Stevens, through Welch, refused to give Mundt this out, refused to cast his proxy for him, said that he had not changed his mind, that he thought it was best for everyone concerned to be heard in public. Army reaction came as great surprise to everyone on Hill and at the White House— not to Sherman Adams and myself, however, but to many others."

That May 11, the day the Dirksen plan went down to defeat, Karl Mundt replied to a letter from his old friend Governor Alf Landon of Kansas, who had written in to report Milton Eisenhower's objection to the harmfulness of the hearing: "I am beginning to wish that Milton Eisenhower would talk to his brother in the White House and then have President Eisenhower make it clear to the country and to Secretary Stevens whether they actually want these hearings to continue on and on and on and on into a dismal and distant future, or whether they will cooperate and try to bring about a formula to shorten them to which all hands can agree. . . ." Ike had not given Stevens an outright order to continue the sessions, but had instead permitted the Secretary to follow his own conscience. Without question, however, Eisenhower did not like this particular Dirksen plan for closed-door sessions. When Jerry Persons, in Hagerty's presence, said Stevens had done the wrong thing in urging that the hearings continue, the President shot back: "I think Stevens did exactly right. Here he had been on the stand for thirteen days and if [this] plan [had] been successful the other witnesses, except McCarthy, would have been testifying behind closed doors. McCarthy would then be at liberty to come out of the hearings and tell reporters anything he wanted even though they had [been given a] transcript. He would have [a] forum while [the] Army would not. Anyway, I'm glad the Army is fighting him right down the line."

Eisenhower that same day stiffened Stevens's resolve on a second decision—to release the details of who promoted Peress. Back in February after the fried chicken lunch Eisenhower told Stevens to "admit that the handling of the Peress case was bungled in the Army. Tell the entire truth in connection with the affair and hold back no information unless the security of the country might be involved in some way. Along with these two things stand upon your rights. . . ." Now at last the Inspector General's report on Peress had been completed. On May 7, Stevens announced that though all of it would not be made public, he would, as he promised, release to the subcommittee the "pertinent information." Army Chief of Staff Matthew Ridgway violently objected. Fred Seaton insisted that the President's instruction to Stevens be followed to the letter. Ridgway came to Seaton's office and the two had "a hell of a row," in Seaton's words, which ended with the General's "clomping out, madder than a wet hornet." The argument escalated to Secretary of Defense Charlie Wilson and, as he frequently did, Wilson bucked it to Eisenhower. On May 11, the President wrote in his diary: "Secretary Wilson called me to ask me about a report that the Mundt investigating committee had requested the Army to provide to the committee the names of all military personnel who had any connection with the so-called Peress case. . . . The purpose of Mr. Wilson's call was to seek my advice as to the wisdom of giving this kind of information to the committee. It appears that Secretary Stevens had already tentatively agreed to provide the information, but that General Ridgway violently objected on the ground that to give away this kind of information and to establish a practice of subjecting officers to cross-examination and virtual persecution by Congressional committees would practically destroy discipline in the Army.

"I disagree with this rather extreme view taken by General Ridgway and I feel that this particular case has to be handled strictly on its merits. Of these I know nothing. I have not followed the hearings either in the press or by television or radio; I have no knowledge whatsoever of the connection between the so-called Peress case and the charges that have been apparently flung back and forth between McCarthy and the Army.

"My own belief is that the Army would be well advised to provide every possible bit of information in this case where the security of the country and efficient administration will permit. They must not be in the position of appearing to 'cover up.' "

Two days later Stevens sent Jenkins the names.

Stevens had become ill with a virus infection, and for the moment he left center stage. He had shown many faults as a witness. Because of the many demands of his office—including budget headaches and procurement wrangles—he had been unable to confine his attention to the quarrel with McCarthy. He had become weary on the stand. He had a bad memory. He looked at the big picture, not at crucial details. He insisted on responding to questions he couldn't answer instead of deferring to John Adams, who knew the answers inside out. He would wander off the question and engage in his own elaborations, which would offer the questioners new openings ("Those were anxious moments," James St. Clair recalled years later).

Every night Welch and St. Clair would spend long hours coaching Stevens at Fort McNair or the Pentagon, going over every possible subject that might come up the next day. And when the next day arrived, the two lawyers would sit behind their shaky witness, pretending to whisper to each other, but in fact prompting Stevens on what to answer. At times Ken BeLieu and Major Ivan, who carried a briefcase chock full of documents, would do the same thing.

But despite the ineptitude of much of his performance, Stevens on television, somehow, through his honesty, evoked public sympathy. Driving home in his long black Packard after a particularly grueling session, Stevens wearily turned to BeLieu: "Ken, you're a clever fellow, give me a couple of bright remarks that I can use next time." And Welch suddenly turned on both of them: "Don't you do it, Ken. You should stay in character, Bob, just the way you are."

So Stevens did, despite the strain it put on him through long hours in the Caucus Room and the strain it put on his staff in the long evenings afterward: "You could follow the cocktail hour across the country," BeLieu recalled many years later. "The phone would ring. First came the nut calls from New York, then Chicago, then Denver, and finally the West Coast. I remember one late in the evening from a Los Angeles lady who had obviously been enjoying a long happy hour. She wanted Joe McCarthy's unlisted home telephone number, and she knew I of all people would have it. 'Sure,' I told her, 'here it is. Give him a call.' By that time in Washington it was 1:00 in the morning."

With Stevens momentarily on the sidelines, John Adams took the stand. Adams had no generals in retinue behind him. At home he had a shy, sweet wife who watched all the hearings on television and day and night took care of their infant daughter, constantly ill with colic and the croup. Adams didn't even have access to the recollections he had dictated for his original chronology. He felt cut off from the other members of the Pentagon team—from Fred Seaton, who he felt avoided him, and from Joe Welch, who would meet in executive session with McCarthy's representatives without him. In the Pentagon, Adams recalled years later, only Struve Hensel remained approachable; and far away in the White House, John Adams believed he had only one friend, Governor Sherman Adams—a man he had seldom seen but who always came across as "the soul of civility."

The minute John Adams took the stand on the morning of Wednesday May 12, however, the Army's tempo picked up. In contrast to his boss, he showed himself crisp and credible and articulate under fire, with a sure command of facts and dates. He began to reel off the chronological record, in fascinating and spellbinding detail. He recalled the October evening on the subway when McCarthy had told him that Schine was useless to the committee, that he only wanted to get his face in photographs (but don't tell Roy).

He vividly described the explosive December 17 lunch at Gasner's Restaurant, "an experience similar to none which I have had in my life."

For a fascinated audience, Adams recalled Cohn's agitation ("He cursed me and then Senator McCarthy. The abuse went in waves. He would be very abusive and then it would kind of abate and things would be friendly for a few moments. Everybody would eat a little bit more, and then it would start in again"); McCarthy's curious passivity ("At first [he] seemed . . . to be trying to conciliate Cohn. . . . But then he more or less lapsed into silence"); the final mad dash in Cohn's car toward the train station, with Cohn pouring out invective, and McCarthy urging, as a solution, a New York assignment for Schine); and Adams's ejection from the car in the middle of Park Avenue, with Cohn's parting words: "Get [to the station] however you can."

Adams described Cohn's phone call to Amherst, to get Schine out of Sunday KP. He recounted how Cohn, learning later that Schine might be assigned overseas, responded, "Stevens is through as Secretary of the Army. . . . We will wreck the Army." He recalled going to McCarthy's apartment on the night of January 22; parrying the Senator's request for a special New York City assignment for Schine; nibbling on hors d'oeuvres with Joe and Jean; and leaving after an "easy, friendly" evening with "a nice big slice of cream cheese and a big hunk of sausage which I took home with me."

Suddenly, almost imperceptibly, Adams's inexorable chronology crossed a boundary line. When McCarthy issued his January 19 ultimatum—produce the members of the Loyalty Board for interrogation within three days, or have them subpoenaed—Adams recalled that he first talked with Hensel, then with Rogers, then (at Rogers's suggestion) with Senator McClellan, and then, on January 21 in the Attorney General's office, with Brownell, Rogers, Sherman Adams, Gerald Morgan and UN Ambassador Henry Cabot Lodge.

"At this meeting," John Adams added, "Governor Adams asked me if I had a written record of all of the incidents with reference to Private Schine which I had discussed with them that day . . . , and when I replied in the negative he stated he thought I should prepare one."

Why had John Adams crossed the divide—the line separating the Army from the outlying reaches of the administration? Why had he brought in Justice and the White House? One answer is that in testifying honestly—in telling the whole truth, in refusing any appearance of a cover-up—he had no choice. A second answer is that he wanted the entire record out: the record of the efforts for Schine; but also the record of the men elsewhere in the administration who pulled the strings in the background. Under questioning the next day Adams admitted showing all his original chronology to columnist Joe Alsop and parts of it to reporters Phil Potter of the *Baltimore Sun*, Homer Bigart of the *New York Herald Tribune*, and Murray Marder of the *Washington Post*. Adams rationalized the leakage: by the time he showed the papers to the reporters—in early February—his experiences "were no secret." Between thirty and fifty people, he said, had firsthand knowledge of them, including members of his family, who had heard him dictating his memos on his Dictaphone at home; friends; associates in the Pentagon; congressmen and senators; and various newsmen.

John Adams had helped spread the information around. And now under questioning he was widening his and Stevens's circle of accomplices, extending it for the first time across the Potomac to the Department of Justice and 1600 Pennsylvania Avenue. After all, why should he be stuck out there all by himself?

Incredibly, Adams's interrogators did not immediately see the bait. They continued to fixate on other things. But the White House saw the implications of his revelation at once. As Hagerty wrote in his secret diary that May 12: "Adams in testimony mentioned the fact that he had conferred with Brownell, Rogers, Governor Adams, Gerry Morgan, and that Governor Adams had told him to prepare a memorandum on case. Believe this to be opening of White House action in case and probably have to face question soon as to whether we will stand for subpoena before committee of White House personnel. President is opposed and will probably not permit it."

Since early March, when the President first asked Rogers for constitutional precedents, the White House had been expecting something like this—some test of presidential powers against congressional powers. After the Army revealed its cache of transcripts of monitored phone calls, in a memo to Sherman Adams dated May 3 Attorney General Herbert Brownell drew a specific line: If the subcommittee tries to require the Department of Defense to turn over monitored phone conversations with the White House or Department of Justice, the administration should refuse.

On May 7, Cabot Lodge reported to Eisenhower Welch's warning that Lodge might be called to testify on that January 21 meeting, and told the President of his intention to decline, in his capacity as a presidential advisor. Eisenhower agreed completely. And with eagerness, at his May 12 news conference, the President—glancing at the J. Edgar Hoover–Bolling documents—denounced the disclosure of confidential data to unauthorized people.

Immediately after that press conference, and only a few hours before John Adams went public on the January 21 meeting, Sherman Adams was huddling with Jerry Persons and Assistant Attorney General J. Lee Rankin, the Justice Department's resident authority on presidential privilege. Ike had made up his mind. The next day, Thursday, May 13, Jim Hagerty wrote in his diary: "Had several discussions during the day with President and [Sherman] Adams on Counselor [John] Adams' testimony at hearing in which he mentioned Governor Adams, Lodge, Morgan, Rogers and Brownell as participating in a conference with him and urging him to put down on paper Cohn-Carr-McCarthy threats against Army—*Daily Mirror* carried story quoting McCarthy that he was going to subpoena White House personnel—Official stand here through my office is 'No Comment.' Attorney General is readying a decision that White House personnel in advisory position to the President cannot testify before Congressional committees—President feels very strongly and said, 'This is one we will fight out right up and down the line.' In conference with Governor Adams and myself President said that it might be necessary to send one White House man, probably Adams, before committee to give his name, his title and then refuse to answer all questions under Presidential order to prove our point—that he was acting in a confidential capacity to the President. He would say that he is under Presidential directive not to answer and let the chips fall where they may. Another alternative is that the Attorney General appear and explain the same position. McCarthy, of course, may be bluffing but if attempt is made to subpoena White House personnel, we will fight it. . . ."

Not only people but papers now lay open to attack by subpoena. Speed became imperative. That same day, May 13, in Charlie Wilson's absence, Acting Defense Secretary Robert Anderson was writing Stevens: "At the instruction of The Honorable Sherman Adams, the Department of the Army is to deliver at once to the Honorable Fred A. Seaton, Assistant Secretary of Defense, for his prompt transmittal to the White House each and all stenographic notes, transcriptions, or other records or memoranda concerning conversations and communications between any of the principals of the McCarthy-Army hearings, employed in the Defense Department and persons employed within this Department or within the Executive Branch of the Government, regarding any matters which are involved in the subject of inquiry before the Subcommittee of the Senate Committee on Government Operations.

"This direction does not include such records with respect to communications between persons employed in the Executive Branch of the Government concerning such matters and the principals who are not employed in the Executive Branch." The Congress, in other words, was not to get from Stevens internal executive branch memoranda.

Anderson signed the letter. An emissary hand carried copies to Stevens and Seaton. And a massive sweep-up began. John Adams's office began carting his documents to Colonel Jean Wood in the office of the Secretary of the Army. Struve Hensel's office did also. Wood assembled these papers with those of Stevens himself, including the transcripts of the monitored telephone conversations. Over many weeks Jack Lucas and the other shorthand artists had been reducing these to writing—dredging every relevant call from their notebooks, typing them up, in Lucas's words years later, like "a bat out of hell," rigorously checking their accuracy, making sure they contained "no phony baloney."

From Wood all these papers began to flow to Seaton. And before nightfall Seaton's agent Phil Mullin, carrying a precious bundle the size of a shirt box wrapped in manila paper, climbed into Seaton's black Buick, told the sergeant to head for the White House, and personally put the documents into the hands of Sherman Adams, getting a signed receipt from the Assistant to the President himself.

At the hearings Friday morning, May 14, in a damaging switch, two Republican committee members turned on Stevens and Adams, who had scuttled the Dirksen compromise. Republicans were being clobbered. One by one they came forward as witnesses to testify on the Army's alleged attempt at blackmail. First, the wounded Dirksen. John Adams, he said, had come with Gerald Morgan to Dirksen's office on January 22. They were trying to kill the subpoena of Loyalty Board members. Did Adams threaten to issue a report on Roy Cohn, McCarthy asked, if the subpoenas were not killed? John Adams awaited the answer in terror. But Dirksen shied from taking the ultimate step: "My recollection is slightly vague on that point." But he did say that in that meeting for the first time the question of the subpoenas was coupled with a discussion of Cohn's efforts for Schine.

Next, Chairman Mundt took the stand. Adams had come to see him also on January 22, and he "felt a little bit uneasy about the juxtaposition" of the unrelated subjects of the subpoenas and the Roy Cohn machinations. Did John Adams, McCarthy continued, tell Mundt the committee wanted the Loyalty Board members also for graft and corruption? "I do not recall he did," Mundt replied.

This squall, however, was only a temporary diversion from the main subject of the day, which at last dawned on the interrogators: that January 21 meeting in Brownell's office.

The inquiry started with a relaxed question by Stuart Symington: "Why was Ambassador Lodge at the meeting on January 21?"

"I don't know, sir. I didn't arrange for his presence."

"Was there anything," Symington persisted, "that you discussed that had to do with the United Nations?"

Welch burst in with a point of order. "This was a high level discussion of the Executive Department," he said, "and this witness has been instructed [by Acting Defense Secretary Robert Anderson] not to testify as to the interchange of views [of] people at that high level at that meeting."

Symington posed a common-sense question: "Does that mean we are going to get the information about low-level discussions but not about high-level discussions?"

Welch could not budge. That very morning the President had laid down the law to his Cabinet: Executive branch officials should not testify before congressional committees on (1) security information or (2) personal advice exchanged between a superior and a subordinate; the consideration of possible publicity, he asserted, would inevitably destroy the advisor's value. Acting Secretary Robert Anderson had relayed this directive to Fred Seaton. And Seaton had told Adams.

Symington continued to probe. Where did Acting Secretary Anderson's instructions come from? John Adams didn't know. He promised to find out.

Now Scoop Jackson joined Symington's attack: Adams had waived his immunity, he said, when he himself brought up the January 21 meeting. Now perhaps it appeared this testimony would embarrass the administration. But that shouldn't keep the committee from hearing it. We should get all the facts, Jackson insisted, not just those favorable to the Army.

The committee demanded that Adams return that afternoon after the lunch hour with a written directive. He returned empty-handed.

The noon hour, Welch said, had just not provided enough time to resolve the question.

Symington refused to relent. In the absence of a presidential directive, he urged Mundt to instruct Adams to answer. The clock was running. Welch turned on the humble charm: "I am the world's leading amateur, I should say, in this field. . . . We are toward the end of an adjournment, with the weekend coming up, and I should say that with more time before us, the position with respect to this witness should be susceptible of clarification at the hands of people wiser than Welch is. So, Senator, if you would not mind passing the thing for the moment, we have a weekend coming up, and on Monday morning it would seem entirely proper for you to press that. I would appreciate the courtesy if you didn't press it now, but I have only the right to say 'please.'"

Symington melted: "Mr. Chairman, I am beginning to fall for Welch, too."

The question would hang there until Monday morning. But it would hang there under an ominous warning from the senior Democratic member of the committee, John McClellan: "Unless there is some reason that I cannot now conceive that will be advanced why others should be excused from testifying in this hearing, or if any matter relevant to developing the whole facts and truth is being withheld by someone else . . . , I shall insist, Mr. Chairman, that those witnesses be subpoenaed and brought here. . . ." He was demanding all the facts. And he was playing constitutional hardball.

Against that insistence from the Democrats—not McCarthy, who so far sat in silence—the White House now moved. By two-thirty that Friday afternoon, Sherman Adams had already met with congressional and constitutional consultants—Brownell, Morgan, Martin, Persons. Word of McClellan's threat to subpoena White House staff members arrived. "The President said," Hagerty recorded in his diary, "that he would not stand for this one minute. He explained that he looked upon his staff members as confidential advisors and that the Congress had absolutely no right to ask them to testify in any way, shape or form about the advice that they were giving to him at any time on any subject—'If they want to make a test of this principle, I'll fight them tooth and nail and up and down the country. It is a matter of principle with me and I will never permit it'— The President reiterated his belief that Stevens was dead right by refusing to permit the hearings to go into closed sessions and said that he would once again tell all members of the staff to keep out of this controversy, to have nothing to say on it, and to let my office, and my office alone, be the spokesman on all questions dealing with McCarthy."

The next day, Saturday, May 15, McCarthy, as expected, told reporters that, like McClellan, he demanded that all participants in the January 21 meeting testify. Hagerty "spent most of [that] morning in conference in Governor Adams' office with the Governor, Herb Brownell, Lee Rankin, Persons, Morgan, Martin, Shanley on draft of letter President to send Monday to Secretary of Defense ordering him to refuse to permit employees in the Defense Department to testify concerning confidential and personal matters relating to advice within the Executive departments—Attorney General also brought over excellent historical memorand[um] outlining similar action taken by twelve Presidents—Washington, Jefferson, Jackson, Tyler, Buchanan, Grant, Cleveland, Theodore Roosevelt, Coolidge, Hoover, Franklin D. Roosevelt, Truman—in which they refused to surrender to Congress on this principle. I recommended that memorandum be attached to letter and made public by the White House. At first, there was some feeling in the meeting that it should be made public by the Defense Department or at the hearing, but when I pointed out that that would mean [John] Adams would make the announcement at the hearing, everyone agreed that we should do it from the White House. . . ."

At seven-fifteen on the morning of Monday, May 17, the President met for breakfast with Brownell, Lee Rankin, Sherman Adams, Hagerty, Persons, Shanley, Morgan, and Martin. He approved the letter and the Brownell memorandum. He agreed to sign the letter at eight-thirty and send it over at once to Robert Anderson in the Pentagon.

"Also agreed," Hagerty recorded, "for me to release correspondence at 9:00 from White House and to say in answer to any questions relating to subpoena (not mentioned in letter) that 'the principle applied equally.' Everyone at meeting unanimously agreed on step and only discussion concerned how to handle it at [Republican congressional] leaders' meeting at 8:30. It was finally agreed that the President would tell the leaders that he had sent this letter and that it was being made public—Would present it as an accomplished fact so that they would not have an opportunity either to oppose it or to offer changes."

The White House breakfast broke up. At eight-thirty the leaders arrived: Senators Knowland, Millikin of Colorado, Saltonstall, Ferguson of Michigan, and Bridges; Representatives Joe Martin, Halleck, Les Arends of Illinois, Leo Allen, and Dan Reed of New York—a largely conservative crowd—along with Treasury Secretary George Humphrey, Republican National Chairman Len Hall, and his assistant, Jim Bassett. "Turning to his letter," Hagerty reported, "the President announced that they all knew that he had been trying to stay out of the 'damn business on the Hill,' that many people have been begging him to get into the struggle, to attack McCarthy personally but that he had refused to do so. However, he said, a situation had come up in the threatened subpoena of his confidential advisers that made it necessary for him to act. He said that he had written a letter to the Secretary of Defense ordering him to refuse to permit their people to discuss confidential matters with the committee and that he had also attached the Attorney General's memorandum outlining the precedents taken by twelve of his predecessors[.] 'Pseudo liberals all over the country have been urging me to raise hell. I have not done that, but I have issued instructions to the Secretary of Defense which order him to keep confidential any advisory discussions in the administrative side of this government[.]' 'Any man who testifies as to the advice he gave me won't be working for me that night'—'I will not allow people around me to be subpoenaed and you might just as well know it now.' "

Majority Leader Knowland, ever maintaining that the Congress should not become a rubber stamp for the executive, had an objection: "He believed," Hagerty wrote, "executive discussions and papers should be protected, but that he would hate to see the subpoena power of Congress challenged. . . . The President [retorted] that he had not mentioned subpoena in his letter but [added] 'let me make one thing clear—Those people who have a position here in this government because of me, those people who are my confidential advisers are not going to be subpoenaed. Governor Adams' official job is really a part of me and he's not going up on the Hill'— 'I've gone to utmost lengths to be cooperative with Congress. I have declined to get into this mess even when I have been needled by the press, but this is one thing I will fight with all my power—I will not have my men subpoenaed.' "

The leaders found the President persuasive. Halleck and Ferguson said they believed Congress would have to do something about investigations; there was a limit on what congressional committees could ask witnesses. Len Hall urged everybody present to stand behind the President on this issue. Knowland told reporters that the President had discussed the letter with the leaders and "that everyone in the room had agreed that the President was perfectly within his rights in ordering Administration personnel to refuse to discuss confidential and advisory matters of the administrative side of the government."

John Adams entered the Pentagon pool car with Jim St. Clair to head for the Hill. A copy of the President's letter to Wilson was placed in his hands. The morning session of the hearing opened. Adams took the stand. He read the letter aloud: It enunciated a sweeping claim of executive privilege: "It has long been recognized that to assist the Congress in achieving its legislative purposes every Executive Department or Agency must, upon the request of a Congressional Committee, expeditiously furnish information relating to any matter within the jurisdiction of the Committee, with certain historical exceptions—some of which are pointed out in the attached memorandum from the Attorney General. This Administration has been and will continue to be diligent in following this principle. However, it is essential to the successful working of our system that the persons entrusted with power in any one of the three great branches of Government shall not encroach upon the authority confided to the others. The ultimate responsibility for the conduct of the Executive Branch rests with the President.

"Within this Constitutional framework each branch should cooperate fully with each other for the common good. However, throughout our history the President has withheld information whenever he found that what was sought was confidential or its disclosure would be incompatible with the public interest or jeopardize the safety of the Nation.

"Because it is essential to efficient and effective administration that employees of the Executive Branch be in a position to be completely candid in advising with each other on official matters, and because it is not in the public interest that any of their conversations or communications, or any documents or reproductions, concerning such advice be disclosed, you will instruct employees of your Department that in all of their appearances before the Subcommittee of the Senate Committee on Government Operations regarding the inquiry now before it they are not to testify to any such conversations or communications or to produce any such documents or reproductions. This principle must be maintained regardless of who would be benefited by such disclosures. . . . By this action I am not in any way restricting the testimony of such witnesses as to what occurred regarding any matters where the communication was directly between any of the principals in the controversy within the Executive Branch on the one hand and a member of the Subcommittee or its staff on the other." (As Jim Hagerty had urged, the President's letter carried with it the Brownell memorandum of March 2 citing Presidential assertions of the right to keep information confidential, beginning with George Washington in 1796).

At last the confrontation had become constitutional. At last McCarthy had entered into presidential territory. And at last the President had hit him. "Put a Constitutional issue before the President," Brownell recalled years later, "and he'd respond to it. At last he felt he'd got his teeth into something significant—principle, not personality."

In asserting this principle, Brownell continued, Eisenhower was not enunciating a rigid rule outlawing the disclosure of all such executive branch information to all congressmen at all times. He knew he could not go by an iron-clad automatic connect-the-dots code. He knew that the President—any President—had to make judgments in a gray area.

He was aware, on one side, that the President had a duty not to engage in a cover-up. On suspicion of corruption or crime, his policy—as Brownell himself had enunciated it at the January 21 meeting—was "give them everything." And short of that, Eisenhower had repeatedly permitted the release of information that he could have withheld, as he did when he let Senators Taft and Sparkman examine the FBI report on Chip Bohlen, when he had let Brownell reveal the history of Harry Dexter White, and when he had overridden General Matthew Ridgway and directed Robert Stevens to give the senate committee everything possible on the promotion and the discharge of Irving Peress.

But Eisenhower also recognized that he had a duty to prevent the disruption of the government. The McCarthy-Army investigation, already nearly a month old, and now taking a first step on what could turn out to be an endless expedition into the Department of Justice and ultimately into the White House itself—this posed a clear and present threat to the government's orderly conduct. The time had come to draw a line. So Eisenhower exercised his constitutional option, as predecessors back to George Washington had exercised it many times before him—he enunciated his right, at his own discretion, to refuse the disclosure of information which now, in these *particular circumstances,* would impede the functioning of government.

To Welch and St. Clair—and Stevens and Adams—this decision was "imposed from on high." They had had no part in framing it. Those who had framed it, in the Department of Justice, knew nothing of the Army lawyers' strategy, of all the specific information in specific documents—like the transcripts of monitored phone calls—that the order might suppress. The President and Brownell were not engaging in a ploy in accordance with any Army plan. They were drawing a constitutional line.

Liberals from coast to coast united in wild applause for Eisenhower's resistance to what Harry Truman called "legislative dictatorship." He had drawn a boundary, not between the Army and McCarthy but between the President and Congress—Republicans and Democrats alike.

Now on that morning of May 17, John McClellan took the first step toward this boundary: "Was the action . . . after that conference [on January 21]," he asked John Adams, "taken on the basis of the independent decision and judgment of the Secretary of the Army, or was it taken as the result of decisions made at that conference?" Adams declined to answer, citing the President's letter.

McClellan tried a second tack: "Did you [and Secretary Stevens] act on your own responsibility . . . prior to January the 21st in the decisions and actions you took?"

"Our negotiations prior to January 20, sir, were strictly within the responsibility of the Army."

McClellan now defined his constitutional ground with incisiveness and caution: "For the present, at least, I am not disagreeing with the Executive directive, with respect to conversations that may have taken place at this meeting. The President may be within his rights to say that you cannot inquire how a decision was arrived at in the Executive Branch of the Government at the President's level. But . . . I wholly disagree, and I shall insist upon making this record clear with respect to what was the result of the decision made at that time, whether responsibility shifted from the Secretary of the Army to higher authorities. That we are entitled to know, because unless we can get that information, we will not have the evidence here upon which to make a decision that will place the responsibility."

Senator Scoop Jackson also modified his aggressiveness. Though he disagreed with the President's use of his discretionary power in this instance, he believed the President did have a right to withhold information from the Congress. And Senator Symington wanted more time to study the issue before going further. When he'd first questioned Adams, he said, he believed that Adams had brought up the January 21 meeting in order to have it discussed. So Symington had tried to cooperate. Now, for the moment, he was backing off. All three Democrats were leaving room for their retreat.

But then for the first time McCarthy began to talk. And the more he talked, the more he widened the distance between him and three men—McClellan, Jackson, and Symington—who might have given his constitutional objection respectability. He had earlier thought, he said, that John Adams and Struve Hensel had instigated this whole fracas. Now he didn't know who was behind it. He no longer was sure who had succeeded in blocking the investigation of Communist infiltration in the federal government.

"Now for some fantastically strange reason, the iron curtain is pulled down so we can't tell what happened at that [January 21] meeting. I don't think the President is responsible for this. I don't think his judgment is that bad. . . ." But, McCarthy went on, the senators now faced "a tremendously important question. . . . How far can the President go? Who all can he order not to testify? If he can order the Ambassador to the UN not to testify about something having nothing to do with the UN, but a deliberate smear against my staff, then any President . . . can, by an Executive order, keep the facts from the American people."

Someone, McCarthy went on, should get to Eisenhower immediately "and point out to him, perhaps, that he and I and many of us campaigned and promised the American people that if they would remove our Democrat friends from the control of this government, then we would no longer engage in government by secrecy, whitewash and coverup."

The American people "will not stand for a coverup halfway through a hearing," McCarthy continued. "Who was responsible," he demanded to know, "for the issuance of the smear that has held this committee up for weeks and weeks and weeks, and has allowed Communists to continue in our defense plants, Mr. Chairman, handling top secret material . . . with a razor poised over the jugular vein of this nation?

"Who is responsible for keeping all these Army officers down here and all the Senators tied up while the world is going up in flames?"

Dirksen recommended a recess. The Democrats dissented. By a 4 to 3 party-line vote, once again, the committee decided to recess for a week, until Monday, May 24, instructing Mundt to try in the interim to get the White House to modify its order. The committee then disappeared into executive session. There McCarthy admitted he was guessing when he labled Hensel architect of the Army's charges.

The next morning at eleven o'clock Hagerty left the White House with the President for a one-day flight to Charlotte, North Carolina. "Rode out with the President after first announcing to newsmen that Secretary Stevens would accompany us on the plane to Charlotte to take part in Armed Forces Week celebration. . . . Newsmen, of course, did not believe this was the only reason—and they were right. President deliberately invited Secretary so he could give public support to him by having him as guest on plane and appearing with him on platform. . . . At Charlotte President pointedly said, 'We have confidence in our Armed Forces from their Secretaries and commanding officers down to the last private.' On way out in car to airport President and I again discussed the press conference [scheduled for the next day]. . . . On hearings President agreed that three points should be cleared up: namely a) that he did not intend to modify in the slightest degree his order to the Defense Department, b) that the January 21st meeting was held for advice on subpoenaing members of the Loyalty Boards and not to take over from Stevens the conduct of the investigation, and c) that any stories that his order was issued to close the hearings were just stupid and silly. . . .

"The President asked me to discuss these matters with Stevens on the plane, and I did so. The Secretary was very pleased at our feeling on the matter and also expressed his willingness to issue a statement . . . and say he would never give up the responsibility to anyone for conducting the hearings. The President and I talked to Stevens alone on the plane and outlined this plan and procedure— Stevens got a big hand when introduced at Charlotte and President supported him to the hilt with photographs eating together . . . a box lunch and also shaking hands both at the Charlotte Airport and Washington Airport on our return. . . ."

"What did the President say to you?" Adams recalls asking Stevens. "Hardly anything," Stevens replied. "We sat in different parts of the plane and rode home in separate cars."

Given the record, Stevens's shouldering of responsibility would entail a bit of fancy footwork, but he agreed. Before nightfall Seaton and Welch were going over a draft of a declaration to be made by the Secretary the next day.

On the morning of Wednesday, May 19, in a one-two punch of news conferences, the President and Stevens announced their conclusion. Eisenhower went first, telling reporters he has issued his May 17 letter to keep the investigation from going off on a long sidetrack into a relationship between President and advisors, that the White House had not approved the preparation and release of the charges against McCarthy and Cohn, that he had no recollection of the January 21 meeting, and that he wanted the hearings to get all the facts out, thus putting himself crosswise to Dirksen, who continued his maneuverings to make the recess permanent. Then Stevens, in the statement edited by Seaton, took on the whole load. The Army alone, he said, had prepared and presented the case against McCarthy.

To Hagerty, the administration had scored. Before the President's news conference, Adams, Persons and Morgan joined Hagerty for a briefing on the McCarthy problem. "The Vice President and Persons had discussed this earlier in the morning," Hagerty wrote in his diary, "and had reached the same conclusion that we had; namely, that we should flatly state that we would not modify [the] Presidential directive, that it was not intended to close the hearings and that the hearings must be continued until the truth had been learned and all principals testified publicly. . . ."

The press conference itself, Jim reflected, "was one of the best the President had ever held. . . . It was forceful and to the point. Called Brownell at the conclusion of the conference and reported to him what the President had said. Mundt and Jenkins were coming to lunch with Brownell, and when I told him of the President's statement he said, 'That makes my job a lot easier.' Subsequently Brownell called me back and said Mundt and Jenkins had dropped their request for modification of Executive Order when they heard what President had said in press conference and had also dropped most of their opposition when informed of Secretary Stevens's statement issued at 11:30 that the Army had sole responsibility in that matter and no 'higher ups' had taken over. Brownell reported that Mundt and Jenkins left in good spirits . . . and as Brownell put it 'they were in favor of the Administration, at least when they walked out of my door. I don't know what Mundt will be when they get back on the Hill.'"

Though Mundt was mollified (Stevens's explanation, he said publicly, "minimized the impact" of Eisenhower's order), McCarthy was not. He continued deepening the moat that now divided him from nearly everybody else. He denounced Eisenhower's "gag order." He threatened to boycott the hearings ("a stacked deck"). He resuscitated his hoary accusations against American Allies who shipped to Red China, and declared he'd now for the first time seen a whole administration "take the fifth." For that one, Hagerty wrote, "I hope [the President] lets me burn McCarthy's ears off."

On Monday, May 24, the hearings started up again. Stevens and Adams began their agile dance, maintaining the innocence of the White House and the Justice Department in the launching of the chronology and subsequent investigation. McCarthy went for the obvious opening. He made Stevens squirm. He reminded Stevens that back on May 6 he had said he didn't know for sure who decided to prepare the charges; now he was saying he, the Secretary of the Army, did.

In addition to Hensel and Brown, McCarthy wanted to know, who else in the executive branch had advised Stevens? Welch refused to let Stevens answer. Mundt broke in with the obvious question: Why should Stevens name some advisors and not others? Barreling forward, McCarthy drove Stevens to declarations out on the ragged edge of the truth: for example, that he had had no discussion of the chronology with anyone—he did not cite his monitored conversations with Lodge and Clay—outside the Pentagon; that he himself had taken the responsibility for sending the charges to the members of Congress; that that very day, May 21, he had learned for the first time of a high administration official's request that Charlie Potter write Charlie Wilson his letter asking for the Army's report on Schine; that he didn't recall whether Adams told him about the three other reporters who received the leaked information in addition to Alsop; that he had at times ignored suggestions made by Sherman Adams, though at the moment he couldn't think of one.

On that Monday afternoon, May 24, manfully maintaining his responsibility to the end, Stevens at last stepped down. John Adams followed him for a short while, and then he too completed his testimony. The two men, their relations never close, were becoming increasingly estranged. A few days earlier, on May 21, Adams had sent a couple of suggestion memoranda to Joe Welch—ideas on what to do when cross-examining McCarthy and Cohn. (On October 21, 1953, Adams said, he had gone to the prizefight with Cohn, Carr, and a mysterious unidentified man named "Oscar." Maybe "Oscar" gave Cohn the phony FBI letter. Why not ask Cohn to identify "Oscar"?) But more and more Adams felt himself "beaten down," cut out of the Army strategy. He no longer sat in on meetings. He felt that Welch was making deals behind his back. He never received a single word or gesture of encouragement from above. He continued terrified at the possibility of going to prison for perjury. He detected informants following him about as he walked through the streets of Washington. An offhand remark by Ken BeLieu confirmed his suspicion that somebody was tapping his telephone wire.

After Adams finished testifying, a parade of officers—armed with charts and statistics—described Schine's behavior at Fort Dix. General Ryan, the Commanding General, recounted how after December 1, 1953, Schine's proliferation of passes left him so exhausted that Ryan discontinued his leave during weeknights. The General's aide-de-camp testified that after the KP episode in January, Roy Cohn ominously informed him of his "long memory"; he would never, he assured the aide, forget the names of those who had made trouble for Schine.

Back in the Oval Office, disgust with the Republican Old Guard—especially on the subcommittee—boiled over. First the target was the Republican Senate Leaders on the Hill. The trouble with them, the President told Hagerty and Gabe Hauge, was that they didn't have the "guts to defend the Administration. Boy! We really need a few good hatchet men on our side up there!!"

Then, on May 25, the target was Karl Mundt. "As usual," Hagerty wrote in his diary, "we discussed the Army-McCarthy row and as usual, the President thought Senator Mundt was a weak chairman—'I use to think he was just a weak man but now it is obvious that he is playing on McCarthy's side. How I wish we had run Mrs. [Barbara] Gunderson in the primaries. She could have [beat] him hands down. Why don't we run some of our young people against the Old Guard and give them a lesson once and for all?' "

Then it was Ev Dirksen. On Wednesday, May 26, the subcommittee voted 4 Republicans to 3 Democrats—over Welch's objections—to dismiss all charges against Hensel and Carr. Ike was infuriated. He agreed with Hagerty that by this move the Republicans on the committee had "just cut their throats. . . . If they were going to drop the charges on Hensel and Carr," the President went on, "they should have made McCarthy publicly admit then and there that he was withdrawing his [accusations]. I would have settled for nothing less. Anything less is just stupid and cowardly."

"I agreed with him," Hagerty wrote in his diary, "and said that I thought the news stories would interpret this as a deal by Republican senators to get McCarthy off the spot, particularly since it had been reported to me by newsmen covering the hearings that Mc-Carthy and his people were especially worried that Carr, who apparently isn't so smart, would break down on [the] witness stand and spill a lot of beans. The President was thoroughly disgusted and said, 'I hope you tell all our people at the White House that it's about time they stopped trying to have me work with guys like Mundt and the rest. They are not for us, they never were, and never will be.' I told the President I would be glad to relay this information."

Hours later Hagerty found out what had happened: Potter had voted to dismiss the Hensel-Carr charges only because Dirksen had told him "that was the way the President wanted it." Hagerty broke the news to the President the next day. Ike exploded. "He said that at no time had he agreed to such a thing, and that he had never gone further with anyone than the public statements he had made at his press conferences. . . . On all those occasions he had expressed the hope that the investigations would be completed as soon as possible—but only after all the principals had an opportunity to tell their story openly and fully. The President suggested that I have Jerry Persons and Jack Martin have Senator Dirksen come down to his office immediately so that he could tell Dirksen to his face the same thing. . . ."

Jack Martin conveyed the message to the Senator. Dirksen apologized for the error. But Hagerty's suspicions remained: "Think it is a good thing that those Senators on the committee realize we are checking closely on everything. . . . It will also serve to warn them that they can't pull fast ones without our hearing about it."

The next day McCarthy poured hot coals on Eisenhower's wrath. He demanded the committee subpoena not just the phone transcripts but all the Army files bearing on the dispute. And then he took the ultimate step. He demanded that federal employees ignore the President's order; bring to him, Joe McCarthy, information— even classified information—revealing corruption and treason in the executive branch. "The oath," McCarthy said, "which every person in this government takes, to protect and defend the country against all enemies, foreign and domestic, that oath towers far above any Presidential secrecy directive. And I will continue to receive information such as I received the other day. . . . I would like to notify those two million Federal employees that I feel it is their duty to give us any information which they have about graft, corruption, Communism, treason and that there is no loyalty to a superior officer which can tower above and beyond their loyalty to their country. . . ."

The White House struck back. On the morning of May 28, Hagerty drafted a flat condemnation. He cleared it with Brownell and his White House associates, got Eisenhower's approval, and at eleven o'clock issued it—at Ike's suggestion—in the name of the Attorney General. The "Executive Branch . . . responsibility," it declared, "cannot be usurped by any individual who may seek to set himself above the laws. . . ." A few minutes later Ike summoned Hagerty to his office: "Walking up and down behind his desk," Hagerty wrote in his diary, "and speaking in rapid-fire order he said . . . : 'This amounts to nothing but a wholesale subversion of public service. McCarthy is making exactly the same plea of loyalty to him that Hitler made to the German people. Both tried to set up personal loyalty within the Government while both were using the pretense of fighting Communism. McCarthy is trying deliberately to subvert the people we have in Government, people who are sworn to obey the law, the Constitution and their superior officers. I think this is the most disloyal act we have ever had by anyone in the Government of the United States.' " When the question came up at his next news conference, the President said, "I am going to . . . say that if such an invitation is accepted by any employee of the Government and we find out who that employee is, he will be fired on the spot if a civilian and court-martialed on the spot if a military man. I won't stand for it for one minute."

Together the President and Hagerty agreed that Hagerty should phone key people in radio, TV, and the print media and that he should press on them this constitutional message. "The President . . . told me that I should do this on my own and should not let anyone even in the White House know what I was doing." Hagerty wasted no time. Late in the afternoon he suggested particularly that Eisenhower listen "to Ed Murrow's program at 7:45 tonight. . . ."

McCarthy, unregenerate in his arrogance ("I hope to remain in the Senate and see many presidents come and go"), was losing allies everywhere. By now John McClellan was not only deserting McCarthy; he was attacking him. In possessing and holding classified information, McClellan asserted in the hearings, McCarthy was possibly committing a crime.

Republican Senator H. Alexander Smith of New Jersey branded McCarthy's utterance "beyond belief"; this country, he said, could not tolerate one-man government. Jackson and Symington abandoned ship, wanting no part in encouraging federal employees to turn over information to people not lawfully entitled to have it. As they taunted their silent Republican committee colleagues, Senator Potter tried feebly to maintain a faint neutrality. Though he admired Eisenhower, he affirmed, he recognized that the executive branch sometimes did overstep its responsibilities. But by now even right-winger Bill Knowland had sided with Eisenhower: by inviting employees to disregard a presidential security order, Knowland asserted, McCarthy had put himself on "highly dangerous and doubtful grounds."

To the President and Hagerty the fight was now joined. Ed Murrow and other commentators, Jim noted in his diary on May 29, had "picked up Brownell's statement of yesterday and characterized it quite properly as a fundamental Constitutional fight between the Administration and McCarthy. Newspaper editorials also supporting our position. . . . Fight is . . . one which we can really go to the people on since it is simple and can be understood. The basic question we are making a fight on is simply this: Has a United States Senator, or anyone, a right to publicly urge the formation of a personal Gestapo within the Administrative Branch of the Government, including the military?"

The President had chosen his ground. And now, determined "to make this a finished fight with McCarthy," determined to "go to the people with it," he spoke out in his own voice. On Monday, May 31, in New York City, he addressed the National Bicentennial Dinner of Columbia University, an anniversary which had taken for its theme "Man's Right to Knowledge and the Free Use Thereof." In ringing

words interrupted again and again by applause, Eisenhower reaffirmed this right and denounced his detested antagonist; "Whenever, and for whatever alleged reason, people attempt to crush ideas,
to mask their convictions, to view every neighbor as a possible enemy,
to seek some kind of divining rod by which to test for conformity, a
free society is in danger. Whenever man's right to knowledge and
the use thereof is restricted, man's freedom in the same measure
disappears.

"Here in America we are descended in blood and in spirit from
revolutionaries and rebels—men and women who dared to dissent
from accepted doctrine. As their heirs, may we never confuse honest dissent with disloyal subversion.

"Without exhaustive debate—even heated debate—of ideas and
programs, free government would weaken and wither. But if we allow ourselves to be persuaded that every individual, or party, that
takes issue with our own convictions is necessarily wicked or treason-
ous—then indeed we are approaching the end of freedom's road. . . .

"As [the Founding Fathers] roused in mankind the determination to win political freedom from dynastic tyranny, we can ignite
in mankind the will to win intellectual freedom from the false propaganda and enforced ignorance of Communist tyranny. Through
knowledge and understanding, we will drive from the temple of
freedom all who seek to establish over us thought control—whether
they be agents of a foreign state or demagogues thirsty for personal
power and public notice."

With these heroic words etched in the nation's consciousness,
Mrs. Mary Driscoll, McCarthy's personal confidential secretary—she
was the sister of David Brinkley, and she'd worked for McCarthy
six years—took the stand on June 1. Jenkins had been probing
lightly Roy Cohn's contention that, to get some of the eleven Mc-
Carthy memos typed, he had left his own office on the ground floor
of the Senate Office Building, declined to use the ample stenographic help there, and gone upstairs to dictate to Mrs. Driscoll
in the fourth floor office of the Senator—a trip that entailed walking
nearly two city blocks and riding an elevator up three flights. Now,
given a half hour to powder her nose and get ready for an unexpected and unrehearsed appearance, the full-cheeked middle-aged
lady herself faced the interrogators. She was nervous and defensive. Ray Jenkins began the preliminaries, extracting from her the

admission that her work habits included systematic destruction of all her shorthand notebooks—the notebooks that contained the origins of the eleven McCarthy memoranda introduced in evidence. Then Welch bored in, one deft and elegant step at a time.

"Mrs. Driscoll, it is always somewhat awkward and difficult to cross examine a lady," he began, "but I must ask you one or two or perhaps more questions about this file. . . . Will you look at your copies of these memorandums that you have in front of you and, taking the one of October 2, 1953, tell us, if you will, on what machine that was typed?"

The lady replied in a mild southern accent. "I couldn't tell you, I don't know. . . . There is an IBM at my desk now."

"Was there then?"

"I don't recall. I don't know."

"Can't you—the secretaries in our office are very talkative about their typewriters. Don't you know when you got the one you got now?"

"No."

"You don't know how long you have had it?"

"No."

"You can't tell us whether you have had it a month or two or longer than that?"

"No."

"And you don't know, Mrs. Driscoll, what kind of a machine you were using in October 1953?"

"No, Mr. Welch, I don't."

"You have no memory at all?"

"No. A typewriter is a typewriter, and I don't pay any attention to the type of typewriter."

Welch bowed a deep bow. "You are a paragon of virtue. My secretaries are always kicking about them and wanting a new one. You don't pay any attention to them. . . ."

Welch then began to tease Mrs. Driscoll's assertion that she had thrown all eleven of the McCarthy memoranda into one file folder, including the last one, dictated to her by Frank Carr, which contained these words: "Senator McCarthy advised Mr. Seaton that the writer [Carr] was searching the files for memorandums dictated concerning Schine."

"Were you startled," Welch asked her, "when Carr dictated that to you? . . ."

"No."

"Well, did you say to him, 'Mr. Carr, look no further, I have got them all in the slickest little package here you ever saw'?"

"Absolutely not."

"Did you tell him his search was silly? . . ."

"Of course I didn't."

"Well, his search was silly when you had them all together, was it not . . . ?"

"I am not going to tell Mr. Carr that his search was silly or that I have all of them. Maybe I have overlooked one."

"Mrs. Driscoll, it is awfully simple. You had them all together, did you not?"

"Maybe I overlooked one."

McCarthy broke in with cumbersome heaviness. He denounced Welch's "brow beating this young lady. Does someone think this is funny? . . . Mr. Welch, you know this, even in your office you can't months later know just who typed a particular letter."

Welch came back razor-sharp: "Mr. Chairman, I would like to say in my office you bet your life you can, because the dictation marks are right on it as they should be in any workman-like office. . . ." And then he said outright: "I do not wish to conceal from anyone in this room that I have grave suspicions about the authenticity of these memoranda. . . ."

"From the start," James St. Clair recalled years later, "we were convinced the memos were phony. But we couldn't prove they were, at least not in ten-minute segments. We tried like hell, for example, to locate an airplane passenger list to prove McCarthy was on that plane and not where one of the memos said he was. But we couldn't get the list. Of course, there was no jury to convince, only public opinion. And Joe Welch went a long way toward convincing public opinion."

He had indeed. In his gentle, courtly manner, Welch had gone to the absolute verge of demonstrating that Mrs. Driscoll was lying under oath, and that McCarthy and his staff had committed perjury.

Thirty years later—despite Mrs. Driscoll's continuing affirmation of her testimony—the skepticism would be corroborated by the *Chicago Tribune*'s Willard Edwards, a McCarthy staff intimate, who recalled in an interview with me that he had personally seen a half dozen secretaries frantically typing the eleven memoranda—constructed from memory and backdated—in a hideaway office at the Congressional Hotel, and that former FBI agent Frank Carr provided technical advice, warning that the paper used must be of a type in existence at the time of the memos' false dates.

In the same interview Edwards, his memory refreshed by a loose yellowed one-page undated single-spaced typescript for his own files, went on to recall a conversation with a drunk Pentagon lawyer—not Welch, not St. Clair, not John Adams, not Hensel, not Eaton—who claimed at a Georgetown cocktail party some two years after the hearings ended that some of the McCarthy team's forgeries responded to documents forged by the Army.

Edwards himself always refused to print this charge without additional substantiation, which he never got. And he agreed on the flimsiness of the accusation when I informed him of something that his faded memorandum showed he clearly did not know—that the Army never released any documents to anybody before March 12, when McCarthy released his eleven memoranda, and that the Army never used any documents whatsoever to validate its charges publicly.

Driven toward the edge of the cliff, McCarthy again and again tried diversions, wild leaps to different subjects. He took hearing time to denounce Senator Ralph Flanders—"senility or viciousness"—for a speech on the Senate floor that very day—a speech that itself rivaled McCarthy's worst as a smear. McCarthy demanded all major witnesses in the hearings take lie detector tests. He reasserted that the Congress should ignore Eisenhower's secrecy order. And, as he'd done repeatedly, he railed against all this waste of time on one private in the Army while Communists continued their subversion undeterred—for example, in the nation's defense plants.

He had given Welch another opening. On the afternoon of June 2, the sixty-three-year-old lawyer deftly baited McCarthy's earnest young Communist-hunting assistant. Roy Cohn had already under oath denied various charges against him—for example, that he had said, "We will wreck the Army" and "Stevens is through as Secretary of the Army"; that he had exerted improper pressure to get Schine a commission; that he had lost his head when Schine was put on KP; and that he had engaged in vituperation, though he conceded he might at times have used a word he would not use on TV. Now he faced a new thrust of attack.

"Mr. Cohn," Welch began, "what is the exact number of Communists or subversives that are loose today in those defense plants? . . . 130, is that right."

"Yes sir. I am going to try to particularize for you, if I can."

Welch cut him off. "I am in a hurry. I don't want the sun to go down while they are still in there, if we can get them out."

"I am afraid we won't be able to work that fast, sir."

"I have a suggestion about it, sir. How many are there?"

"I believe the figure is approximately 130. . . . Those are people, Mr. Welch—"

Welch once again cut in with mock impatience: "I don't care. You told us who they are. In how many plants are they?"

". . . I see 16 offhand, sir."

"Sixteen plants?"

"Yes sir."

"Where are they, sir? . . . Reel off the cities."

Cohn swiftly went down the list, ending: "Cambridge, Mass.; New Bedford, Mass.; Boston, Mass.; Quincy, Mass.; Lynn, Mass.; Pittsfield, Mass.; Boston, Mass."

Welch found the opportunity irresistible: "Mr. Cohn, you not only frighten me, you make me ashamed when there are so many in Massachusetts." The audience laughed. Welch silenced them with mock seriousness: "This is not a laughing matter, believe me. Are you alarmed at that situation, Mr. Cohn?"

"Yes sir; I am."

"Nothing could be more alarming, could it?"

Cohn had to concur: "It certainly is a very alarming thing."

Welch came to the natural conclusion: "Will you not, before the sun goes down, give those names to the FBI and at least have those men put under surveillance?"

McCarthy rode to the rescue: "Mr. Chairman, let's not be ridiculous. Mr. Welch knows, as I have told him a dozen times, that the FBI has all of this information. The defense plants have the information. The only thing we can do is to try and publicly expose these individuals and hope that they will be gotten rid of. And you know that, Mr. Welch."

Welch refused to be ruffled by this dark roll of thunder. "I do not know that." He turned back to Cohn. "Mr. Cohn, do you mean to tell us that J. Edgar Hoover and the FBI know the names of these men and are doing nothing about them?"

"No sir. . . ."

"Do you mean to tell us they are doing something about them?"

"Yes sir."

"What are they doing about them?"

372 | William Ewald, Jr.

Cohn returned a plausible answer: "They notify the Defense Department. . . . All the FBI can do is give the information. Their power ends right there."

"Cannot the FBI put these 130 men under surveillance before sundown tomorrow?"

"Sir, if there is need for surveillance in the case of espionage or anything like that, I can well assure you that Mr. John Edgar Hoover and his men know a lot better than I. . . . I do not propose to tell the FBI how to run its shop. It does it very well."

". . . Are you sure they know every one of them?"

"I would take an oath on it, sir. . . ."

Welch sprang the trap: "That being true, Mr. Cohn, can you and I both rest easy tonight? . . . If the FBI has got a firm grasp on these 130 men, I will go to sleep. . . ."

McCarthy came booming in, ranting about Alger Hiss, Harry Dexter White and other traitors, reiterating the limitations on the power of the FBI.

Welch picked up the theme: "Well, Mr. Chairman, my confidence in the FBI is simply limitless, and I think Mr. Cohn's confidence is similar; is that right, sir?"

Cohn could only part company with McCarthy: "Yes sir; that is right."

"All I am suggesting," Welch continued puckishly, "is that we just nudge them a little and be sure they are busy on these 130. Would you mind helping nudge them?"

Cohn balked, trying to retain his balance: "Sir, you do not have to nudge the FBI about this or about anything else."

"Then they have got the whole 130, have they, Mr. Cohn?"

"I am sure of it, sir. . . ."

"Then what is all the excitement about, if J. Edgar Hoover is on the job chasing these 130 Communists?"

Once again, with folksy humor, Welch had appropriated the FBI to the Army and the Administration. And that same day in a news conference the President was underscoring the liaison, putting out Justice Department statistics on security risks routed, reporting on the results of the administration's antisubversion program, masterminded by Hoover and his forces in the Bureau.

At six thirty-five that evening the phone rang in Fred Seaton's office. His aide Phil Mullin picked it up. Mrs. Driscoll was calling. McCarthy's beleaguered secretary had a proposition: The next day during the noon recess, McCarthy would meet with Seaton or his designee and "discuss in some detail" information the Defense Department probably didn't have on Communists in defense plants.

Mullin took the message down. But Fred didn't rush to accept. ("He was a smoothie. *He* would never have gone to a fried chicken lunch.") Instead there followed thrust and counterthrust phone calls between Seaton and McCarthy, with Mrs. Driscoll sometimes in the middle (on his side Seaton would at times have Mullin get the Senator to the phone; he didn't want "Seaton-is-calling" messages floating around the hearing room). McCarthy made adulatory comments on nationwide TV about Seaton's sterling anticommunism. And the wily Assistant Secretary wrote the Senator an exquisitely fly-specked letter: The Pentagon, he said, of course wanted to receive such information, and fast; Seaton would meet with McCarthy for this purpose with—as the Senator had later suggested—a stenographic reporter present; but the Pentagon would not agree in advance, as McCarthy insisted and as his subcommittee rules required, to keep the names secret. "The Department," Seaton wrote, "must be free to act without consulting you." Impasse.

For many weeks those monitored phone calls had been inching their way through the underground pipeline. Before the hearings even began, Jenkins and Welch had conferred on their introduction. They had been subpoenaed on April 22. From the start McCarthy had insisted that all of them, including those within the executive branch, go into evidence, or none. Welch had agreed to the introduction of all relevant information; he and St. Clair had no strategy either to force or to bar the admission of the Army's documents. But by May 17 the transcripts had not yet been delivered. Then came the President's directive, slamming down the portcullis.

On May 22, out of the mass of impounded records now locked up within the iron fence of the White House, White House Staff Secretary General Paul T. Carroll had turned back to Fred Seaton a single folder of documents the President specifically had declined to withhold—the transcripts of phone conversations between Stevens or Adams on one side, and committee senators or staff (Cohn and Carr) on the other. And at last the tedious process of reading them into the hearing record began. The monitors took the stand—first Jack Lucas, then Jane Pike, then Ted Rhodes, then Eleanor Glancy, followed by a group of lesser stenographic fry. One by one they read—or heard and corroborated Jenkins as he read—each document.

And as the intoning of the conversations began—Dirksen's,

Mundt's, McClellan's—the remaining impounded documents went back from the White House to the Pentagon, specifically to the office of Fred Seaton, designated by Governor Adams as the President's representative for their custody. Thereafter nobody saw them. Even John Adams on May 28 had pleaded in vain with Struve Hensel to get returned to him some of the documents he had surrendered, including several of his memoranda to Stevens, his original chronology, and all the monitored phone calls he'd had with his boss.

The impounders had moved with dispatch and secrecy and effect. The long contemporaneous record—day by day, minute by minute—of the Army's fecklessness and compliance—a record that took the edge off the stridency of their charges and undercut many assertions in Stevens's testimony—this record would remain sealed. It had been sealed by an accident, the happenstance result of a presidential directive designed in the Justice Department by officials who had no inkling of the details of the evidence they were shutting out.

The portcullis had in truth slammed down, and it had slammed down just in time for the Army. McCarthy was pursuing the scent. While Jack Lucas testified, McCarthy and Cohn explored the existence of other Stevens's calls—to Hensel and Rogers and Brownell and the men in the White House.

In the transcripts that were now entering the hearing record, McCarthy saw another opening, and he rushed into it. Symington, he declared, should disqualify himself because of his now-revealed complicity in trying to help Stevens—help him in conspiracy with Clark Clifford, Truman Democrat. McCarthy and Symington had been caterwauling at each other for weeks. Now the cold fury between the two became a blaze of enmity. To the man from Wisconsin, the distinguished gentleman from Missouri became "Sanctimonious Stu."

Cohn continued to testify, all seriousness. Welch continued to question, with occasional flippancy. He labeled Irving Peress as a "no good Communist," a dentist who drills Communism into patients. Welch compelled the earnest young witness to admit that the Army, Navy, and Air Force were "wonderful"; ready to fight Communists on land, on sea, and in the air. He baited him on the eleven memos. He baited him on the Communists in defense plants. He baited him on the desperate need for speed in rooting out traitors in this time of national peril: "May I add my small voice, sir,"

Welch concluded in mock serious tones, "and say whenever you know about a subversive or a Communist or a spy, please hurry. Will you remember those words?"

McCarthy could stand no more. Suddenly he broke in with a climactic and fatal rejoinder: "In view of Mr. Welch's request that the information be given once we know of anyone who might be performing any work for the Communist Party, I think we should tell him that he has in his law firm a young man named Fisher whom he recommended, incidentally, to do work on this committee, who has been for a number of years a member of an organization which was named, oh, years and years ago, as the legal bullwork of the Communist Party, an organization which always swings to the defense [sic] of anyone who dares to expose Communists.

"I certainly assume that Mr. Welch did not know of this young man at the time he recommended him as the Assistant Counsel for this committee, but he has such terror and such a great desire to know where anyone is located who may be serving the Communist cause, Mr. Welch, that I thought we should just call to your attention the fact that your Mr. Fisher, who is still in your law firm today, whom you asked to have down here looking over . . . secret and classified material, is a member of an organization, not named by me but named by various committees, named by the Attorney General, as I recall, . . . as 'the legal bullwork of the Communist Party.' He belonged to that for a sizeable number of years, according to his own admission, and he belonged to it long after it had been exposed as the legal arm of the Communist Party.

"Knowing that, Mr. Welch, I just felt that I had a duty to respond to your urgent request that before sundown, when we know of anyone serving the Communist cause, we let the agency know. We are now letting you know that your man did belong to this organization for either three or four years, belonged to it long after he was out of law school. . . .

"I have hesitated bringing that up, but I have been rather bored with your phony requests to Mr. Cohn here that he personally get every Communist out of government before sundown. Therefore, we will give you information about the young man in your own organization.

"I am not asking you at this time to explain why you tried to foist him on this committee. Whether you knew he was a member of that Communist organization or not, I don't know. I assume you did not, Mr. Welch, because I get the impression that while you are quite an actor, you play for a laugh, I don't think you have any conception of the danger of the Communist Party. I don't think you yourself would ever knowingly aid the Communist cause. I think you are unknowingly aiding it when you try to burlesque this hearing in which we are attempting to bring out the facts, however."

The onslaught, the torrent of twisted words, caught Welch and St. Clair by complete surprise. The fact of Frederick Fisher's National Lawyers Guild membership had for nearly two months rested unnoticed in the public record, first in newspaper accounts of Welch's April 15 press conference about Fisher's separation from the Army's defense, then in McCarthy's April 20 formal charges. (The additional fact of Fisher's organizing activity with Greenberg which had decided Hagerty's vote to dismiss him—that fact had never come out, and McCarthy undoubtedly did not know it.) In James St. Clair's recollection, there had never been, as Roy Cohn has claimed, and John Adams surmised, a deal—a flat quid-pro-quo agreement—that if McCarthy's side would not mention Fisher, the Army would not delve publicly into allegations, which Cohn denied, that Cohn had tried to dodge the draft during and after the war. There was simply, on the Army's side, a self-imposed decision to eschew the subject of Cohn's draft status (as they eschewed the subject of McCarthy's alleged sexual deviation, including a bizarre lead slipped secretly by a respected congressman to Welch one evening in the Pentagon massage room); and the expectation that because the subject of Fisher had already come up and receded twice, it would not come up again.

For weeks, indiscriminately, McCarthy had been laying about him, sporadically slashing not only at Joe Alsop and the *New York Post* and the *New York Times* and the *Washington Post* and Eisenhower and Brownell, but also at Symington and McClellan and Dworshak and Ray Jenkins—nearly everybody but J. Edgar Hoover.

Welch had cudgeled no one. He'd been courteous, even courtly, to everyone, from the hapless Mrs. Driscoll to Roy Cohn to McCarthy himself. He had endeared himself to millions watching television as he had to a shy young Pentagon receptionist who once asked how he felt after a long, wearing day. "I'm so glad you asked me," Welch replied. "I feel *wonderful.*"

McCarthy had squandered his right to aggressive attack. Welch had left his untouched. But now in a single instant Welch would expend it all.

"Mr. Chairman, under the circumstances I must have something approaching a personal privilege."

Mundt granted Welch's request.

"Senator McCarthy, I did not know—" Welch began. Then he stopped. McCarthy was looking elsewhere, pretending to have something more urgent on his mind.

"Senator," Welch continued, graciously reminding his antagonist of his many and repeated interruptions, "sometimes you say, 'may I have your attention?'"

"I am listening to you," McCarthy replied. "I can listen with one ear."

Welch riveted him. "This time I want you to listen with both."

"Yes."

Welch began again: "Senator McCarthy, I think until this moment—"

McCarthy curtly cut him off with an order to his aide Juliana: "Jim, will you get the news story to the effect that this man belonged to this Communist-front organization? Will you get the citation showing that this was the legal arm of the Communist Party, and the length of time that he belonged, and the fact that he was recommended by Mr. Welch? I think that should be in the record."

Welch swept the diversion off the board. "You won't need anything in the record when I have finished telling you this.

"Until this moment, Senator, I think I never really gauged your cruelty or your recklessness. Fred Fisher is a young man who went to the Harvard Law School and came into my firm and is starting what looks to be a brilliant career with us.

"When I decided to work for this committee, I asked Jim St. Clair, who sits on my right, to be my first assistant. I said to Jim, 'Pick somebody in the firm who works under you that you would like.' He chose Fred Fisher, and they came down on an afternoon plane. That night, when he had taken a little stab at trying to see what the case was about, Fred Fisher and Jim St. Clair and I went to dinner together. I then said to these two young men, 'Boys, I don't know anything about you except I have always liked you, but if there is anything funny in the life of either one of you that would hurt anybody in this case, you speak up quick.'

"Fred Fisher said, 'Mr. Welch, when I was in law school and for a period of months after, I belonged to the Lawyers Guild,' as you have suggested, Senator. He went on to say, 'I am Secretary of the

Young Republicans League in Newton with the son of Massachusetts' Governor, and I have the respect and admiration of my community and I am sure I have the respect and admiration of the twenty-five lawyers or so in Hale and Dorr.'

"I said, 'Fred, I just don't think I am going to ask you to work on the case. If I do, one of these days that will come out and go over national television, and it will just hurt like the dickens.'

"So, Senator, I asked him to go back to Boston.

"Little did I dream that you could be so reckless and so cruel as to do an injury to that lad. It is true he is still with Hale and Dorr. It is true that he will continue to be with Hale and Dorr. It is, I regret to say, equally true that I fear he shall always bear a scar needlessly inflicted by you. If it were in my power to forgive you for your reckless cruelty, I would do so. I like to think I am a gentleman, but your forgiveness will have to come from someone other than me."

McCarthy had no comprehension of what was happening. As the nation watched horrified, he went crashing ahead, denouncing Welch for baiting Cohn hour after hour, insisting on reading facts about Fisher into the record.

Welch cut him short: "Senator, may we not drop this? We know he belonged to the Lawyers Guild, and Mr. Cohn nods his head at me."

The gesture introduced the final severing by the scalpel: "I did you, I think, no personal injury, Mr. Cohn."

"No, sir."

Welch sealed the assent with a gesture of magnanimity: "I meant to do you no personal injury, and if I did, I beg your pardon."

Then with two lightning rapier strokes, he turned back to the Senator: "Let us not assassinate this lad further, Senator. You have done enough. Have you no sense of decency, sir, at long last? Have you left no sense of decency?"

At that electric moment, blinding in its brilliance, McCarthy stood at bay, alone, all all alone—without even the ashen-faced Roy Cohn—a man in total isolation from all things true, just, worthy, and of good report.

Epilogue

WHO KILLED JOE McCARTHY?

The Eisenhower strategy against McCarthy was a strategy, exactly, to produce impotent isolation.

It was not a strategy that turned on McCarthy's issue of anticommunism. McCarthy and Eisenhower and indeed most of the American people—given the evidence—saw the possibility of domestic Communist subversion as a significant problem. They saw it as a problem in 1948 with the indictment of Alger Hiss; in 1950 with the revelation of the espionage of physicist Klaus Fuchs; in 1951 with the conviction of Julius and Ethel Rosenberg; in 1952 when Eisenhower won in a landslide as a man who would clean up all the messes—including this one—in Washington.

And they saw it as a continuing problem in the late spring of 1954. In one study made during and just after the Army-McCarthy hearings, only 7 percent of those polled said they believed no Communists remained in government; and only 2 percent said they would consider Communists in government no threat whatsoever. "Could the President," Governor Sherman Adams asked reflectively years later, "have convinced the American people that all of McCarthy's allegations were frauds? I doubt it."

The Eisenhower strategy against McCarthy was thus not a strategy of flat denial of the existence of a problem of internal subversion. It was a strategy of detachment—of separating the decent anti-Communist centrist followers from their indecent anti-Communist leader. It was a strategy that paralleled the one Eisenhower had been following for more than a year in his attempt to get legislation through the Senate—the strategy, he confided to his diary on April 1, 1953, of winning "away from the McCarthy-Malone axis about five or six of their members," and thus reducing the "splinter group . . . to impotence." By June of 1954, less than a year and a half after Ei-

379

senhower entered office, that anti-McCarthy strategy of isolation had largely succeeded.

The hearings ground on. McCarthy himself took the stand. He denied he had ever sought favors for Schine. He dug in stubbornly as Senator Scoop Jackson of Washington, prompted by Bob Kennedy, ridiculed a sweeping psychological warfare plan of David Schine, a ridiculing that brought Cohn and Kennedy to a near fistfight right there in the conference room. And to the end McCarthy maintained he had, sitting in New York City, dictated a memo to Cohn and Carr, also in New York City, by long distance telephone to his secretary Mrs. Driscoll, in Washington.

Frank Carr took the stand. Under avid grilling, he affirmed and reaffirmed the authenticity of McCarthy's eleven memoranda. He had indeed, he said, taken an elevator up three flights from his first-floor office to dictate to Mrs. Driscoll on the fourth floor. He had indeed in one memo, he claimed, said that John Adams "came *down* [italics added] here" to Senate Office Building Room 101, though Carr was allegedly dictating in Mrs. Driscoll's office upstairs. McCarthy had one last name-calling clash with Senator Symington, and he had also one last round of wildly sprayed threats to probe the CIA, the Loyalty Security Board malefactors, and the perpetrators of the promotion of Peress. Then on June 17, at 6:32 P.M., after seventy-one half-day sessions, two million words of testimony, thirty-two witnesses, 187 hours of television time, and more than 100 thousand live attendees, the hearings sputtered to an end.

Still fuming with purple indignation on the sidelines, Struve Hensel finally filed with the committee and then made public on June 20 his affidavit refuting in toto McCarthy's accusations against him. Hensel revealed McCarthy's admission in the May 17 executive session of the committee that he had no evidence whatsoever for his charge that Hensel had masterminded the Army attack in order to stop McCarthy's investigation of Hensel himself. He revealed McCarthy's offer to withdraw all his accusations against Hensel if in doing so he would not appear to be a "damn fool." And he revealed McCarthy's kick-below-the-belt Indian Charlie story.

On June 18, Welch and St. Clair for the first time went to the White House. "The President," Jim Hagerty wrote in his diary, "congratulated Welch for a very fine job. Welch told the President that he thought that if the hearings had accomplished nothing else, the Army had been able to keep McCarthy in front of the television sets for quite a while, long enough to permit the public to see how disgracefully he acted. He said he was sure this would be helpful in the long run. The President agreed with him. . . ." A few days later, on the evening of Friday, June 25, White House Chief-of-Staff Sherman Adams arrived at the home of Fred Seaton for a relaxed buffet supper of the Friendly Sons and Daughters of Franklin Pierce.

The attention of the nation, held mesmerized all those weeks by the spectacle on the tube, began to turn elsewhere. By late August and early September the Congress at last was passing Eisenhower's legislative requests—the biggest volume in his entire eight years. By October the President was campaigning coast to coast for the election of Republican senators and congressmen, campaigning on a scale and with an intensity unmatched by any other President in American history in an off-year election. By November, though the Republicans lost control of the Senate and House, they lost it by an eyelash, in an election in which the issues of McCarthy and McCarthyism and domestic communism had virtually disappeared.

Finally, on December 2, in response to a resolution introduced by Ralph Flanders of Vermont and reported out by a committee headed by conservative Republican Arthur V. Watkins of Utah, the United States Senate—in the third such action in its entire 165 years—voted to condemn McCarthy for "conduct contrary to Senatorial traditions." The vote was 67–22 (all the negative votes were Republicans, including majority leader William Knowland). The conduct condemned was McCarthy's abuse of a Senate subcommittee on privileges and elections that had been looking into his financial activities; and his abuse of the Watkins censure committee itself—a committee McCarthy had branded the "unwitting handmaiden" of the Communist party. These Senate charges had no direct connection whatsoever with the Army-McCarthy controversy. Two days after the censure vote, Eisenhower invited Chairman Watkins to the White House and—in words eagerly released to the press by Jim Hagerty—praised him for "a very splendid job."

So Joseph McCarthy, senator from Wisconsin, was politically dead. He had been brought down by many people and many forces, including the force of fortuitous accident. But above all he had been defeated by Dwight Eisenhower.

It is wrong, of course, to ascribe the political demise of McCarthy to a grand strategy furtively and flawlessly masterminded in the Oval Office by Eisenhower himself. The President had no master plan, no week-by-week, month-by-month blueprint for carefully controlled action. After the McCarthy browbeating of Zwicker, for example, while one of his top lieutenants—Cabot Lodge—was urging, with the President's enthusiastic approval, a fighting denunciation by Stevens in an open hearing, another top Eisenhower lieutenant— Jerry Persons—was setting up the fried chicken lunch. Eisenhower did not convene, with keen foresight, the January 21 meeting in Brownell's office; he did not order the writing of the Adams chronology; he did not supervise its leakage to the press to put McCarthy on the defensive; and he did not plan the hearings as a means of exposing the loathsome foe to the TV viewing public, thus destroying him. Indeed, Eisenhower expected the hearings to last only a few days. And at the end of the first week, disgusted, he wanted them stopped.

Moreover, Eisenhower did not issue his May 17 directive to Charlie Wilson as a grand stroke to help the Army in its argumentation with McCarthy. Welch and St. Clair had no idea the directive was coming. In complete independence and isolation, Herbert Brownell and Bill Rogers had devised it as a constitutional answer to a constitutional problem. The time had come, in their view and that of the President, to shut off an endless trail of inquiry which was beginning to lead away from the Pentagon and into the Justice Department and the White House.

Eisenhower, nevertheless, did win. He won because, first, he and his administration took the anti-Communist issue away from McCarthy. Truman had tried to do the same thing. He had established an elaborate mechanism of boards to test and decide the loyalty of government employees. Some of the most conspicuous departures from the State Department—particularly among the old China hands—occurred not under Eisenhower and Dulles but under Truman and Acheson. For example, by the time Eisenhower took over, O. Edmund Clubb had left. So had the first of the three Johns—John Stewart Service. A second John, John Carter Vincent, had been looked into again and again and again. Perhaps, if Acheson had remained Secretary of State, Vincent would have been cleared. Perhaps he would have been found, once again, a man of dubious loyalty. In any event, Foster Dulles permitted him to resign with a full pension, and McCarthy howled. The third John, John Paton Davies, did depart in 1954, two years into Dulles's term as Secretary of State, but only after Dulles had taken a searing from McCarthy on nationwide television for having kept this perfidious holdover so long.

But despite his loyalty apparatus, Truman had failed to appropriate the antisubversion issue. By the time Truman left office, despite the State Department purges, McCarthy as a symbol of anti-Communist cleanup was galloping faster than ever. In contrast to Truman, Eisenhower succeeded. By the time the hearings ended, Eisenhower had on his side of the sharp line separating him from McCarthy the three most salient anti-Communists in America: Richard Nixon, who had got Alger Hiss; Herbert Brownell, who had devised the administration's toughened loyalty-security procedures and exposed Harry Dexter White; and the greatest prize of all, J. Edgar Hoover. All three had declared themselves, in the spotlight of public attention, allies of the President.

Eisenhower won, next, because he never engaged in a personal vituperative attack on McCarthy as an individual, which might have swelled McCarthy's press coverage and forced his followers to rally behind a man they saw as a martyr. Truman and Acheson had engaged in such personal attack. And after three long years, they had helped produce millions of words for McCarthy in headlines and front-page news. And the more they tried to slug it out, the more suspicion of stonewalling and complicity they brought down on their own heads, the more inviting targets of attack they became, and the more lustily the demagogue's followers would bellow: "McCarthy is my leader, I shall not be moved. . . ." Ike from the start saw this trap and evaded it. "I really believe," he wrote in his diary April 1, 1953, "that nothing will be so effective in combatting [McCarthy's] particular kind of troublemaking as to ignore him. This he cannot stand."

Eisenhower won, further, because he never engaged in an attack on McCarthy as a member of Congress, thus forcing senators and representatives—ever touchy about their powers in an independent branch of government—to coalesce in an institutional defense of an injured fellow member. Though at least one citizen wrote in urging Eisenhower to "fire McCarthy," Eisenhower could not. He could not deprive a congressional committee of its constitutional right to investigate the executive branch. He could insist on a measure of courtesy. But he had no power to stop vigorous inquiry. "Only the United States Senate," the President told his brother Milton, "can deal with McCarthy." And "only the people of Wisconsin," he told Jim Hagerty, "can get rid of him."

Given these limitations, Eisenhower won because through a devoted, canny, and streetwise organization—notably Sherman Adams, Jim Hagerty, Struve Hensel, and Fred Seaton, an organization that forthrightly improvised much of its own way—he chipped and sliced and cut at the detested foe until the combined forces—including, memorably, the forces of Justice under Brownell and Rogers—finally brought him down.

As this process came to its climax, Eisenhower won because his cohorts, most visible on nationwide television, became convincing and believable symbols of simple human decency. By the time the hearings ended, the American people had indelibly in their consciousness the stark distinction between Stevens (patently honest, bumbling, good-hearted, guileless), John Adams (meticulous with fact, scrupulous, sincere, impressive in testimony) and, supremely, Joe Welch (dapper, courtly, and kind), and the barracudas ranged against them, from McCarthy and Cohn to the back-room boys with their cropped photos and their memos of questionable authenticity.

And Eisenhower won, above all, because he constantly held up before his fellow countrymen a standard to which—in the words of his great hero, George Washington—wise and good men, weary of niggling negative controversy, could repair: a standard of abstract principles of freedom of the mind, fidelity to the Constitution, fair play, honesty, magnanimity; of legislation to be passed and work to be done to move the country forward.

"The militarists in Berlin, Rome and Tokyo started this war," Franklin Roosevelt declared in a magnificent utterance at the heart of the great worldwide conflict, "but the massed, angered forces of common humanity will finish it." Led by the President of the United States, the massive awakened forces of common humanity also ended McCarthyism.

The curtain descended. The principal actors drifted away. First John Adams, then Robert Stevens—after decent intervals and appropriate kind words of farewell—left the Department of the Army. Stevens returned to his business, his ranch, and relative obscurity; Adams to difficult years in the private practice of law in Washington, then to a staff job and ultimately to board membership at the CAB, where, as a quirk of fate would have it, he found himself a colleague of G. Joseph Minetti, the second husband of the widow of Joe McCarthy.

Others returned to the practice of law: in Washington, Struve Hensel; in New York City, Roy Cohn, Herbert Brownell, and William Rogers (who in 1969 became Richard Nixon's Secretary of

State); and in Boston, Joseph Welch and James St. Clair (the latter of whom served as counsel to President Richard Nixon during the Watergate crisis in 1974).

Two men made a name for themselves in the movies: Joe Welch, who in 1959 starred in *Anatomy of a Murder* with Jimmy Stewart and Lee Remick; and G. David Schine, who among his other considerable business interests became "producer" of a highly meritorious film called *The French Connection*.

And three went home to the news media: C. D. Jackson, who returned to the Luce publishing empire; Jim Hagerty, who, after serving out Eisenhower's entire administration as Press Secretary, became a Vice President of ABC; and Fred Seaton, who went back to the Seaton newspapers and broadcasting stations headquartered in Hastings, Nebraska.

The wheels of governmental process continued to turn. All thirty-three suspended Fort Monmouth employees were cleared and reinstated, twenty-five of them through the workings of the Army's security system; among others, Aaron Coleman—like discharged State Department China expert John Stewart Service—had to win his vindication in court. The animosities began to diminish. Roy Cohn dedicated a book to Joseph Welch. Colonel Ken BeLieu, who rose to the post of Under Secretary of the Navy under Lyndon Johnson and Under Secretary of the Army under Richard Nixon, became a good friend of McCarthy staffer Jim Juliana, who left the government but stayed on in Washington. Even Joe McCarthy, in his last years of decline, alcoholism, and press neglect before his death in 1957, made awkward attempts at reconciliation with Stuart Symington and John Adams.

Many of the central characters are dead: Eisenhower, McCarthy, Stevens, Seaton, Hagerty, Persons, Morgan, Martin, C. D. Jackson, Welch, Jenkins, Dirksen (who did indeed eventually become Eisenhower's knight in armor in the Senate), McClellan, Mundt, Henry Jackson.

But for those still alive—Sherman Adams at his New Hampshire ski resort, Brownell, Rogers, St. Clair, BeLieu, John Adams—the memory of those days remains forever vibrant. Like Struve Hensel—pugnacious and combative as ever—they will always be proud they fought the good fight.

Sources and Acknowledgments

I have used three types of sources:

(1) *Unpublished papers: e.g.*, transcripts and records of telephone conversations, memoranda for the record, diary entries, minutes of meetings, memoranda from one person to another, letters, records of appointments. Because these documents themselves play a central part in the story, they are ordinarily identifiable in the text by writer or speaker, person written or spoken to, date, and frequently hour and minute.

These papers reside principally in the Dwight D. Eisenhower Library in Abilene, Kansas, which houses the files of Fred Seaton, including the impounded Pentagon documents; of President Eisenhower, Jim Hagerty, and C. D. Jackson. I have also drawn on other repositories: the files of the Department of the Army in the National Archives; the files of the Department of Justice, particularly the Federal Bureau of Investigation; and the papers of Sherman Adams in the Baker Library of Dartmouth College, of John Foster Dulles and Arthur Krock in the Mudd Library of Princeton University, of Karl Mundt in the Karl E. Mundt Library of Dakota State College, and of Elmer Davis and Robert A. Taft in the Library of Congress. From Frederick Eaton, Willard Edwards, Frederick Fisher, Robert S. Kieve, and Bernard M. Shanley, I have received copies of manuscripts in their own possession.

To all the custodians of all these collections, particularly the Eisenhower Library, my warm thanks for their generosity and help. My special thanks to Senator Ted Stevens. My thanks also to David C. Acheson, John S. D. Eisenhower, Milton S. Eisenhower, Mrs. C. D. Jackson, Robert S. Kieve, Bernard Shanley, Robert A. Taft, Jr., and Mrs. Eugene Wilson for permission to use direct quotations.

(2) *Interviews:* with John G. Adams, Sherman Adams, Kenneth BeLieu, Herbert Brownell, Violet Bryan, Mrs. Prescott H. Bush, Sr., Lucius Clay, Charles Corddry, Edwin Darby, Frederick Eaton, Willard Edwards, Milton Eisenhower, John Finney, James R. Franklin, Jack Garrabrant, Arthur Hadley, Jim Hagerty, Marjorie Hagerty, Bryce Harlow, Gabriel Hauge, H. Struve Hensel, Isabel Hensel, Robert Humphreys, Peter Kohler, Arthur Larson, Henry Cabot Lodge, John J. Lucas, Jr., Kevin McCann, Barbara Martin, Robert Montgomery, Gerald D. Morgan, Philip J. Mullin, Mary Nelson, Philip Potter, J. Lee Rankin, William P. Rogers, James D. St. Clair, C. Herschel Schooley, Fred A. Seaton, Gladys Seaton, Bernard Shanley, Betty Snyder, Mary Caffrey Stephens, Thomas E. Stephens, Stuyvesant Wainwright, Abbott Washburn, and one who wishes to remain anonymous. I have supplemented these inter-

views of my own with a number of oral history interviews, with Sherman Adams, Thomas E. Dewey, Milton Eisenhower, Gabriel Hauge, William F. Knowland, Walter Kohler, and Wilton B. Persons. For access to these and permission to quote I extend my thanks to the staff of the Oral History Research Office of Columbia University and to Sherman Adams, R. Burdell Bixby, Milton Eisenhower, Mrs. Gabriel Hauge, and the Trustees of Columbia University.

To distinguish these sources from the contemporaneous records, I have ordinarily identified interviews in the text by speaker and by mention of the fact that he is engaging in recollection "years later."

(3) *Published writings,* including: John G. Adams, *Without Precedent: The Story of the Death of McCarthyism* (New York: Norton, 1983); Sherman Adams, *Firsthand Report* (New York: Harper, 1961); Edwin R. Bayley, *Joe McCarthy and the Press* (Madison: University of Wisconsin Press, 1981); Charles E. Bohlen, *Witness to History* (New York: Norton, 1973); Roy M. Cohn, *McCarthy* (New York: New American Library, 1968); Robert Cutler, *No Time for Rest* (Boston: Atlantic-Little Brown, 1965); Elmer J. Davis, *But We Were Born Free* (Indianapolis: Bobbs-Merrill, 1954); Ovid Demaris, *The Director: An Oral Biography of J. Edgar Hoover* (New York: Harper's Magazine Press, 1975); Robert J. Donovan, *Eisenhower: The Inside Story* (New York: Harper, 1956), *Tumultuous Years: The Presidency of Harry S. Truman, 1949–53* (New York: Norton, 1982); Dwight D. Eisenhower, *At Ease: Stories I Tell to Friends* (Garden City, N.Y.: Doubleday, 1967), *Mandate for Change* (Garden City, N.Y.: Doubleday, 1963); Robert H. Ferrell, ed., *The Eisenhower Diaries* (New York: Norton, 1981); *The Gallup Poll, 1953–71,* II (New York: Random House, 1971); Fred I. Greenstein, *The Hidden-Hand Presidency: Eisenhower as a Leader* (New York: Basic Books, 1982); Robert Griffith, *The Politics of Fear* (Lexington: University Press of Kentucky, 1970); Townsend Hoopes, *The Devil and John Foster Dulles* (Boston: Atlantic-Little Brown, 1973); Emmet John Hughes, *The Living Presidency* (New York: Coward, McCann and Geoghegan, 1972), *The Ordeal of Power: a Political Memoir of the Eisenhower Years* (New York: Athenuem, 1963); Ray H. Jenkins, *The Terror of Tellico Plains* (Knoxville: East Tennessee Historical Society, 1978); Arthur Krock, *Memoirs: Sixty Years on the Firing Line* (New York: Funk and Wagnalls, 1968); Earl Latham, *Communist Controversy in Washington: From the New Deal to McCarthy* (New York: Atheneum, 1969); Bill (William H.) Lawrence, *Six Presidents, Too Many Wars* (New York: Saturday Review Press, 1972); Henry Cabot Lodge, *As It Was* (New York: Norton, 1976), *The Storm Has Many Eyes* (New York: Norton, 1973); Gary May, *China Scapegoat: The Diplomatic Ordeal of John Carter Vincent* (New York: New Republic Books, 1979); Richard Nixon, *RN: The Memoirs of Richard Nixon* (New York: Grosset and Dunlap, 1978); David M. Oshinsky, *A Conspiracy So Immense: The World of Joe McCarthy* (New York: Free Press, 1983); James T. Patterson, *Mr. Republican: A Biography of Robert A. Taft* (Boston: Houghton Mifflin, 1972); Charles E. Potter, *Days of Shame* (New York: Coward-McCann, 1965); *Public Papers of the Presidents of the United States,* vols. 1953, 1954 (Washington, D.C.: U.S. Government Printing Office); Thomas C. Reeves, *The Life and Times of Joe McCarthy* (New York: Stein and Day, 1982); Richard Rovere, *Senator Joe McCarthy* (New York: Harcourt Brace, 1959); Arthur M. Schlesinger, Jr., *Robert Kennedy and His Times* (Boston: Houghton Mifflin, 1978); Michael Straight, *Trial by Television* (Boston: Beacon Press, 1954); William C. Sullivan, *The Bureau: My Thirty Years in Hoover's FBI* (New York: Norton, 1979); Harry S. Truman, *Years of Trial and Hope* (Garden City, N.Y.: Doubleday, 1956); U.S.

Senate (Eighty-third Congress), Permanent Subcommittee on Investigations and Special Subcommittee on Investigations of the Committee on Government Operations: Hearings and Reports, 1953–54.

For access to these publications I thank the staffs of the libraries of George Washington University, Harvard University, the State University of New York at Purchase, and Yale University; and of the Greenwich Library.

I extend warm appreciation to two men of impressive professional distinction—Knox Burger, agent, and Herman Gollob, editor. I am endlessly grateful for their association with this book.

I add my thanks to Marie Eimmerman, who typed every word of a difficult manuscript with great rapidity and skill.

And I close with my gratitude to my closest collaborators—my own family. Our three sons—Dr. William Bragg Ewald III, Charles Ross Ewald, and Thomas Hart Benton Ewald—made valuable suggestions all along the way, and Tom in addition undertook some particularly demanding clerical work.

My wife, Dr. Mary T. Ewald, contributed more than anyone in thought, word, and deed from the beginning to the end. And to her, as always, the book is dedicated.

Greenwich, Connecticut
October 12, 1983

Index

Acheson, Dean, 19, 21–25, 53, 56, 73, 122–23, 133, 382, 383

Adams, John G., 99, 119, 134, 158, 162, 174, 183, 202, 208, 236, 254, 256, 281, 288, 289, 294, 346, 348, 361, 374, 384, 385; appointed Army counselor, 83–85; in Army defense, 292, 296–97, 316; in Army-McCarthy hearings, 300, 306, 315, 318, 320, 323, 327, 328, 331–32, 336, 342, 344, 347–54, 356, 358–59, 362–63, 373, 376, 380; background of, 96–97; Brownell's views on, 297; Carr's relationship with, 223, 239–40, 244–45, 255, 336; chronology leaked by, 232, 277–78; chronology written by, 176–87, 215, 222–223, 229, 232, 234–35, 248–50, 253, 256, 257–60, 277, 307, 382; Cohn's threats and accusations against, 156–57, 173, 198, 217–18, 282–83, 348; diminishing influence of, 297, 319; ejection of, from McCarthy hearing, 194, 196, 205; in Fort Monmouth investigation, 91, 93–96, 126–31, 156; at Justice Department meeting (January 21, 1954), 171–72, 350; in Lawton controversy, 135; in loyalty boards dispute, 102, 154–55, 166–67; McCarthy memos reviewed by, 279–83; McCarthy subcommittee members and, 197–99; at Pentagon luncheon (November 6, 1953), 119, 257–58, 263–64; in Peress controversy, 188, 189, 194–196; pressure for firing of, 262, 284, 314; Rogers and, 83, 168, 170; in Schine affair, 158–61, 163, 173–175, 190–92, 213, 257–60, 308; Sherman Adams's views on, 297; Stevens and, 83–85, 210, 273–77

Adams, Margaret, 97

Adams, Rachel, 320

Adams, Sherman, 72, 81, 89, 140, 141, 144, 187, 204, 217, 229, 231, 238, 269, 362, 374, 379, 381, 383–384, 385; Adams chronology and, 175, 192, 222, 232, 250, 292, 348–349; Army-McCarthy hearings and, 344, 350; Charles Wilson as viewed by, 249–50; Communist Chinese trade policy as viewed by, 60; drafting of Eisenhower's Milwaukee Arena speech and, 46–47; as Eisenhower's floor manager, 40–42; on Eisenhower's Wisconsin campaign, 12; Hensels' personal relations with, 320–21; John Adams as viewed by, 297; Justice Department meeting as viewed by (January 21, 1954), 171; McCarthy as viewed by, 170; McCarthy-Stevens agreement and, 221, 222; McLeod's firing opposed by, 58; subpoena issue and, 353–355; in Peress controversy, 193; Stevens as viewed by, 246; as White House liberal, 143, 227–28

Adler, Julius Ochs, 245

Agronsky, Martin, 207

Air Force, U.S., 71, 263, 268, 271, 272, 275, 279–80, 306, 341

Akers, Floyd, 320

Allen, Leo, 355

Alsop, Joseph, 232, 233, 235, 242, 277–78, 287, 342, 349, 362, 376

Alsop, Stewart, 235

Ames, Paulette, 282

Anastos, George, 329

Anderson, Jack, 233

Anderson, Robert, 71, 77, 350–52, 354

Andrews, Bert, 61

Arends, Les, 355

389

Army-McCarthy hearings, 313–78; committee members in, 313–15; cropped-photograph episode in, 324–30; Dirksen's proposals for, 343–44; Fisher episode in, 375–78; Hensel-Carr charges dismissed in, 364; Hoover-Bolling letter in, 335–339; McCarthy memoranda in, 367–70; plans for truncation of, 333–34; subpoena issue in, 318, 340, 349–62, 365–67; television coverage of, 315; *see also specific individuals*

Arnold, Thurmond, 288

Auchincloss, Jim, 130, 134, 154, 196, 274, 276

Awalt, William J., 89

Back, George I., 90–91, 94, 130, 131, 177, 274, 276, 277

Baldwin, Hanson W., 77

Bassett, Jim, 355

Beach, Ned, 145

BeLieu, Kenneth, 79, 85, 208, 210, 217, 274, 298, 301, 305–6, 315, 319, 320, 346–47, 363, 385

Bennett, James, 64

Bentley, Elizabeth, 17, 22, 50, 119, 168

Berding, Andrew, 82–83

Berg, Aaron, 303

Bergin, General, 184, 185

Bernau, Phyllis, 81

Berry, Lewis, 172, 254

Biddle, Anthony Drexel, 320

Bigart, Homer, 125–26, 232, 349

Bishop, Joseph W., Jr., 74–75, 79, 83

Blount, John B., 278, 292–93, 308

Bohlen, Charles E. ("Chip"), 56–59, 65, 168, 357

Bolling, Alexander, 335, 337

Bradley, Colonel, 325, 326, 328–29

Bradley, Omar, 146

Bricker, John, 41, 224, 238, 254

Bricker, Amendment, 224

Bridges, Styles, 54, 57, 224, 355

Briggs, Dean, 45

Brinkley, David, 367

Bromley, Bruce, 299

Brown, Frank, 235, 256, 322, 362

Brownell, Herbert, 139, 140, 143, 151, 163, 220, 253, 286, 301, 303, 339, 374, 384, 385; appointed attorney general, 49, 71; Army officials as viewed by, 167–68; background of, 117–18; in Eisenhower's presidential campaign (1952), 30, 37, 40, 117–18, 137, 299; Harry Dexter White accused by, 116–17, 118–19, 121–22, 125, 275, 336, 357, 383; Hoover's relationship with, 336; John Adams as viewed by, 297; at Justice Department meeting (January 21, 1954), 167, 170–71, 348–350; liberalism of, 118; in loyalty-boards dispute, 115–16, 154–58, 167; McCarthy's attacks on, 376; in Oppenheimer investigation, 152; subpoena issue and, 353–58, 362, 365, 382; Truman's denunciation of, 123–24

Bryan, Freddie, 321, 333

Bryan, Violet, 255, 288

Buckley, William F., Jr., 55, 65

Bullis, Harry, 343

Bundy, McGeorge, 36

Bundy, William P., 73

Burress, W. A., 194, 196

Bush, Prescott, 237

Butler, John Marshall, 296, 331

Byrnes, James F., 21, 121, 123, 124

Cabot, Paul, 207, 209

Camp Gordon (Ga.), 160, 183–85, 245, 260, 289, 295

Camp Kilmer (N.J.), 187, 189, 193, 260

Capehart, Homer, 159

Cardozo, Benjamin, 49, 163

Carr, Frank, 93, 195, 219, 309, 340, 363, 364; Army–Ford Foundation link explored by, 189; in Army-McCarthy hearings, 315, 327, 329, 332, 334, 335, 342–43, 373, 380; dismissal of charges against, 364; in Fort Monmouth investigation, 90, 94, 130, 180; John Adams's relationship with, 223, 239–40, 244–45, 254, 336; in loyalty-boards dispute, 166, 175–76, 185; McCarthy memoranda and, 263–68, 283, 368–69; at Pentagon luncheon (November 6, 1953), 119, 257–58, 263–64; in Peress controversy, 187–88, 190, 192; in Schine episode, 157–58, 166, 175, 181–84, 186, 191, 257–60, 273–76, 280, 282, 307–8

Carroll, Paul T., 373

Carroll, Pete, 145, 148

Catledge, Turner, 38

Caudle, T. Lamar, 168

Central Intelligence Agency (CIA), 73, 289, 317, 380
Chadwick, John, 289–90
Chambers, Whittaker, 18–19, 22, 62
Chesney, Earle, 295
Chiang Kai-shek, 16, 20, 48
China, 16, 19–20, 59–60, 148
Chou En-lai, 20
Churchill, Winston, 30
Clark, Tom, 121, 123, 124
Clay, Lucius, 30, 117, 118, 219–22, 232, 299, 342, 362
Cleary, Tom, 275–76, 280, 296
Clifford, Clark, 198, 200, 374
Clubb, O. Edmund, 55, 382
Cochran, Jacqueline, 30
Cohn, Albert, 49, 273
Cohn, Roy, 52, 55, 67, 91, 92, 134, 158, 174, 183, 232, 244–45, 268, 280, 282, 294, 335, 361, 384, 385; in Army-McCarthy hearings, 288, 304, 309, 315, 320, 322–23, 325–327, 329–32, 334, 340–44, 351–52, 363, 370–76, 378, 380; background of, 49–50; in Fort Monmouth investigation, 90, 94, 125, 128–31; in investigation of pamphlet on Soviet Siberia, 85–89; John Adams accused by, 156–57, 173, 198, 217–18, 282–83, 348; in loyalty-boards dispute, 102; McCarthy memoranda and, 263–67, 367; McCarthy's refusal to fire, 262; overseas libraries investigated by, 62–63, 316; at Pentagon luncheon (November 6, 1953), 257–58, 263–64, 271; in Peress controversy, 187, 194–95; pressure for firing of, 208, 221, 250, 254, 284, 314; Rogers's view of, 168; in Schine episode, 97, 99–100, 115, 120, 155–58, 160, 166, 171–72, 175–85, 198, 258–60, 273–78, 280–82, 291, 292, 295, 297, 307–8, 351; Schine commission sought by, 69, 292, 317; Stevens's view of, 165; Stevens threatened by, 184–85, 370; on Welch, 300
Coleman, Aaron H., 92–93, 99, 129, 258, 337, 385
Coleman, Tom, 11, 39, 41, 46
Collier, Robert A., 337
Collingwood, Charles, 245
Conant, James Bryant, 55–56, 65
Connell, Byron, 139
Connelly, Mathew, 168

Criminal Investigations Division (CID), 160, 184, 189, 192, 213, 276, 295
Currie, Lauchlin, 17
Cutler, Robert, 32, 34, 44, 46, 60, 138, 159, 285

Dalton, Harry, 209
Davies, John Paton, 133–34, 148, 382
Davis, Bob, 27
Davis, Elmer, 36, 68–69, 122–23, 252
Davis, John W., 286
Dean, Vera Micheles, 61
Defense Department, U.S., 71
Democratic party, 221
Dempsey, Jack, 89
Dewey, Thomas E., 28, 40–41, 42, 53, 117, 137, 168, 198, 228, 298–299
Dirksen, Everett M., 80, 172, 174, 198–99, 200, 204, 221, 236, 268, 272, 286, 351, 361, 364, 385; Adams chronology and, 233; in Army-McCarthy hearings, 252, 314, 333–34, 343–44, 360, 373; Cohn's firing discussed by, 250; Eisenhower's appeals to, 244; in Fort Monmouth investigation, 92; fried-chicken lunch and, 208, 210; Hensel on, 211; Jenkins recommended by, 303; McCarthy-Stevens agreement and, 215–16, 218; necessity of public hearings questioned by, 284–85
Doctors Draft Act (1950), 188, 190
Dodge, Joe, 138
Donovan, Bob, 246
Driscoll, Alfred, 41
Driscoll, Mary, 242, 269, 367–69, 372–73, 376, 380
Dulles, Allen W., 73, 99–100, 289
Dulles, John Foster, 18, 48–49, 53–62, 71, 81, 121, 138, 140, 148, 150, 237, 240, 289, 382
Dworshak, Henry, 309, 314, 331, 376

Eaton, Frederick, 297, 315, 324
Eder, Shirley, 283
Edwards, Willard, 21, 94, 242, 369–370
Eisenhower, Dwight D., 26–29, 70–72, 139–40, 225; Army-McCarthy hearings as viewed by, 319, 332–

Eisenhower, Dwight D.—*Continued*
334, 343, 345, 363–65; Atoms
for Peace advanced by, 154,
203; B'nai B'rith speech of (November 23, 1953), 132; Bohlen
nominated Soviet ambassador by,
56–59; C. D. Jackson and, 138;
Cohn's firing favored by, 223; on
Communism as election issue, 126–
127; Conant nominated high commissioner by, 55–56; Dewey's relationship with, 299; first State of the
Union message of (January 7, 1954),
163; Hagerty on, 70, 252; in Harry
Dexter White controversy, 121–22;
on H-bomb development, 303; and
Hoffman's defense of Stevens, 207;
Hoover's relationship with, 336,
339; Knowland placated by, 261;
legislative program of (1954), 144,
208, 242; on McCarthy, 221–22,
238, 239, 365–66; McCarthy ignored by, 66–67, 144, 379–84; on
McCarthyism, 146–48, 150–51;
McCarthy's campaign appearances
with, 35–38; and McCarthy's
library attacks, 67–68; McCarthy's
meeting with (October 2, 1952),
11–12, 32–34; McCarthy's praise
of, 290; McCarthy-Stevens agreement and, 219–21; McCarthy subcommittee membership questioned by, 286, 295; Milton Eisenhower's report to, 288–89; Milwaukee speech of (October 3, 1952),
36–47, 140, 141, 145; on Mundt,
314, 364; as NATO Commander,
26, 30; Nixon advised by, on Stevenson response, 269–70; in Oppenheimer investigation, 151–54,
304; on Peress controversy, 240;
personal attacks shunned by, 29,
251; in presidential campaign of
1952, 11–12, 30–32, 48, 117–18,
137; at Republican Convention
(1952), 25–26, 141; and Republican legislators (March 1,
1954), 236; on Republican right,
224–25, 270; Rogers's advice to, on
McCarthy, 169; Rosenbergs' clemency appeal denied by, 64–65;
Seaton's relationship with, 227–32;
Stevens backed by, 235, 240, 245–
246, 285, 288, 344, 353, 360–61;
Stevenson's Miami speech as
viewed by, 246–47; subpoena issue

and, 349–50, 354–58; Symington's
relationship with, 197; Truman as
viewed by, 29; as viewed by press,
243; "which clause" opposed by,
224; White House organization
under, 226–27; Wilson-McCarthy
lunch as viewed by, 252–53; Zwicker
commended by, 193, 241
Eisenhower, John, 64
Eisenhower, Milton, 66–68, 147, 288–
289, 344–45, 383
Elicher, Max, 128–29
Ellender, Allen, 207
Emory, Alan, 126
Ernst, Morris, 201, 206, 232, 306
Executive Order 10450 (April 27,
1953), 54, 116, 127

Falkenburg, Jinx, 33
Fast, Howard, 61
Federal Bureau of Investigation
(FBI), 22–23, 95, 124, 335, 339,
340, 371–72
Ferguson, Homer, 243, 290, 355
Finney, John, 217
Fisher, Frederick G., Jr., 301, 302,
305, 308, 309, 375–78
Flanagan, Francis, 52
Flanders, Ralph, 250–52, 370, 381
Fleeson, Doris, 243
Flores, Iris, 341
Folliard, Eddie, 33, 141, 243
Ford, Gerald R., 157
Ford Foundation, 189
Fortas, Abe, 201
Fort Bragg (N.C.), 280
Fort Dix (N.J.), 120, 125, 155, 160,
175–76, 178–79, 182–84, 186,
258–59, 278, 289, 291–94, 304,
307–8, 363
Fort Monmouth (N.J.), 90–95, 97,
98–99, 123, 127–31, 154–56, 159,
258, 263–66, 273, 275, 307–8, 335,
337, 342, 385
Foster, John Watson, 53
Franklin, James, 319–20, 330
fried-chicken lunch (February 24,
1954), 208–11, 314, 382
Fuchs, Klaus, 20, 22, 63–64, 379

Glancy, Eleanor, 244, 373
Glassman, Vivian, 128
Gold, Harry, 63–64
Government Printing Office, 282;
McCarthy's investigation of, 73

Greenblum, Carl, 127
Greenglass, David, 63–64, 93, 94, 130
Griswold, Dwight, 296
Grover, Allen, 245
Gruenther, Alfred M., 27, 124, 141, 145
Gruenther, Homer, 144, 145, 295
Gunderson, Barbara, 363–64
Gurney, Chan, 97

Hadley, Arthur, 205–6, 217, 222, 233, 238, 242, 245, 341
Hagerty, Jim, 34, 38, 148–49, 159, 170, 207, 224, 225, 236, 238, 240, 245, 247–48, 256, 261–62, 286, 295, 299, 304, 314, 360–66, 380–381, 383–84, 385; Army-McCarthy hearings as viewed by, 331, 344–345; Dulles-McLeod dispute and, 58; on Eisenhower, 70, 252; in Fisher controversy, 301–2, 376; McCarthy as viewed by, 134, 144, 145; McCarthy-Stevens agreement and, 217, 221–23; on Mundt, 363–364; on Oppenheimer case, 303; on opposition to Cohn, 250; press leaks discouraged by, 141; press as viewed by, 242–43; subpoena issue and, 349–50, 353–55, 357; as White House liberal, 143; White House role of, 227–29, 231; Wilson-McCarthy lunch as viewed by, 252–53
Hagerty, Marge, 302
Hall, Leonard, 143, 238–39, 244, 246–247, 290, 355
Hallanan, Walter, 40
Halleck, Charles, 236, 355
Hannah, John, 247
Harkness, Richard, 207
Harlow, Bryce, 141, 142, 144–46, 148, 149, 151, 203, 295
Harris, Bob, 209
Harris, Reed, 62
Harsch, Joe, 139, 141
Haskins, Charles, 267
Hauck, C. J., 256
Hauge, Gabriel, 34, 45, 46, 71, 140, 227, 363
Hazlett, Swede, 332
Heald, Henry, 52
Hearing Boards, 100, 128, 166
Heiskell, Andrew, 136
Helms, Paul, 251

Hensel, H. Struve, 75, 79, 196, 197, 207, 210, 212, 215, 227, 230–31, 245, 247, 254, 262, 271, 277, 287, 289, 301, 304, 305, 307, 343, 347, 348, 359–60, 362, 374, 380, 384, 385; Adams chronology and, 231–235, 256–57; in Army defense, 291–294, 296–97, 302; in Army-McCarthy hearings, 315–23, 328, 333, 341–42, 351, 364; Charles Wilson as viewed by, 249; coordinated response to McCarthy sought by, 82, 102, 126, 155, 156, 158; on Dirksen and Mundt, 211; dismissal of charges against, 364; in drafting of chronology, 231, 248, 253; Hoover as viewed by, 335; Inspector General's report as viewed by, 278–79; John Adams recommended by, 83, 85; on Joseph Alsop article (March 15, 1954), 278; McCarthy memoranda and, 268–69; McCarthy's attack on, 309–10; McCarthy-Stevens agreement and, 219; Seaton's relationship with, 230, 249; in selection of Welch, 299; Stevens's relationship with, 206
Hensel, Isabel, 230–31, 302, 316, 320–21, 335
Hickenlooper, Bourke, 58, 296
Hiss, Alger, 18–19, 21, 23, 73, 372, 379, 383
Hobby, Oveta Culp, 41
Hoffman, Paul, 28, 207, 304
Holland, Spessard, 249
Hoover, Herbert, 30
Hoover, J. Edgar, 22, 24, 50, 59, 95, 124, 151–52, 218, 233, 262, 305, 335–40, 371–72, 376, 383
House Un-American Activities Committee, 17–18, 121, 168, 314
Howard, Robert A., Jr., 74, 75, 79
Hughes, Emmet John, 29, 37, 44, 72, 137, 142, 144, 146
Hull, John, 277
Humphrey, George M., 49, 71, 83, 139, 272, 355
Hunt, Lester, 236–37
Hurley, Patrick, 16
Hyman, Harry, 129

Information Agency, U.S., 247
Interior Department, U.S., 228
Internal Security Act (1950), 24
International Information Administration (IIA), 60–63, 65–66

International Monetary Fund (IMF), 119, 124, 139
Ivan, Gabby, 301, 317, 346

Jackson, C. D., 37, 44, 60, 62, 70, 136–50, 154, 159, 203, 269, 283, 285–86, 295, 317, 385
Jackson, Henry M. ("Scoop"), 72, 197, 198, 315, 337, 352, 359, 366, 380, 385
Jenkins, Ray H., 303, 304, 306, 314–318, 320, 321–22, 324–25, 327–29, 332, 334, 336–37, 340, 341, 346, 361, 362, 367, 373, 376, 385
Jenner, William, 31, 46, 225, 238
Johnson, Earl, 75, 79, 93
Johnson, Leroy, 207
Johnson, Lyndon B., 44, 162, 246, 385
Jones, Robert L., 206
Juliana, Jim, 98, 304, 310, 329, 330, 335, 341, 377
Justice Department, U.S., 71, 239
Justice Department meeting (January 21, 1954), 167–72

Kaghan, Theodore, 63, 316
Kaltenborn, H. V., 237–38
Kane, John F., 243
Kaplan, Raymond, 62
Kefauver, Estes, 313
Kennan, George F., 56
Kennedy, John F., 51–52, 170, 320
Kennedy, Joseph P., 51–52
Kennedy, Patricia, 182, 279, 281
Kennedy, Robert F., 51–52, 59, 60, 72, 197, 278–79, 282, 380
Kiermas, Ed, 34
Kieve, Robert, 144, 149
Kimball, John, Jr., 305
Kitty, Fred, 129
Kline, General, 183
Klutznick, Philip M., 304
Knowland, William F., 42–44, 58, 199, 204, 208, 236, 240, 241–43, 252, 254, 260–61, 286, 290, 296, 355, 356, 366, 381
Kohler, Walter Jodok, 11–12, 35, 38–44, 46–47, 93–94
Krock, Arthur, 223
Kyes, Roger, 203–5, 207, 215, 222, 233, 261, 301, 331, 341

La Follette, Robert M., 16
Lamont, Corliss, 82
Landon, Alf, 212, 344
Langlie, Arthur, 41

Lansing, Robert, 53
Larsen, Roy, 136
Lattimore, Owen, 24, 50
LaVenia, Thomas, 176
Lawford, Peter, 182, 281–82
Lawrence, Bill, 34, 37, 38, 47, 83, 209
Lawton, Kirke, 90, 91, 94, 97, 130, 131, 134–35, 177, 263, 265, 269, 274, 276, 277, 281–82, 304, 323, 328, 341
Lee, Robert E., 28
Lehman, Herbert H., 127, 189, 306
Lehrbas, Lloyd, 133, 255
Lemnitzer, Lyman, 315
Levitsky, Joseph, 94, 128, 130
Lippmann, Walter, 36, 235
Lodge, Henry Cabot, Jr., 30, 41, 49, 170, 171, 213–15, 222, 232, 253, 302, 342, 348–50, 352, 362, 382
Lodge, John, 41
Longworth, Alice Roosevelt, 298
Lotz, Colonel, 128, 130
Lourie, Donald B., 54
Love, Francis J., 20
loyalty-boards dispute, 99–102, 115–116, 166, 175–76, 185
Loyalty-Security Appeals Board, 166, 185
Lucas, John J., Jr., 73, 80–81, 85, 100, 187, 291, 301, 317–18, 320, 351, 373, 374
Luce, Clare Boothe, 37, 245
Lyons, Roger, 62

MacArthur, Douglas, 25, 27, 30, 40, 43, 133
McCann, Kevin, 33, 34, 42
McCardle, Carl, 61
McCarran Act (1950), 24
McCarran Internal Security Subcommittee, 50, 134
McCarthy, Al, 185, 276–77, 306
McCarthy, Jean Kerr, 89, 169, 172, 176, 192, 257, 272–73, 275–76, 348
McCarthy, Joseph Raymond: childhood of, 13, 15; as circuit judge, 14–15; drinking habits of, 25; friendliness of, toward adversaries, 25, 139, 165–66; investigation staff selected by, 49–52; in Marines, 15; at Marquette University, 13, 14; medical problems of, 32; public approval of, 290–91, 312; in Senate election (1946), 16; in Senate re-election campaign (1952), 11–12,

McCarthy, Joseph Raymond—
Continued
49; Stevens memorandum of under-
standing with, 211–23; wedding of,
89, 272
McClellan, John, 72, 167, 197, 200,
237, 246, 254, 284–85, 314, 316,
318, 323, 348, 353–54, 358–59,
366, 374, 376, 385
McCloy, John, 189
McCluney, Forest, 139
McCrum, Marie, 139
McGranery, James P., 50
McKee, Samuel, 87
McKeldin, Theodore Roosevelt, 41
McLeod, Scott, 54, 57, 58, 132, 237,
240, 311
McNeil, Marshall, 247–48
McNeil, Wilfred J., 206, 230
Maglin, General, 184, 185, 295
Malone, George, 67, 296
Mao Tse-tung, 16, 20
Marder, Murray, 232, 349
Marshall, George C., 16, 24, 25, 28,
31, 36, 42–46, 70, 142
Martin, I. Jack, 89, 141–43, 145,
148–50, 208, 221, 225, 295–96,
353–54, 364, 385
Martin, Joe, 40, 355
Mathews, Troup, 62
Matthews, J. B., 72, 90, 167, 170,
197
Menjou, Adolphe, 17
Meyers, Benny, 287
Miller, Joseph J. M., 308
Millikin, Eugene D., 224, 243, 355
Milne, Edward, 121–22
Milwaukee Arena speech (October 3,
1952), 36–47, 140, 141, 145
Minetti, G. Joseph, 384
Mitchell, Jim, 318–19
Montgomery, George, 208
Montgomery, Robert, 17, 30
Moore, Harriet, 86–87
Morgan, Jerry, 60, 141–50, 170–72,
221, 225, 229, 238, 240, 295–96,
348–54, 361, 385
Morris, Bob, 285
Morse, Wayne, 52–53
Moss, Annie Lee, 209, 262, 296
Mudgett, G. C., 180, 264, 271
Mullin, Phil, 230, 231, 255, 351,
372–73
Mundt, Karl, 22, 95–96, 169, 172,
174, 199, 200, 201, 206, 236, 244,
268, 284–85, 296, 306–7, 336, 361,
385; in Army-McCarthy hearings,

313, 315–16, 320, 330, 337, 339,
342, 344, 352, 353, 360, 362–64,
374, 377; Cohn's firing discussed by,
250; committee rules and, 252;
Eisenhower on, 314, 364; fried-
chicken lunch and, 208, 210–11,
314; Hagerty on, 363–64; Hensel
on, 211; McCarthy-Stevens agreement and, 215–16; McCarthy subcommittee role as viewed by, 286,
290, 309
Murray, John, 308
Murrow, Edward R., 231, 251–52,
303, 366

Navy, U.S., 71, 263, 268, 271, 272,
275, 279–80, 306, 341
Neely, Matthew, 207
Nellor, Ed, 21
Nichols, Louis B., 339–40
Nimitz, Chester, 16
Nixon, Pat, 89
Nixon, Richard M., 22, 42, 50, 72, 89,
159, 204, 229, 237, 238, 260–61,
290, 300, 303, 383, 384–85; Adams
chronology and, 222–23, 232;
Army counsels' views on, 301;
Checkers speech of, 31; contain-
ment policy opposed by, 48; as
Eisenhower's running mate, 30–31;
Hiss's testimony doubted by, 19,
270; McCarthy's CIA probe re-
sisted by, 73; McCarthy's restraint
urged by, 60, 161, 169; McCarthy-
Stevens relationship and, 208, 211,
216–17, 221; as mediator between
McCarthy and administration, 59,
67; Stevenson answered by, 246–
247, 269–71

Ochs, Adolph, 36
Office of the Chief of Legislative
Liaison (OCLL), 177, 257, 307,
316
Office of the Surgeon General, 188
Office of War Information (OWI),
62, 66
Okun, Jack, 129
Olney, Warren, 94
Oppenheimer, J. Robert, 151–54, 159,
303, 304

Paley, William S., 247
Partridge, Richard C., 82, 85–87, 88,
90, 115, 131
Patterson, Robert, 33
Patton, George S., 28–29

Pearson, Drew, 13, 25, 69, 210
Pegler, Westbrook, 173
Peress, Irving, 187–89, 190–94, 199,
    345–46, 357, 374, 380
Persons, Wilton Burton ("Jerry"), 34,
    48, 141–44, 148, 201, 204, 216,
    225, 238, 252, 269, 296, 345, 350,
    361, 364, 382, 385; Adams chronol-
    ogy and, 232; background of, 43;
    Communist Chinese trade policy
    and, 60; conciliatory tendencies of,
    67, 140, 159, 171, 207–8, 215;
    Dirksen compromise favored by,
    344; and drafting of Eisenhower's
    Milwaukee speech, 44, 46; Mc-
    Carthy-Stevens agreement and, 220,
    221; McLeod's consultation with,
    58; personality of, 43–44; subpoena
    issue and, 353–54; White House
    role of, 227–29
Peterson, Val, 41
Peurifoy, John, 23
Pierson, Arthur, 310
Pike, James A., 290
Pike, Jane R., 81, 373
Popper, Karl, 138
Potter, Charles, 172, 174, 199, 200,
    206, 208, 211, 216, 236, 243, 249–
    254, 262, 268, 284, 286, 306, 311,
    314, 319, 334, 342–43, 362, 364
Potter, Phil, 232, 249, 260, 349, 366
Prewitt, Tom, 341
Purtell, William, 296
Pusey, Merlo, 47
Pusey, Nathan M., 35

Rankin, J. Lee, 79, 82, 102, 155, 350,
    354
Reagan, Ronald, 17
Reber, Miles, 75, 80, 176, 257, 307,
    316
Reber, Sam, 316, 319
Reed, Dan, 355
Reichelderfer, General, 99
Reid, Mrs. Ogden, 39
Remington, William, 17, 50, 168
Republican party, 11–12, 25, 28, 30–
    32, 36, 40–41, 48–49, 117–18,
    137, 141, 252
Reston, James, 140, 141, 162, 202,
    205, 233, 243, 341
Reuss, Henry, 39
Rhodes, Theodore R., 81, 206, 373
Ridgway, Matthew B., 82, 180, 195,
    212, 222, 249, 264, 296, 315,
    345–46, 357
Ringler, Earl L., 294, 308

Ringling, Henry, 11–12
Robinson, Bill, 225, 270
Rogers, Adele, 149
Rogers, William P., 80, 81, 94, 162,
    225, 285, 287, 299, 301, 339, 374,
    382, 384, 385; Adams chronology
    and, 187, 222, 232, 253, 292, 348–
    350; Army officials as viewed by,
    168; attempts by, to placate Mc-
    Carthy, 67, 72, 161; Eisenhower
    advised by, on McCarthy, 169–70;
    Hoover as viewed by, 336; on
    John Adams, 83, 168; in Justice
    Department meeting (January 21,
    1954), 171; in loyalty-boards dis-
    pute, 155, 158–59, 166–67; Mc-
    Carthy's relationship with, 168–69;
    McCarthy-Stevens agreement and,
    221; in McCarthy-Stevens dispute,
    208; Stevens as viewed by, 168,
    196–97; Symington on, 201
Roosevelt, Eleanor, 61
Roosevelt, Franklin D., 30, 49, 52,
    66, 298, 306, 384
Roosevelt, Theodore, 41
Rosenberg, Ethel, 50, 63–65, 379
Rosenberg, Julius, 50, 63–65, 92–94,
    128, 379
Rovere, Richard, 51
Rowley, Don, 65
Russell, Richard, 249, 250
Ryan, Cornelius, 164, 176, 181, 184,
    276, 278, 293–94, 363

Sabath, Adolph, 21
Safchik, Irwin, 207
St. Clair, James, 300–301, 304–5,
    307, 309, 311, 315, 317, 319, 320,
    333–35, 346, 356, 358, 369, 373,
    376, 377, 380, 382, 385
Saltonstall, John, 94
Saltonstall, Leverett, 224–25, 236,
    243, 284, 355
Sarant, Louise, 129
Sarnoff, David, 247
Sartre, Jean-Paul, 61
Sayre, Francis B., 290
Schine, G. David, 50, 52, 67, 73, 85,
    273, 304, 306, 332, 333, 362, 385;
    in Army-McCarthy hearings, 321–
    330, 342–43, 380; background of,
    51; Bishop questioned by, 74–75;
    at Camp Gordon, 244; chronology
    of controversy over, 178–87, 215,
    222–23, 229, 232, 234–35, 248–
    250, 253, 256, 257–60, 277, 307,

Schine, G. David—*Continued*
382; CID appointment sought by,
160, 163–65, 190, 192, 213, 276,
295; Cohn's interventions in behalf
of, 69, 97, 99–100, 115, 155–58,
160, 166, 171–72, 175–85, 198,
258–60, 277–78, 280–82, 292, 295,
297, 307–8, 351; commission sought
by, 69, 176–77, 257, 277, 292, 307,
316, 317, 370; draft eligibility of,
69, 97–98, 176–78, 269, 297; at
Fort Dix, 120, 125, 155, 159, 160,
175–76, 178–79, 182–84, 186,
278–79, 289, 291, 293–94, 363;
McCarthy memoranda on, 263–68,
279, 283, 304, 318, 367–69, 374;
McCarthy irritated by, 177–78,
347; McCarthy's interventions in
behalf of, 119–20, 173–75, 348;
overseas libraries investigated by,
62–63, 316; Sokolsky's interventions in behalf of, 131, 173, 189,
192; Stevens approached by, 97–
98
Schine, J. Meyer, 340
Schmitt, Len, 11, 41
Schooley, Hersch, 125–26
Sears, Samuel, 303
Seaton, Fred A., 84, 123, 125–26,
133, 162, 193, 215, 245, 247–48,
249, 253, 256, 261, 262, 269, 305,
307, 311, 317, 320, 347, 361, 374,
381, 384, 385; appointed assistant
secretary of defense, 83; in Army
defense, 283–84, 291, 295–97, 302,
319; Army-McCarthy hearings and,
333–34, 341, 344, 345, 350–52,
368; Eisenhower's Milwaukee
speech plans leaked by, 38, 47; Eisenhower's relationship with, 227–
232; Hensel's relationship with, 230,
249; in loyalty-boards dispute,
100–102; McCarthy's relationship
with, 254–55, 267–68, 372–73;
McCarthy-Stevens agreement as
viewed by, 212–13, 216; St. Clair's
relationship with, 301; in Schine
episode, 163–65; Stevens as viewed
by, 229, 284; and Symington, 286–
288; Welch's relationship with,
299–300
Seaton, Gladys, 230, 300
Security Review Board, 100, 128,
166
Security Screening Board, 100, 166
Senate Armed Services Committee,
284

Senate Foreign Relations Committee,
57–58
Senate Internal Security Subcom-
mittee, 285, 340
Service, John Stewart, 20, 21, 24, 55,
170, 382, 385
Shanley, Bernard, 27, 31, 65, 67, 72,
77, 143–44, 146, 148–49, 159, 299,
304, 354
Shanley, Maureen, 149, 159
Shapley, Harlow, 24
Sheil, Bernard J., 304
Sherwood, Robert E., 153
Simmons, Francis, 209
Smathers, George, 249
Smith, H. Alexander, 95, 165, 274,
366
Smith, John Thomas, 143
Smith, Margaret Chase, 198, 206
Smith, Walter Bedell, 138, 148, 277,
291, 317
Smith Act (1940), 50
Snyder, Betty, 67
Snyder, Murray, 67, 143, 148, 150
Sobell, Morton, 92
Sokolsky, George, 50, 125, 131, 172–
173, 189, 190, 191–92, 195, 275–
276, 278, 280, 341
Sparkman, John, 58, 357
Spellman, Francis Cardinal, 245
Stalin, Joseph, 70
Stassen, Harold, 37, 59, 60, 137, 143,
228
State Department, U.S., 21–25, 53–
54, 71, 383
Steinman, Louise Tinsley, 13
Stephens, Thomas E., 29, 32–33, 64,
143, 148, 150, 159, 299
Stevens, Dorothy Goodwin Whitney,
78
Stevens, Joan, 78
Stevens, Robert T., 71, 73, 79–82, 133,
166, 242, 247–48, 252, 268–69, 280,
287, 296, 297, 301, 305, 314, 349,
382, 384, 385; Adams chronology
and, 254–60; on alleged destruction
of Communist files, 189; in Army
defense, 232–38, 245, 302, 309; in
Army-McCarthy hearings, 300,
306, 311–12, 316–37, 339–42,
344–47, 350, 358, 362–63, 373;
background of, 76–77; Cabot's assistance to, 209–10; Charles Wilson's views on, 262; Cohn's alleged
threats against, 184–85, 370; and
approval of chronology, 253;
Eisenhower's backing of, 235, 240,

Stevens, Robert T.—*Continued*
245–46, 285, 288, 344, 353, 360–
361; first months as secretary of
the army, 77–79; in Fort Monmouth
investigation, 90–95, 97, 123, 125–
128; fried-chicken lunch and, 208–
212; Hensel's relationship with,
206; Inspector General's report and,
278–79; John Adams appointed by,
83–85; Kyes consulted by, 203–
205; in Lawton controversy, 130,
131, 134–35; Lodge's assistance
to, 213–15; in loyalty-boards dispute, 100–102, 115–16; in Mc-
Carthy memoranda, 263–68, 280;
McCarthy's memorandum of understanding with, 211–23; McCarthy's
relationship with, 93, 119, 165–66;
McCarthy subcommittee members
and, 197–99; at Pentagon luncheon
(November 6, 1953), 119, 257–58,
263–64, 271; in Peress controversy,
193, 199–201, 357; Peress court-
martial suggested to, by McCarthy,
187; Potter as viewed by, 249;
public perception of, 226; Rogers's
views on, 168, 196–97; in Schine
episode, 97–100, 115, 119–20, 131,
156–61, 163–65, 178, 180–83, 186,
190–91, 250, 257–60, 292–93, 308;
Schine episode as recalled by, 272–
277; Seaton's view of, 229, 284;
Sherman Adams on, 246;
in Siberia pamphlet probe, 87–89;
Zwicker backed by, 195–96, 205–7
Stevens, Robert T., Jr., 208
Stevenson, Adlai E., 39, 42, 70, 123,
246–47, 250, 269–71, 290, 335–36
Stimson, Henry, 36, 189
Strauss, Lewis, 151–52
Streibert, Ted, 247
Suchow, Lawrence, 127
Sulzberger, Arthur Hays, 36–38
Summerfield, Arthur E., 12, 35, 42,
44, 46, 47, 249
Surine, Don, 310, 329, 335
Swan, Walter, 319
Symington, W. Stuart, 60, 72, 197,
307, 385; Adams chronology and,
248–49, 260, 278, 287–88; in Army-
McCarthy hearings, 314–15, 324,
337, 339, 352–53, 359, 366, 374;
Eisenhower's relationship with,
197; McCarthy's attacks on, 376,
380; open hearings favored by,
284; on Rogers, 201; Zwicker hear-
ing and, 198, 200–201, 205, 214

Taber, John, 60
Taft, Robert A., 25, 28, 30–31, 36,
40–41, 46, 58–59, 62, 65, 117–18,
141–42, 357
Taft, William Howard, 41
Talbott, Harold, 37, 71, 77
Thomas, J. Parnell, 17, 168
Thomas, Norman, 132
Thornton, Dan, 41
Tolson, Clyde, 339–40
Treasury Department, U.S., 71, 119
Trice, Mark, 296
Trudeau, Arthur, 115, 180, 264
Truman, Harry S, 16, 18, 37, 56, 70,
121, 123, 139, 163, 306, 358; Brow-
nell denounced by, 123–24; Eisen-
hower's view of, 29; in Harry Dexter
White controversy, 118–19, 336;
Lattimore FBI report released by,
24; loyalty files closed by, 23; Mac-
Arthur fired by, 25; McCarthy's
attacks on, 133, 339; McCarthy
strategy of, 382–83; Rosenbergs'
clemency appeal made to, 64
Tydings, Millard, 24, 169

Vaughan, Harry H., 118–19, 124
Velde, Harold, 120–21
Vincent, John Carter, 54–55, 170,
382
Vinson, Carl, 142, 203
Vinson, Fred, 124
Voice of America (VOA), 60, 62, 65

Wadsworth, James, 197
Wainwright, Jonathan M., 272
Walsh, Edmund, 20
Warren, Earl, 41, 286
Washington, George, 28, 384
Waters, George, 21
Watkins, Arthur V., 381
Weber, Janet, 306
Wechsler, James, 62
Welch, Joseph N., 298–302, 304,
306–9, 315, 317, 319–20, 324–31,
333–35, 337–40, 344, 346–47, 349,
352, 353, 358, 361, 362–64, 369,
370–78, 380, 382, 384, 385
Welker, Herman, 215, 296
Wheeling (W.Va.) speech, 20–22
Wherry, Ken, 229
White, Harry Dexter, 17, 117–19,
121–22, 124, 125, 139, 155, 336,
339, 357, 372, 383
White, Theodore H., 61

Whitman, Ann, 81, 121, 139, 147, 285
Willis, Charlie, 141, 144, 301
Wilson, Arthur R., 304
Wilson, Charles E., 49, 77, 82, 83, 138, 203, 209, 247, 272, 284, 300, 302, 305, 332, 334, 342, 344–46, 350, 362, 382; Adams chronology and, 250; in Army defense, 319; bluntness of, 226–27, 249; Cohn's firing urged by, 262; in Fort Monmouth investigation, 92; McCarthy answered by, 244, 311; McCarthy's luncheon with (March 10, 1954), 252–53; on Oppenheimer investiga-tion, 151–52; in Schine episode, 98; in selection of Welch, 299; subpoena issue and, 354–56; Stevens as viewed by, 262
Wilson, Eugene, 269
Winchell, Walter, 50
Wood, Jean, 298, 315, 320, 351

Young, Robert N., 185, 190, 315

Zhukov, Georgi, 28
Zwicker, Ralph W., 191–205, 211, 214, 216, 218, 222, 233, 241, 260, 296, 306, 382

During the Eisenhower Administration, William Bragg Ewald, Jr., served as a member of the White House staff and as assistant to Secretary of the Interior Fred A. Seaton. When the Administration ended, he went with Eisenhower to Gettysburg to assist on his two volumes of White House memoirs, *Mandate for Change* and *Waging Peace*. Out of these experiences and exhaustive additional research into the Eisenhower years, Dr. Ewald wrote *Eisenhower the President: Crucial Days, 1951–60*, which Dr. Arthur Burns called "a literary masterpiece and a work of superb scholarship."

Dr. Ewald received his doctorate from Harvard University. He is the author of two books on eighteenth-century English literature, *The Masks of Jonathan Swift* and *Rogues, Royalty and Reporters: The Age of Queen Anne Through its Newspapers*. He and his wife, Dr. Mary T. Ewald, live in Greenwich, Connecticut, near the headquarters of the International Business Machines Corporation, which he joined after leaving Washington. They have three sons.